STATEBUILDING
BY IMPOSITION

Studies of the Weatherhead East Asian Institute, Columbia University

The Studies of the Weatherhead East Asian Institute of Columbia University were inaugurated in 1962 to bring to a wider public the results of significant new research on modern and contemporary East Asia.

STATEBUILDING BY IMPOSITION

Resistance and Control in Colonial Taiwan and the Philippines

Reo Matsuzaki

CORNELL UNIVERSITY PRESS   ITHACA AND LONDON

Cornell University Press gratefully acknowledges receipt of a subvention from the Office of the Dean of Faculty, Trinity College, which aided in the publication of this book.

First published 2019 by Cornell University Press

Library of Congress Cataloging-in-Publication Data

Names: Matsuzaki, Reo, author.
Title: Statebuilding by imposition : resistance and control in colonial Taiwan
    and the Philippines / Reo Matsuzaki.
Description: Ithaca : Cornell University Press, 2019. | Series: Studies of the
    Weatherhead East Asian Institute, Columbia University | Includes
    bibliographical references and index.
Identifiers: LCCN 2018035595 (print) | LCCN 2018037765 (ebook) |
    ISBN 9781501734847 (pdf) | ISBN 9781501734854 (epub/mobi)
    | ISBN 9781501734830 | ISBN 9781501734830 (cloth)
Subjects: LCSH: Taiwan—Politics and government—1895-1945. | Philippines—
    Politics and government—1898-1935. | Nation-building—Taiwan—History. |
    Nation-building—Philippines—History. | Nation-building—Japan—History. |
    Nation-building—United States—History.
Classification: LCC DS799.716 (ebook) | LCC DS799.716 .M38 2019 (print) |
    DDC 951.249/04—dc23
LC record available at https://lccn.loc.gov/2018035595

For my wife, Katy, and my mother, Michiko

Contents

Acknowledgments

This book is a culmination of the support and advice that I received from my professors, colleagues, friends, and family over the past two decades. As an undergraduate student at Georgetown University, I was inspired to make political science not just my major, but my profession, by Joseph Lepgold and Victor Cha. Daniel Nexon, my senior thesis adviser, introduced me to the body of literature on empires and statebuilding that shaped the direction of my intellectual inquiry in graduate school and beyond. I am also profoundly grateful for the mentorship I received from Mitch Kaneda.

The genesis of this book lies in the research I conducted at MIT. This book would not exist if not for the tremendous support, and patience, given by Christopher Capozzola, Alexis Dudden, Roger Petersen, Kathleen Thelen, and, especially, Richard Samuels. The role my friends—particularly Nathan Cisneros, Kristin Fabbe, Jennifer Ferng, Llewelyn Hughes, Andrew Radin, Paul Staniland, Jessica Trisko-Darden, and Adam Ziegfeld—played in the development of my project at this stage was enormous. I would above all like to thank Miriam Kingsberg Kadia, who was extremely generous with her time, reading multiple drafts of my work at every stage of its development.

My archival research in Japan, Taiwan, and various locations across the United States was made possible by funding provided by the Matsushita International Foundation, the Society for Historians of American Foreign Relations, and the Smith Richardson Foundation. I am grateful to Nobuhiro Hiwatari, who arranged my affiliation with the Institute of Social Science at the University of Tokyo, as I conducted preliminary research. Thereafter, it was through the sponsorship of Naoyuki Umemori that I was able to participate in a yearlong fellowship at Waseda University's Center for Global Political Economy. During this time, I was fortunate to meet Toyomi Asano and Meitetsu Haruyama, who kindly invited me to partake in their workshops and seminars and allowed me to test out my ideas in front of a Japanese academic audience. Michael Liu and Caroline Ts'ai graciously hosted me in Taiwan so that I could conduct research at the Archives of the Institute of Taiwan History, Academia Sinica. I would also like to thank the various librarians and support staff, and in particular Akiko Watanabe, who provided crucial logistical assistance. Nami-san, chef-owner of a splendid eatery in Waseda, which remains among the best-kept culinary secrets of Tokyo, ensured that I ate and drank well in fine company while engaging in research in Japan.

A turning point in both my career and the development of this book was my fellowship at Stanford University's Center for Democracy, Development, and the Rule of Law. I am grateful to Francis Fukuyama, who brought me to Stanford as a postdoctoral fellow and subsequently entrusted me to manage CDDRL's governance project during its inaugural year. Many of the theoretical and conceptual ideas underpinning this book were developed through my experience managing the governance project, as well as the many conversations with, and feedback from, my fellow pre- and postdoctoral scholars at Stanford: Michael Albertus, Toshihiro Higuchi, Reyko Huang, Eric Kramon, and Aila Matanock. I would also like to thank Larry Diamond, Karl Eikenberry, Erik Jensen, Stephen Krasner, Lucan Way, and Daniel Ziblatt for participating in my first book workshop and Samantha Maskey and Jason Wu for their help in ensuring its success. The critiques and suggestions I received during this workshop led me to largely abandon my first full manuscript, and write the book anew. This lengthened the time I would ultimately spend on this project, but the result—at least I hope— has been the writing of a much better book.

In the process of developing the arguments advanced in this book, I received helpful feedback from Yuen Yuen Ang, Séverine Autesserre, Jason Brownlee, John Dower, Sheena Chestnut Greitens, Konrad Kaliki, Daniel Koss, Leonid Peisakhin, Shohei Sato, Dan Slater, and Tuong Vu. Mary Alice Haddad, Shinju Fujihara, Yuko Kasuya, Ariyoshi Ogawa, Susan Pharr, Jeremy Pressman, and Ryan Sheely afforded me valuable opportunities to present my work to a wide array of scholars from multiple disciplines and countries. I would especially like to thank Erik Kuhonta, Zachariah Mampilly, Melissa Lee, and Hillel Soifer for participating in my second book workshop held at Trinity College and Daniella Salazar for taking excellent notes of the discussion. Their comments and suggestions allowed me to sharpen my argument, improve the organization of my narrative, and think through the ethical implications of my work. Melissa Lee, in particular, read numerous drafts of my manuscript and spent many hours discussing and debating with me the various theoretical and empirical components of the book, both large and small.

The contributions of my wonderful colleagues at Trinity College must also be recognized. Andrew Flibbert, Isaac Kamola, Jennifer Regan-Lefebvre, Lida Maxwell, and Abby Fisher Williamson were kind enough to read early iterations of my chapters. In addition, Zayde Antrim, Jeff Bayliss, Ben Carbonetti, Sonia Cardenas, Xiangming Chen, Diana Evans, Serena Laws, Thomas Lefebvre, Kevin McMahon, Vijay Prashad, Anna Terwiel, and Mary Beth White have helped make Trinity an ideal environment for me to pursue my research, while teaching on topics that inspire my thinking and writing. I am especially indebted to Stefanie Chambers and Anthony Messina for the advice, encouragement, and mentorship they provided not only in matters pertaining to the publication of this book but also in all aspects of my academic career. I was greatly aided in my research by Yingfang Chen, Steven Craney, and Ellen Xinyi Liu. The maps contained in this book were created by David Tatem.

I would also like to thank the reviewers for providing me with helpful suggestions for improving the manuscript, the editors and staff at Cornell University Press and Westchester Publishing Services for all of their help in the book's production, and Roger Haydon of Cornell University Press and Kenneth Ross Yelsey of Columbia University's Weatherhead East Asia Institute for taking interest in my project and guiding and advising me throughout the publication process.

I am forever grateful to my mother, Michiko, who supported all of my pursuits and took pride in my accomplishments, despite this resulting in her only son ending up with a career and family across the globe. My daughter, Anna, deserves credit for providing the extra motivation needed to get this book written, and my wonderful in-laws, Greg and Ina Handlir, for helping with child and dog care when I was away on research trips and conferences. Finally, my greatest gratitude goes to my wife, Katy. I could not have done this without her. She gave me emotional support during times of struggle. She read every iteration of the manuscript, and thanks to her superior understanding of the English language, ensured that what I wrote was intelligible. Moreover, without the many sacrifices she made, it would not have been possible to write this book while teaching a full course load and raising a small child. I alone am responsible for all errors and mistakes that remain in this book, but any credit belongs to us both.

Note on Transliteration

To aid in making the text accessible to nonspecialists, I have written Taiwanese geographic names according to transliterations used today in Taiwan, rather than by the Japanese pronunciations employed during the colonial period (e.g., Taipei, not Taihoku). All Chinese phrases and names have been transliterated using Pin-Yin conventions, except for historical figures and places commonly known in their Wade-Giles versions, as well as when authors have themselves transliterated their names in Wade-Giles. Chinese and Japanese names have been written in the order of last name first, reflecting how names would appear in these languages. However, for Chinese and Japanese authors writing in English, and for those whose work has been translated and published in English, I have written their names according to the Western convention of first name first.

Glossary

baojia	Qing-era community-based system of enforcing rules and regulations
baoliangju	system of indirect rule through a hierarchy of gentry-managed administrative offices that was briefly used by the Japanese to govern Taiwan in 1895
barrio	neighborhoods and surrounding villages that constitute a Philippine municipality (pueblo)
benmusho	subcounty administrative offices employed in Taiwan during the initial period of Japanese rule
cacique/caciquism	political boss/bossism
cédula	head tax
dazu hu	"large-rent household": the landed elite in Qing-era Taiwan who typically resided in urban areas while leasing their agricultural lots to the xiaozu hu (small-rent households)
dohi	"bandit": a term used by the Japanese colonial regime to refer to Taiwanese insurgents
dōka	cultural assimilation
Federalista	members of the Federal Party in the Philippines
gobernadorcillo	municipal mayor in the Philippines under Spanish rule
goningumi	"five-man group": community-based system of enforcing rules and regulations in Japan during the Tokugawa period
hannin kan	nonmanagerial civil servants within the Japanese bureaucracy
hokō	community-based system of enforcing rules and regulations in Taiwan under Japanese rule composed of approximately one hundred households
hosei	head of a hokō
ilustrado	Filipino elites distinguished by their educational achievements
jichi	"self-rule": a term used in Taiwan under Japanese rule to connote a system of local and community-based enforcement of the state's rules and regulations
jiei kumiai	village-level self-defense militias employed in Taiwan during the initial period of Japanese rule
junsa	patrolman
junsaho	assistant patrolman

kō	ten-household teams that constitute a hokō
kōchō	head of a kō
kōminka	policy of forced Japanization
kōtō kan	individuals who successfully passed the higher civil service exam for appointment to managerial positions within the Japanese bureaucracy
ladrone/ladronism	bandits/banditry
naichi enchō shugi	"homeland extensionism": principle of institutional assimilation and political integration of a colonial territory
polizeistaat	"police state": Prussian model of local governance whereby police officers are placed at the center of administration
presidente	municipal mayor in the Philippines under American rule
principales/principalía	class of political elites in the Philippines composed of current and former local officeholders
pueblo	Philippine municipality composed of barrios
seibutsugaku no gensoku	"principles of biology": theory and practice of applying social Darwinism to colonial administration
shinshō	"gentleman": honorary title given to former members of the scholar-gentry in Taiwan under Japanese rule
sōteidan	"able-bodied corps": village-level self-defense militias established as part of the hokō system to succeed the jiei kumiai
tuhao	"local strongmen": individuals in positions of authority through their control over private instruments of coercion
xiaozu hu	"small-rent household": tenants of dazu hu (large-rent households) in Qing-era Taiwan, who themselves behaved as landlords by subleasing agricultural lots to peasant families
zongli	"overseer": quasi-bureaucratic official placed in charge of enforcing rules and regulations at the township level in Qing-era Taiwan

STATEBUILDING
BY IMPOSITION

TAIWAN, THE PHILIPPINES, AND THE PUZZLE OF STATEBUILDING

Military planners once imagined war among the great powers and nuclear annihilation as the gravest threats to humankind. In the current era, this fear has given way to preoccupation with the dangers of ungoverned and undergoverned spaces, which threaten lives across the globe as incubators of warlordism, terrorist cells, illicit trafficking, pandemics, and famine. At the same time, the strength and weakness of the state has also become a pressing concern for economists, who—having moved away from their earlier consensus that macroeconomic stability, fiscal responsibility, and private sector dynamism were sufficient for economic growth—have increasingly emphasized that bad governmental institutions are the foremost cause of economic stagnation and decline. Consequently, statebuilding has now become the United Nation's core agenda and the World Bank's top priority. It was the ultimate strategic objective of the United States in Iraq after toppling the Baathist regime in 2003 and is the raison d'être of continued U.S. troop presence in Afghanistan, now two decades after the 9/11 attacks. However, despite the dedication of humanitarian workers and development experts, the many books and policy papers written on this subject, and the billions of dollars spent on statebuilding across the globe, little progress has been made in transforming ungoverned and undergoverned spaces into strong states.[1]

Recent failures in statebuilding, it is argued, are products of their impositional nature. Although the United States, the United Nations, the World Bank, and other international actors involved in statebuilding may believe that their vision of modernity will necessarily lead to the betterment of people's lives, such faith is often not shared by those on the receiving end of institutional reform. Instead, efforts by contemporary statebuilders to remake ungoverned and undergoverned spaces in their own liberal-democratic image are regarded by subject populations as unwelcome intrusions into political, economic, and social affairs. Just as the "well-intended schemes to improve the human condition"[2] by authoritarian and colonial rulers of the past were met with widespread resistance, so too have today's statebuilders encountered feigned acquiescence, sabotage, and outright armed opposition from those they have set out to help. Accordingly, with newly constructed institutions enjoying little legitimacy in the eyes of the governed, they are ignored or simply absorbed into existing institutional structures and practices, with limited long-term behavioral impact. At worst, statebuilding irreparably damages, and even destroys, traditional political, economic, and social systems, resulting in worse governance outcomes for local peoples and communities.[3]

As I contend in this book, imposition has indeed been the defining feature of statebuilding in the contemporary era. Critics of statebuilding are correct in their assessment that when new governance institutions are imposed on localities amid widespread resistance, they will lack local ownership, and any associated rules and regulations are unlikely to be obeyed or respected, at least voluntarily. Yet, my analysis also critically departs from prevailing accounts that characterize statebuilding by imposition as an infeasible proposition that is destined to fail. Recent statebuilders have undoubtedly struggled to remake occupied territories in their liberal and democratic image. However, let us not forget that modern governance institutions have been successfully imposed in the past in places such as China, Russia, and, as we will see shortly, Taiwan.[4] Although imposition may not be the easiest way to forge strong and modern institutions, and we may object to the oppressive and violent methods through which strong states are typically created amid resistance, the historical record demonstrates that it is hardly impossible. Why, then, has statebuilding by imposition been so unsuccessful in *recent* decades? What has stood in the way of American and United Nations officials in their quest to transform ungoverned and undergoverned spaces in their image? The principal obstacle to the success of statebuilding by imposition has been, for better or for worse, the commitment of recent statebuilders to liberal and democratic models of governance.

Our beliefs and values on how modern states ought to be constructed have also stifled development of an empirically grounded theory of statebuilding by imposition. Due to the oppressive and violent methods employed by the most effective statebuilders of the past, scholars have tended to view their endeavors as categorically different from those undertaken by contemporary liberal-democratic statebuilders and hence irrelevant to the study of statebuilding in today's ungoverned and undergoverned spaces.[5] Yet, as long as statebuilding is pursued amid resistance, the underlying process through which new governance institutions are established within the locality is similar regardless of the statebuilders' vision of modernity or the degree to which they rely on oppression and violence to achieve their ends. Hence, even if we find the strategies employed by successful autocratic or colonial statebuilders objectionable, by studying them we will come to a better understanding of how modern states may be effectively imposed on those who resist. Such an exercise will inevitably lead us to conclusions that are normatively unappealing, or outright unacceptable. But this is precisely the point. It is only then that we may understand what it would *actually* take to establish strong states within the structural and political conditions found in today's ungoverned and undergoverned spaces and problemize our faith in statebuilding as the best way to advance security and welfare across the globe.

To this end, this book engages in comparative analysis of Taiwan under Japanese rule (1895–1945) and the Philippines under U.S. rule (1898–1941): two contemporaneous cases of statebuilding by imposition that produced contrasting outcomes despite comparable underlying structural and institutional conditions. Under the Qing and Spanish administrations, nineteenth-century Taiwan and Philippines, respectively, were shallowly governed polities wherein the exercise of governmental authority, as through the collection of taxes, maintenance of law and order, and provision of public goods, was highly uneven. The socioeconomic structures and conditions of Taiwan and the Philippines—ethnic diversity, rising inequality, and frequent conflict over land—also made these territories inherently difficult to govern. Like today's ungoverned and undergoverned spaces, Taiwan and the Philippines were therefore hardly conducive to the construction of strong states. Yet, despite commonalities in the conditions under which these parallel statebuilding projects began, the outcomes were anything but similar. Whereas the enforcement of rules and regulations in colonial Taiwan became systematic and rule-bound under Japanese administration, it remained uneven and prone to corruption in the Philippine Islands.

I advance two interrelated claims. First, I highlight attainment of systematic compliance with rules and regulations as the central challenge of statebuilding by imposition. For individuals residing in strong and established states, who have been socialized into behaving as law-abiding citizens, rules and regulations enacted by the state are, for the most part, unquestioningly accepted. Such is not the case with ungoverned and undergoverned spaces, where expectations and views of government are shaped by the performance and behavior of a minimalist—and often predatory—state, and the people are thus likely to react with fear and anxiety to any attempt by the government to expand its scope. It is for this reason that societal actors, as intermediaries between state and society, come to play an important role in the statebuilding process. Through relying on such administrative intermediaries, and taking advantage of the power and authority that they exert locally, government officials can obtain systematic compliance from the people. However, when modern governance institutions are imposed on the subject population, the very individuals who are most capable of fulfilling this mediational function—local elites, and especially community leaders—are themselves, by definition, opposed to the endeavor, thus increasing the difficulty of statebuilding. If statebuilding is to have any chance of success, uncooperative, and even openly hostile, community leaders must be made to behave as obedient intermediaries.

Second, I argue that the effectiveness and cooperativeness of administrative intermediaries are determined by the structure of mediational institutions that regulate their interactions with government officials at the interface of state and society. These institutions—such as clientelistic networks, neighborhood associations, and government-administered mass organizations—decide who is empowered to represent local communities as officially sanctioned intermediaries, the duties and responsibilities of these individuals, the special privileges that they may enjoy, and any punishments associated with noncompliance. In turn, the extent to which mediational institutions constrain the behavior of administrative intermediaries and compel their adherence to the statebuilder's modernist agenda varies according to the constitution of these institutions. In some instances mediational institutions are structured in ways that advance the interests of local elites at the government's expense, but in others they function as highly effective instruments of discipline. Whether mediational institutions become inadvertent sources of state weakness, or mechanisms through which community leaders can be made to behave obediently, is not historically or structurally predetermined; rather, the mediational institution's constitution, and hence its effect on statebuilding, is endogenous to the process of imposing new governance institutions on the subject population.

Specifically, mediational institutions can be configured by statebuilders into effective disciplinary instruments through two types of institutional interventions. First, by formalizing rules that regulate interactions between government officials and administrative intermediaries, society itself becomes intelligible to the state and thus closely surveillable by bureaucrats. Formalization also allows for the routinization of punishments and rewards by standardizing and codifying acceptable and unacceptable behavior. Second, by disaggregating institutions of state-society mediation to the most basic units of sociopolitical organization, administrative intermediaries are themselves made more disciplinable. It is, after all, much easier for frontline government officials to exercise disciplinary power over intermediaries who have limited influence, wealth, and coercive capacity. Those at lower levels of sociopolitical aggregation are also more interchangeable, making it less likely that rulers become dependent on any one individual for the enforcement of rules and regulations. Ungoverned and undergoverned spaces are, in short, transformed into strong states by reconstituting the very fabric of society in ways that advance the government's capacity for disciplining community leaders into obedient intermediaries.

Recent and ongoing statebuilding missions have been pursued under the premise that strong states are constructed by establishing representative governmental institutions, holding free and fair elections, liberalizing the economy, and enacting laws that protect private property and advance personal liberties. In actuality, there is an inherent contradiction between the liberal-democratic model of governance advanced by today's statebuilders and the process through which a strong state may be successfully established amid widespread resistance. The implication is not necessarily that the United States or the United Nations should adopt illiberal and undemocratic statebuilding strategies for the sake of success. Rather, I demonstrate what successful statebuilding by imposition has entailed historically, so that we may engage in informed discussion of whether the tremendous costs associated with this endeavor are worth the benefits of transforming the world's ungoverned and undergoverned spaces into strong states.

A Tale of Contrasting Outcomes in Statebuilding by Imposition

Regardless of the vision of modernity undergirding a polity's governance system, modern states are distinguished by their expansive reach over the lives of their subject populations.[6] Whereas traditional rulers sought merely to count the number of inhabitants and record the extent of their most valuable possessions (land, castles, etc.), modern states expend considerable effort in collecting detailed statistics on the socioeconomic characteristics and behaviors of the population. People's interactions with the state were once largely limited to fulfilling tax and labor obligations; otherwise, most individuals went about their lives without much attention from the authorities. In the contemporary era, the presence of government is felt from the moment of birth to the end of one's life, as the state intervenes in the health and education of children, working conditions within farms and factories, care of the sick and elderly, and treatment of human bodies during and after death. Today's rulers provide much more for their populations than the kings and queens of centuries past—in the form of communication and transportation infrastructures, public education, healthcare, retirement benefits, and the like—but in exchange, they expect the people to contribute to the provision of public goods and services by paying burdensome taxes and following an array of rules and regulations. The modern state, in short, knows more about, does more for, and demands greater participation and contributions from its people than political orders that came before it.[7]

Modern states nonetheless vary across two key dimensions of stateness. First, they may be differentiated based on the extent to which they attempt to exercise control over, and extract resources from, the subject population—that is, the *scope* of government. European colonies in the late nineteenth and early twentieth centuries, for instance, were distinctly modern in that their populations were subjected to new labor and land regimes that integrated local economies into the world capitalist system; the codification of customary law, meanwhile, led to concentration of judicial and political authority in the hands of traditional leaders (chiefs, sultans, and the like) in the locality, reification of ethnic and tribal categories, and overall expansion of social and economic interactions placed under official purview.[8] Yet, the scope of colonial governments was still far more limited than that sought and achieved by statebuilders in Europe itself. A major challenge of decolonization thus became one of constructing and developing new governmental institutions and capacities that would make former colonized territories more like European nation-states in both form and function. Indeed, what makes Taiwan under Japanese rule and the Philippines under U.S. rule unique among colonized territories concerns this dimension of stateness: Unlike European rulers in Africa and Asia, Japanese and American statebuilders attempted to construct a modern state in their respective colonies that were similar in scope to their home territories.

Second, while all modern states seek, in varying degrees, to exert greater authority over a wide range of human activities and interactions in contrast to traditional polities, not all will succeed in actually obtaining systematic compliance with an expansive and intrusive set of rules and regulations. This variation in the *strength* of the state is what makes a statebuilding enterprise, irrespective of the scope of government sought by modernist reformers, a success or failure.[9] Here, state strength is defined as the *evenness* with which compliance with rules and regulations is obtained throughout the realm. A strong state, under this formulation, is one that can compel inhabitants to abide by the state's rules and regulations regardless of how rich or politically well-connected they may be; whether they live in cities or the hinterlands; or the extent to which the government's policies advance their material interests. A weak state, by contrast, is one wherein compliance is uneven across individuals, social forces, territorial spaces, or policy areas. Yet, even in the weakest of states, there is at least nominal recognition by local populations that a government, rightfully or otherwise, exercises political authority over them, even if rules and regulations are unevenly, and sometimes seldom, enforced. Weak states should therefore be distinguished from collapsed states or ungoverned spaces, in which the government and its administrative institutions have completely disintegrated due to war, or were never present.

It is in the sense of state strength and weakness that I refer to colonial Taiwan as a successful case of statebuilding and the Philippines as one of failure. This variation in statebuilding outcomes can be seen by comparing the abilities of the Government-General of Taiwan (GGT) and the Insular Government of the Philippine Islands (IGP) to undertake two basic administrative tasks that any modern state must do to achieve its larger policy goals and objectives: (1) collect statistical information on the characteristics, behaviors, and assets of inhabitants—that is, "see like a state"[10] and (2) mobilize citizens and subjects for the purpose of providing public goods and services.

"Seeing Like a State"

Among the various administrative tasks performed by a modern state, "seeing" is arguably the most foundational, as the government's ability to do anything else depends on its collection of accurate information. Even the crudest forms of taxation, such as the head tax, require data on the number of taxable inhabitants in a given district, which in turn is made possible by tracking any changes in a person's place of residence and knowing the person's age, sex, and other factors that affect one's ability to do manual labor.[11] Insofar as effective provision of public goods and services rests on people's cooperation and contributions, the state must have the capacity to monitor this and punish those who fail to comply. In this way people are deterred from freeriding on the labor and sacrifices of others and have confidence that the costs associated with providing a public good or service are equitably distributed across the population.[12]

Stark differences in the ability of the GGT and the IGP to "see" their inhabitants are apparent in the efforts they similarly put forth to collect data on land ownership. In Taiwan, despite desire by the landed elite to guard as best they could information on landholdings and their productive capacities—so as to lessen their tax burden—the Japanese succeeded in implementing an island-wide cadastral survey in 1898, just three years after Japan took control of Taiwan. As a result of this survey, which was completed in 1903, the Land Investigation Bureau discovered that the amount of cultivated land on the island was twice as much as previously recorded by the Qing administration: 361,447 *chia* (one chia = 0.97 hectares) in 1887 vis-à-vis 777,850 chia in 1903.[13] In addition to producing detailed cadastral maps, the bureau also recorded various information on individual lots that was previously unknown to government officials, such as land type, the date and method by which the lot came under possession of the current owner(s), and information pertaining to mortgage agreements. Most important, detailed information on land grade was painstakingly collected so that tax rates for each lot could be accurately calculated.[14]

Although it is not possible to know the extent to which the results of the 1898–1903 cadastral survey were truly accurate, in the sense that they captured land relations as understood by the Taiwanese people at the time, the endeavor nonetheless created a set of detailed maps and data on land ownership and usage that made the Taiwanese countryside intelligible to the colonial state. Moreover, that the Japanese were able to uncover such a large amount of previously unreported land suggests that the GGT exhibited considerable capacity to penetrate Taiwanese society and systematically enforce its rules and regulations. The survey was also completed in five years—an astonishingly short period of time, even given Taiwan's small size. Finally, it is significant that the survey did not lead to rural unrest, either in the form of rich landlords protesting increases in effective tax rates or small-scale cultivators accusing the landed elite of land-grabbing, as property rights were assigned and the size of each agricultural lot demarcated.

In contrast, the IGP demonstrated an acute inability to conduct cadastral surveys quickly and widely throughout the archipelago. First, it is important to note that the cadastral surveys, which began in 1913, were never completed under American rule: in 1935, when direct U.S. control over the archipelago ended with the creation of the Commonwealth of the Philippine Islands, approximately half of the privately owned land had not yet been formally surveyed and registered.[15] Given the much larger size of the Philippines compared to Taiwan, one would expect that such surveys would take longer than the five years that the Japanese needed. Nonetheless, that after more than twenty years the colonial government had yet to survey even half of privately owned land suggests considerable weakness compared to the GGT.[16] Also, much of the surveying in Taiwan was conducted in the midst of a colonial war between Japanese forces and militia armies led by the Taiwanese landed elite. In contrast, by 1913, when the United States implemented the Cadastral Survey Act, the Philippines were largely at peace (with the exception of the administratively separate island of Mindanao, which was not included in the data), and various governmental institutions had been in place for more than a decade.

Moreover, there is considerable evidence to suggest that the Filipino landed elite corrupted the process of surveying and registering land and that the Cadastral Act was made into a vehicle for land-grabbing. This was in direct contradiction to the explicit goal of the United States to protect the property rights of small-scale cultivators. Data collected by the Americans show a rise in tenancy and concentration of land in the hands of a small number of elites between the census years of 1918 and 1939—that is, after the adoption of the Cadastral Act.

Whereas the percentage of farmers who were landowners was relatively stable between 1903 and 1918 at 80.76 percent and 77.74 percent, respectively, it declined substantially to 49.23 percent in the 1939 survey.[17] Greater integration of the Philippines into the world economy during this period, and the resulting commodity boom of the 1920s, also likely helped to effect this change in land ownership.[18] Nonetheless, the IGP's own reports, newspaper editorials, and memoirs of American colonial officials, as well as postwar analyses by Filipino scholars, substantiate the notion that abuse of the Cadastral Act by Filipino elites was an important cause of the rapid rise in land inequality.[19]

Providing Public Goods and Services

In addition to extracting information and resources, a strong and modern state must be able to systematically provide a wide range of public goods and services. Since this often necessitates the people's cooperation and contributions, effective provision of public goods and services in turn rests on systematic compliance with rules and regulations. The level of support and assistance that the government obtains in containing the spread of infectious diseases is especially indicative of this capacity, as such often involves policies that go against people's habits and beliefs.

During the first decade of the twentieth century, twenty thousand lives were lost every year, on average, from infectious diseases in Taiwan. This amounted to more than 20 percent of the total number of deaths recorded annually, making improvement to Taiwan's hygienic environment among the most pressing concerns of the colonial government.[20] In particular, the Japanese were determined to eradicate bubonic plague—a disease that killed anywhere from one thousand to three thousand Taiwanese per year—from the island, and the campaign against this deadly disease became an early test of the colonial state's capacity to mobilize the Taiwanese population and provide public goods and services. The antiplague campaign stood on three pillars: capturing plague-carrying rodents, quarantining those infected with the disease, and burning dwellings where plague victims had lived.[21]

Successful implementation of these policies was logistically and politically difficult, as it required wide-scale cooperation between the colonial state and the Taiwanese population for measures that were highly unpopular. Indeed, as a *New York Times* reporter who visited the island in May 1901 reported, "Few Chinese families will let the authorities know when the plague visits them. . . . Funerals do not help to answer this question, for . . . it is always possible to dig a hole under the floor of a residence and deposit [the deceased] there. . . . They had rather suffer with a disease and die with it than to let it come to official notice."[22] Yet, despite evidence of initial resistance from the population, the antiplague campaign eventually ended in success, with the virus completely eradicated by 1917. Significantly, as revealed in the journal of Zhang Lijun, a local notable from the town of Huludun in central Taiwan, colonial officials relied on individuals like him to rally the local residents in capturing rodents, report any suspected cases of the plague, and burn the homes of those infected.[23]

The contrast in outcomes vis-à-vis comparable health campaigns in the Philippines is striking. During the time that Japanese colonial officials pursued the antiplague campaign, cholera was the primary disease of concern in the archipelago. The spread of the sixth cholera pandemic (which originated in India) to the Philippines in November 1902 led to, according to official figures, 109,461 deaths before it subsided in early 1904—a figure that, given the weakness of the colonial state, likely grossly underreported the true magnitude of the epidemic. Furthermore, with the IGP unable to eradicate this deadly disease, cholera lingered and became an endemic, leading to nearly twenty thousand deaths in 1908, and again in 1919. As late as 1930, just over three thousand people died of cholera despite decades of attempts to rid the islands of the disease.[24]

Accounts by U.S. colonial officials, while they should be accepted with caution, blame the uncooperativeness of Filipino elites for the IGP's failure at addressing the cholera epidemic. Health officials reported that efforts to isolate the sick, first in specialized hospitals and later within their own homes, proved futile in the face of family and friends routinely ignoring the government's orders, and with local Filipino authorities doing little to help enforce such regulations. Filipinos concealed sickness within their homes and communities and had rather flee, spreading the disease in the process, than seek treatment by American physicians.[25] Widespread disobedience during this period was perhaps to be expected, given that the 1902–4 cholera epidemic took place immediately following the end of the brutal counterinsurgency campaign. However, unlike in Taiwan, compliance with health and sanitation regulations hardly improved in subsequent years. In 1919, with the Philippines suffering from yet another devastating cholera epidemic, the Bureau of Health reported: "The people did not coöperate with the sanitary authorities. The first cholera case is usually reported late or not at all . . . the tendency of the majority of the people is to conceal the cases in order to avoid quarantine, hospitalization and disinfection."[26]

The cause of this unevenness in enforcement was certainly not a lack of manpower on the part of the IGP's Bureau of Health. With the maintenance of sanitary conditions having become an utmost priority of the colonial regime in light of the 1902–4 cholera epidemic, considerable resources were in fact devoted to this end. By the early 1910s, the staff of the Bureau of Health had grown to well over three thousand officials, with two hundred of them being physicians. Health inspectors were deployed throughout the archipelago and made weekly inspections (daily during epidemics) within their jurisdiction.[27] Yet, because successful implementation of the Bureau of Health's rules and regulations required a degree of voluntary compliance on the part of the local population, even an abundant bureaucratic presence was insufficient for the IGP to be able to enforce its rules and regulations evenly throughout the realm.

Divergent Outcomes from Similar Beginnings

The variation in statebuilding outcomes between colonial Taiwan and the Philippines, as illustrated previously, was substantial. It is also important to note that it did not take long for this difference to emerge: within a decade of Japanese rule in Taiwan, the colonial government had already begun to exhibit the capacity to evenly enforce rules and regulations. In contrast, the colonial state in the Philippines demonstrated considerable weakness until the very end of the American period.

There are three possible explanations for this outcome. First, underlying structural conditions—climate, geography, factor endowments, population density, level of economic inequality, ethnic diversity, and the like—might have made it much easier for any modernist ruler to construct a strong state in Taiwan. In contrast, the Philippines could have been burdened with structural disadvantages that would have made it difficult for anyone to succeed at statebuilding. Second, it is possible that Taiwan was already on its way to becoming a strong state before Japanese rule, thanks to reforms instituted by the Qing authorities in previous decades. Under this scenario, the Japanese merely built on a favorable institutional foundation, rather than construct a strong state anew. Conversely, it may be that the Philippines under Spanish rule was especially poorly governed, and this legacy of bad institutions proved to be an insurmountable constraint on American statebuilders. The third possible explanation, which is the focus of this analysis, places causal weight on Japanese and American statebuilding efforts. Although underlying structural conditions and existing institutions necessarily define the realm of the possible, statebuilders still retain considerable leeway to displace existing institutions, engineer their atrophy through purposeful neglect, layer new institutions on top of the old, or reappropriate entrenched norms and practices in ways that advance their modernist agenda.[28]

Underlying Geographic and Socioeconomic Structural Conditions

Without a doubt, underlying structural conditions affect the ease with which modern state institutions can be established in a given territory. Statebuilding proceeds more smoothly in smaller territories with geographic features that allow for ease of travel and in cooler climates, which are less prone to deadly tropical diseases.[29] Another potentially important factor is the territory's level of socioeconomic inequality. Landlords with large holdings, who rely on their own financial and coercive resources to maintain control over vast tracts of land and their inhabitants, are likely to fear losing their authority, wealth, and way of life under the centralized institutional structure of a modern state. The capacity for landed elites to resist statebuilding also increases with higher income inequality, because wealth and the influence it generates within local communities provide the means to undermine any attempt to build strong and modern governmental institutions.[30] Finally, ethnic diversity may have a negative impact on statebuilding, insofar as it can lead to takeover of the central government by one ethnic group or another and the alienation of rival groups from the state, its institutions, and its distributional networks.[31]

Comparing Taiwan and the Philippines across a set of key geographic and socioeconomic variables demonstrates their striking similarities. As shown in Table 1.1, Taiwan and the Philippines were both ethnically heterogeneous societies with similar climate and terrain. The amount of land devoted to cash crops conducive to large plantations was limited in the Philippines and negligible in Taiwan, and rice was the primary agricultural product of both territories. The late nineteenth century was a period of rapid economic growth in these territories—a development made possible by the integration of their domestic markets into the world economy, as well as changes to local laws that allowed greater economic and political participation by the Taiwanese and Filipino peoples—which led to the emergence of a native landed elite and increased socioeconomic inequality.[32]

This is not to suggest that there were no differences in underlying structural conditions across the two territories. Comparability, after all, does not imply sameness. With a much higher percentage of tenant farmers at the turn of the twentieth century, Taiwanese society was initially more unequal, and thus less favorable to statebuilding in this regard. Meanwhile, the Philippines was larger than Taiwan in both territorial size and total population, making it more difficult for rulers to project their power and authority across the realm. Yet, with population centers in both Taiwan and the Philippines concentrated along the coastal plains, it was still relatively easy for authorities to access the vast majority of people in comparison to landlocked territories with few navigable rivers. Also,

TABLE 1.1. Comparison of Structural Conditions in Taiwan and the Philippines

	TAIWAN	THE PHILIPPINES
Territorial size (in square miles)	13,795	115,026
Total population (at first census year)	1905: 3,039,751 (220 per square mile)	1903: 7,635,426 (66 per square mile)
Terrain	Mostly mountainous with plains in west	Mostly mountainous with coastal plains
Climate	Tropical in the south; semitropical in the north	Tropical
Ethnic structure	Five Han Chinese groups and nine aboriginal communities	Eight "Christianized" ethnic groups and sixteen "non-Christian tribes," including a large Muslim population in the south
Land use for agricultural production (as percentage of cultivated land)	1901: Rice (73.9); Sweet potato (11.1); Tea (5.3); Peanut (2.6); Tobacco (0.1)	1902: Rice (45.5); Abaca (16.5); Coconut (11.5); Corn (8.0); Sugar (5.5); Tobacco (2.5)
Primary commodity goods (as percentage of export value)	1890–94: Tea (59.1); Sugar (27.0); Camphor (7.9)	1890–94: Abaca (39.0); Sugar (36.5); Tobacco (11.0); Coconut (3.0)
Tenant farms as percentage of total	1900: 43%	1903: 18%

Sources: Harrell, "From *Xiedou* to *Yijun*": 110; Ho, *Economic Development of Taiwan*, 356; Ka, *Japanese Colonialism in Taiwan*, 64; Owen, "Philippine Economic Development and American Policy," 120–21; Takekoshi, *Japanese Rule in Formosa*, 105–14; Taiwan, Bureau of Aboriginal Affairs, *Report on the Control of Aborigines in Formosa*, 1; Taiwan, Committee of the Formosan Special Census Investigation, *The Special Population Census of Formosa, 1905*, 38; United States, Bureau of the Census, *Census of the Philippine Islands: 1903*, vol. 1, 263, 468–77, vol. 2, 15–16, vol. 4, 254–76; Wickberg, "Continuities in Land Tenure," 214.

although the Philippines was larger than Taiwan, it was still smaller than most other polities of East and Southeast Asia, such as French Indochina, Dutch Indonesia, British Malaya, Thailand, Japan, and China. Given that strong states were eventually forged in many of these larger territories, it should also have been possible in the Philippines.[33]

Another important difference—one that made Taiwan a more challenging site for statebuilding—was the way in which socioeconomic cleavages intersected with patterns of violence. The ethnic composition of the Philippines at the turn of the twentieth century was certainly more heterogeneous. Among the so-called Christianized populations, Filipino peoples, according to American colonial anthropologists, consisted of eight distinct language groups: Tagalog, Visayan, Ibanag, Ilocano, Bicol, Pampangan, Pangasinan, and Zambalan. In addition, the "non-Christian" peoples were grouped into sixteen tribes and placed under special military-controlled administrative jurisdictions.[34] In contrast, there were five self-identified Han ethnic groups in Taiwan—Hakka, Zhangzhou, Anxi, Tongan, and Sanyi—along with nine aboriginal tribes.[35] (Similarly to the Philippines, the aboriginal tribes were governed separately from the majority Han peoples, and under special and militarized administrative structures.) Yet, despite the Philippines' greater diversity, perceived ethnic differences were far more politicized, and violently so, in Taiwan: while Taiwan and the Philippines both witnessed large-scale armed uprisings and intercommunal violence through the course of the nineteenth century, conflicts in Taiwan took place across ethnic and lineage lines, whereas in the Philippines, it was largely class based or inspired by messianic movements.[36]

In sum, despite differences in underlying structural conditions, comparison across these geographic and socioeconomic variables leaves little reason to believe that statebuilding was substantially more difficult in the Philippines than in Taiwan.

The Legacy of Existing Institutions?

Underlying structural conditions are not the only factors that constrain the behavior of statebuilders and define the realm of the possible when they design new institutions. In imposing a new and modern governance system, statebuilders must contend with the fact that it is necessarily built alongside, and layered atop, an existing institutional foundation. Insofar as the old institutions are favorable to those already in positions of power, as is typically the case, they are not easily displaced. Moreover, even if statebuilders succeed in removing or altering existing formal institutions, it is much harder to change entrenched beliefs, norms, and habits, all of which affect how people react to new rules and regulations.[37] As such, it is hardly surprising that among the most important determinants of variation in political, economic, and social outcomes within postcolonial countries are the legacies of colonial-era institutions.[38] Similarly, as shown recently by political scientists and economists, colonial institutions are themselves shaped by precolonial political and socioeconomic systems.[39] In explaining differences in statebuilding outcomes across colonial Taiwan and the Philippines, or any statebuilding effort for that matter, it is therefore prudent to examine the extent to which existing institutions might have made Taiwan a more favorable setting for imposing a modern governance system.

When the Japanese took possession of Taiwan in 1895, the territory had been under Qing rule for just over three centuries. For much of this period, Taiwan was a frontier territory where migrants from Fujian and Guangdong fought native aboriginal tribes for possession of the island's fertile soil. Rebellions against the government and violence between rival ethnic and lineage groups were so frequent that a common saying held that at least one small insurrection occurred every three years and a major disturbance every five.[40] Starting in the late nineteenth century, land relations became more stable and conflict among the transplant Han communities, as well as between them and Taiwan's aboriginal peoples, subsided considerably. In turn, the original landed elite gradually became culturally and politically assimilated into the Qing ruling class. Yet, this socioeconomic development also had the pernicious effect of concentrating wealth and power in the hands of a few landed families.[41]

Turning to Taiwan's formal governmental institutions during this period, the most notable feature, at least from the perspective of this study, was its bureaucracy. Much like the rest of China at the time, meritocratically chosen civil servants—that is, individuals who entered government service via passage of a rigorous civil service exam—staffed the upper ranks of the subprovincial (and later, provincial) government in Taiwan.[42] In this sense, the Qing administrative apparatus exhibited some elements that approximated the modern bureaucratic ideal type found in the writings of Max Weber.[43] However, lacking most other characteristics typically associated with Weber's conceptualization of modern forms of political authority, and having been completely displaced after Taiwan's annexation by Japan, the Qing administrative apparatus hardly furnished the Japanese with an institutional foundation on which to construct a modern bureaucracy.

In the first place, the Qing provincial administration was not functionally differentiated, with the local magistrate serving both executive and judicial responsibilities. The government's scope was also narrowly defined, and the duties of the magistrate did not go much beyond tax collection, maintenance of security (with the help of privately financed and organized militias), and adjudication of justice. Most significantly, its reach into Taiwanese society was limited because of the small size of the formal bureaucratic apparatus at the subprefectural level. Having to make do without much of an administrative staff, Qing magistrates had little choice but to depend on local strongmen (*tuhao*) or the scholar-gentry—typically wealthy and landowning men distinguished by their scholarly achievement or military service—to undertake even those functions that were regarded as within the government's jurisdiction. Provision of relief and aid to the poor and disabled, construction of administrative buildings and city walls, regulation of opium, implementation of land surveys, suppression of rebellions, pacification of aboriginal lands, and defense against foreign invasions were all undertaken via direct leadership by a local strongman or scholar-gentry, or through their close collaboration and financial assistance.[44]

Furthermore, although recruitment into the bureaucracy was itself merito-cratic, advancement was highly influenced by one's personal ties and political loyalties. To the detriment of bureaucratic autonomy and impartiality, bureau-crats forged close collaborative ties with powerful societal actors—in particular, wealthy heads of lineage groups with the capacity to command large peasant militias—and by relying on their financial resources and coercive capacity, Qing officials advanced their own careers by implementing public works projects, pro-tecting towns and trade routes from bandits, and suppressing rebel forces. Tai-wanese elites also had much to gain personally from their collaborative ties with Qing bureaucrats. With the help of patrons in the Qing officialdom, Taiwanese elites could hope to obtain honorary titles, which afforded social prestige and priv-ileges, increase prospects for governmental employment, and gain access to vari-ous opportunities for self-aggrandizement.[45]

The meritocratic rise of Lin Wencha of Wufeng is a case in point. From the head of a modest lineage group in central Taiwan, he became one of the largest landowners on the island through his collaboration with Zuo Zongtang, the governor-general of Zhejiang and Fujian Provinces during the final years of the Taiping Rebellion (1850–1864). Originally recruited by Qing officials to raise a volunteer force to suppress rebels in Fujian, it did not take long for Lin Wencha to demonstrate his military prowess and capability as a field commander. When Taiwan itself became engulfed in the rebellion, Lin was therefore the natural choice to lead the counterinsurgency campaign. Yet, rather than dedicate himself to cap-turing the leaders of anti-government forces, he went about settling old scores with rival lineage groups in his home region. Labeling his personal enemies as rebels of the empire, he seized their lands and added them to his family's hold-ings; he also forced others to sell their land at significantly discounted prices by threatening outright confiscation. After Lin Wencha's death, his brothers and sons faced reprisals from their foes within officialdom, but the family's continued ties to powerful Qing administrators, most notably Taiwan governor Liu Mingchuan (1884–1891), allowed the Lins of Wufeng to maintain, and even legitimate, their family's ill-begotten wealth and prestige.[46]

The exploits of Lin Wencha were extraordinary in many ways, but they were consistent with the general pattern of state-society relations found within this shallowly and unevenly governed polity. In a more typical late-nineteenth-century case from the Hsinchu region in northern Taiwan, a large absentee landowner (*dazu hu*) by the name of Wu-Shun-Ji filed charges against the family's perpetual tenants for their nonpayment of rent. The leases were sizable and these tenants, known as *xiaozu hu*, behaved as landlords in their own right by subleasing the land to peasant families. The subprefect ruled in favor of the Wu family, but get-ting their xiaozu hu to comply with this decision was no easy task, given that they were heads of lineage groups themselves, commanded gangs of at least a few dozen men, and resided within heavily fortified villages. The subprefect thus resorted to extralegal means to enforce his ruling. In trying to get Fan Linxiang, one of the guilty xiaozu hu, to pay rent owed to Wu-Shun-Ji, the subprefect captured and held hostage his grandson, Fan Atian, who had nothing to do with the case at hand but could be apprehended because he was traveling outside of the family's stronghold. Just as telling as these documented instances of state weakness in late-Qing Taiwan is the absence of archival documents pertaining to disputes between the xiaozu hu and their peasant tenants. With government officials able to exercise their authority only in urban centers, the state was simply absent from the towns and villages where the majority of Taiwanese people lived.[47]

Like the Qing bureaucracy in Taiwan, the Spanish counterpart in the Philippines (1565–1898) was a mix of traditional and modern administrative institutions and practices. Although it lacked the competitive examination system of Qing-era Taiwan, the bureaucracy itself was much larger. According to 1883 records, 5,552 officials staffed the civil administration, while the army employed another 14,545 individuals. To this, we must add local Catholic parishes, composed of 1,962 clergy members, which were formally integrated into the state starting in the mid-nineteenth century.[48] The extensiveness of the Spanish government's scope, compared to that of the Qing administration in Taiwan, was notable. In contrast to Qing officials, who did not see the state as having a role in providing primary education, promoting industry, and regulating the population's health and hygiene, governmental councils were created in the Philippines pertaining to all of these areas at the central, provincial, and municipal levels. Although this certainly did not mean that officials could evenly provide or regulate education, industry, and health and hygiene across the realm, at least there was recognition within the local elite stratum that these were appropriate areas of governmental oversight and intervention.[49] Reflecting bureaucratic reforms that took place in Spain itself during the course of the nineteenth century, the Philippine bureaucracy also underwent significant differentiation and specialization in administrative functions and responsibilities during the final decades of the Spanish era. Most notably, the reorganization of the Royal Audiencia (its president having simultaneously served as governor-general and chief justice prior to the reform) into an exclusively judicial institution in 1861 led, at least in theory, to the separation of the government's executive and judicial powers and subsequently the creation of an autonomous judicial hierarchy of courts that reached down to the provincial level.[50]

Furthermore, Spanish officials had the capacity to exercise far greater coercive and policing power over the subject population than did Qing administrators. The primary coercive arm of the Spanish regime was the Guardia Civil, a paramilitary force created in 1868 and deployed in strategic locations throughout the archipelago. Numbering 156 officers and 3,352 men in its final year of existence, the Guardia Civil's basic operational unit was composed of twenty to thirty-five men. Originally created to fight banditry and suppress rebellious activity, it eventually superseded municipal-level police forces (which were organized and led by local Filipino officials) and became involved in enforcement of everyday rules and regulations concerning gambling, payment of taxes, and the like. The state had therefore largely succeeded in monopolizing coercive power by the end of the Spanish period—a development that would later benefit American statebuilders. Indeed, when U.S. officials established the Philippine Constabulary in 1901, the Guardia Civil provided not only the know-how and the organizational template for a new national police force but also the constabulary's initial manpower.[51]

In addition to the Guardia Civil, the Spanish regime exercised its policing powers by a second, and arguably more important, institution: the Spanish priests and their local parishes. Given the religiosity of the Filipino population, parish priests wielded considerable moral authority within the locality, but this was not all. Owning some of the largest estates in the archipelago, Catholic priests controlled the lives of ordinary Filipinos as landlords.[52] As keepers of people's birth, baptismal, marriage, and death records, they were custodians of demographic data. In fact, it was by relying on the church's records that the government was able to institute an early form of income tax, whereby the amount of head tax one paid was a function of the *cédula* bracket to which one belonged. The requirement that every able-bodied adult male (except for those possessing special privileges) contribute forty (later fifteen) days of labor, or its equivalent, to the state was also made enforceable thanks to statistics maintained by the church. The immense power enjoyed by the church within the locality also came from the various formal administrative duties assigned to it by the Spanish regime. Possessing the right to publicly disgrace and shame individuals, parish priests exercised quasi-judicial authority. They ascertained the political and spiritual fitness of a locally elected individual to serve as *gobernadorcillo*, as the municipal mayor was called, and also sat on all local governmental councils (on schooling, public works, agriculture, public health, etc.) as president or vice president.[53]

Nonetheless, because the interests of the state and church did not fully align, parish priests were not always reliable agents of policing. The church's primary role as defender of the Catholic faith led it to oppose primary education in Spanish for the Filipino masses, for fear that it would erode the church's ability to remain the sole provider of knowledge. As large landlords, Catholic priests resisted reforms that would have made it easier for small-scale landowners to obtain secure titles to their land. Believing that supernatural forces caused epidemics, they opposed the use of modern medicine to treat those suffering from smallpox, cholera, and other infectious diseases—a position that directly contradicted their leadership roles in local health boards.[54] Yet, despite such conflicts of interest, the presence of a parish priest in each Philippine municipality gave the state abilities to penetrate and regulate society that far exceeded those of Qing officials in Taiwan.

The Spanish state in the Philippines was, in short, institutionally more modern than the provincial government of Taiwan. This did not necessarily mean, however, that the Spanish colonial state exhibited greater strength than its northern neighbor. Indeed, beyond the foremost priorities of the Spanish regime—security and taxation—enforcement of rules and regulations was highly uneven. This can be illustrated by examining, as was done previously for the American period, the Spanish regime's attempt at combating the spread of infectious diseases and collecting information pertaining to land ownership.

The smallpox vaccine was introduced in the Philippines as early as 1805, and the Spanish regime touted its vaccination program as among its most important accomplishments. Indeed, records show that the Central Board of Vaccination and its regional and municipal branch offices dedicated tremendous amounts of energy to combating smallpox. Yet, despite their efforts, actual enforcement of the vaccination program was poor. The problem was that, with local customs and beliefs clashing with Western medical knowledge and practices, the government's health inspectors could not get elected municipal officials to comply with laws mandating vaccinations. It also did not help that the local parishes were indifferent, if not outright hostile, to Western medical practices. The government's attempt to control the spread of cholera also failed for similar reasons. Local customs pertaining to the care of the sick and burial of the dead contributed to the spread of cholera, and health officials could do little to convince the populace to change its ways, or to compel Filipino municipal officials to enforce quarantines during epidemics. The law mandated that a local health board be maintained at all times for the purpose of instilling sanitary habits among the townspeople and villagers, but this practice was rarely observed.[55]

The Spanish regime was equally unsuccessful in instituting an effective land ownership regime in which those without political or economic clout could be protected by obtaining secure titles to their land. In 1877, for example, Teodoro Benedicto, a Chinese mestizo landowner in the sugar-growing province of Negros Occidental, was accused by his Spanish neighbors of acquiring much of his vast estate through illegal means. His tactics were both simple and effective: After legally purchasing three hundred hectares in La Carlota, he allegedly acquired the land of neighboring small-scale Filipino rice growers through unfair loan agreements or by outright intimidation, thus expanding his La Carlota estate to seven thousand hectares. In addition, his accusers charged that Teodoro used similar methods to possess the entire barrio of Antipolo in neighboring Pontevedra, sixteen hundred hectares in La Castellana, and twenty-six hundred in Isabela. Without ever having obtained secure titles to their land, and with local Filipino officials acting as Teodoro's collaborators and enablers, the peasants had little recourse but to retreat to the mountains in defeat—that is, until Spanish landowners, out of spite, jealousy, or perhaps because they were genuinely horrified by the astonishing scale of the injustice, reported Teodoro's abuses on the peasants' behalf. Yet, for every such case that was brought to the authorities' attention, there were many more that went unreported and unpunished.[56]

Spanish officials were in fact well aware of how lack of security over land ownership was becoming both a source of economic inefficiency and cause of injustice against the peasantry. The result was an 1880 royal decree that established general procedures for providing landowners with secure titles. However, foreshadowing the U.S. failure at instituting a similar land registry system three decades later, this reform made matters worse for peasants. Prioritizing administrative efficiency, the state assigned the task of processing paperwork for landholdings of less than ten hectares to the gobernadorcillos, but they were seldom neutral agents in this matter. Closely allied with, and even subordinate to, the newly emergent mestizo landed elites, they abused their office to facilitate the interests of these "neo-caciques."[57] Furthermore, once an individual served a term as gobernadorcillo, he joined the *principalía* class of present and former Filipino officeholders and obtained the permanent right to be one of the small number of voters who participated in local elections. It therefore comes as little surprise that among the ranks of the landowning elite during the late Spanish period were many former gobernadorcillos, who parlayed their service to enrich themselves and their families after their time in office.[58] In essence, what the 1880 royal decree did, as the 1913 Cadastral Act would later do on a much wider scale, was to provide the socioeconomic elite the means to secure titles to land that they had usurped from the peasantry.

In sum, despite its larger size and greater capacity to penetrate local society, the Spanish colonial government in the Philippines, like its Taiwanese counterpart, was ultimately a weak state governing over a strong society.[59] Yet, this did not mean that the Philippines, or Taiwan for that matter, was inherently impermeable to modern governance practices. Both polities contained the societal building blocks of a strong state. When Japanese and American invaders arrived in the late nineteenth century to impose on Taiwan and the Philippines their own vision of modernity, the critical difference between their statebuilding campaigns was not the underlying potential for these territories to become strong and modern states. Rather, it was the territories' colonization by countries that employed vastly different statebuilding strategies under similar structural conditions and institutional endowments.

The Analysis to Come

This chapter has provided the empirical groundwork for a comparative analysis of statebuilding by imposition in Taiwan and the Philippines. Ruled by two empires, the Qing and the Spanish, with dissimilar worldviews and administrative structures, these neighboring islands of the Asian littoral inhabited different worlds. And yet, their political development progressed in a remarkably parallel manner—that is, up until their respective annexation by Japan and the United States at the turn of the twentieth century. The analysis to come develops a theory of statebuilding by imposition to explain this variation in outcome.

But why examine these two polities with a single study in the first place? If the Taiwan case helps us observe how modern political institutions were successfully imposed on a subject population amid widespread resistance, what exactly is the analytical benefit of comparing statebuilding in Taiwan and the Philippines, which remained a weak state across the Spanish and American periods? What is to be gained by studying a case in which the outcome of interest—that is, state strength—remained largely unchanged? What can a comparative investigation of colonial Taiwan and the Philippines reveal that we cannot obtain from examining these cases alone, or as part of a larger study of the Japanese and American imperial systems?

First, comparing colonial Taiwan and the Philippines allows one to see with greater clarity what the Japanese did differently to make Taiwan a case of statebuilding success, whereas American administrators in the Philippines aided in empowering and entrenching a landed elite at the expense of political unity and governmental effectiveness. Because Japanese and American statebuilding efforts involved wholesale imposition of new institutional models, the effects of their endeavors were numerous and far-reaching. By examining these cases within a comparative framework, we can isolate and focus attention on the factors that mattered most in producing divergent outcomes from similar underlying structural conditions and institutional endowments.[60]

Second, as intriguing as stories of change may be, especially those as dramatic as in colonial Taiwan, continuity is not an uninteresting or unproblematic outcome.[61] This is especially true when, as with the U.S. statebuilding mission in the Philippines, a tremendous amount of time, resources, and coercive power are expended on institutional transformation. The Philippines remained a weak state at the end of U.S. rule not because colonial officials attempted very little, but because the many measures they undertook to transform the Philippines in their image inadvertently reproduced and entrenched the very sources of weakness. To understand the causes of statebuilding success and failure, one must understand not only how Japanese officials reimagined and reconstituted Taiwan's seemingly unruly local governance system into an effective instrument of disciplinary power but also why so little progress came out of the many reforms instituted by U.S. officials in the archipelago. All too often, statebuilding failure is seen as a reflection of inaction, or a result of insufficient money, manpower, and the will to construct good institutions in target territories.[62] This work examines how the perpetuation of state weakness may also be a consequence of too much commitment to a set of well-intended, but misguided, statebuilding strategies and institutional models.[63]

Finally, the Philippines, when placed in the context of similar efforts to impose modern state institutions under colonial rule, serves as a bridge linking statebuilding under colonialism with recent attempts by the United States and the United Nations to impose modern governmental institutions in today's ungoverned and undergoverned spaces. It was in this archipelago of seven million inhabitants that the United States first introduced and innovated the ideas and strategies, as well as the rhetoric, that have since characterized its statebuilding missions across the globe.[64] Furthermore, with the exception of Puerto Rico and a number of small Pacific island territories—which remain a part of the United States today—the total time that the United States exercised control over the Philippines (a little over forty years) was far longer than any of its subsequent efforts to construct modern (and democratic) states abroad. It was not just the duration that made U.S. statebuilding efforts in the Philippines particularly intense: unlike in places such as South Vietnam, and more recently Iraq and Afghanistan, the United States directly ruled the Philippines via a colonial government led by an American governor-general until 1935, when the Philippines became a commonwealth of the United States. Hence, if the ideas and strategies that the United States has persistently employed in its statebuilding missions from the late nineteenth century to today could have succeeded anywhere, it was arguably the Philippines. As such, beyond the theoretical insights that one can glean from comparing colonial Taiwan and the Philippines, understanding why this *particular* case failed has important implications for contemporary policy debates.

In the analysis to follow, chapter 2 presents a theory of statebuilding by imposition, which will guide the ensuing comparative investigation of colonial Taiwan and the Philippines. I argue in this chapter that when new governmental institutions are imposed on a subject population amid resistance, genuine cooperation from societal actors in the enforcement of rules and regulations is unlikely. Statebuilding success will therefore depend on whether institutions of state-society mediation can function as effective instruments for disciplining locally authoritative individuals into obedient administrative intermediaries, thus compelling them to behave as if they fully support the statebuilding project. This is advanced, in turn, through institutional reforms that alter the very constitution of society to make intermediaries more disciplinable. On one hand, by formalizing institutions of state-society mediation, their behavior is made more visible to the state. On the other, by disaggregating the scale at which mediation occurs, and confining the power and influence of intermediaries to the locality, it becomes possible for the state to maintain autonomy from its societal collaborators and to punish and reward them in a systematic manner.

The four subsequent chapters constitute the empirical core of the book, wherein I apply this theory of statebuilding by imposition to explain what led to the considerable variation in state strength across colonial Taiwan and the Philippines. Chapter 3 details the contours of Japan's statebuilding campaign in the years immediately following its annexation of Taiwan in 1895. The discussion begins by examining the debate on how Japan should govern Taiwan, and why the Japanese were determined to depart from European colonial precedence of indirect rule. Japan's campaign to reshape Taiwan in its image started out disastrously, however, with the colonial government unable to defeat insurgent forces and maintain effective control over the territory. The situation was so dire, and prospects of success so dim, that Japanese policymakers even contemplated abandoning Taiwan altogether, despite its strategic and symbolic importance. It was out of these initial struggles that the plan to remake Taiwan into a *polizeistaat* (police state) emerged. The colonial police force was rapidly expanded into an imposing bureaucratic presence, with branch offices established throughout the territory. This not only made noncompliance with rules and regulations costly for the Taiwanese people but also ensured that the GGT would have the capacity to effectively oversee and discipline local administrative intermediaries. After chapter 3 traces the development of formal governmental institutions during the early colonial period, chapter 4 examines the evolution of Taiwan's mediational institutions under Japanese rule. It demonstrates that although the system of state-society mediation that came to define the GGT's local governance structure, known as *hokō*, had its roots in the Qing-era institution of *baojia*, its effectiveness at substantiating governmental authority was largely a product of Japanese institutional reforms that reconstituted Taiwanese society into one that could be "seen" and disciplined.

Chapter 5, which analyzes colonial Philippines, shows that the level of local resistance, the way that the colonial war progressed, and even the coercive measures employed by the U.S. military to defeat the insurgency were similar to how events unfolded in Taiwan during the initial years. Yet, the two cases part ways once statebuilding began in earnest and new institutions reflecting American political ideals and practices were imposed onto the Filipino population. Blindly believing in the confluence of interests between U.S. rulers and Filipino elites, U.S. officials did not concern themselves with the problem of compliance and instead concentrated their efforts on drafting a multitude of new laws inspired by American institutions and practices. The result was something that might have resembled a strong state on paper, but it scarcely functioned as such. Indeed, it did not take long for colonial officials to realize that their mission to transform the archipelago in their image was failing. However, as detailed in chapter 6, their beliefs on good government, as well as U.S. domestic political necessities, which produced America's initial statebuilding strategy, would continue to constrain the behavior of U.S. officials and lead them to stay the course. Refusing to fundamentally rethink their approach to statebuilding, and convinced that the problem was with the civilizational level of the Filipinos rather than with the design of their rules and regulations, colonial officials instituted reforms that somewhat improved the governability of the archipelago in the short term, but at the expense of statebuilding's long-term success.

The final chapter (chapter 7) explores the question of why Japan and the United States came to adopt such contrasting reform strategies and institutional designs vis-à-vis their respective territories despite the comparability of Taiwan and the Philippines at the turn of the twentieth century. It contends that the strategic choices and institutional models adopted by Japanese and American colonial officials had little to do with antecedent structural conditions in the target territories or nature of existing Taiwanese and Filipino mediational institutions; rather, they reflected the political constraints and ideological biases of their home countries. Specifically, Japan succeeded at statebuilding by imposition because it was an autocracy. In contrast, America's commitment to democratic institutions and processes at home and abroad led its statebuilders to adopt strategies and models in the Philippines that ultimately proved self-defeating, resulting in both a weak state *and* a dysfunctional democratic system.

This observation has important implications for the way that statebuilding by imposition is conducted in today's ungoverned and undergoverned spaces. Statebuilding efforts by the United States, the United Nations, and other international actors start from the premise that strong states can be constructed in ungoverned and undergovered spaces through democratizing and liberalizing reforms. Yet, this analysis suggests that when statebuilding is undertaken amid widespread resistance, its success depends on the illiberal act of reconfiguring the very fabric of society, such that it becomes more intelligible and disciplinable by government officials. Rather than letting civil society flourish as a counterweight to the state, as is the norm in today's prosperous and well-governed democracies, statebuilding by imposition is advanced through curtailing the autonomy enjoyed by local communities. In the long run, the presence of strong state institutions is more likely to allow democratic forms of governance to function effectively, but in the short term such a polity is necessarily undemocratic in its constitution.

Does this mean that the United States, the United Nations, and other actors engaged in statebuilding today should draw inspiration from the strategies employed by Japanese colonial officials in Taiwan? If we are indeed committed to transforming ungoverned and undergoverned spaces into strong and modern states, then yes. Yet, rather than advance the Japanese statebuilding campaign in Taiwan as a model to be emulated, I aim instead to problemize the very premise that Western countries and organizations ought to be engaged in statebuilding in today's ungoverned and undergoverned spaces in the first place. Too much of the existing analysis on statebuilding is based on wishful thinking for how strong and modern states can be established amid widespread opposition and resistance from local communities and their leaders. Let us examine, instead, what successful statebuilding by imposition has actually entailed, so that we may have an informed debate on the true costs and benefits of this endeavor.

A THEORY OF STATEBUILDING BY IMPOSITION

At the heart of statebuilding by imposition is a dilemma. During its initial stages, when expansion of the state's regulatory scope over the population is received with considerable fear and suspicion, administrative intermediaries play an invaluable role in the statebuilding process as everyday enforcers of rules and regulation within the locality. It is through their assistance that taxes are collected, public goods and services are provided, and, in general, compliance with rules and regulations is obtained. Yet, when statebuilding is undertaken by way of imposition—that is, when construction of a strong and modern state is pursued amid widespread opposition by local communities *and* their leaders—the very individuals whose support rulers need to establish modern political institutions are themselves opposed to the endeavor. Discontented elites, including local community leaders, may not always outwardly resist the statebuilders out of fear of being punished, but their opposition implies that they are unlikely to serve as effective and obedient intermediaries. At best, rules and regulations will remain unevenly enforced, and only in a manner that personally benefits local communities or their leaders; at worst, these elites will become an uncontrollable force within society and the very cause of state weakness.

This is why statebuilding by imposition often fails. Yet, a higher probability of failure does not imply its inevitability. Underlying structural or political conditions may make the establishment of a strong and modern state more or less difficult, but there is much to the outcome of statebuilding that is determined by the actions of the statebuilders themselves. Indeed, while Japanese and American colonial administrators faced similar obstacles in imposing modern governance institutions in Taiwan and the Philippines, respectively, the results of their state-building campaigns, as discussed in the preceding chapter, diverged greatly. Whereas Taiwan was reconstituted into a strong and modern state, with rules and regulations evenly enforced throughout the realm, state weakness became entrenched in the Philippines under U.S. rule as a direct consequence of America's well-intended, but ill-conceived, effort to remake the archipelago in its image. Similarly, failures by the United States, the United Nations, and an array of international development agencies to transform today's ungoverned and undergoverned spaces into strong states cannot be explained simply by the various adverse antecedent conditions found within these territories, nor by lack of commitment of time, manpower, and financial resources on the part of the statebuilders. Strategic choices and institutional models employed by statebuilders are also to blame for recent struggles with statebuilding.

This chapter presents an institutional theory of statebuilding. Unlike much of the social scientific scholarship on this topic, the focus is not on the variables that motivate rulers to initiate statebuilding; nor does the discussion dwell on the various structural conditions, such as climate, geography, factor endowments, population density, economic inequality, and ethnic diversity, that affect the probability of statebuilding success in any given territory. Furthermore, in exploring the institutional foundation of a modern state, the analysis goes beyond the formal political, judicial, and administrative institutions that constitute what scholars typically refer to as "the state." Although establishing a bureaucracy approximating Max Weber's modern ideal type is a critical and necessary component of statebuilding, there is much more to this process than bureaucracy building.[1] In particular, the chapter highlights the critical function that institutions of state-society mediation play in shaping the behavior of administrative intermediaries, whose assistance the state needs to obtain systematic compliance with rules and regulations from the subject population.

The purpose of mediational institutions, and hence their optimal structural characteristics, differs depending on the context in which statebuilding is undertaken. When the interests of statebuilders and socioeconomic elites align and synergetic relations exist among them, the primary function of a mediational institution is to coordinate their activities and to ensure the smooth flow of information and resources between state and society. In contrast, under statebuilding by imposition, the foremost purpose of mediational institutions is to serve as instruments of discipline, such that administrative intermediaries are compelled to behave as obedient enforcers of rules and regulations regardless of their interests. To this end, mediational institutions should be designed to maximize the state's capacity to monitor administrative intermediaries and shape their behavior through clear and consistent application of sanctions.

Significantly, these claims contradict the way that the statebuilding process is commonly perceived by Western scholars and practitioners. Because statebuilding, properly conceived, extends to institutions at the interface of state and society that regulate people's social and economic behaviors and interactions, its success, when pursued amid resistance, necessitates some degree of social engineering. The objective of such institutional reforms is to furnish rulers with the capacity to compel systematic compliance with rules and regulations that go against people's self-interest. Statebuilding by imposition, in this way, demands construction of a societal structure that is diametrically opposed to the autonomous civil society model that has become accepted as the standard of good governance in Western democratic theory and practice.

Statebuilding and the Limits of Bureaucratization

Statebuilding is the process through which rulers seek to expand the scope of government over a wide array of people's political, social, and economic behaviors. Whereas various political and socioeconomic actors—such as religious orders, guilds and corporations, and warlords and aristocrats—once made binding rules over subject populations, fielded their own armies and militias, and autonomously maintained law and order within their territorial sphere of influence, an ideal-typical modern state monopolizes legislative, coercive, and judicial power and authority. In the economic sphere, a modern state ensures that all economic transactions that take place within its jurisdiction are subject to a common set of rules and regulations, and that weights and measures are standardized across the realm; it negotiates trade treaties with other sovereign actors with a single voice and compels all businesses operating within its borders to abide by these agreements.[2]

Although some of the foregoing features of political modernity were already present in classical antiquity and ancient China, it is in the social sphere that modern states are most clearly distinguishable from their predecessors. Viewing any individual behavior or social interaction with consequences for the wider community as within the rightful bounds of public policy, modern states have extended their regulatory scope into matters previously controlled by societal actors, as well as those considered to lie within the private sphere of the family or individual. Education, which was once predominantly provided and managed by religious entities or private institutions, thus became subject to various government regulations on pedagogical content, accessibility, and faculty training.[3] Rather than allow custom and family preferences to determine whether children were educated, some level of schooling became universal and compulsory. Even more intrusive were regulations over health and hygiene, which dictated the shape and layout of houses, streets, public spaces, and neighborhoods, as well as the materials and methods used for their construction and maintenance. In the name of public health, how people prepared, sold, and ate food, used water, disposed of excrements, and buried the dead were all made subject to government control or oversight; mothers were told what they should and should not feed their children, and vaccinations became mandatory—or at least strongly encouraged—such that people's bodies, and the body politic, would be protected from deadly viruses.[4]

Such expansion in the scope of government, in turn, necessitated greater administrative capacity to obtain quantifiable data on economic and social phenomena; to analyze this data and formulate public policy; to craft and enact relevant regulations and legislations; and finally, to compel the subject population to abide by these rules. Yet, this was hardly straightforward for governments to accomplish, and even states that eventually became known for their commitment to, and success in, statebuilding initially struggled to expand their regulatory scope over society.

Between 1800 and 1801, for example, France's newly created Bureau de Statistique sought to gather detailed information on the French population and economy to demonstrate that people's lives had improved under the republican regime. By collecting social and economic data and presenting it as a description of *French* society and economy, bureau officials sought to advance the notion that the various peoples of the republic in fact composed a single national community. Without the manpower to collect this information itself, however, the bureau sent a detailed questionnaire to the newly installed prefects of each department (province) on the occupation, property holdings, and wealth of the local population. Also of interest were data on the arability of land and its use, as well as statistics on domestic animals and the type and amount of goods produced on farms. The prefects were baffled and overwhelmed by these demands, for they too did not possess the staff or the know-how to collect such data. They sought assistance from local notables, scholars, and village elders, but cooperation was not always forthcoming. Even when prefects succeeded in gathering information with the help of individuals with deep knowledge of local customs and traditions, it was not the kind of information that the central government had requested, nor was it organized in a way that was of any use to the state. What the authorities had sought was quantitative data that they could analyze, rather than long and qualitative descriptions of local economy and society.[5]

As this account of the French Republic's struggle with implementing its first national census demonstrates, statebuilders' attempts to expand the scope of government were stymied, in the first place by the ineffectiveness of the bureaucratic apparatus. Before the late nineteenth century, the French bureaucracy, like those elsewhere in Europe, was simply too small, and its officials were without the necessary training, expertise, and organizational incentives to effectively enforce the rules and regulations of a modern, high-scope state. In 1800, France's civilian bureaucracy hovered at around 1 percent of the total population and remained at this level for much of the century. Its great power competitors were even further behind in bureaucratic development, with Austria, Great Britain, and Prussia possessing civilian bureaucracies that were 0.45, 0.41, and 0.33 percent of the total population, respectively, in 1850. It was not until the last three decades of the nineteenth century that the bureaucracies of these countries underwent meaningful expansion—with the Habsburgs of Austria leading the way with a sevenfold increase in per capita size of the bureaucracy—as rulers sought to make their modernist vision a concrete reality.[6]

The ineffectiveness of Europe's protobureaucracies was not only a product of their small size but also a function of traditional practices of hiring, training, and promoting government officials. On one hand, individuals were arbitrarily hired, fired, and promoted based on whatever criterion the ruler deemed most pertinent, be it possession of specialized knowledge and skills, perceived loyalty and devotion to the ruler, or need to maintain balance among competing factions and interests within the court. On the other, government positions often came to be regarded as hereditary property of the officeholder and, as such, were bought and sold as a source of wealth and power. Employment in these early bureaucracies was also seldom seen as constituting a profession, and for most individuals government service was not a full-time occupation. It would indeed be a mistake to describe those employed by government agencies in most European countries before the late nineteenth century as bureaucrats, for this terminology assumes a degree of professionalism and specialization of the government's administrative apparatus that simply did not exist at the time.[7]

Although the institutional hallmarks of a rationally constituted bureaucracy—specialized education for aspiring bureaucrats, use of examinations for hiring, and cultivation of a professional class of self-identifying civil servants—were first innovated in China in the second century BC, it was not until the nineteenth century that this was widely adopted by European states to meet the complex administrative needs of a modern state.[8] The first European country to institute these reforms was Prussia, which introduced, albeit on a limited basis, use of examinations for entry, tenure in office, seniority-based promotion, and a set schedule of salaries in the late eighteenth century. Britain, meanwhile, adopted a basic examination system for its Treasury Department in the 1830s, and after decades of gradual and piecemeal introduction of administrative reforms, government-wide civil service rules and procedures were enacted in the

1870s. It was in nineteenth-century France, where a degree from one of the *grandes écoles* ("great schools") became a key criterion for entry into the civil service, that bureaucratization of administration advanced the furthest among European countries at the time. By essentially requiring that aspiring bureaucrats all attend the same elite schools and receive formal instruction in subjects pertinent to government service, the French system achieved standardization and homogenization in training and outlook and cultivated a strong esprit de corps among bureaucrats.[9]

However, despite the critical role that bureaucrats play in a modern state, systematic enforcement of rules and regulations of a high-scope state cannot be achieved through their efforts alone. The problem is that the primary method through which bureaucrats obtain compliance with rules and regulations when public and private interests diverge is by the threat of punishment.[10] Yet, the cost of maintaining a bureaucracy large enough for the state to directly monitor the behavior of each individual is prohibitive. And even if this were financially and logistically feasible, saturating society with bureaucrats would not eliminate the asymmetry of information that naturally exists between state and society. Indeed, even in societies dominated by a large bureaucratic apparatus, people still find ways to conceal their assets and profits, get around health inspections and quarantines, and enjoy prohibited vices. Individuals may moreover feel empowered to openly disobey rules and regulations if enough people engage in such behaviors, calculating that the state has neither the capacity nor the will to punish every act of disobedience, especially in matters that do not meaningfully impact its security or fiscal health.[11]

Hence, bureaucratic expansion and rationalization was necessary for the success of statebuilding in nineteenth-century Europe and later in East Asia and elsewhere,[12] but it was hardly sufficient. Something critical is missing in accounts that reduce, explicitly or otherwise, statebuilding to bureaucracy building: an institutional mechanism at the interface of state and society that gives bureaucrats the authority to demand and receive compliance with an array of new, and oftentimes locally unintelligible, rules and regulations. For modern states to realize their wide-ranging public policy objectives, they need most people to *voluntarily* comply with most rules and regulations most of the time. This not only allows the government to employ punitive sanctions sparingly and with greater effectiveness but also, when the majority of people are compliant with the law, noncompliance is made much easier and less costly to detect.[13]

Voluntary compliance is especially hard to obtain during the initial stages of statebuilding, when modernist rulers seek to drastically expand the scope of government for the first time, or in weak states characterized by decades of misrule. For individuals residing in strong and modern states, who have benefited from

goods and services provided by government agencies, it may seem reasonable—
and even instinctual—to trust the authorities, meet their tax obligations, and follow the law. Such is not the case where people's expectations of government were
shaped under a minimalist or predatory state. As James Scott writes, "Living
within the [early modern] state meant, virtually by definition, taxes, conscription, corvée labor, and, for most, a condition of servitude."[14] It was thus in areas
where the state's administrative reach was the strongest (rather than in the so-
called state of nature) that the life of an average individual was "poore, nasty, brut-
ish, and short."[15] Similarly, in today's ungoverned and undergoverned spaces, the
state, or its substitute, is by no means a commonwealth born out of a social contract between ruler and subject. Instead, it is more akin to *bula matari* (he who
crushes rocks)—a metaphor originally used by the Congolese population to describe Belgian king Leopold's highly extractive and violent colonial regime.[16] For
such peoples, expansion of the government's scope implies greater hardship and
less freedom; statebuilding, therefore, is something to be feared and resisted, rather
than welcomed as a development that would better their lives and livelihood.

As a result, something seemingly ordinary to a modern and law-abiding subject, such as a national census, could arouse anxiety and become the cause of unrest in a polity undergoing statebuilding. The aforementioned difficulties in data
collection experienced by France's Bureau de Statistique in 1800 would indeed
be repeated all over the world whenever modernist rulers attempted to collect socioeconomic data from skeptical and fearful peoples. When British colonial officials in India attempted to undertake a census for the first time in the province
of Awadh in 1869, for instance, people questioned the government's intentions
and resisted the collection of demographic data. One rumor had it that the census was being taken in preparation for a policy whereby "one man from each
family, or every fourth man, was to be taken as a recruit, an emigrant, or a la-
bourer on the roads or to build an enormous fort." According to another, "England
had suddenly become so hot that the Queen had desired that two virgins might
be sent from each village to fan her night and day."[17] Similar types of rumors also
swirled around the Qing dynasty's 1909 census. In Jiangxi Province, violence
erupted when enumerators were accused of stealing souls to use in the construction of railroads.[18] Frustrated government officials dismissed such rumors as
symptomatic of the peasants' ignorance. Nonetheless, although these rumors
might have been based on misconceptions and untruths, they were rational responses from those accustomed to being treated as little more than sources of revenue and labor for the state, and who had come to trust only their family and
local community for their welfare.[19]

Furthermore, even when statebuilding is advanced by rulers who enjoy legitimacy from the subject population, people may still selectively engage in disobe-

dient behavior when new rules and regulations contradict customs and traditions, or go against their material interests. For example, establishment of a public education system, along with enactment of laws mandating some degree of compulsory education, is a common undertaking for modernist rulers. From the statebuilders' perspective, mass education contributes to the wealth and power of the state, as it leads to citizens who are more economically productive and, having internalized the myth of belonging to a national community, more likely to sacrifice their welfare and lives for the nation's prosperity.[20] Yet, to a farming household, children are important sources of labor, and parents would much rather see them work in the field or the kitchen, than study subjects in the classroom that are seemingly superfluous for life as a farmer. Similarly, modern concepts of public health and sanitation are likely to make little sense to those accustomed to using traditional remedies to cure illness and who see epidemics as having supernatural causes. To those unfamiliar with germ theory, rules that prohibit people from using the same water source for drinking, washing, and sewage will be seen as nuisances that are best ignored; vaccinations will be feared as likely causing the very sickness they are meant to prevent; and quarantines will be resisted so that family and friends can care for the sick and bury the dead according to local custom.

Compliance with rules and regulations may also suffer due to people's confusion and misunderstandings about what is being asked of them and why. Returning to the census example, most types of information that states seek to gather—ethnicity, land ownership, vital statistics, and the like—derive meaning and value from socially constructed categories. As such, for census takers to accurately ascertain the ethnic or racial composition of the population, people must first understand and accept the meanings associated with ethnic and racial categories found in the census forms; for land surveyors to exactly determine the boundaries of agricultural lots, people must view land as something that is privately owned, rather than communally shared. In general, categories that are meaningful to modernist reformers, but not necessarily to the subject population, must somehow be conveyed in a way that can be locally comprehended and accepted. The bureaucracy may have expertise in surveying techniques, the manpower to survey each household, and the ability to store, calculate, and analyze information, but if it cannot get people to actually perceive themselves and the world around them according to modern socioeconomic concepts and categories, the resulting data will be woefully inaccurate. For rulers to "see like a state,"[21] so too must those providing the data.

Indeed, it was precisely because of people's fears, anxieties, concerns, and confusions about the census—in addition to the provincial government's organizational shortcomings—that French prefects, as discussed earlier, sought the help of local notables in collecting demographic and economic data. In this particular instance, administrative intermediaries proved unable or unwilling to provide the necessary assistance. Nonetheless, this observation leads to the second component of a state's governance structure that determines its ability to systematically enforce rules and regulations: institutions of state-society mediation. While much of the scholarship on statebuilding has focused on the expansion and bureaucratization of public administration, mediational institutions play an equally important role in the statebuilding process. To fully understand variation in statebuilding by imposition, one must therefore go beyond existing analyses of the modern bureaucracy and its development and examine the conditions under which mediational institutions become effective instruments of policy enforcement.

The Administrative Intermediary

Mediational institutions—such as clientelistic networks,[22] neighborhood associations,[23] and government-administered mass organizations[24]—are the formal and informal rules and organizational structures that regulate interactions between government officials and local communities at the intersection of state and society. Unlike the modern Weberian bureaucracy, the specific structural and organizational form that mediational institutions take varies widely in formality, scale, membership, and social and economic functions across polities. Nonetheless, they all serve a similar role within the governance structure in that they facilitate coordination and relationships of domination and control between formal agents of the state and locally authoritative or powerful individuals in enforcing rules and regulations.

The central figure in a mediational institution is the administrative intermediary: the societal actor—such as a village headman, parish priest, president of a guild, or boss of a clientelistic network—who is formally or informally designated by the authorities as responsible for policy implementation within the locality. Of particular interest here are the various functions administrative intermediaries perform to assist the authorities in obtaining local compliance with rules and regulations. The first is their role in helping the state access local knowledge and extract any information relevant for policymaking. Intermediaries—at least those with strong local roots and ties—possess knowledge on native climate, geography, customs, and traditions, as well as information on people's demographic characteristics and interpersonal relationships. Such knowledge and information is vital not only to government officials who are tasked with collecting such data— census takers, land surveyors, and the like—but also to any frontline bureaucrat charged with policy enforcement, be it the schoolteacher, the health inspector, or the police officer.

Second, the knowledge that administrative intermediaries possess on local socioeconomic conditions and traditions, especially when they are sympathetic to people's fears, anxieties, concerns, and confusions, allows them to serve as effective disseminators of information and translators of a policy's content and intent.[25] As discussed earlier, the ideas and rationales underlying a modernist regime's social and economic policies are often nonsensical or unintelligible to those who are unversed in modern forms of knowledge. New rules and regulations may ask people to provide information in a form that is unfamiliar to them or to adopt unconventional behaviors and practices. It is the responsibility, then, of administrative intermediaries to ensure that confusion, misinformation, and misunderstandings are addressed and that people have a clear sense of exactly what they are being asked to do by the state. It is with their assistance that the subject population will learn the purpose of gathering census data; the way to correctly report the productivity of their land; the standard weights and measures to be used for commerce; new and efficient farming techniques; the hygienically proper methods for treating water and disposing of waste; and much else.

Third, it is the administrative intermediary's responsibility to persuade people to willingly comply with a rule or regulation. People oftentimes fail to obey not because they are confused or misinformed about a rule or regulation but because the government's new policies contradict what they believe to be appropriate behavior based on custom or tradition, or out of self-interest. Indeed, a landowner may blame his ignorance or confusion for "incorrectly" reporting the extent of his landholdings or the yield of his crops, when his actual intent was to hide wealth from the tax authorities all along. Parents may very well understand the benefits of education in the abstract but, belonging to a farming or artisan household, may elect to keep their children out of schools and in the field or the workshop based on what they perceive to be in the best interests of the family. Administrative intermediaries, to the extent that their authority is morally and socially derived and that they enjoy the trust of the community, are much more likely than a frontline bureaucrat to succeed in persuading such individuals that the government's policies are in the household's or the wider community's best interests.[26]

Fourth, if community members cannot be persuaded to follow a rule or regulation, it is up to the administrative intermediary to obtain their compliance through the threat of punishment. Such punishment may rely on coercive or remunerative instruments, but compliance is likely to be most effectively and efficiently obtained if it takes the form of moral or social sanctions. The village headmen in early modern Japan, for example, had the power to ostracize any household that failed to pay their share of the village's annual tax obligation, or that engaged in the type of behavior that would subject the village to official re-buke and punishment. An ostracized household would be ignored by its neigh-bors, denied assistance during harvest, and subjected to exclusion from social ac-tivities, such as feasts and festivals. Essentially, members of an ostracized family would have no means of maintaining their livelihood, or their sanity, within their community and thus little choice but to leave the village in shame and ruin.[27] Sim-ilar types of morally and socially derived sanctions are available to administra-tive intermediaries in tight-knit communities whose members have a strong sense of moral obligation to one another—what Lily Tsai terms "solidary groups"[28]—and can be employed to obtain systematic compliance with rules and regulations without the intermediary's resorting to outright coercion.

The fifth and final function of an administrative intermediary, at least in po-litical systems characterized by effective governance, is to serve the interests of the local community and to obtain the support of the state in pursuit of objectives that are important to the welfare and livelihood of community members. The duties of administrative intermediaries discussed thus far—collection and dissemina-tion of information and enforcement of rules and regulations through persua-sion and punitive action—are those that promote the interests and goals of the state, often at the expense of local communities. Yet, if enforcement of unwanted and burdensome rules and regulations was all that intermediaries did, it is likely that they would quickly lose the trust of community members and be seen no dif-ferently from a frontline bureaucrat. The ability of administrative intermediaries to obtain compliance, either by appealing to collective interests or through the threat of moral or social sanctions, would in turn diminish.

Furthermore, if administrative intermediaries are reduced to nothing more than disciplinary agents of the state, serving in this capacity is unlikely to appeal to those belonging to local communities who possess the capacity to collect and disseminate information, as well as the moral and social standing to compel people to follow the government's rules and regulations. Instead, the role will likely be-come filled by individuals outside of the solidary group, who are attracted solely by the financial rewards and political influence that come from being tasked with tax collection, distribution of government resources, and enforcement of various rules and regulations on economic transactions and social vices. An administra-tive intermediary who enjoys little legitimacy in the eyes of the people will still be able to obtain some degree of compliance through remunerative or coercive means to the extent that the intermediary controls valuable economic resources (such as land, water, and capital) or employs private security forces. The intermediary can also call in the police or the military for help. However, such an individual is much less effective in performing the aforementioned governance functions than an actual community *leader* with moral standing within the locality. Lacking normative bonds with community members, the intermediary is likely to engage in abusive behavior, become the object of hatred, and further erode any willingness on the part of the subject population to comply with new rules and regulations.[29] It is for this reason that, in order to maximize the contribution of mediational institutions to policy enforcement, the state should allow, and even encourage, administrative intermediaries to serve the interests of their communities within the bounds set by the statebuilders' goals and objectives.[30]

The most obvious way administrative intermediaries serve the community is by obtaining government support for the provision of popular welfare services, such as aid for the poor, elderly, and disabled, and for the construction and repair of roads, schools, hospitals, temples, and other public buildings and infrastructures.[31] In addition, administrative intermediaries advance local interests by negotiating with the authorities on how a new rule or regulation is implemented so as to prevent, blunt, or diffuse any negative effects of the policy on people's well-being. They may also decide not to strictly enforce a rule or regulation in order to protect people's interests. Insofar as such behavior is limited, discrete, done in a way that respects the state's authority, and helps to improve the locality's overall governability, the state may even purposefully overlook such acts of noncompliance.[32]

Administrative intermediaries, in short, play a critical role in local policy enforcement, especially during the initial stages of statebuilding, when confusion over new rules and regulations and resistance to them are widespread. However, such reliance on societal actors is not costless to the state or without its risks. At the basic level, the costs and risks associated with state-society mediation are similar to those found in any situation in which principals rely on agents for policy implementation: asymmetry in information between principals and agents allows the latter to selectively enforce rules and regulations in a way that benefits them personally, while disregarding those that are cumbersome or otherwise disadvantageous, leading to unevenness in rule enforcement across space and issue areas.[33]

Nonetheless, agency costs within a hierarchical organization—such as a bureaucracy—are mitigated to some extent by larger organizational interests, as well as a sense of esprit de corps among principals and agents. Such is not the case for principal-agent relations that are forged across different organizational structures, especially when they cross the state-society divide. For a typical administrative intermediary, his or her wealth, power, and authority are not dependent on the strength of the state itself. Intermediaries who are members of the local solidary group will likely seek to collect as little tax as possible and selectively enforce rules and regulations in ways that advance the interests of the local community rather than those of the state. As for the profit-motivated and predatory intermediaries who are unbounded by membership in solidary groups, they possess every incentive to take advantage of the power and privileges afforded to them to aggrandize wealth, buttress their coercive capabilities, and construct a web of clientelistic ties that promote their personal interests above all else. There are indeed numerous examples in the historical record of administrative intermediaries ultimately becoming the foremost obstacles to statebuilding.[34]

Taiwan during the late Qing period, as discussed in chapter 1, exemplified this dynamic. By collaborating with the scholar-gentry in cities and strongmen in the countryside, Qing administrators succeeded in maintaining their political authority through the course of the nineteenth century despite a multitude of rebellions and foreign incursions. However, these intermediaries often abused their ties with government officials to settle local scores and confiscate land from rivals, and through these actions they corrupted Taiwan's administrative and judicial institutions. The most extraordinary example of this was the rise of Lin Wencha of Wufeng, but the underlying process through which he gained his tremendous wealth and power was not uncommon. Unable to control the actions of administrative intermediaries, the government could only enforce rules and regulations that served the private interests of powerful strongmen and scholar-gentry families. The result was a high degree of unevenness in tax collection, provision of public goods and services, and law enforcement.[35]

What, then, determines whether administrative intermediaries serve the state as obedient agents of statebuilding, or become the very cause of state weakness? What explains the variation in the ability of the Qing and Japanese regimes to manage and discipline their intermediaries such that landed elites routinely skirted their obligations and eluded government control during the Qing period but served as effective enforcers of rules and regulations under Japanese rule? Although the Spanish and American administrations in the Philippines were equally unable to systematically enforce rules and regulations, bossism at the provincial level became a notable source of state weakness only in the latter period. Why? Such variation in governance outcomes within and across Taiwan and the Philippines, as well as in instances of statebuilding more broadly, might be explained in part by the extent to which the interests of government officials and socioeconomic elites align. Yet, interests alone do not explain behavior. Just as important, if not more so, are the informal and formal rules and organizational structures at the interface of state and society that constrain the behavior of administrative intermediaries and compel them to act against, or even reconceptualize, what they regard as serving their best interests.

Making State-Society Mediation Work under Imposition

To understand the cause of variation in the effectiveness of administrative inter-mediaries as agents of statebuilding, we must look at both interests and institutions. Starting with the former, the more that intermediaries see statebuilding as advancing their interests, and the more they benefit from the public goods and services provided by a high-scope state, the greater the likelihood that they will behave as obedient enforcers of rules and regulations. Conversely, when interests of statebuilders and administrative intermediaries are unaligned, the latter are more prone to shirk their responsibilities, enforce only those rules and regulations that benefit them personally, or sabotage policy implementation altogether. This is precisely why statebuilding campaigns have typically (but not always) seen greater success in polities where political and economic events and developments led various political and socioeconomic elites, including community leaders, to view, and even demand, construction of modern state institutions as a means to advance their personal or class interests.

Elites may support, even enthusiastically, expansion of the government's scope for a variety of reasons. Hendrik Spruyt argues that the development of modern state institutions in Europe reflected the desire of the merchant class for a strong central government with the capacity to enforce a standard set of rules regulating economic transactions internally and externally to advance long-distance commerce.[36] Other scholars have traced variation in statebuilding outcomes to the interests of the landowning elite, with factor endowments, degree of inequality in land ownership, and labor mobility determining their level of support.[37] Fear of foreign invasion and subjugation has also been an important factor in compelling elites to accept the narrative of the necessity of modern governance institutions, with total war arguably serving as history's greatest instigator of statebuilding. Conversely, limited wars have tended to divide rather than unite, and to motivate elites to seek self-preservation instead of contributing to statebuilding.[38] According to Dan Slater, various elite groups are more likely to favor statebuilding when the threat of social revolution becomes endemic and unmanageable under the state's existing governance structure.[39] If the political order actually collapses from internal strife, Tuong Vu has contended, statebuilding is more likely to succeed if one side achieves decisive victory, such that the successor regime is marked by interelite coherence in values, beliefs, and interests.[40] In short, although considerable disagreement exists among scholars as to why statebuilding is pursued in the first place, as well as why broad modernist coalitions of political and socioeconomic elites are forged in some polities but not in others, a common thread through most accounts of statebuilding is that it tends to succeed when widely supported by the territory's elite stratum.

Herein lies the fundamental problem of statebuilding by imposition: Contrary to the dynamics described above, in instances in which modern political and administrative institutions are *imposed* on local communities *and* their leaders by a small group of modernist rulers or by a foreign power, socioeconomic elites will be skeptical of, if not outright hostile toward, statebuilding. Rather than seeing the state's monopolization of coercion, greater government oversight and intervention in economic and social affairs, and increase in the size of civilian and military bureaucracies as serving their personal or class interests, various elite groups will regard such expansion in the scope of government as a threat to their political authority, social status, or material well-being. Hence, instead of supporting the statebuilders in their quest to construct a strong and modern state, socioeconomic elites will be motivated to prevent the systematic enforcement of new rules and regulations. To the extent that the government succeeds in defeating all armed resistance and establishes its dominance over coercive capacity throughout the realm, socioeconomic elites are likely to put on an outward show of loyalty and obedience to the new regime.[41] However, the incentive for community leaders, in their capacity as administrative intermediaries, to engage in shirking, selective policy enforcement, and sabotage will remain strong. It is precisely for this reason that statebuilding by imposition often fails.

Yet, even when the interests of community leaders are initially unaligned with those of statebuilders, behavior conducive to statebuilding success may still be induced. State-society mediation takes place within an *institutional space* that determines what kind of individuals are chosen or self-selected as administrative intermediaries, as well as the nature of their relationship with government officials. The specific form that mediational institutions take will also have distributional implications, affecting how, and to what extent, government officials and societal actors exercise power over one another. A confluence of interests between statebuilders and administrative intermediaries will increase the likelihood of systematic enforcement of rules and regulations, but so too will an institutional structure that incentivizes intermediaries, regardless of their underlying interests, to behave as though they support the endeavor of constructing a strong and modern state. Outward behavior does not always reflect one's actual wants and desires, and although preference falsification may produce emotional distress and agony to the individual, it is a perfectly acceptable outcome to rulers. Ultimately, for statebuilding to succeed, what is important is that rules and regulations are systematically observed—and not why this occurs.[42]

What type of institutional structure, then, increases the likelihood that administrative intermediaries will behave obediently regardless of their personal or class interests? How can institutions of state-society mediation be designed to advance statebuilding by imposition? To address these questions, one must first understand that the primary function of a mediational institution differs depending on whether statebuilding is widely supported by socioeconomic elites, or is forced on them by imposition. If elites are generally supportive of statebuilding, then the primary purpose of a mediational institution is to serve a coordinating function. Ideally, mediational institutions would therefore be organized in a way that enables easy communication among administrative intermediaries, and between them and bureaucratic officials. Mediational institutions should also ensure that government and societal actors understand their duties and responsibilities and that any joint effort in tax collection, provision of public goods, or policing goes smoothly.

In contrast, although mediational institutions necessarily play a coordinating role under statebuilding by imposition as well, this is not their foremost function. Rather, it is to serve as instruments of discipline. It thus becomes important that mediational institutions aid the state's surveillance capacity by increasing the *visibility* of administrative intermediaries and their behaviors. In addition to advancing coordination between governmental and societal actors by clarifying the administrative duties and responsibilities of the latter, mediational institutions, as disciplinary instruments, must institute a clear and credible system of rewards and punishments. They may still serve as a mechanism for distributing goods and services to local communities, but they should also ensure that this does not lead to intermediaries becoming too wealthy and powerful for frontline bureaucrats to oversee and control their actions. When statebuilding serves the interests of socioeconomic elites, effective coordination between them and government officials in the enforcement of rules and regulations may take place regardless of the balance of power between the state and social forces. Such is not the case, however, under statebuilding by imposition. For individuals to be effective intermediaries, they must be locally authoritative but should also be limited in their ability to exercise coercive and remunerative power, such that they may be disciplinable through rewards and punishments.

This is achieved by structuring institutions of state-society mediation around two basic organizational principles: formalization and cellularization.[43] Formalization entails the codification and standardization of (1) rules pertaining to the duties and responsibilities administrative intermediaries are expected to perform; (2) punishments and rewards associated with performing these duties and responsibilities; (3) the criteria and methods through which individuals are selected to serve as administrative intermediaries; and finally, (4) organizational structures within which interactions between administrative intermediaries and disciplinary agents of the state, and between the former and members of the local community, take place.

Formalization serves a twofold purpose. First, it enhances the state's monitoring capacity.[44] As James Scott has argued, in order for the state to "see" its subject population and its members' behaviors, society itself must be made intelligible to bureaucrats. Just as cadastral surveys translate and reconstruct locally specific and socially derived norms and knowledge of land relations according to standard units of measurement and official categories and relationships—that is, information that bureaucrats can easily digest and record—state-society mediation can be better monitored if it is reconstituted in a manner by which bureaucrats can see exactly what intermediaries are doing (or not doing) to enforce rules and regulations.[45] The second purpose of formalization is to foster self-discipline on the part of administrative intermediaries. With clearly defined rules pertaining to the duties and responsibilities expected of them, as well as consequences for failing to perform such duties, intermediaries can develop unambiguous and universal expectations regarding what they must do to avoid punishments or receive rewards. Such a set of rules also allows bureaucrats to apply punishments and rewards in a consistent and impartial manner. Furthermore, predictability in the application of punishments and rewards not only deters noncompliant behavior due to a desire to avoid punishments or receive material rewards but also generates compliance out of a sense of fairness. Even intermediaries who view statebuilders as illegitimate intruders and disagree with the content of the government's policies will obtain satisfaction from the fact that rules are enforced (or at least, appear to be enforced) predictably, consistently, and hence justly. This will not only make it more likely that an individual will comply with rules and regulations for normative, rather than material, reasons but also that the individual will report acts of noncompliance by others for the sake of fairness.

Second, the government's ability to discipline administrative intermediaries is enhanced through cellularization—that is, the disaggregation of state-society mediation into the most basic units of sociopolitical organization, such as villages and neighborhoods. For reasons discussed earlier, administrative intermediaries are likely to be more effective enforcers of rules and regulations when they are community *leaders*, but a wide array of individuals may enjoy authority within the locality. A village elder, who might possess little more than the wisdom of old age; a religious figure, who exercises considerable moral authority within the community; and a wealthy and regionally prominent individual, who controls vast tracts of land, water, and the people who depend on them for their livelihood, could all potentially possess the ability to persuade constituents to follow a rule or regulation, or employ moral or social sanctions on those who fail to comply. Institutions of state-society mediation can therefore vary substantially in scale across polities: from systems organized around regionally prominent landed elites at the provincial level to those that take place on the small scale of individual villages and neighborhoods.

Although organizing state-society mediation at a larger scale requires a smaller bureaucratic apparatus to maintain effective governance—the fewer intermediaries there are to monitor, the smaller the staff is needed to maintain a robust surveillance system—and is therefore more economical, there are at least three distinct benefits to cellularization that relate to the state's sanctioning capacity.[46] First, it is much easier for frontline bureaucrats to discipline intermediaries with limited influence, wealth, and coercive capacity. Administrative intermediaries at lower levels of sociopolitical aggregation are also more interchangeable, and for this reason, the government is less likely to become dependent on any one individual for the enforcement of rules and regulations. Second, any personal profit and influence, as well as prestige, that comes from serving as tax collectors, distributors of state resources, or enforcers of public policies diminish accordingly with scale. Consequently, intermediaries in a cellularized system are less likely to accumulate the influence, wealth, and coercive capacity needed to corrupt or undermine the government's bureaucratic agents than those who mediate between state and society at higher levels of sociopolitical aggregation.

The third and, in the long run, most transformative effect of cellularization is that while it may even strengthen existing communal relationships and norms *within* villages and neighborhoods, it weakens traditional ties and networks that bind geographically proximate, economically codependent, or ethnically similar villages, towns, and cities into larger sociopolitical entities. Since each village or neighborhood in a cellularized system interacts directly and individually with government officials via administrative intermediaries to address local needs and solve collective action problems, the demand or necessity for nonstate mechanisms of facilitating *inter*community coordination and public goods provision declines. In turn, as traditional regionwide social and economic networks and community structures diminish in importance, so too do opportunities for socioeconomic elites to maintain clientelistic ties across multiple villages, towns, and cities and to challenge the power and authority of the state as autonomous political bosses. Furthermore, as the exercise of traditional and personalistic authority is constrained to interactions within villages and neighborhoods, people will be compelled to participate in, and acclimate to, depersonalized and rationally constituted political and economic institutions and relationships at higher levels of sociopolitical aggregation.

The goal of both formalization and cellularization, in short, is to increase the ability of the state to see and discipline administrative intermediaries. Yet, regardless of the effectiveness of mediational institutions as disciplinary instruments vis-à-vis the intermediaries, if the capacity of these individuals to obtain people's compliance with rules and regulations becomes compromised as a result of institutional reforms, the state will remain weak. For this reason, as discussed above, an important underlying factor in establishing effective mediational institutions is the authoritativeness of the administrative intermediary in the eyes of community members. At least during the initial stages of statebuilding, this typically implies the belonging of administrative intermediaries to the local solidary group, such that they have access to moral and social instruments of persuasion and sanction. If statebuilding is to succeed, rulers have to therefore attract the right kind of individuals to serve as intermediaries. To the extent that the state succeeds in getting true community leaders to serve as administrative intermediaries, statebuilders should then ensure that any attempts to strengthen a mediational institution's disciplinary capacity—whether this entails formalization, cellularization, or some other institutional reform—does not lead to the erosion of community leaders' authority in the eyes of the governed. Such a balance is indeed hard to achieve, and there are numerous historical instances in which compliance with rules and regulations suffered precisely because institutions and policies designed to enhance the loyalty or obedience of administrative intermediaries led to a decline in the locality's governability.[47]

Finally, what if traumatic and socially destructive events, such as war, slavery, warlordism, or rapid industrialization, led to the weakening or destruction of solidary groups and traditional mechanisms of moral and social sanctions before, or during, the initial phases of statebuilding? As discussed in the ensuing analysis, despite the destructiveness of colonial war, village- and neighborhood-level solidary groups remained robust in both Taiwan and the Philippines at the turn of the twentieth century. This is not necessarily the case, however, in all, or perhaps even most, of today's ungoverned and undergovered spaces. In such territories, the challenges associated with statebuilding by imposition are therefore likely to be even greater. Rather than grafting modern state institutions onto existing structures of local governance, an entirely new and formal, yet locally meaningful, system of enforcement and mobilization would have to be constructed at the foundation of society.[48] Nonetheless, while the *specific* solutions the Japanese devised in obtaining systematic compliance with rules and regulations may not apply to contemporary ungoverned and undergoverned spaces that lack strong solidary groups, the fundamental problem of statebuilding by imposition remains the same regardless of variation in socioeconomic conditions and communal structures within the locality.

Conclusion: From Theory to Practice of Contemporary Statebuilding

What explains variation in the outcomes of statebuilding by imposition? Why is success more likely with the support of socioeconomic elites? What role do elites play in the statebuilding process, and how can statebuilders obtain their cooperation when self-interest motivates them to oppose statebuilding? In the foregoing analysis, I advanced the following claims: (1) that statebuilding is made possible by a large and professional bureaucratic apparatus and mediational institutions that work in concert to obtain systematic compliance with new rules and regulations within localities; (2) that when statebuilding is pursued by way of imposition, and thus lacks the support of local communities and their leaders, the primary function of a mediational institution is to serve as an instrument for disciplining administrative intermediaries into obedient enforcers of rules and regulations; and (3) that mediational institutions are more likely to perform this disciplinary function effectively, minimizing agency costs associated with relying on administrative intermediaries for policy enforcement, when they are formalized and cellularized. Eventually, as people accept the state's claim to authority over a wide range of social and economic interactions and behaviors and internalize various norms, mores, and habits associated with modern subject-hood and citizenship, the state will be able to obtain systematic compliance with rules and regulations without the help of administrative intermediaries. At this point in the state's development, variation in a government's capacity to formulate and implement public policies will depend in large part on the effectiveness and efficiency of formal political, administrative, and judicial institutions. Until then, however, the structure of mediational institutions, and the resulting behavior of administrative intermediaries, will be among the key determinants of state strength.

The ensuing chapters substantiate these claims through a comparative historical analysis of statebuilding in colonial Taiwan and the Philippines. Before turning to the case studies, however, I would like to preview three broad implications of my argument as they pertain to recent and ongoing efforts by Western countries and organizations to reconstruct ungoverned and undergoverned spaces in their own image. The first concerns the claim that statebuilding by imposition is made possible through institutional reforms that change the constitution of society, making it disciplinable by government officials. By this, I do not mean that statebuilding by imposition can only be achieved when society is completely structured by, and subsumed under, the state. It is indeed precisely so that statebuilders may productively allow people to govern themselves (within limits) and engage in private and communal initiatives, interactions, and exchanges that

the need arises for *mediation* between state and society through institutions designed to discipline administrative intermediaries. Moreover, as discussed, the
most effective intermediaries are not merely disciplinary agents of the state, but
rather, local authority figures who see themselves as representing the interests of
their constituents.

Nonetheless, changing the composition of existing institutions of state-society
mediation or imposing new mediational structures on the subject population fundamentally alters power relations and hierarchies in society and the way that
people interact within and between local communities. As such, instead of society's
development being exogenous to the process of constructing modern governance institutions, social engineering becomes an integral component of statebuilding itself. My argument, therefore, departs from prevailing theoretical accounts of statebuilding that focus on what Theda Skocpol called "the state properly
conceived"—that is, "a set of administrative, policing, and military organizations
headed, and more or less well coordinated by, an executive authority."[49] It also
deviates from that which contemporary statebuilders, such as the United States,
the United Nations, and various international development organizations, see as
within the appropriate and legitimate boundaries of their missions.

The second implication relates to what is commonly known as regime type:
the extent to which a polity is democratic or authoritarian in its institutional constitution. An autonomous civil society, according to democratic theorists, plays
an important role in keeping the government accountable to the people and providing individuals the opportunity to formulate their own independent identities, interests, and policy preferences free of political interference.[50] In contrast,
the purpose of mediational institutions, at least in the context of statebuilding by
imposition, is to assist the state in penetrating society, compelling subjects to act
against their wants and desires, and, in the long run, shaping people's identities
and interests such that they coincide with those of the modernist rulers. Hence,
even if society is not completely subsumed by the state, it is still dominated by it.
"Self-rule," in turn, becomes a practice of communal self-enforcement of rules
and regulations formulated and imposed by the state.

If statebuilding is achievable simply by modernizing and strengthening the
polity's administrative apparatus (that is, bureaucracy building), then there is no
reason why statebuilders cannot also pursue reforms that democratize and liber-
alize the polity's political, economic, and social spheres. The most well-governed
and prosperous states of the contemporary period, with a few exceptions, are in
fact all liberal democracies. Yet, if successful imposition of modern governance
institutions necessitates an authoritarian societal structure, an irreconcilable
conflict emerges between the logic of statebuilding and that of democracy building. As the ensuing analysis of America's statebuilding mission in the Philippines

shows, the inability (or perhaps, impossibility) of American officials to resolve this conundrum lay at the center of the archipelago's descent into, in the words of Alfred McCoy, "an anarchy of families."[51] This observation leads to my argument's final implication: what stands in the way of statebuilding by imposition in today's ungoverned and undergoverned spaces is less the adverse structural or institutional conditions found within target territories, and more, for better or for worse, our inability to pursue the types of institutional reforms that would lead to its success.

THE *POLIZEISTAAT*

If one were transported back to late nineteenth-century Taiwan, the person would likely conclude that this frontier territory of the Qing Empire was a poor candidate for successful statebuilding. The ethnically diverse island was home to a multitude of lineage-based communities that were tight-knit and thus distrustful and cautious of outsiders. Such distrust between communities, combined with scarcity of land and unequal access to water, led to frequent intercommunal violence that made Taiwan inherently difficult to control, let alone govern. Moreover, because of the shallowness of the state's presence outside of market towns and its lack of coercive capacity, law enforcement, along with suppression of rebellions and banditry, largely relied on private means and efforts. The result was that Taiwan, before Japanese rule, was an unevenly governed polity where powerful societal actors, rather than government officials, dominated the political arena. It was a quintessential weak state, comparable to the so-called ungoverned and undergoverned spaces of the contemporary era.

What also decreased the likelihood of statebuilding success in Taiwan under Japanese rule was that Japan's attempt at transforming Taiwan into a strong and modern state took the form of institutional imposition. Whereas statebuilding is typically made possible through a broad coalition of political and socioeconomic elites, the Japanese statebuilding campaign was met with considerable opposition by the island's traditional administrative intermediaries—the scholar-gentry and the strongmen—who rejected, at least initially, the colonizer's claims to political authority, as well as its modernist goal of dramatically increasing the scope of government.

Yet, despite lacking many of the structural and institutional antecedent conditions historically associated with statebuilding success, and despite wide-scale armed resistance at the start of the colonial occupation, Taiwan was rapidly transformed into a strong and modern state. Within its first two decades, the new colonial regime succeeded in dismantling long-standing militia forces and monopolizing coercion; implementing a cadastral survey that doubled the amount of privately owned land recorded in official documents; compelling landowners, including the island's most powerful landed elites, to pay taxes based on these updated records; mobilizing the subject population in a campaign against bubonic plague; and much else.

What explains this unlikely outcome? Through what institutional structures and practices were the Japanese able to compel local elites, in their role as administrative intermediaries, to behave as if they believed in the legitimacy of the colonial government and its statebuilding agenda? As discussed in the previous chapter, there are two components to statebuilding by imposition: (1) construction of a large bureaucratic apparatus with the capacity to undertake many of the administrative functions of a modern state and (2) reconstitution of mediational institutions as instruments for disciplining administrative intermediaries into obedient and effective enforcers of rules and regulations.

This chapter examines the former of these two dynamics in the context of colonial Taiwan: how, after much trial and error, Japanese colonial officials adopted the *polizeistaat* model of bureaucratic administration, wherein the police became the most important organ of the state. But first, the analysis begins by setting the larger political, geostrategic, and ideological context within which Japan's colonization of Taiwan unfolded to explain why the Japanese, departing from European (especially British) colonial theory and practice, became so committed to statebuilding when they could have much more easily governed Taiwan indirectly and shallowly through native elites.[1] The discussion then turns to Japan's counterinsurgency campaign and how this initial period of conquest proved highly consequential to the long-term progress of statebuilding. Through this analysis, the close relationship that exists between counterinsurgency and statebuilding is highlighted. Military strategies that minimize the costs associated with conquest and occupation of territory amid resistance are not necessarily those that lead to development of a strong and modern state in the long run. Conversely, those that are costly to both statebuilders and local communities in the immediate term are more likely to engender the institutional foundation for statebuilding's ultimate success.

Japanese Colonial Policy as Expression of Pragmatism

The annexation of Taiwan was not within the Japanese government's strategic plan when it went to war against the Qing Empire in July 1894. Rather, it resulted from opportunism when the complete collapse of Chinese defenses in Manchuria allowed Japan's army and navy to expand their field of operations from the Liaodong Peninsula (with its strategically placed Port Arthur) to Weihaiwei (the Qing Empire's second most important naval base) and finally to the Penghu Islands. (See Map 3.1.) In this way, a war that Japan started to secure Korean "autonomy"—by installing a pro-Japanese government in Korea—led to Japan's annexation of Taiwan, after the island was included in Japan's territorial demands in the 1895 Treaty of Shimonoseki. Japan's peace terms with the Qing Empire were partially undone, however, when the so-called Triple Intervention by France, Russia, and Germany forced Japan to cede Liaodong Peninsula and Weihaiwei, which eventually came under the control of Russia and Great Britain, respectively.[2]

The Triple Intervention turned what was supposed to be a moment of national triumph into one of humiliation. Whereas Japanese policymakers believed that victory over China would demonstrate Japan's worth as a great power to the West, its aftermath became a reminder that Japan was still a junior power and a country that could be bullied into submission by the truly powerful. It was also a tremendous blow to Japanese strategic planning, as possession of Liaodong Peninsula and Weihaiwei would have positioned Japan for further imperialist advances in Korea and northern China. Instead, the intervention led Russia, Japan's greatest threat at the time, to further expand and consolidate its sphere of influence in Northeast Asia and place its army and navy in a position to militarily threaten Japan itself. Taiwan—a potential base for naval operations and international trade to Japan's south—was the sole bright spot in an otherwise disappointing and humiliating outcome. As General Katsura Tarō wrote in 1896, "Taiwan looks over the Pescadores [Penghu Islands] to the China coast and is linked, through Amoy, to all of southern China. It leads onto the South Sea islands and offers potential for controlling the distant South Seas in the same way that Tsushima joins Kyushu to Pusan and helps us control Korea."[3] Katsura—a member of the Japanese army's inner leadership circle, who would later become one of Japan's longest-serving prime ministers—reasoned that it was through Taiwan that Japan could extend its influence into China, now that the northern route was blocked. Japanese leaders, for both geostrategic and emotive reasons, were determined to make the most of this opportunity.

Realization of this geostrategic objective of "northern defense and southern advance" (*hokushu nanshin*) was of course contingent on Japan's success in

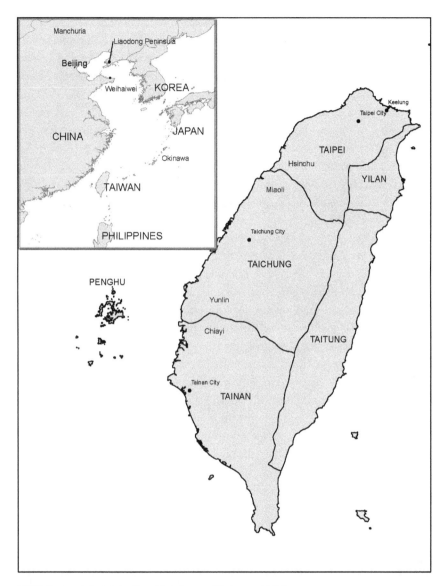

MAP 3.1. Administrative Divisions of Taiwan, 1901

Note: In 1901, Taiwan was divided into three first-class prefectures of Taipei (Japanese, Taihoku), Taichung (Taichū), and Tainan (Tainan) and three second-class prefectures of Yilan (Giran), Taitung (Taitō), and Penghu (Hōko). Prefectures, subprefectural regions, and cities in Taiwan are all transliterated according to contemporary convention, rather than those employed by Japan in 1901.

securing control over Taiwan and mobilizing the island's people and resources for its imperialist ambitions. Yet, because Taiwan was a late addition to Japan's wartime strategic planning, little preparation had been made for governing Taiwan. In fact, when Taiwan was formally annexed in May 1895, policymakers had not even decided on the most basic legal and political framework for Taiwan's administration and incorporation into the Japanese Empire.[4] Would it be governed directly by Tokyo, like Hokkaido and Okinawa—territories that were incorporated into the Japanese nation-state in the late nineteenth century—until it was deemed ready to be made into a regular Japanese province? Or would Taiwan become Japan's first overseas colonial possession? Japanese policymakers were united in their desire to make Taiwan a permanent part of the Japanese Empire, but what was the best model for achieving this goal: Ireland, Algeria, and Alsace-Lorraine, which were governed as integral parts of the national territories of Britain, France, and Germany, respectively, or British Crown colonies such as India, which were designated as administratively, politically, and culturally distinct domains of the empire?

As Japan had repeatedly done since American gunships forcefully ended its three-century-long self-imposed isolation from the international community in 1853, Prime Minister Itō Hirobumi turned to Western precedent and sought advice from Montague Kirkwood (an Englishman) and Michel Revon (a Frenchman) on the matter. Their views, in turn, presented Japanese policymakers with two contrasting options: (1) govern Taiwan through native rulers and by relying on existing political and judicial institutions and practices—that is, the model of indirect rule; or (2) impose modern governance institutions onto Taiwan with the aim of incorporating and assimilating the island as an integral part of the home territory.

Kirkwood argued that Japan should treat Taiwan as a foreign territory and thus govern it according to proven methods of colonial administration.[5] Using the British Crown colonies of India, Ceylon (present-day Sri Lanka), and Jamaica as examples, Kirkwood recommended that the Japanese government institute a governance structure for Taiwan that positioned it as a politically and culturally distinct entity from Japan. Departing from administrative institutions that were adopted in Japan's newly incorporated territories of Okinawa and Hokkaido—where the local bureaucracy was composed of bureaucrats from the central administration in Tokyo—an autonomous colonial civil service should be created. Taiwan would also be politically severed from Japan through creation of an indigenous legislative body, and unlike in Okinawa and Hokkaido, its inhabitants would never attain representation in the Imperial Diet. As for the judicial system, existing Qing-era statutes and legal procedures, as well as the island's own customary laws, were to be preserved as much as possible and used as the basis of

Taiwan's unique legal code. The legitimacy of Japan's domination over Taiwan was to largely come from its ability to provide the Taiwanese people with good governance, rather than from the notion that they could be absorbed into the Japanese nation so as to construct a single and inseparable political and cultural community.[6]

If Kirkwood's argument assumed that racial differences between the Japanese and the Taiwanese prevented the island's complete and permanent integration into Japan's national community, Revon took the position that Japan could and should "assimilate Formosa [Taiwan] and the Pescadores [Penghu Islands] as fully as possible ... [and] plan on making these islands a prefecture of the empire in the future."[7] Revon's suggestion was essentially to pursue a set of policies that would lead to both the cultural assimilation of the Taiwanese people and the political and institutional absorption of Taiwan into the Japanese nation-state. The former principle came to be known as *dōka* (cultural assimilation) and the latter as *naichi enchō shugi* (homeland extensionism). In promoting dōka and naichi enchō shugi, Revon did not suggest, however, that Japanese laws, or the various constitutional rights and duties of the Japanese, should be transferred immediately to Taiwan.[8] Instead, his recommendation was to put in place a framework through which Japanese institutions could be introduced in Taiwan over time, just as Japan had done in Hokkaido and Okinawa. Indeed, with Hokkaido considered a frontier territory inhabited by the "barbaric" Ainu people, prefectural-level elections were not introduced until 1901, and it remained unrepresented by elected officials in the Imperial Diet until 1902. In Okinawa—which was a semiautonomous kingdom that paid tribute to both Japanese and Qing overlords before its incorporation into Japan as a prefecture in 1879—the granting of the franchise was delayed even further; it was in 1909 that the first prefectural-level elections took place, and Okinawans had to wait until 1912 to finally obtain representation in the Imperial Diet.[9] Similarly, dōka was to be Japan's long-term goal for Taiwan, rather than its governing strategy.

The implications of the policy advocated by Revon for the lives of the Taiwanese were therefore not too different from the approach proposed by Kirkwood in the immediate term. At the outset, Taiwanese subjects would continue to be governed by their own laws and customs. However, the two contrasting governing schemes had radically different consequences for the long-term development of Taiwan's internal institutional order, as well as for the structure of the Japanese Empire as a whole. Under Revon's assimilationist vision, traditional Taiwanese laws and customs were impediments to the eventual imposition of modern institutions. The Taiwanese would be initially governed under familiar institutions to avoid confusion and unrest, but the objective was to completely rid Taiwan of its "backward" customs and traditions in favor of Japan's modern laws and administrative structures. Kirkwood's proposal also started from the notion that existing Taiwanese institutions were barbaric, but he assumed that they could form the foundation on which to forge a distinctly Taiwanese version of colonial modernity. Whereas Kirkwood's approach sought to keep Qing-era political and legal order unchanged in the locality, with the Japanese simply replacing Qing officials in Taipei, Revon's assimilationist position implied the transformation of Taiwan into a modern high-scope state.

Presented with these two contrasting visions for Taiwan, Japanese policymakers chose the path that maximized Japan's larger foreign policy objectives, as well as its long-term geostrategic interests—that is, Revon's assimilationist proposal. As a result of Japan's decisive victory against the Qing Empire in the Sino-Japanese War, Japan could now confidently consider itself the most powerful *Asian* country in the region. However, Japan was not yet among the ranks of the great powers, and its position in Northeast Asia was still relatively weak, as evidenced by Japan's quick capitulation to the Triple Intervention by France, Germany, and Russia. Hence, Japan's Taiwan policy could not simply be about Taiwan. In the view of Japan's top civilian and military leaders, the way by which Japan governed Taiwan should support Japan's immediate foreign policy concerns—such as ensuring that it did not derail ongoing negotiations with Western powers to reverse the unfair trade treaties and extraterritorial agreements that Japan was forced to sign in 1858—while buttressing Japan's long-term geostrategic interests.[10]

From this perspective, presented most clearly in Deputy Foreign Minister Hara Takashi's influential February 1896 position paper,[11] dōka and naichi enchō shugi were deemed the more strategically sensible approach to statebuilding: A thoroughly Japanized Taiwan—assuming that this was possible—was much more likely to become a strategic asset than a Taiwan with its own distinct national identity, or one where its population saw itself as part of a larger Chinese imagined community. Having successfully challenged Western aggression in Asia, Japanese policymakers were keenly aware that in an era increasingly defined by national self-determination, the colonial form of political organization had become fundamentally brittle. Only when the Taiwanese were culturally, administratively, legally, and politically assimilated into the Japanese nation-state was Taiwan's future as an integral component of the Japanese Empire secure against irredentist claims by China or an indigenous nationalist movement (which in turn could provoke Western intervention). Kirkwood's proposal might have allowed Japan to govern the island with greater efficiency and less friction in the short term, but it also would have created the preconditions for Taiwan's independence in the long run. As Hara wrote in a January 1899 editorial, "The doctrine of appeasement [as practiced by the British in their colonies] may buy peace in the short term, but brews calamity in the future, and will lead to our nation's demise."[12]

Hence, Japan's decision to pursue assimilationist goals in Taiwan did not result from preexisting ideological beliefs about how colonial territories should be governed, or from a normatively driven crusade to civilize the Taiwanese people. Rather, it was born out of realpolitik. Japan's commitment to statebuilding was thus devoid of ideological and normative content. All that mattered was that Taiwan would *eventually* become a seamless part of the Japanese national community; *how*—that is, through what institutional models and statebuilding strategies—this would be realized was unimportant. As such, just as pragmatism guided Japan's selection of dōka and naichi enchō shugi as its basic approach to statebuilding, pragmatism would also come to guide how these visions were put into practice.

Without an ideological or normative compass guiding them, the Japanese, perhaps naturally, initially looked to their own experience in their quest to transform Taiwan into a modern state and eventually incorporate the island into the Japanese national community. Specifically, they sought to mimic models and strategies employed vis-à-vis Okinawa and Hokkaido, where, as noted earlier, the Japanese engaged in "internal" colonization during the decades before Japan's annexation of Taiwan. First, officials imagined Taiwan as a possible settler colony, like Hokkaido, that could absorb Japan's rapidly expanding population. Accordingly, ethnic Han inhabitants of Taiwan were given two years to decide whether to remain on the island and become Japanese subjects or to sell their property and migrate to mainland China. The hope was that a large number of Taiwanese would leave, creating an opening for Japanese settlers to become farmers and landowners in Taiwan.[13]

Second, as in Okinawa, the full extension of the rights and duties associated with Japanese citizenship to Taiwan was made contingent on the success of the Taiwanese people in adopting and internalizing Japanese norms, habits, traditions, and language—that is, dōka was to precede Taiwan's full political and institutional integration into the Japanese nation-state.[14] As such, although Japanese civil, commercial, and criminal codes, as well as codes of civil and criminal procedures, were officially extended to Taiwan in June 1898, the new laws and legal procedures were applied only to Japanese nationals and foreign residents from Western countries. The Taiwanese people also did not enjoy the right to elect delegates to the Imperial Diet, nor were they obliged to serve in the military during times of war.[15] Meanwhile, in an attempt to expedite cultural assimilation of the Taiwanese, a number of Japanese-language schools were established immediately after annexation with plans to create an elaborate public school system in the ensuing years. The plan, drafted by Izawa Shūji, chief of Education Affairs, called for providing free primary and secondary education to the Taiwanese masses that would mirror the Japanese school system in length (that is, ten years in total).

As for the content of the curriculum, Izawa proposed the initial use of Confucian classics as core texts to ease the transition. Otherwise, subjects taught in the new colonial schools, including ethics, Japanese national language, writing, arithmetic, geography, history, art, music, and exercise, would mirror Japan's public school curriculum.[16]

It did not take long, however, for Japanese colonial officials to realize that these policies, while they may have contributed to cultural assimilation and political integration in Okinawa and Hokkaido, were faltering in the Taiwanese context. Despite the government's efforts to promote Japanese migration to Taiwan, the island's climate and its disease environment proved far too hostile for Japanese farmers—at least during the early years of Taiwan's colonization—who regarded Hawai'i, the United States, Canada, and eventually Latin American countries as superior destinations to start a new life.[17] Any hope that assimilation of Taiwan could be rapidly advanced via settler colonialism was quickly abandoned as the realization set in that the Taiwanese people, rather than Japanese settlers, would compose the vast majority of the island's population. In turn, efforts to understand Taiwan's existing legal, political, and socioeconomic systems were redoubled so that the Government-General of Taiwan (GGT) could institute new laws and regulations that took into account local customs and traditions.[18]

Izawa's education policy, moreover, was never fully adopted due to difficulties convincing Taiwanese elites to send their children to the new public schools, as well as concerns that the system proposed by Izawa would be far too expensive to implement and maintain. Observing that independence movements in colonized territories across the globe were being led by the educated elite, top colonial officials also feared that Izawa's proposal to give the Taiwanese people the same quality education as Japanese settlers could undermine Japan's control over Taiwan; if the goal was to ensure that Taiwan remained a perpetual part of Japan, it was better to keep the island's native inhabitants uneducated or undereducated for the time being.[19] The system that was eventually adopted in 1898 therefore shortened the length of public school education (primary and secondary combined) from the original ten years to six. Additionally, whereas Izawa's proposal called for public education to be free of charge, new schools would be established only in areas where communities were willing to fund them through local taxation and private donations.[20] In essence, this implied that dōka, at least initially, would not be pursued as a matter of public policy. In turn, although the colonial government retained its commitment to naichi enchō shugi as its ultimate vision for Taiwan, this was to happen after a "natural" multigenerational process of cultural assimilation.

In sum, motivated by what they saw as a pressing geostrategic rationale to integrate Taiwan into the Japanese national community, Japanese policymakers were committed to statebuilding à la dōka and naichi enchō shugi, but they were also pragmatic and flexible in how they achieved these outcomes. This commitment, no matter how strong it might have been, did not mean that the Japanese would succeed in making Taiwan into a strong state, or that they would be able to assimilate and integrate the Taiwanese people into the Japanese nation-state. The outcome of Japanese colonial policy during the initial period from 1895 to 1897 was in fact a catastrophe for all parties involved. The draconian counterinsurgency strategies that the imperial army adopted to suppress Taiwanese resistance led to the loss of tens of thousands of lives and only served to fuel greater opposition to Japanese rule. The administrative structure designed by GGT officials proved both inefficient and ineffective and failed to obtain systematic compliance with new rules and regulations. So seemingly hopeless was the situation in 1897 that a growing number of politicians advocated abandoning Taiwan altogether.

Nonetheless, the GGT's pragmatic orientation did mean that colonial officials were more likely to flexibly adopt and readjust policies based on realities on the ground, rather than become constrained by popular ideological currents or domestically oriented political calculations in Tokyo. Most policymakers, and especially the country's military leaders, also remained firmly committed to Taiwan and determined to do whatever it took to make Japan's statebuilding mission there a success. This combination of commitment to statebuilding and pragmatism in approach would eventually lead Japanese colonial officials to focus their attention on institutions of state-society mediation and lead them to forge the foundations of a strong state.

The War of Conquest and the Demise of the Scholar-Gentry

If the outcome of the Sino-Japanese War was a moment of national humiliation for the Japanese, it was an act of treachery for Taiwan's scholar-gentry and for Qing generals and administrators serving on the island. Whereas territories such as Liaodong Peninsula and Weihaiwei had actually been conquered and occupied by the Japanese during the 1894–95 war, the closest the imperial army and navy ever got to Taiwan was Penghu. Taiwanese elites were therefore rightfully outraged that the Qing court so easily conceded their homeland as part of the peace settlements, especially when they had successfully defended against the French a decade earlier and were confident that they could do so again. Indeed, from the moment that word of Taiwan's inclusion in the terms of the peace treaty arrived in Taiwan, the island's scholar-gentry wrote letters of protest to Qing governor Tang

Jingsong expressing anger and frustration at being abandoned. Although they were born in Taiwan, the local gentry viewed themselves as part of the larger Chinese civilization, and in the case of the upper gentry, retained family, lineage, and business ties with their ancestral homes in Fujian and Guangdong. As members of the Qing intellectual elite, and as individuals who administratively and militarily helped uphold Qing authority in Taiwan (as well as in China itself), the thought of being severed from their homeland and ruled by the Japanese was more than they could bear.[21]

The news of Taiwan's abandonment was equally disheartening to Qing officials serving in Taiwan, who had previously fought against the French to protect Chinese sovereignty and influence and were prepared to defend Taiwan against the Japanese. Hence, rather than abide by Beijing's orders to transfer control over Taiwan to the Japanese peacefully, Governor Tang, with the support of the island's scholar-gentry, declared Taiwan to be an independent and democratic republic and sought foreign assistance in preventing the newly formed Republic of Taiwan from being annexed by Japan. To the chagrin of the republic's leaders, Western powers were unmoved by their call for help, however. Soon after Japanese warships landed in Keelung, Tang fled to mainland China, predicting that without foreign assistance, the fledgling republic did not have a chance against the better-equipped and better-trained Japanese forces. Yet, while Tang's betrayal and departure led to confusion and desertion among the republic's forces in the north, others—in particular, Liu Yongfu, who led the Qing army and navy in southern Taiwan, as well as heads of some of Taiwan's most prominent scholar-gentry families—remained committed to the struggle.[22]

The ensuing war between Japan and the Taiwan Republic would last only five months, from May to October 1895, but its impact on Japan's statebuilding effort in Taiwan was far-reaching, due to two critical decisions made by the imperial army's commanders. First, after seeking the help of the island's scholar-gentry in the pacification effort when they first arrived, Japanese military officials soon determined that their interests were better served by excluding the former political elite from the colonial administration. It was indeed the case that most of Taiwan's scholar-gentry had initially supported the creation of the Taiwan Republic and mobilized militia armies to defend against the Japanese invasion. They were nonetheless fundamentally conservative individuals whose personal well-being—as landlords, capitalists, and guardians of traditional Qing culture—depended on peace being quickly restored. As such, after the republic's northern defenses swiftly collapsed with Tang's departure and Japanese forces easily captured Keelung and Taipei, members of the scholar-gentry in northern Taiwan—now facing the reality of living under Japanese occupied rule—shifted their stance from that of resistance to accommodation. Their goal was to maintain the existing Qing-era governance structure as much as possible, so that they could continue to enjoy political power and social prestige under Japanese rule.

To this end, in August 1895 Taipei's scholar-gentry and wealthy merchants presented to Governor-General Kabayama Sukenori a plan to set up a system of state-society mediation called *baoliangju*, which was to be organized around the scholar-gentry's existing clientelistic networks. The plan called for setting up baoliangju offices, each headed by members of the local gentry, throughout Taiwan, as well as a central coordinating baoliangju headquarters in Taipei to be led by a group of the island's most influential scholar-gentry. The purpose of these offices was to assist Japanese officials in maintaining law and order and to mediate any disputes and misunderstandings between colonial bureaucrats and local community members. In exchange for their collaboration, the scholar-gentry would be granted special political, social, and economic privileges—essentially those they had enjoyed under Qing rule—and be treated with respect and dignity as corulers of Taiwan. The proposal, in short, was one that sought to preserve the scholar-gentry's political and economic interests, as well as their way of life, under Japanese rule.[23]

Japanese officials, who arrived in Taiwan with little knowledge of the local population and having yet to devise a concrete strategy as to how they would govern the island, initially welcomed this plan, and baoliangju offices were created in the greater Taipei area and surrounding regions. The Japanese did not see this arrangement as a permanent solution to governing Taiwan, however; it was simply a stopgap measure that was put into place during the initial months when the colonial bureaucracy had not yet been fully established. Moreover, policymakers in Tokyo, as discussed earlier, were coalescing around naichi enchō shugi as their vision for Taiwan, and the baoliangju system simply did not fit within this framework. Consequently, despite baoliangju offices' playing a critical role in maintaining peace and stability in northern Taiwan, as well as preventing misunderstandings and disputes between Japanese officials and the Taiwanese people from spiraling out of control, Governor-General Kabayama terminated his support for the baoliangju initiative in October.[24] This ended the first and only attempt by the Japanese to rely on prominent gentry elites as administrative intermediaries. From then on, individuals selected to mediate interactions between state and society would be those of much lesser means and influence; rather than organizing state-society mediation at the national and regional levels, as outlined in the baoliangju proposal, it would thenceforth occur at the level of villages and neighborhoods.

Second, just as consequential as Kabayama's decision to end the baoliangju experiment and to sideline the scholar-gentry was the approach he and other Japanese military officials adopted in pacifying the island. After Japanese forces occupied the provincial capital of Taipei, their initial plan to attack by sea the southern city of Tainan, the new de facto capital of the Taiwan Republic, was set aside in favor of an overland campaign, in which the army would conquer one Taiwanese city and town at a time down the two-hundred-mile stretch connecting Taipei and Tainan. Although the Japanese ultimately succeeded in their march to Tainan, the campaign turned out to be costlier and required much more manpower—over seventy thousand troops in total—than anticipated. The middle portion of this route traversed a mountainous region that saw many peasant uprisings, rebel activity, and banditry during the Qing period. As such, towns and villages located there were heavily fortified with impenetrable bamboo groves interwoven with thorny plants; their inhabitants were also hardened individuals, accustomed to protecting themselves against outsiders who threatened their security and livelihood.[25]

The inability of the Japanese to distinguish between friend and foe, and between villages that harbored the enemy and those that sought only to stay out of harm's way, further contributed to the difficulty of defeating rebel forces and controlling Taiwanese towns and villages. As James Davidson, the U.S. consul in Taiwan at the time of the invasion, observed:

> The greatest obstacle that the Japanese encountered was the smiling villagers who stood in their doorways, over which they had flown a white flag, watching the troops pass by. . . . But scarcely were the troops out of sight before guns were brought out through the same doorways and shots fired at the first unfortunate party whose numbers were sufficiently small to make it appear safe to the treacherous occupants. Troops now return and find the mutilated bodies of their companions in the streets; while at the doors and windows of the houses near, are the same grinning friends and the same little white flag, an emblem of peace, still floating over their guilty heads.[26]

Davidson was hardly an unbiased observer of Japan's military campaign against the Taiwanese people. Precisely for this reason, and because his views reflected those of the Japanese, both the content and tone of his account reveal how the continual ambushes, heavy rain, heat, and spread of infectious diseases, combined with inherent prejudices that the Japanese held toward the native population, led them to treat the Taiwanese with cruelty. Exhibiting little sympathy toward those caught between the warring parties, the Japanese shelled rebel-controlled towns from afar with artillery and burned to the ground entire villages suspected of aiding forces allied with the Taiwan Republic.[27]

By the time Liu Yongfu fled to mainland China and the scholar-gentry and merchants of Tainan surrendered in October 1895, the Japanese had done irreparable damage to their image among a sizable segment of the Taiwanese population. Hence, instead of Tainan's fall ushering in a period of peace, it merely served as a transition to a new phase in the conflict between the Japanese occupiers and the Taiwanese population. This time, rather than engaging in conventional battles against renegade Qing forces and the scholar-gentry's well-organized militia armies, the Japanese faced the daunting task of suppressing a multitude of small-scale uprisings, insurrections, and ambushes led by disgruntled members of the lower gentry, commoner leaders radicalized by the brutal actions of the invaders, and criminal elements seeking to profit from the instability. Uninterested in carefully diagnosing the cause of continued anti-Japanese sentiment and distinguishing among the various insurgent forces, Governor-General Kabayama simply labeled all armed opponents as *dohi* (bandits) and proceeded to punish them, along with any individuals and communities suspected of aiding them, with excessive violence.[28]

A downward spiral of uprisings begetting vicious reprisals begetting more uprisings made large swaths of Taiwan ungovernable. In December 1895, several cities, towns, and military installments came under rebel attack in northern Taiwan, and with the bulk of the imperial army having returned to Japan following the capture of Tainan in October, much of this region fell to rebel control. Reinforcements from Japan arrived in February 1896, and in the process of reestablishing Japanese authority in the north, many innocent people were killed as entire villages were again burned during the punitive expedition.[29] "Though the punishment was intended for portions of the population involved, it is unavoidable that the misfortune might have been extended to the whole village during the process," Kabayama wrote in May 1896, reflecting on the damage inflicted on the innocent during the counterinsurgency operations. "To conceal wicked elements, or to refrain from reporting what you know is not to be forgiven," he continued, and one "must bear the past in mind as a lesson for the future."[30]

The belief that indiscriminate violence was the solution to bringing peace to Taiwan was widely shared among Japanese military officials, and this destructive and counterproductive strategy continued even after the end of Kabayama's governor-generalship in early June 1896. From June 16 to 22, Japanese troops undertook a punitive campaign in the Yunlin region of central Taiwan, where 4,295 houses across thirty villages were incinerated. Unsurprisingly, such acts of wanton violence drove even more Taiwanese to join the insurrection outright or to secretly sympathize with the rebel cause. From late June to early July 1896, virtually all of Yunlin came under rebel control before Japanese reinforcements recaptured the region's towns.[31]

The ferocious resistance and the vicious counterinsurgency campaign had many lasting effects on Taiwan and its people. At the most fundamental level, more than thirty thousand Taiwanese—a little over 1 percent of the entire population—perished as a result of the war.[32] Moreover, the conduct of Japanese colonial officials during the armed conflict, the contemptuous attitude they displayed toward the Taiwanese people and their culture, and their rejection of the baoliangju system made it clear that there was no political future for Taiwan's scholar-gentry. The most prestigious position a scholar-gentry could now assume was that of *sangi* (counselor) at the provincial level—a symbolic advisory role that came with no real power—and the best employment most members of this former ruling class could hope for under Japanese rule was as schoolteachers.[33]

Politically marginalized, the majority of the scholar-gentry, following the example of Tang Jingsong and Liu Yongfu, fled Taiwan to the mainland. Whereas approximately 350 individuals holding upper gentry ranks in the Qing bureaucratic system resided in Taiwan before Japanese takeover, only 47 such individuals could be identified in 1900. Overall, about two thousand members of the larger scholar-gentry stratum and their families migrated to mainland China immediately following Japanese invasion of Taiwan in 1895, and their migration to China continued unabated for the next several years.[34] In the short term, the resulting political vacuum made it difficult for the Japanese to govern the Taiwanese people, as evidenced by the intensification of the resistance. In the long term, however, this presented the Japanese with an opportunity to put into place a new system of state-society mediation that served their statebuilding goals. Even as the scholar-gentry fled, remaining in Taiwan was a class of local notables composed of rural strongmen (*tuhao*), commoner landlords, and merchants who enjoyed power and authority at the level of villages, towns, and urban neighborhoods. As the Japanese would soon discover, precisely because they were less wealthy and less influential than the scholar-gentry, these local-level community leaders would prove to be far better partners in statebuilding.

The Failure of Japan's First Attempt at Statebuilding

By late 1897, it was clear that the Japanese military occupation of Taiwan, as well as Japan's attempt to reconstitute the island into a strong and modern state, had gone awry. Instead of Taiwan serving as Japan's strategic outpost and economic gateway into southern China and Southeast Asia, the various administrative costs associated with its occupation were draining the national treasury, and the unyielding peasant rebellions and insurgent attacks had taken a considerable toll on the morale of the Japanese army.[35] Given this dismal state, some even advocated selling Taiwan to France, which had shown an interest in taking over control of

Taiwan a decade earlier.[36] If Taiwan did not seem like a promising candidate for statebuilding in May 1895, by the end of 1897, even the prospect of maintaining a modicum of control over the island looked dim.

The problem was that the Japanese army proved inept at governing. Untrained in the science of administration or the art of governing, viewing themselves as culturally and racially superior, and having come to thoroughly distrust the motives of the local population, Japanese military officials interacted with the Taiwanese people with contempt and disrespect, and they knew only how to use excessive force in attempting to obtain compliance with rules and regulations.[37] Also proving to be problematic, at least in the short run, was Governor-General Kabayama's decision to sideline and malign the scholar-gentry. These wealthy and regionally prominent individuals were uniquely qualified to obtain the cooperation of the Taiwanese people, as shown by the successful baoliangju experiment in northern Taiwan. Had the Japanese decided to govern Taiwan indirectly through these wealthy and powerful gentry elites, it is likely that Kabayama and his successors could have avoided the costly counterinsurgency war that immediately followed the collapse of the Republic of Taiwan. The GGT's decision to partner with community leaders of limited wealth and influence, rather than the scholar-gentry, would ultimately contribute to statebuilding, but in the short run, this decision prolonged the war, led to more deaths on both sides, and brought Japan to the brink of abandoning Taiwan altogether.

Administrative reform, and in particular creation of a civilian bureaucracy to replace the military as colonial administrators, was therefore the top priority of General Nogi Maresuke when he assumed the governor-generalship in October 1896. To this end, Nogi expanded the size of the colonial bureaucracy from a full-time staff of 3,308 in 1896 to 5,838 in just one year.[38] He also sought to bring government closer to the people by doing away with the existing twelve subdistricts and replacing them with smaller management offices (*benmusho*), seventy-eight in total, each containing three sections: general, police, and tax affairs. In an attempt to reduce military involvement in civil affairs, Nogi moreover adopted the so-called triple guard system (*sandan keibi sei*), wherein Taiwan was divided into three security regions: the mountain and forest zone assigned to regular military units and gendarmerie (the military police); cities, towns, and villages, which came under the jurisdiction of the civilian police; and intermediate areas, where police and gendarmerie were jointly responsible. Furthermore, so that the civil administration would have sufficient coercive capacity to govern the Taiwanese population without military assistance, eighty-four police offices and eleven aboriginal pacification offices were created at the same administrative level as the benmusho as separate bureaucratic structures.[39]

Yet, despite these reforms, small-scale insurrections continued across Taiwan, and the island remained an unevenly governed territory where compliance with rules and regulations was low. In part, this was because Nogi's bureaucratic reforms—especially the way in which he designed Taiwan's new policing apparatus—were poorly executed, such that even Nogi's own staff were critical of the personnel costs, redundancies, confusion, and buck-passing arising under the new administrative structure.[40] In particular, the triple guard system became a source of friction between the army and the civil administration, and due to jurisdictional ambiguities surrounding the intermediate zone, it did little to prevent gendarmes, or regular military units, from intervening in matters of civil administration.

The police force was also not deployed in a way that maximized its capacity to punish lawbreakers or to contribute to monitoring community leaders. Given unstable conditions throughout Taiwan, and with insurgents often targeting symbols of Japanese political authority (like the police), the Nogi administration adopted the collective disposition model of police deployment. Accordingly, even the smallest police offices were manned by a sizable detachment of twelve to thirteen policemen, and in areas considered to be hotbeds of insurgent activity, police deployments ranged anywhere from forty to one hundred men. The hope was that this would deter insurgent attacks against the police, and if attacked, provide them with sufficient defensive capacity. However, this approach, while maximizing the police's coercive capacity, was not suited to making it an effective instrument of everyday policing. Although the number of police and gendarmes in Taiwan exceeded six thousand by the end of 1897, and their per capita numerical density surpassed that of Japan itself, the police—because they were deployed in large clusters within towns, rather than spread out across the countryside—were seldom a regular presence in peoples' lives, especially in the villages.[41]

Another contributing factor to the police force's ineffectiveness was its poor quality. To staff the seventy-eight police sections within the benmusho, in addition to the administratively separate eighty-four police offices, the meager colonial police force, totaling 230 inspectors and 1,200 patrolmen in March 1896, was rapidly expanded. By June 1897, the force had nearly tripled in size to 275 inspectors and 3,020 patrolmen, exceeding the 3,000-man gendarmerie. Under any circumstances, such a dramatic influx of new recruits would have strained bureaucratic quality, but this was particularly problematic in the context of colonial Taiwan. Since the GGT refused to hire any Taiwanese subjects as regular employees of the colonial bureaucracy, the police became staffed exclusively by Japanese individuals who, for the most part, knew nothing about Taiwan—its geography, history, culture, or customs—and had no understanding of the island's spoken languages. Meanwhile, by 1897 approximately four hundred Taiwanese subjects were employed on an ad hoc basis by individual police offices to serve as assistants, but these Taiwanese assistants, who were known by a more Chinese-sounding title (at least to Japanese ears) of *keiri* or *junri* rather than that of *junsa* (as the Japanese patrolmen were called), were not given any serious policing tasks. Largely used as coolies, they wore a special cap designating their status rather than an official uniform.[42]

The insurgency and high mortality rate among the Japanese in Taiwan (caused by their lack of immunity against tropical diseases) also made the island an undesirable location for Japanese citizens to pursue a career in civil service, especially as low-level government functionaries. The GGT was thus compelled to hire anyone, regardless of background or qualifications, who—attracted by the higher salary and bonuses paid to GGT bureaucrats compared to civil servants in Japan—was willing to migrate to Taiwan and enter the colonial service.[43] Predictably, those who joined the police force were hardly equipped to undertake the wide-ranging responsibilities demanded of them, and like the military, were prone to abusive treatment of the local population. Some even came with a criminal background. Reflecting the low quality of the colonial police, between April and December 1896, one hundred twenty-three patrolmen were relieved of their duties, two inspectors and seventy-nine patrolmen were fined, and twelve were admonished. It was estimated that the crime rate among the police was as high as 10 percent. Yet, little effort was made by the Nogi administration to address this problem through language instruction or training in police work before recruits were assigned to local police offices.[44]

Moreover, simply saturating a territory with colonial bureaucrats and bringing government closer to the people did not automatically lead to improved governance. Expanding bureaucracy alone was not enough to motivate systematic compliance with rules and regulations from the subject population. For the Japanese to substantiate their authority in a locality, it was critical that they obtain the cooperation of Taiwanese community leaders. This much Nogi and his fellow administrators understood. They lacked, however, a clear sense of how best to organize mediational institutions between state and society to achieve this end. They knew what they did not want—that is, the baoliangju or any other mediational structure that preserved and institutionalized the power and status of the scholar-gentry as autonomous political bosses—but not how to attract local community leaders as administrative intermediaries and turn them into obedient enforcers of new rules and regulations.

In the absence of formal and standardized rules and organizational structures regulating state-society mediation, the GGT had little choice but to rely on individual ad hoc efforts by colonial administrators to forge personal working relations between themselves and Taiwanese elites. For example, the upper gentry of

Taichung Prefecture in central Taiwan, among them Wu Degong and Wang Xueq-
ian, were initially unwilling to collaborate with the Japanese. This changed when
Murakami Yoshio became prefect of Taichung in 1897 and held poetry readings
and banquets in honor of the local gentry. He personally ensured that villages
damaged by flood received government aid and assisted in establishing schools
in the area. Both Wu and Wang greatly appreciated Murakami's gestures of
respect toward the scholar-gentry and his care for the general welfare of the
people. In return, they informally assisted the GGT in restoring peace and order
in Taichung. Similarly, Shirai Shintarō, a businessman who had studied *kangaku*
(Chinese studies) in his youth and had come to Taiwan to serve as an adviser to
the GGT's chief civil administrator, played an instrumental role in obtaining
the support of the gentry in the northeastern prefecture of Yilan to negotiate the
surrender of insurgent forces.[45] In such cases, members of the local gentry who
assisted the Japanese in defeating the insurgency and maintaining order were given
the honorary title of *shinshō* (gentleman), but this, unlike the defunct baoliangju
system, came with no social privileges or material benefits. There were also no
formal rules detailing the responsibilities of a shinshō, and no punishments were,
or could be, specified for failure to behave as obedient intermediaries.[46]

The informality of the shinshō system also meant that collaborative relationships between specific individuals often did not survive the death or departure
of one or both of the parties involved; practices of state-society mediation based
on personal ties in one locale were also not easily transferable to another. A notable instance of the latter was the GGT's inability to replicate the self-defense
associations (*jiei kumiai*) model of local policing employed in the Chiayi and Yunlin
subprefectural regions of central Taiwan, where it was originally conceived
with the support of local notables, elsewhere on the island. In the summer of 1986,
Furushō Kamon, head of the GGT's Home Affairs Bureau, met with members of
the local gentry and other prominent individuals during an inspection tour of
Chiayi. Chiayi and neighboring Yunlin were sites of considerable rebel activity
earlier in the summer, and Furushō had come to the region to seek advice from
local Taiwanese elites on how best to govern this hotbed of anti-Japanese sentiment. Upon learning that during Qing times, households in Chiayi and Yunlin
contributed able-bodied individuals to serve in a multivillage self-defense militia
(*lianzhuang baojia*) under the *baojia* system of household organization—wherein
each household was supposedly part of a one-hundred-household unit of *jia*,
which in turn contained a thousand-unit *bao* at the subregional level—Furushō
sought the assistance of community leaders in reviving this institution.[47]

With the establishment of jiei kumiai—the Japanized name Furushō gave
this institution—seemingly leading to lower levels of rebel activity in Chiayi
and Yunlin, Furushō sought to extend the system across Taiwan. However,

because baojia had atrophied in most other regions and been replaced by a system of strongmen rule before the Japanese period, and because the impetus for creating jiei kumiai had not come from local community leaders outside of Chiayi and Yunlin, the GGT's initial attempt in making baojia the foundation of its local governance structure failed everywhere else that it was attempted. What Furushō's experimentation with baojia critically lacked was a formalized set of rules and regulations that could be instituted throughout the island regardless of local customs, experience (or lack thereof) with baojia, or the extent to which community leaders were supportive of the initiative and willing to work with the Japanese.[48]

Where Nogi and his staff failed was not in the overall approach to statebuilding, but in institutional design. The large colonial police force did little to contribute to state strength, due to its poor training and ineffective deployment system. Meanwhile, given the existence of various traditions of governance across Taiwanese localities, the inability of the Japanese to access local knowledge or information, and the illegitimacy of the Japanese colonial regime, a formalized system of state-society mediation would have done much to improve Taiwan's governability. However, the Nogi administration was without a model for how to achieve this. What would come to distinguish the subsequent tenure of Governor-General Kodama Gentarō and Chief Civil Administrator Gotō Shimpei—the duo commonly regarded as having built the institutional foundations of a strong and modern state in colonial Taiwan—from their predecessors was their attention to the details and mechanics of forging an effective system of administration, not just within the state's bureaucratic apparatus, but in society as a whole.

Laying the Bureaucratic Foundations of State Strength

By late 1897, no improvement in Taiwan's security condition, coupled with high-profile corruption scandals within the GGT, led to the collapse of Tokyo's confidence in Governor-General Nogi. However, abandoning Taiwan was out of the question for reasons discussed earlier. Hence, rather than divesting in Taiwan, the military brass redoubled its efforts to make statebuilding successful by nominating General Kodama Gentarō as Taiwan's new governor-general. Kodama, having previously spearheaded the modernization of the Japanese army based on the Prussian model, was a seasoned administrator, widely regarded as the military's top intellect and strategist. Kodama was therefore arguably the most qualified individual to serve as governor-general—a position that, by law, had to be occupied by an admiral or vice admiral in the navy or a general or lieutenant general in the army.[49] In contrast, the individual handpicked by Army Minister Katsura Tarō to serve as Kodama's civilian deputy was Gotō Shimpei, who—as head of the Home Ministry's Sanitation Bureau—was hardly an obvious choice to lead Taiwan's civil administration at this critical juncture.[50]

Although Gotō had prior experience with Taiwan—having helped formulate the GGT's policy regarding the widespread use of opium among the island's elites—he seemed, to many, unqualified to become the GGT's top civilian official.[51] A medical doctor by training, Gotō was a graduate of a provincial medical school, and not the prestigious Law Faculty of the University of Tokyo, which typically produced Japan's top administrators. Having spent his entire government career as a bureaucrat in the Sanitation Bureau before his appointment as the GGT's chief civil administrator, he also did not have the experience, such as in financial or legal affairs, that was regarded as vital in leading a colonial administration. Katsura was nonetheless well acquainted with Gotō through their mutual participation in a conservative study group (composed of those who had studied abroad in Germany) and was impressed with Gotō's intellect and industriousness. Katsura, in fact, had sought to appoint Gotō to a prominent position in the GGT for some time. When Katsura briefly served as absentee governor-general of Taiwan in the summer of 1896, he had Gotō join him, along with Prime Minister Itō Hirobumi and Navy Minister Saigō Tsugumichi, on an inspection tour of Taiwan. And although Kodama was not personally familiar with Gotō, he had witnessed Gotō's capability as an innovative administrator when they worked together to establish an immunization system for Japanese soldiers during the First Sino-Japanese War, and thus supported Katsura's unusual choice for the top civilian official. Once they began working together, it indeed did not take long for Kodama, like Katsura, to become thoroughly impressed with the abilities of his new deputy, giving Gotō complete discretion over the GGT's state-building strategy.[52]

Gotō's approach to remaking Taiwan into a strong and modern colonial state stood on three pillars. First, even more so than Nogi, he believed that the police should be placed at the center of local administration. Specifically, the policing system most appropriate for Taiwan, Gotō argued, was not of the contemporary vintage, but one modeled on the "police prior to the eighteenth century; that is, a police organization whose duties are wide-ranging."[53] As a student of German administrative practices, what Gotō had in mind was the Prussian polizeistaat model, whereby the police were placed in charge of overseeing all aspects of local administration.[54] Second, although a committed modernizer, Gotō believed that a polity's laws should be founded on its own customs, traditions, and historical experiences. Hence, while it was desirable that Taiwan eventually become assimilated into the Japanese national community, assimilation was rejected as a guiding principle for institutional reform. The final component of his statebuilding strategy was what Gotō called *jichi*—a term that may be literally translated as "self-rule." Yet, in arguing that "the restoration of the traditional Taiwanese systems of self-rule is the most important priority in the rehabilitation of the Taiwan administration,"[55] Gotō did not imply that the Taiwanese should autonomously govern themselves through traditional political institutions and practices. Instead, what he had in mind was a local governance structure that relied less on direct bureaucratic rule and more on self-enforcement of government-imposed rules and regulations by local communities.

These three pillars of Gotō's statebuilding strategy roughly correspond to institutional reforms concerning (1) the bureaucracy, in particular the police; (2) the legal sphere; and (3) institutions of state-society mediation. The following pages discuss the first of these reforms, given the centrality of the bureaucracy in prevailing analyses of statebuilding, while Gotō's reforms on Taiwan's laws and legal procedures, as well as mediational institutions, are examined in chapter 4.

Colonial Taiwan as a *Polizeistaat*

Under the Nogi governor-generalship, the colonial police underwent considerable growth in size and role in local administration, but as mentioned, it suffered from inefficient organization and poor quality. Nogi also failed to completely extricate the military from civil administration, leaving the most abusive element of the colonial regime in charge of maintaining order and enforcing policy precisely in those mountainous and intermediate areas where the local population distrusted and feared the Japanese the most. The result was a policing apparatus that had plenty of coercive power but was without the means to wield it effectively so that compliance with rules and regulations was systematically obtained.

In transforming Taiwan into a polizeistaat, Gotō undertook a series of organizational reforms that reshaped both the structure and character of the colonial police. First, he strengthened the police by way of subtraction—by reducing the manpower of the army and gendarmerie and eliminating their role in everyday policing. In early 1898, the total number of gendarmes, at 3,400 men, was greater than that of the civil police. By 1900, however, the size of the gendarmerie had been reduced by half, and in 1905, only one company (composed of 230 men) remained. Meanwhile, the Japanese army stationed in Taiwan, which stood at roughly 20,000 men throughout the Nogi years, was scaled back to a single mixed brigade of 5,000 in 1898.[56] In addition, Gotō eliminated the triple guard system and prohibited the army from interfering in the suppression of dohi unless the police explicitly requested their assistance.[57]

Gotō also changed how the colonial police were deployed from the previous collective disposition to that of scattered disposition. As noted earlier, the colonial police force during the Nogi administration was stationed in one of eighty-four police offices or seventy-eight benmusho, and in units ranging from twelve to one hundred men. Under the new system, average police deployments per police office, which stood at around twenty-five under Nogi, were reduced to four or five. In addition, the number of police offices was increased to more than three hundred in 1899, seven hundred fifty in 1900, and nine hundred thirty by the end of 1901. With the total population of Taiwan just shy of three million at the time, Gotō's reforms ensured that there was roughly one police office, each staffed with at least three officials, for every three thousand inhabitants.[58] This diminished the potency of the police as a fighting force against insurgents, but in return, greatly enhanced its capacity to monitor and discipline the subject population.

The rapid expansion in the number of police offices was made possible in part by reducing the average size of police deployments, but this alone was not enough to supply the number of new police offices. An increase in the overall size of the force was unavoidable, and it was expanded from 3,290 in 1897 to 5,607 in 1900. The challenge, then, was to ensure that this did not result in deterioration in the quality of the police. Gotō's solution was twofold. Soon after arriving in Taiwan, he overhauled the existing meager police training facility into a full-fledged police academy. The academy offered a basic twenty-week curriculum for patrolmen (junsa), while those seeking to serve as inspector or lieutenant inspector were required to complete a forty-week course. Reflecting their wide-ranging duties as both law enforcement officials and local administrators, police recruits took courses in administrative law, criminal procedure, accounting, opium policy, household registration, jailing, and the *hokō* code (discussed in chapter 4), among other subjects. An important component of both programs was Taiwanese language instruction. To incentivize patrolmen to learn the local language, the GGT gave salary bonuses to those who learned to speak one of several Taiwanese dialects.[59]

Second, starting in 1900, Taiwanese individuals were formally recruited into the police force as assistant patrolmen (*junsaho*) and given uniforms and badges signifying their official rank within the Japanese bureaucratic hierarchy. In this way, Gotō was able to dramatically increase the size of the police without having to rely on unqualified recruits from Japan. Thereafter, approximately 20 to 30 percent of the police force consisted of local recruits, who were generally better educated and came from wealthier families than their Japanese superiors. This also allowed for the presence of at least one Taiwanese junsaho in every police office and greatly improved the state's ability to monitor the Taiwanese people, to mobilize them in the provision of public goods and services, and to alleviate any misunderstanding concerning new rules and regulations. Later, when the police organization was overhauled in 1920, the position of junsaho was abolished and patrolmen were divided into two separate ranks. Under the new system, although de facto racial segregation continued and Taiwanese subjects were largely relegated to the rank of second-class patrolmen, they were nonetheless given opportunities for career advancement. A handful of Taiwanese became police captains, and about 4 percent of first-class patrolmen were from the local population. Meanwhile, some Japanese junsa were demoted to second-class patrolmen, leaving a third of this lower rank thereafter composed of Japanese nationals.[60]

In addition to improving police effectiveness, Gotō's reforms strengthened and expanded the position and the role of the police in the colonial administration. Under the previous system, prefectural governors were responsible for overseeing the conduct of the police in their districts, making it difficult for the police to address problems, such as well-organized rebel groups, that spanned several jurisdictions. Gotō decided that a more centralized police structure was needed. A powerful police headquarters (*keisatsu honsho*) was created in Taipei, and Taiwan was divided into two police divisions, each containing ten district police bureaus. The district police bureaus, in turn, jurisdictionally corresponded to the newly created counties, which replaced the previous six prefectures as the largest units of local administration. Furthermore, in accordance with the polizeistaat model, Gotō subsumed institutions of local government below the county level under the police hierarchy by appointing police inspectors as heads of the subcounty offices (which had taken the place of the benmusho as the lowest rung of the colonial bureaucracy in the new local government system). He also created a cadre of specially trained policemen to undertake administrative tasks that went well beyond matters of everyday policing, such as management of public lands, economic production, public monopolies (namely, opium and camphor), education, and transportation and communication. In this way, the police department became not just a powerful branch of government, but the local administration itself.[61]

This expansion in the breadth of police duties and responsibilities was accompanied by reforms that intensified the depth of the patrolmen's interaction with the population. Much of a patrolman's day, true to his title, was spent patrolling the neighborhood. Police patrols occurred twice daily, and in strategically important locations as much as six times a day. During these patrols, the police would look for any suspicious behaviors and objects, as well as inspect the cleanliness of public spaces and ensure that individuals respected rules concerning hygienic behavior. The police jotted down their observations on whether rules and regulations were being followed, on any changes in the cultural habits of the population (in particular, whether they were adopting Japanese customs), as well as on the area's general economic conditions. They also conducted household investigations during the daily patrols to correct or update information contained in the household register, such as the birth of a child and people's employment status and occupations. In addition, patrolmen recorded anything that stood out regarding the personalities and behaviors of household members, relations among household members and their neighbors, and living conditions—both in terms of a household's cleanliness as well as its relative poverty or opulence. Such inspections were conducted without warning and as frequently as the patrolmen deemed necessary.[62]

A major shortcoming of the policing system under Nogi was its arbitrariness in the use of coercion. Before the arrival of Kodama and Gotō, all rebels were labeled as dohi and treated alike, regardless of whether they were actual bandits and criminal elements, or villagers motivated to resist the state and its state-building agenda out of fear or indignation. This approach made it impossible to employ moral suasion and material rewards to obtain the surrender of some groups while repressing others depending on their underlying interests and motivations. Aiming to facilitate the surrender of those amenable to living under Japanese colonial rule, Kodama publicly announced his belief that many of those who were engaging in rebellious activities were doing so because of abuse they suffered from the military under previous administrations, and that he had no intention of punishing legitimately aggrieved individuals if they disarmed and swore allegiance to the colonial regime. Recognizing that many of those who joined militias were often young men without any prospect for employment, Kodama further promised that the GGT would provide those who surrendered with jobs.[63]

Such efforts to entice surrender were coupled with reforms that made punishment for continued resistance more rule bound. Statutory punishments for subversive and rebellious activities against the state were not very severe under the Japanese criminal code, and those found guilty of endangering Japan's internal security were typically handed prison sentences of varied lengths. Capital punishment was infrequently employed by the courts. As such, although a large number of dohi leaders were killed during the Nogi administration, this was not because they were found to be guilty in a court of law. Rather, they died in combat or, as was more often the case, by arbitrary execution at the hands of the colonial state's security forces under the pretext of "urgent disposition."[64]

Gotō had no qualms about using capital punishment against those who challenged the political authority of the GGT; what he did find unhelpful was the arbitrariness with which violence was used by the state to compel obedience. In November 1898, Gotō therefore enacted the Bandit Punishment Ordinance, which overrode relevant Japanese criminal laws to make acts of "banditry"—that is, any rebellious activities against the state—punishable by death. GGT officials, under the direction of Gotō, used this law liberally (in combination with promises of leniency toward those who surrendered) to compel rebel leaders to submit to the authorities. Consequently, although instances of arbitrary executions by the military disappeared almost entirely, legal executions increased exponentially.[65] In 1898, even though the Bandit Punishment Ordinance had been in effect for only two months, the number of legally sanctioned executions increased more than fivefold compared to the previous year, from 54 to 282. Thereafter, the GGT averaged 716 executions per year between 1899 and 1902 during the height of Kodama and Gotō's counterinsurgency campaign.

The final round of reforms to the criminal code came in 1904, as Gotō, confident in the government's victory against rebels, shifted his attention to Taiwan's system of everyday police work. The most notable reform was the Fine and Flogging Ordinance, which made low-level offenses that had previously carried a statutory punishment of a short prison term punishable instead by a fine or flogging. The introduction of flogging as a form of punishment was controversial, as it had been banned as barbaric in Japan. Yet, in Gotō's mind, this system was far more humane than incarcerating people while their families languished. The law's provision to allow those who were unable to pay a fine to instead choose flogging— one lash of the whip was the standard rate for one yen in fine—was also seen by the GGT as benefiting the poor by providing them and their families a way to escape indebtedness and bankruptcy. Finally, the law expanded the range of offenses that fell under the police's summary judgment authority to include all offenses for which the statutory punishment was a fine or flogging. The average time from arrest to punishment was subsequently reduced to four days for most offenses. In this way, the police were not only a ubiquitous presence in people's lives, but they had the authority to efficiently punish those suspected of disobeying GGT's rules and regulations.[66]

In sum, by increasing the size of the police force and dispersing patrolmen widely across localities, improving the quality of the patrolmen, and reforming the criminal code and legal procedures, Gotō refashioned Taiwan into a polizeistaat. Yet, in doing so, his aim was not to make the GGT more violent toward the population or reliant on coercion for policy enforcement. Indeed, after 1902, use of the Bandit Punishment Ordinance decreased dramatically, and so too did the sentencing of dohi to death. The function of the police was instead to serve as a constant reminder of the state's expanded presence and role in people's lives. Moreover, as demonstrated in chapter 4, it became the principal bureaucratic organ that oversaw the behavior of administrative intermediaries and managed institutions of state-society mediation. The police's role as purveyors of lawful violence against the population was but a small part of their overall role as agents of discipline.

Conclusion:
The Limits of Bureaucracy Building

The bureaucracy of a state is often, and for good reason, viewed as the primary source of the state's strength: In a modern state, whether the objective is to collect statistical information, extract tax revenue, or ensure people's cooperation in providing public goods and services, it is the bureaucrat—the census taker, the tax collector, the health inspector—who is tasked with policy implementation.[67] This insight, which lies at the heart of the Weberian approach to the study of the state,[68] was indeed the central pillar of Japan's statebuilding strategy in Taiwan from the outset, and the reason why the Japanese invested considerable resources in constructing a large bureaucratic presence. In 1900, a total of 7,088 regularly and permanently appointed bureaucrats were employed by the GGT, which amounted to 2.5 bureaucrats per thousand inhabitants. By 1920, with a full-time staff of 15,282, bureaucratic density had increased to 4.1 per thousand.[69] Particularly notable, as mentioned, was the size of the colonial police force, which maintained a density, following Gotō's reforms, of approximately one patrolman for every six hundred people.[70] It was not just the size that reveals evidence of wholehearted commitment to bureaucracy building: The Japanese transplanted several administrative models in organizational structure, technical training, and record keeping to buttress the state's capacity for direct policy implementation.[71]

Yet, there are reasons to be skeptical of attributing Japan's statebuilding success solely to its efforts at constructing a large and modern bureaucracy. Japanese bureaucrats, especially the higher civil servants (*kōtō kan*), were perhaps among the most qualified in the world; they were Japan's best and brightest, given the prestige associated with government service and its rigorous examination-based selection method.[72] However, the extent to which this quality translated to Taiwan, even after Gotō's reforms, is debatable. Rules for recruitment remained considerably loose in Taiwan at the lower rungs of the bureaucracy for the duration of the Japanese period, because it was difficult for the GGT to attract Japanese civil servants to serve in Taiwan. During the *entire* Japanese period, only 2,628 individuals passed the GGT's regular civil service exam for the nonmanagerial rank of *hannin kan*, suggesting that most colonial bureaucrats were without the minimum qualifications mandated by the GGT's own rules.[73] In addition, even the competency and effectiveness of well-qualified Japanese bureaucrats were likely compromised by their superficial understanding of local customs, their sense of racial and cultural superiority, and the inability of most to communicate in any of the island's spoken languages. Direct interactions between Japanese colonial officials and the Taiwanese people often resulted in misunderstandings, resentment, and even violence at the outset of colonial rule.

The GGT, due to its racist attitudes and distrust of the Taiwanese population, did not attempt to solve these problems by recruiting locally in any meaningful way either. It was not until the 1920s that a Taiwanese individual rose to the rank of kōtō kan for the first time; and as late as 1931, only forty-four Taiwanese were employed by the GGT at the rank of hannin kan, and four as kōtō kan. The surge in the number of Taiwanese serving as formal GGT officials began in 1937, as the need for experienced colonial bureaucrats in Japan's newly occupied territories in China led to a shortage of administrative personnel in Taiwan.[74] One is therefore left to wonder how the Japanese managed to govern the island for so long and so effectively, transforming Taiwan into a strong and modern state, without relying on the Taiwanese as colonial bureaucrats.

What these observations suggest is that although the expansion and bureaucratization of Taiwan's administrative apparatus, and in particular its large police presence, contributed to statebuilding, it was unlikely to have been the only, or even the most important, reason for its success. Max Weber is well known for his analysis of the bureaucracy and its centrality in the functioning of a modern (legal-rational) state. But as the foremost scholar of political legitimacy, he also persuasively argued that the strength of a political order is not a function of coercive power alone; rather, states are able to collect taxes, provide public goods and services through people's cooperation and contributions, and motivate individuals to go into battle for national interests because the populace sees the state as authoritative.

"If a state is to exist," Weber wrote, "the dominated must obey the authority claimed by the powers that be."[75] To explain Japanese statebuilding success in Taiwan necessitates an account of how the island's new rulers acquired this authority, despite the colonizers' lack of legitimacy in the eyes of the Taiwanese and their doing little—as seen from the violent counterinsurgency campaign and exclusion of Taiwan's traditional political elite from colonial administration—to seek legitimation during the early years of colonial rule. Hence, to fully understand why Japan succeeded in transforming Taiwan—a seemingly ungovernable territory by the end of 1897—into a modern state, one must examine reforms directed at institutions of state-society mediation. The ubiquitous presence of the bureaucracy was certainly a key component of the colonial state's strength. Yet, just as important were institutional reforms at the interface of state and society, which compelled community leaders to behave as obedient administrative intermediaries and assist in obtaining systematic compliance with rules and regulations from their fellow subjects.

THE ADMINISTERED COMMUNITY

Although a substantial bureaucratic presence is necessary for the development of a strong and modern state, it is not sufficient. As discussed in chapter 3, the Taiwanese under Japanese colonial rule were among the most closely monitored peoples in the world, with police density reaching one patrolman for every six hundred individuals. Yet, this still was not enough for the police to ensure systematic compliance with rules and regulations by their efforts alone. The police possessed plenty of coercive power to punish those who disobeyed, but the problem was uneven access to local information and knowledge. Even with the government possessing advanced tools for information gathering, measurement, and record keeping, officials had little choice but to rely on local informants and collaborators to furnish them with the raw data necessary to "see like a state."[1]

It is for this reason that administrative intermediaries play a critical role in the construction of a strong state. In particular, community leaders possess the knowledge and capacity to provide authorities with information to monitor people's movements, assess value of possessions for tax purposes, and punish those who fail to abide by the state's rules and regulations. Yet, community leaders' privileged access to information, as well as the legitimacy they enjoy, gives them power—power they can use to advance personal interests over that of the state-builders and to weaken the state from below through selective policy enforcement and outright obstruction. When modern state institutions are imposed on a subject population by a small group of modernist rulers, rather than established under a broad coalition of political and socioeconomic elites, such risks associated with relying on community leaders for governance purposes is particularly high. As argued in chapter 2, for statebuilding by imposition to be successful through collaboration with community leaders, government officials must be able to discipline them into behaving as obedient intermediaries. This, in turn, is made possible by reconstituting institutions of state-society mediation into disciplinary instruments.

Whereas Chief Civil Administrator Gotō Shimpei's reforms of the formal policing apparatus are detailed in chapter 3, the focus of this chapter is on the institution of state-society mediation called *hokō*, which was among Gotō's earliest and most important institutional innovations in disciplining administrative intermediaries. Hokō's roots can be traced to the Qing-era system of local governance known as *baojia*—the two terms are in fact different pronunciations of the same Chinese characters. However, by the time the Japanese annexed Taiwan in 1895, baojia, which never functioned effectively as an instrument of state-society mediation in Taiwan, had atrophied and been superseded by alternative institutions of local rule centered on rural strongmen (*tuhao*) and urban scholar-gentry. As such, hokō's success in compelling systematic compliance with rules and regulations under Japanese rule cannot be explained as an institutional legacy of baojia. As this chapter demonstrates, it was rather a product of the alterations Japanese colonial officials made to baojia's basic constitution in its resurrection as hokō.

First, in reconstituting baojia into hokō, previously informal rules governing interactions between government officials and administrative intermediaries underwent *formalization*. By assigning specific duties and responsibilities—from maintaining roads to reporting deaths from contagious diseases—to the intermediaries, the Japanese codified and routinized what was expected of them and made it possible for the state, buttressed by its large police presence, to punish the disobedient in a systematic and lawful manner. Second, hokō's principal organizational unit was reduced in scale from one encompassing several economically or ethnically linked villages and towns to that of a single village or neighborhood. The colonial state's exclusive reliance on hokō as an institution of local governance also precipitated the decline of all other existing forms of state-society mediation that operated at a higher level of sociopolitical aggregation. This *cellularization* of Taiwanese society, in turn, made it difficult for intermediaries to abuse their authority, aggrandize personal wealth and power, or challenge the state as entrenched political bosses. By way of formalization and cellularization, Taiwanese society was thus transformed into what may be called an *administered community*: a societal order wherein local communities are structurally autonomous but are nonetheless organized by formal institutions of state-society mediation that allow government officials greater capacity to oversee and discipline administrative intermediaries and to coordinate their efforts in effecting the state's political and developmental goals.[2]

This chapter is divided into four parts. The first part analyzes the overall strategy adopted by Gotō in altering Taiwanese society to serve his statebuilding agenda. The reconstitution of baojia into hokō was the chief innovation to come out of this effort. The second part adds historical context to the discussion by describing the structure of state-society mediation under Qing rule and the ways in which this contributed to the weakness of the Qing provincial administration. Part 3, the heart of the institutional analysis, details the formalizing and cellularizing reforms undertaken by Japanese officials vis-à-vis Taiwan's existing system of state-society mediation to transform hokō into a highly effective instrument of discipline. Finally, part 4 examines how hokō officials helped to substantiate the authority of the Government-General of Taiwan (GGT) in the locality, and contributed to Taiwan's political modernization by integrating the island's multitude of lineage-based communities into a single "imagined community"[3] of imperial subjects.

Statebuilding according to the "Principles of Biology"

Dōka (cultural assimilation) and *naichi enchō shugi* (homeland extensionism), as explored in chapter 3, were the guiding principles of the Japanese government's statebuilding strategy in Taiwan. The former pertained to policies aimed at culturally and linguistically Japanizing the Taiwanese people. This was pursued by forming associations dedicated to eradicating "backward" and "evil" Taiwanese customs, such as footbinding, the styling of men's hair in queues, and opium smoking,[4] as well as through construction of primary schools in which Japanese was the principal language of instruction.[5] Naichi enchō shugi referred to the goal of eventual political and administrative integration of Taiwan into the Japanese nation-state as a regular prefecture, much in the way Okinawa and Hokkaido had been in the late nineteenth century.

In adopting dōka and naichi enchō shugi in principle, the Japanese government did not consider whether the Taiwanese would show any inclination toward becoming part of the Japanese national community. There is also little evidence that policymakers in Tokyo who formulated the government's policy toward Taiwan in 1895 had analyzed how Japan would actually go about assimilating the Taiwanese people.[6] Indeed, the decision to pursue dōka and naichi enchō shugi was more a reflection of larger Japanese strategic interests and concerns, and had little to do with existing conditions on the island. These policies were adopted in light

of the fear that the colonial form of political organization—that is, the designation and treatment of Taiwan as a foreign territory populated by people belonging to a separate nation, rather than as an integral component of Japan's national
community—had become fundamentally unsustainable in an era when colonized peoples around the globe were demanding their right to national self-
determination. Only when the Taiwanese were fully assimilated into the Japanese
nation-state would Taiwan's future as an integral component of Japan be secure.[7]
As Izawa Shūji, who served as the GGT's first chief of educational affairs, surmised, "To maintain order in a new territory . . . it is necessary to conquer its
spirit, dispel its old national dreams, and realize a new national [Japanese] spirit."[8]

Gotō undoubtedly understood the strategic benefits of a *successful* effort to culturally and institutionally assimilate the Taiwanese people into the Japanese
nation-state. But he was skeptical that dōka and naichi enchō shugi should or
could serve as guiding principles for designing new governance institutions.[9]
Underlying his objection was a belief in what he termed *seibutsugaku no gensoku*
(principles of biology). A committed empiricist, Gotō was highly critical of policymakers in Tokyo who, without having familiarized themselves with prevailing
conditions in Taiwan, arrived at dōka and naichi enchō shugi as Japan's statebuilding strategy through legalistic and deductive reasoning alone. Instead, he
advocated using scientific methods to investigate the customs and traditions of
the Taiwanese and the application of this knowledge to colonial policymaking.
He studied how the French, the British, and the Germans administered their
colonies to ascertain the costs and benefits of different administrative models, and
explored their feasibility in the Taiwanese context.[10] Moreover, Gotō believed
that policymaking should be characterized by flexibility and pragmatism and
that effective governance was a product of constantly devising solutions most
appropriate for a particular time, place, and set of conditions through careful
empirical research.[11]

While Gotō's dedication to empiricism and his anthropological approach to
institutional reform in Taiwan may be worthy of praise, seibutsugaku no gensoku
was also undergirded by a thoroughly repulsive set of beliefs. Gotō, whose world-
view was shaped by his reading of Charles Darwin, Julian Huxley, Gustave Le Bon,
and Herbert Spencer, was a believer in social Darwinism and in the notion that
national communities were founded on objective racial differences. Even if the
Taiwanese came to adopt Japanese language and customs, he therefore doubted
that they would truly become Japanese. At minimum, cultural assimilation was
something that took many generations, and even then the question remained of
whether underlying racial differences could actually be erased.[12] As Gotō explained
to Governor-General Kodama Gentarō soon after their arrival in Taiwan, "We
cannot suddenly change the eyes of a halibut to look like those of a sea bream.

Likewise, the fact that we need to respect customs comes from the principles of biology."[13] Taiwan could certainly be transformed into a modern state, but this state would be distinctly Taiwanese, rather than an institutional replica of Japan.

Finally, to Gotō, imperialism was a reflection of the natural process by which strong states grew as they defeated and absorbed weaker ones, as well as a virtuous undertaking whereby civilization and modernity were spread to the barbaric and backward places of the world. It was also of utmost importance for Japan to become a full-fledged and self-conscious imperialist power, since the possession of colonies symbolized great-power status. The problem with naichi enchō shugi was that it imagined Taiwan as constituting the new outermost rim of the Japanese nation-state, and if adopted as the guiding principle of Japanese expansionism writ large, it would limit how far the Japanese empire could grow. Rather than being the last in a chain of islands (including Okinawa) that extended out from the Japanese homeland, Gotō envisioned Taiwan as Japan's first and innermost colonial territory. Its purpose was to serve as "our training ground in colonial policymaking"[14] and to demonstrate Japan's aptitude as an imperialist power.

Rejecting both the feasibility and desirability of dōka and naichi enchō shugi, Gotō deemphasized and defunded policies and programs pursued by the previous Nogi administration that aimed to advance assimilation and set out to govern Taiwan by relying on local customs and traditions.[15] One of the biggest casualties of this shift in colonial policy, as mentioned in chapter 3, was Japanese-language education. Japanese-language instruction was certainly useful in training a cadre of Taiwanese secretaries and functionaries to serve at the lower ranks of the GGT, as well as in Japanese firms. However, any policy aimed at rapid and wholesale Japanization of the Taiwanese people was now deemed a waste of government resources that would only be detested by the local population. Consequently, the Nogi-era plan of providing the Taiwanese people with a six-year elementary education modeled after the Japanese public school system was scrapped in favor of a four-year program focused on vocational training and Japanese-language proficiency. Thereafter, public schools would be built only in places where local Taiwanese elites supported their construction and operation through private donations and collection of tuition. Compulsory primary education, which had been the goal of early colonial administrators and educators, was out of the question for the foreseeable future.[16]

In a further departure from the statebuilding goals and administrative practices of his predecessors, Gotō aimed to draft an entirely new constitution along with a set of civil and criminal law codes for Taiwan based on Qing-era legal practices and with Taiwan's customary laws in mind. The initial steps toward achieving this ambitious undertaking began immediately after Gotō's arrival in 1898 as part of his efforts to implement an island-wide census and to modernize Taiwan's existing system of land ownership.[17] Yet, it was not until April 1901, with the creation of the Commission for the Investigation of Old Laws and Customs (Kyūkan Chōsa Kai), that the work of drafting Taiwan's own constitution and legal codes began in full.

Led by the distinguished law professor Okamatsu Santarō of Kyoto University, the investigation of Taiwan's customary law became a massive undertaking that, in addition to a fifteen-member steering committee, required the employment of a staff of approximately one hundred field researchers and translators. The committee was divided into two divisions. The first studied Taiwan's legal system and administrative procedures. Of particular interest were laws and customs concerning land ownership and kinship relations (such as family structure, lineage, marriage, succession, and inheritance). The second division investigated the traditional economy, with particular emphasis on movable possessions, commerce, and credit. Eventually the two divisions were combined into one, and a third division, responsible for crafting draft legislations, was established in 1909.[18]

Although the Japanese had a long history of studying the Qing legal system, there was no previous research on how abstract Chinese legal principles translated into actual governing practices in Taiwan. Hence, in addition to examining all available Chinese legal treatises and standard Qing-era national and provincial statutes and miscellaneous works (such as local gazetteers and essay compilations), Okamatsu's researchers undertook extensive interviews with Taiwanese elites and collected anything that could help illuminate local norms and practices, such as contracts, ledgers, certifications, and inscriptions. The effort was monumental. It was not until August 1914 that the Kyūkan Chōsa Kai completed its multivolume report and produced a series of draft legislations to serve as the foundation of a new Taiwanese law code.[19]

Unfortunately for those who dedicated over a decade to this task, neither Gotō nor Kodama were in positions to dictate, let alone influence, Japan's statebuilding strategy in Taiwan (Kodama had in fact died in 1906) and to push for implementation of these draft legislations when their work was finally completed. Disregarding the work done by Gotō and his successors, politicians in Tokyo maintained their belief that dōka and naichi enchō shugi were to serve as Japan's guiding principles in administering Taiwan. They saw Gotō's reliance on local customs as a necessary but suboptimal short-term fix before conditions were ripe for the wholesale transfer of Japanese laws and institutions to the island.[20]

This did not mean, however, that the work of Okamatsu and his colleagues was without consequence for the development of Taiwan's governance institutions. Although the GGT did not possess the ability to enact a new constitution for Taiwan, or an entirely new set of law codes and legal procedures—such authority rested with the Imperial Diet in Tokyo—it was permitted to promulgate lawlike ordinances (*ritsurei*) that amended or supplemented Japanese laws to suit special Taiwanese conditions and circumstances until Taiwan was deemed ready for the wholesale transfer of Japanese institutions. Kyūkan Chōsa Kai's findings, as well as those of Gotō's staff prior to the commission's founding, became the basis of these ordinances.[21] Nonetheless, it is important to note that while Japanese colonial institutions, at least during Gotō's tenure as chief civil administrator, drew from research conducted by Japanese colonial anthropologists, by no means were they designed to preserve Taiwan's traditional order. Rather, as a comparison of Qing-era mediational institutions and those established by Gotō will reveal, the purpose of this research was to help Japanese statebuilders reconstitute Taiwanese society so as to make it intelligible and disciplinable.

State-Society Mediation and State Weakness in Qing Taiwan

The Qing state in Taiwan was neither modern nor strong. It was pre- or proto-modern, in the sense that the state intervened very little in the lives of the subject population. Official tax rates were low, and the government did not regard itself as responsible for providing many of the goods and services that we have come to associate with modern statehood.[22] Its weakness, moreover, was reflected by the state's struggle to evenly enforce rules and regulations over matters recognized to be within the proper bounds of government purview. To the extent that the state was able to suppress rebellions, resolve disputes among warring social forces, enforce the magistrate's rulings, and collect taxes on land and trade, it was dependent on the cooperation of societal actors—serving as administrative intermediaries—but this in itself was not what made the state so weak. The problem was that the institutional structures and informal practices Qing authorities relied on to mediate relations between them and Taiwanese community leaders led to unsystematic policy enforcement, development of a class of politically influential and autonomous local bosses, and corruption of the machinery of government.

For much of Taiwan's history as a frontier region of the Qing empire, the control exercised by the Qing state was deliberately shallow, and it was not until the nineteenth century that officials began to formalize—albeit in a manner that allowed for considerable local variation—existing practices of state-society mediation. These efforts came in three forms. The first, and paradoxically least important, was that of baojia. The baojia system was initially developed in China in the eleventh century, but it was not until the early 1700s that it was extended to Taiwan, following the island's incorporation into the Qing Empire. Instead of treating entire townships and villages as self-contained, indivisible, and autonomous entities, baojia, in theory, structured state-society mediation through rationally subdivided groupings of households. As originally conceived, a baojia unit was composed of three layers: ten households constituted a *pai*, ten pai formed a *jia*, and ten jia were grouped together into a thousand-household unit of *bao*. These units were then linked to the bureaucracy through a hierarchy of patron-client ties. Local notables (typically wealthy commoners) were selected as leaders at each administrative level, and the head of the bao reported to the local magistrate. The intention was for baojia to perform two vital governance functions within the locality: collecting census data and maintaining intercommunity peace by organizing a local self-defense force.[23]

Baojia was only superficially instituted during the Qing period, however. The pai unit of ten households was disregarded entirely, and Qing administrators simply relabeled organically constituted towns and villages as jia units. In turn, bao became a geographic designation that referred to locally determined groupings of towns and villages that shared common kinship or ethnic ties or constituted an interdependent socioeconomic unit that relied on a common water source for irrigation and was commercially linked to a single market town. Furthermore, while responsibility for maintaining census records continued to rest with baojia throughout the Qing period (at least in localities where baojia had not completely atrophied due to internal strife or neglect), its function of maintaining intercommunity peace was soon subsumed by a second, and institutionally separate, form of state-society mediation: the *zongli* system, which grew out of Taiwan's longstanding practice of relying on local strongmen to provide security on an island characterized by recurring violence between lineage and ethnic groups.[24]

It may be that the Taiwanese people, many of whom originated from the southeastern region of China, were culturally disposed to glorify fighting prowess, to take insults to their lineage group's honor seriously, and to resort to violence to settle private disputes.[25] Yet, whatever the cultural disposition of the Taiwanese people, socioeconomic conditions on the island certainly contributed to Taiwan's reputation as a violent frontier region of the Qing Empire, at least until the mid-nineteenth century.[26] When Han Chinese settlers arrived in large numbers starting in the seventeenth century, Taiwan had already been settled by peoples of Austronesian origin. It was by way of violence—what we would today call ethnic cleansing—that Taiwan's aboriginal people were pushed out of the coastal plains during the initial phase of Chinese settlement; later, it was again through coercive means that the Chinese extracted camphor and mineral resources from the mountainous regions of Taiwan that were still controlled by Taiwan's aborigines.[27]

The way in which Chinese settlers migrated to Taiwan also contributed to intercommunity conflict. Most of the original migrants from mainland China came to Taiwan as part of cooperatives that settled on uncultivated land, rather than as individuals joining existing communities. These cooperatives were generally composed of individuals belonging to a common ancestral lineage group, or at minimum, hailing from the same geographic region. The result was that each local community was a socially cohesive and tight-knit socioeconomic unit that viewed outsiders with distrust and suspicion. Also contributing to intercommunity tensions was the fact that Chinese migrants originated from different regions across China, each with their own unique traditions and dialects.[28] Given scarcity of land, rural underemployment, and private control over vital water sources, feelings of distrust and suspicion, fueled in part by ethnic differences, easily escalated into violent confrontations over land and water, leading to lingering animosity between lineage groups. The shallowness of the Qing state's military and policing presence, in turn, compelled local Taiwanese communities to rely on their own private efforts to maintain their interests, uphold their lineage group's honor, and settle disputes with rival groups.[29]

While Qing officials, out of necessity, collaborated with the strongmen from the very beginning, their role in maintaining local governance received formal recognition in the early nineteenth century after creation of the semiofficial position—that is, formally recognized by the state, but outside of the Qing bureaucratic officialdom—of zongli (overseer). In theory, any individual who possessed the traits of an ideal zongli, such as honesty, wealth, caution, diligence, and knowledge, could assume this position on nomination by the local community. In practice, however, outside of the commercial centers (where wealthy merchants often served as zongli), the position came to be occupied by local strongmen. For the most part, the zongli, although locally wealthy and prominent, were but minor political figures whose influence extended over no more than a few villages. In the Danshui subprefecture in northern Taiwan, for example, twelve townships containing 295 towns and villages in 1871 were managed by 110 zongli. In localities where more than one lineage or ethnic group resided, it was common to have a dual overseership, such that each lineage or ethnic community could be officially represented.[30]

Under the zongli system, the primary responsibility of the strongmen remained largely unchanged from before: the organization and maintenance of a private militia for the purpose of enforcing the government's orders, upholding the law, and suppressing banditry and rebellious activity. They were also responsible for mediating disputes between villages, such that conflicting groups could come to a mutually acceptable settlement outside of the formal court system (thereby lessening the administrative burden of the magistrate). It was also the zongli's duty to oversee implementation of local public works projects, supervise the baojia in compiling household registers, and inform the people of new laws and government proclamations. However, formal recognition of strongmen as zongli altered the power dynamic between the state and social forces in one important way: It afforded strongmen access to government funds, as well as opportunities to cultivate ties with Qing officials and—for the most cunning and ambitious of them— to significantly increase wealth and political influence. As such, while the average strongman-zongli employed no more than a dozen men in his militia and oversaw the affairs of only a few villages, some of them took advantage of their semi-official standing, as well as ties with Qing administrators, to dramatically increase their family landholdings (by disposing of their rivals as traitors and taking possession of their land) and to field large, privately controlled militias with hundreds of men under arms.[31]

Constituting the third and uppermost form of state-society mediation were the collaborative relationships that emerged between Qing administrators and the island's scholar-gentry class. The scholar-gentry were typically men of considerable wealth, many from Taiwan's large landowning, as well as strongmen, families. Yet, what distinguished them as a social class and gave them political and moral authority was not their wealth or control over coercive instruments per se, but their possession of official rank, typically as a result of passing the highly competitive Qing bureaucratic exam or through military service. Their emergence as a sizable social class in Taiwan did not occur until the latter half of the nineteenth century, but they soon came to play a role in the Qing governance system in Taiwan that far surpassed that of an average strongman. Unlike the strongmen, whose sphere of influence was largely limited to their lineage groups, the respect and prestige attached to the scholar-gentry rank allowed these individuals to operate at a much higher level of sociopolitical aggregation. They therefore had the ability to initiate, finance, and organize large and capital-intensive public works projects, such as construction of government buildings, city walls, temples, and regional communication and transportation infrastructures. When Qing authority was threatened by domestic rebellions and foreign excursions, they led large volunteer armies composed of ethnically related lineage groups to assist the government's war-fighting efforts.[32]

Starting in the late nineteenth century, the authority that the scholar-gentry enjoyed in Taiwanese society was further buttressed by their appointment as heads of ad hoc and quasi-governmental bureaus (*ju*)—an administrative innovation aimed at expanding the scope of government without increasing its size and cost. Intendant Liu Ao (the highest Qing official on the island), for example, established the improvement promotion bureau (*peiyuanju*) in 1882 to manage the sale and distribution of opium, such that the proceeds of the quasi-governmental opium monopoly could be used to finance welfare institutions and large-scale public works projects. His successor, Liu Mingchuan, was even more dependent on such bureaus to initiate many modernizing reforms, as well as to defend Taiwan against internal and foreign threats. Notable examples included the land tax bureau, the pacification and land reclamation bureau, and the local militia bureau. These bureaus were certainly beneficial to reformers such as Liu Ao and Liu Mingchuan, as they could bypass the regular Qing bureaucracy and implement their policies, with the help of the scholar-gentry, while not having to burden the provincial finances. The benefits the scholar-gentry accrued by their participation in such quasi-governmental bureaus were arguably even more substantial. It was through his leadership of the pacification and land reclamation bureau in central Taiwan, for example, that Lin Chaodong (of the Wufeng Lins discussed in chapter 1) came to exercise effective control over the lucrative camphor industry during the final years of Qing rule. Moreover, appointment as heads of local militia bureaus gave the scholar-gentry the opportunity to obtain formal authority, as well as financial resources, from the provincial government to mobilize and command thousands of volunteer troops during times of national crisis, thus expanding their clientelistic network beyond their own lineage group.[33]

This tripartite system of state-society mediation consisting of baojia, zongli, and scholar-gentry-led bureaus, despite enabling provincial administrators to maintain control over Taiwan through the many insurrections and foreign incursions of the late Qing era, had two principal shortcomings. First, it was only in the urban centers that the Qing government maintained a civilian and military presence at all times. The tripartite mediation system was in fact developed precisely to compensate for the smallness of the provincial administration. Hence, the only way by which Qing officials could learn of misbehavior by administrative intermediaries in the countryside was if the intermediaries' rivals brought it to the attention of the local magistrate. In turn, instead of the government's formal policing powers being used to enforce rules and regulations in a systematic and impartial manner, policing became an instrument for local elites to settle personal disputes, extract revenge, and appropriate land from their rivals. Indeed, there is no better example of this dynamic than the meteoric rise of Lin Wencha— the aforementioned Lin Chaodong's father—from a minor zongli in Wufeng to among the wealthiest and most influential strongmen in Taiwan.[34]

The second shortcoming was that because state-society mediation occurred at a high level of sociopolitical aggregation, administrative intermediaries came to rival, and even surpass, Qing prefectural magistrates in political influence. As such, if a Qing magistrate desired to punish an influential strongman or scholar-gentry for whatever reason, it required careful planning, plotting, and the implicit or explicit backing of high-ranking Qing officials in mainland China—that is, the kinds of actions directed at a political equal, rather than an individual whose place within the Qing political hierarchy was supposedly much lower.[35] Moreover, the wealth and political influence of prominent strongmen or scholar-gentry, combined with their direct control over instruments of coercion, made it difficult for Qing officials, even the island's intendant (and later governor, when Taiwan became a full-fledged province in 1887), to obtain their cooperation on policies that did not personally benefit the administrative intermediaries. The result was a high degree of unevenness in enforcement of rules and regulations.

When Liu Ao solicited the scholar-gentry's support of his quasi-governmental opium monopoly, for instance, he was able to obtain the cooperation of individuals based in the southern region of Taiwan, where he enjoyed personal ties with the local gentry, but not in the north. Similarly, when he attempted to raise gentry-led militias across Taiwan for the island's defense against foreign threats, Lin Weiyuan, the most influential scholar-gentry in northern Taiwan, withheld support, which led Lin Weiyuan's scholar-gentry and strongmen supporters and clients to also decline contributing to the island's defense. Conversely, thanks to friendly relations with the scholar-gentry in northern and central Taiwan, such as Lin Chaodong and Lin Weiyuan, Governor Liu Mingchuan (Liu Ao's successor) was able to undertake land reform in these regions. In the south, however, his efforts to modernize Taiwan's convoluted and inefficient system of land ownership and taxation were rebuffed by the region's scholar-gentry, who did not feel that their interests were advanced by Liu Mingchuan's proposed reforms. In all of these examples, it is notable that the Taiwan intendant, and later governor, declined to use force to compel the cooperation of recalcitrant intermediaries. The wide-scale support that individuals such as Lin Weiyuan and Lin Chaodong enjoyed, not just in Taiwan but among the political elites of mainland China, meant that any attempt to punish them for their lack of cooperation could very well lead to the overreaching official's political downfall.[36]

In sum, under the Qing system of state-society mediation, enforcement of rules and regulations was unsystematic and highly dependent on personal ties between government officials and community leaders. When a politically influential strongman or scholar-gentry's private interests or agenda did not overlap with those of the state, policy enforcement was unlikely. As such, the Qing system was not an arrangement, as both Liu Ao and Liu Mingchuan learned, that allowed modernist reformers to successfully implement policies that expanded the scope of government at the expense of Taiwan's political elite.

It therefore comes as little surprise that Japanese colonial officials, who had some knowledge of Qing administrative practices and problems, determined not to restore the scholar-gentry to their former positions of influence after taking control of the island, as discussed in chapter 3. Instead, they preferred to rely on local-level community leaders as administrative intermediaries—merchants and large landlords who might have served as minor zongli under the previous regime or, more commonly, those who had assisted the zongli at the lowest level of sociopolitical aggregation as town managers and village chiefs. Such individuals, the Japanese surmised, would be much easier to oversee and discipline than the regionally influential strongmen and scholar-gentry.

Moreover, by designating hokō as the sole institutional medium for state-society mediation and reducing the scale of each hokō unit to that of a single village or neighborhood, Japanese statebuilders ensured that no community leader could become powerful enough to challenge the authority of even a low-level colonial bureaucrat. Through formalization of rules associated with hokō, duties and responsibilities of administrative intermediaries were also standardized, making it possible for Japanese bureaucrats to oversee and manage each hokō unit in a routine and rule-bound manner. In this way, although the system of state-society mediation that emerged under Japanese rule drew inspiration from mediational institutions found in Taiwan, the degree to which the colonial police were able to obtain the systematic cooperation of community leaders in enforcing new rules and regulations came to surpass by far that obtained through Qing-era practices. What was once a society dominated by prominent strongmen and scholar-gentry families was transformed into an administered community of law-abiding subjects.

Hokō and the Making of an Administered Community

As discussed in chapter 3, Gotō's proposal for transforming Taiwan into a strong and modern state rested on three pillars: the *polizeistaat* model for local administration, seibutsugaku no gensoku, and finally, *jichi* ("self-rule"). For Gotō the concept of jichi did not mean that the Taiwanese people should govern themselves. The GGT was without any institutional mechanism for political representation of the island's inhabitants, with all of its laws drafted by a small circle of colonial bureaucrats in the GGT's consultative assembly. Opportunities for Taiwanese participation in the formal administrative organs of the state were also minimal. Rather, what Gotō had in mind was something akin to the institution of state-society mediation found in Japan during the Tokugawa era (1603–1868): a village governance structure composed of a headman, a committee of elders, and "five-man groups" (*goningumi*) that served as the state's principal disciplinary instrument in the locality.

Under this system, the village headman, with the assistance of elders, was responsible for collecting taxes and implementing any directives from the samurai, which had largely shed its previous function as warriors to constitute the bureaucratic class in the seventeenth century. The headman was to help settle any disputes that arose between villagers and prevent impoverished farmers from fleeing to the mountains to escape their tax obligations. These duties of the headman and elders were supported by the goningumi system, which, despite its name ("five-man group"), was composed of anywhere from two to ten land-owning households. The purpose of goningumi was for households to police one another and to ensure that no household was shirking its obligations to the village and the state. This system was nonetheless "self-ruling" in that the village itself functioned as an autonomous socioeconomic unit and rule enforcement relied on normative and social institutions and relationships within the village. The village headman received some official recognition for his service as an administrative intermediary—he was allowed to carry a small sword and his family was bestowed the honor of possessing a last name and family crest—but he was of the village, not part of the samurai officialdom that resided in cities and castle towns.[37]

Believing Taiwan to be at a level of development similar to that of Japan in the late Tokugawa era, Gotō envisioned that jichi would help outsiders—Japanese colonial officials taking the place of Tokugawa-era samurai bureaucrats—to govern Taiwan with the help of a village headman or town manager and through some institutional equivalent of goningumi.[38] Conveniently for Gotō, Taiwan, as stated earlier, already possessed such a system: the baojia, composed of groups of ten, one hundred, and one thousand households. Yet, rather than simply resurrecting baojia, as Furushō Kamon attempted to do in the summer of 1896, Gotō thoroughly reconstituted it into something quite different from that which was found under Qing rule and more similar to Japan's own goningumi model so that it would better serve Japanese statebuilding objectives.

To this end, under the Hokō Bylaw of August 1898,[39] the original three-tier baojia structure was reduced in scale by making hokō into a hundred-household unit, which was then subdivided into smaller goningumi-like teams of ten households called *kō*. In practice, since the idea was for a single hokō to correspond in size to a typical Taiwanese village or neighborhood, they ranged from fifty households in small villages to three hundred households in urban settings. Both non-Chinese foreigners and Japanese settlers were excluded from participation in hokō, but membership was required of all native Taiwanese inhabitants as well as Chinese nationals from mainland China. To pay for hokō's administrative expense and the salaries of its officers, heads of Taiwanese households were required to pay hokō dues on top of their regular tax obligations. The duties and the selection method of the *hosei* and *kōchō*—heads of hokō and kō, respectively—were also formalized under the Hokō Bylaw. Among other things, these rules stipulated that although the colonial government had ultimate say over who would serve in hokō leadership positions, both hosei and kōchō were to be elected by households of the local hokō unit. Hosei elections—the only opportunity for Taiwanese subjects to participate in some kind of a democratic process—could become heated affairs with different household factions vying for this top position. In all, approximately forty-five thousand Taiwanese community leaders (out of a population of approximately three million) served in leadership positions within hokō in 1903, and over the years the size of the hokō leadership class grew proportionately as Taiwan's population increased.[40]

Given that the hokō system was initially devised during the height of the insurgency, among its most important tasks was to engage in village self-defense against the so-called bandits (*dohi*) and to provide any information to the authorities that would help suppress rebellious activities. Therefore, Gotō required each hokō unit to contribute to the organization of a *sōteidan* (able-bodied corps)—much like how Qing authorities had sought to maintain local peace and security through the formation of village-level militias. However, departing from Qing practices, these local militias, which averaged forty men, were firmly integrated into the state's policing apparatus: Although each sōteidan was led by a Taiwanese corps chief and several assistant chiefs (typically chosen among the leaders of the hokō units contributing to the particular sōteidan's manpower), it was placed under the close supervision of the local police office. Moreover, because the primary responsibility of the sōteidan was to conduct surveillance and to notify the police of any rebel activity, as well as assist the police in their various civil duties, they were not necessarily armed. If local conditions made it necessary to provide sōteidan with armaments, they could temporarily borrow weapons from the authorities. In general, the possession of arms was strictly regulated so as to ensure the state's monopoly over instruments of coercion.[41]

In addition to specifying rules concerning the organization of hokō, as well as the selection method of its leadership, the 1898 Hokō Bylaw mandated that each hokō district draft and adopt a clear set of duties and responsibilities to which its members would be held accountable, based on a template provided by the authorities. There was nonetheless some flexibility as to the precise content of these rules, given considerable variation in local circumstances across Taiwan—both in terms of the level of rebel activity and in existing structures of state-society mediation.[42] In this way, what distinguished the hokō system from previous attempts by the Japanese to structure institutions of state-society mediation within the locality was the focus placed on formalization. Gotō and his subordinates in the colonial bureaucracy believed that the Taiwanese could only be ruled under an authoritarian system, but they also understood that people were more likely to behave obediently when governed by a clear set of impartially enforced rules and regulations.[43]

Furthermore, to give weight to these formal guidelines for proper everyday behavior, a system of fining abrogation of hokō duties and responsibilities was instituted at both the individual household level and the collective level.[44] For example, the Tainan District Hokō Code of 1899 levied fines ranging from 0.05 yen to 5 yen on any household that failed to hang a door placard, report a birth or death within seven days, notify the authorities of overnight visitors and population movements, aid neighboring households in the event of a robbery, and serve in the sōteidan when appointed. A heavier fine of up to 10 yen was levied against any individual who resigned from a hokō leadership position without proper reason. Any household that hid or affiliated with dohi incurred a fine of up to 25 yen. Moreover, the entire kō unit was liable for a fine of 5–10 yen for not taking measures to provide security within strategically important locations, and an even larger fine of 5–50 yen for failing to aid neighboring kō units during emergencies. In the event of a major disturbance, such as a village-wide riot, the entire hokō was liable under the criminal code's joint responsibility (*renza*) provision, which compelled all constituent households, regardless of whether they partook in the disturbance, to contribute an amount commensurate with their wealth. Such was the case when the village of Puzijia in southern Taiwan was forced to pay 2,400 yen in 1901 for failing to preempt a riot.[45]

The organization of hokō as originally established in 1898 had its shortcomings, however. Most problematic was the lack of a formal coordination mechanism among the multitude of hokō units and of an institutional structure through which the local police branch office could exercise its oversight responsibilities. As described in chapter 3, the Japanese colonial police force was a large bureaucratic organization with branch offices throughout Taiwan. Even then, there were three to four hokō units for every police branch office.[46] To complicate matters, an institution that came to be informally known as hokō bureaus (*baojiaju*) emerged across Taiwan, following the Qing tradition of collaboration between the scholar-gentry and the state via semiofficial bureaus. Because hokō bureaus were informal institutions, they were not governed by a clear set of rules and regulations; their relationship to the local police branch office also remained unspecified. The duties and responsibilities of hokō bureaus, as well as their size and organizational structure, thus varied, and in urban centers they grew to become sizable operations. The hokō bureau in the Wanhua district of Taipei, for instance, was composed of a bureau chief, four assistant chiefs, five secretaries, an archive director, an accountant, and a clerk. The last three of these positions were salaried. In addition, local notables were selected to serve as councillors and met whenever the hokō bureau chief needed the advice and help of the wider community.[47]

The effectiveness of hokō bureaus at coordinating actions among their constituent hokō units and with the local police thus differed significantly across localities. Moreover, since hokō bureaus were created through local initiative, rather than via government decree or regulation, they enjoyed considerable autonomy—a development that was advantageous from the Taiwanese perspective, but a cause of concern for colonial administrators.[48] Hokō bureaus also became a source of corruption. Because hokō units and bureaus collected regular fees from households in an amount that was locally determined, and because the levying of hokō fines brought in a steady stream of income, there arose multiple opportunities for leaders of hokō units and bureaus (at times in collaboration with corrupt police officials) to collect excessive fees and fines from the populace and to abuse hokō funds for personal gain.[49]

To address these problems and to further formalize Taiwan's system of state-society mediation, the Working Rules for the Implementation of the Hokō Bylaw (Hokō Jōrei Shikō Kisoku) was enacted in May 1903. The Hokō Working Rules provided greater specificity as to how hokō units across Taiwan should be organized. Minimum and maximum sizes of kō units were set at five and fifteen households, respectively; a hokō unit, similarly, was to be composed of five to fifteen kō. The sōteidan system was also subjected to further standardization. Previously, sōteidan were established as needed, and there were no clear regulations as to their constitution; henceforth, a sōteidan unit was to be created for every police branch office and was to have membership ranging from twenty to sixty men between the ages of seventeen and fifty. Also starting in 1903, those serving in a sōteidan unit were given khaki uniforms, patterned after the design of Japanese military garb. The sleeves of the new uniform indicated the individual's rank in the corps, and the cap was inlaid with the chrysanthemum seal of the Japanese imperial family with the character *sō* (for sōteidan) placed at its center. New rules also addressed the problem of corruption, and in particular the practice of levying excessive fines for official and personal use. They stipulated separate accounting of hokō fees and fines and prohibited fines from being used to cover everyday operational outlays—instead, collected monies were to be used for unanticipated emergency costs and for rewarding those who made notable contributions to local welfare and security.[50]

Most important, the Hokō Working Rules abolished the informal hokō bureaus, which the Japanese authorities feared were becoming an instrument for community leaders to entrench and expand their political influence, much in the way the zongli system had under Qing rule. In their place, allied hokō associations (*hokō rengōkai*) were formally established in each locality so that hokō units could coordinate their activities and receive consistent police oversight. Record keeping was also enhanced through creation of allied hokō associations, which were mandated to employ a paid secretary who would maintain information on household membership, population movement, and other demographic data, as well as keep track of the collection and use of hokō fees and fines. Unlike the hokō bureaus, which, due to their informality, had no physical presence and typically operated out of the bureau chief's private residence, allied hokō associations conducted their duties at permanent public locations, most commonly temples and police branch offices. Police surveillance of the activities of hokō leaders was therefore made much easier. Given that allied hokō association offices came to be used as venues for public meetings and events, their existence also provided the colonial police a window into Taiwanese society more broadly.[51]

Moreover, these reforms not only led to the formalization—and hence, increased visibility and controllability—of state-society mediation in colonial Taiwan but also contributed to its cellularization. As discussed previously, by the late nineteenth century, two types of community leaders had emerged as key administrative intermediaries in Qing-era Taiwan: the strongman and the scholar-gentry. While the sources of their authority within Taiwanese society and the scale at which they operated differed—the former were respected for their military prowess and the latter for their scholarly training—the loyal support they enjoyed from their constituents, as well as their control over coercive instruments, allowed them to behave as autonomous political actors within their respective level of influence. There were also very few formal institutional mechanisms that prevented Qing-era administrative intermediaries from aggrandizing wealth and developing a large web of clientelistic ties that insulated them from the state's disciplinary instruments. Qing officials became especially beholden to the scholar-gentry and were unable to implement policies that aimed at strengthening the power and authority of the state at their expense.

In contrast, although many individuals who served as hosei originated from wealthy families, possession of considerable wealth was not a prerequisite for hokō leadership. The task of hokō officials was not to finance public works projects themselves but to collect funds and recruit labor from the local community. Hokō officials communicated to the authorities local preferences for what public works projects to prioritize and where to build them, but decision-making power over such matters ultimately rested with the colonial bureaucracy.[52] Even the restoration of temples required government permission.[53] Hokō officials did not control the instruments of local coercion either. Sōteidan were armed only during times of crises, and even then were placed under the close supervision of local police branch offices. As such, serving as hosei might have allowed individuals to cultivate socioeconomic networks and increase influence in their local community, but it did not provide opportunities for amassing personal fortune, engaging in land-grabbing, or extending political influence much beyond the hokō unit. At most, individuals occupying hokō leadership positions could expect to obtain some additional income, as they were tasked with the distribution and sale of lucrative monopoly goods, particularly opium.[54]

Through these reforms, Taiwan was transformed during Kodama and Gotō's administration into what one may label an administered community. Instead of state-society mediation being regulated by a wide array of informal practices and semiofficial institutions, as was the case under Qing rule, government officials now oversaw and managed administrative intermediaries under a standard set of rules and regulations that were systematically applied across Taiwan. These rules and regulations not only specified the duties and responsibilities of each hokō unit but also provided guidelines as to their size and organization.

This new system of jichi was also cellularizing in that the basic unit of sociopolitical organization was scaled down to the level of villages and neighborhoods. At the same time, it was precisely because of hokō's cellularizing characteristics, as laid out in the following section, that the GGT was able to integrate Taiwan's multitude of lineage-based and ethnically homogenous communities into a more unified societal space of a modern colonial state. By taking advantage of the hokō system's inherent malleability, Japanese statebuilders could subdivide and recombine natural villages and neighborhoods into new local administrative structures that allowed the state to more efficiently and rationally govern the subject population.

Exercising State Strength through Societal Mediation

As defined in chapter 1, state strength is "the evenness with which compliance with rules and regulations is obtained throughout the realm." The GGT demonstrated this capacity by successfully gathering detailed data on people's landholdings and mobilizing the subject population in its campaign to eradicate the plague, among other achievements. All of this was accomplished not by direct bureaucratic enforcement of rules and regulations, but through the institutional structure of hokō and via the assistance of administrative intermediaries. However, hokō was not simply an instrument for imposing the government's will on the people. As a mediational mechanism between state and society, hokō provided the flexibility to adapt rules and regulations to meet local conditions and was utilized as a channel for communicating to the state the needs and concerns of the community. Taiwan's administered community was hierarchically organized, and hokō leaders were made subservient to the colonial police. Yet, it was able to generate systematic compliance with rules and regulations because the hokō system also left room for local agency.

Specifically, as an institution of state-society mediation, hokō contributed to colonial governance and to the transformation of Taiwan into a strong and modern state in the long run in five distinct ways. The first and most fundamental task assigned to hokō was to assist colonial officials in the collection of various information on the Taiwanese people, their possessions, and their daily behaviors. Although the government provided the bureaucratic capacity and the technical expertise necessary to gather and analyze large amounts of data to make Taiwanese society more visible to the state, it was only with the help of administrative intermediaries that this information could be extracted from the subject population in the first place. The 1898–1903 island-wide land survey is a case in point.

To those such as historian and politician Takekoshi Yosaburō, who observed the survey firsthand, the endeavor was a testament to Japanese mastery of scientific methods and modern administrative techniques. "When I inspected the different maps and ledgers in the Bureau of Surveys, and also had the pleasure of seeing the officials at work," Takekoshi wrote, "I could not but admire the vastness of the undertaking, and the scientific way in which it was being carried through."[55] He marveled at how Japanese engineers used advanced techniques "to make surveys correct in every detail"[56] and was particularly impressed with the detailed survey maps of villages, drawn to a scale of 1 to 600, as well as those compiled at the district level:

> In the village map we saw rice fields, tea plantations, brooks, hills and woods, all drawn with that precision which the trigonometrical survey alone can secure. District maps were then produced. . . . With one of these maps and a pencil it was easy at once to ascertain the size of each village. In that godown it would be almost as easy to examine the physical contour and geographical features of Formosa [Taiwan] as it is to study the palm of one's own hand.[57]

This was not all. Surveyors had also measured and classified fields, ponds, and plantations according to their productivity and had collected information regarding annual rent, crop value, and irrigation charge. "Compared with the gigantic enterprise under review," Takekoshi surmised, "the revision of the land tax which was carried out in Japan in the year 1874 was mere child's play. The whole area of Formosa has now been accurately measured, its hills and valleys carefully surveyed, and its productive capacity ascertained."[58] While Takekoshi, whose book on Taiwan served as GGT propaganda, was prone to exaggerate Japan's achievements, it is nonetheless hard to deny the impressiveness of what the colonial land surveyors had accomplished.

Takekoshi was also correct to point out that the collection of all of this information was made possible by expert knowledge and efficient bureaucratic organization. The actual task of measuring, demarcating, and assessing land was conducted by survey teams of administrative officials, survey technicians, assistant clerks, and translators. Their efforts, in turn, were supervised and coordinated by the newly created Land Investigation Bureau, consisting of a central office in Taipei (headed by Gotō), branch offices in each of the prefectures, and dispatch offices at the subprefectural level. Gotō placed particular emphasis on hiring and training qualified individuals to serve as survey technicians, 780 of them in total. A school for training surveyors was set up in Taiwan, where Taiwanese subjects who had passed the school's entrance exam were enrolled in a six-month course on surveying techniques. Gotō also recruited personnel directly from Japanese vocational schools specializing in math and engineering to supplement the locally hired staff.[59]

Nonetheless, no matter how technically proficient the surveyors might have been, if they had not been able to access local knowledge, their survey maps would have lacked the information that so impressed Takekoshi. Hokō thus allowed the Japanese to apply modern surveying techniques to better "see" Taiwan and to produce highly detailed survey maps. Hired by the government as land survey commissioners, hosei's responsibility was to indicate to the survey technicians the boundaries of privately owned lots and adjudicate disputes over ownership claims. They helped surveyors gather information on harvests, basic farming costs, interest rates, annual rents, and value of cash crops. By combining this information with observations and measurements taken by the surveyors, each lot could be assigned a productivity grade and tax valuation.[60]

It was also through the help of hokō that the colonial government acquired detailed information on Taiwan's inhabitants. When an island-wide census was undertaken in 1905, again in 1915, and every five years thereafter, hokō officials assisted government enumerators in counting Taiwanese subjects and gathering information on their age, sex, race, marital status, occupation, language, education, physical disabilities, household composition, type of dwelling, and habits pertaining to the use of opium.[61] It would not have been possible for the police to maintain its household register—a book containing information on the wealth, occupation, health, and living conditions of households—if not for hokō's assistance either. Under the hokō code, each household was obligated to report overnight trips as well as any extended stays by visitors from outside of the community to the kōchō. The kōchō then communicated this information, along with other changes he noticed concerning the health and status of households, to the hosei as part of his monthly report. Next, it was the hosei's turn to aggregate all of this in a written report, which he submitted to the local police branch office biannually. It was also the hosei's responsibility to report to the police any behavior that disturbed peace and security, such as vandalism, accidents or deaths, rumors of public disobedience or riots, and violations of quarantine measures during epidemics. He was to be on the lookout for prostitutes, professional gamblers, and suspicious individuals. If a person seemed to have become wealthy overnight, possessed items or lived a lifestyle that looked well beyond the person's means, or fell into sudden poverty, it was to be reported. Any failure on the part of households, kōchō, or hosei to fulfill these duties resulted in a fine.[62]

If hokō officials' first duty was to aggregate and translate local knowledge and information into a form that was useful to the colonial state, their second was to convey various types of information from the state to society. During the monthly allied hokō meetings, the police informed hosei about new rules and regulations and changes to existing ones; any difficulties encountered in enforcing rules and regulations were discussed as well. Information on sanitary habits, scientific farming, new seed varietals, and modern husbandry techniques was also disseminated during these daylong meetings. Afterward, each hosei would summon all of the kōchō and sōteidan leaders within his hokō unit to his home and review matters that were discussed during the meeting. It was then the responsibility of the kōchō to pass on any relevant information to the household heads under his watch.[63]

A third hokō duty was to serve as the primary instrument through which an array of new rules and regulations were enforced. By taking advantage of hokō's built-in mobilizational capacity, the colonial state could carry out various public works projects as well as pursue campaigns against dohi, infectious diseases, pests, and social vices. It was with the help of hokō leaders, for example, that the colonial government was able to recruit the manpower necessary to build new highways, bridges, and railway lines as well as expand and update existing ones. The most significant of these early public works projects was the cross-island railroad (completed in 1908) that linked the island's two main cities—Taipei in the north and Tainan in the south—and connected other important population centers via numerous feeder lines. To ensure the smooth and timely completion of these projects and to distribute work equitably among households, logistical matters were discussed during the allied hokō meetings, whereby the specific labor contribution of each household was determined based on the expected timing, duration, and scale of the project. Once these public works projects were completed, it was hokō's responsibility to maintain them on a regular basis. After the north-south railway was built, the hokō code was revised to instruct each hokō unit to supply two inspectors to patrol the rail lines for any problems arising from wear, accidents, or deliberate acts of sabotage. The new hokō code also prohibited villagers near rail lines from letting their animals roam free. Maintenance of bridges and highways was an explicit obligation of hokō units as well.[64]

Public health and sanitation was another area where hokō's contributions proved vital, especially during the early period of colonial rule. Twenty thousand people, on average, died every year from infectious diseases during the first decade of colonial rule, and to address this public health crisis, new regulations on the use of privies and drinking wells were enacted and vaccinations were made compulsory. Public lectures and demonstrations were held in allied hokō offices to make people aware of how the spread of infectious disease could be contained through hygienic habits, such as blowing one's nose in a proper manner, not spitting to clear one's sinuses, and keeping fingernails neatly trimmed. Posters warned of how disease could be spread by sharing clothes and improper disposal of waste. In cities, the police instructed hosei to set up garbage boxes, and in rural areas, disposal yards; the use of antiseptic solutions and mosquito nets was encouraged. Regulations governing marketplaces were put into place and any violation of them resulted in a hokō fine. New building codes mandated that homes have sufficient ventilation and lighting, as well as a proper lavatory. Just as hokō units were mobilized for road building, they were drafted to construct waterways and gutters and to keep streets clear of clutter and garbage.[65]

Various measures undertaken to eradicate bubonic plague from the island were implemented via the hokō structure. In the city of Tainan, for example, hokō spearheaded a rat-catching campaign that began in November 1901, whereby each household was rewarded 0.05 yen for every rat caught, and households that turned in 1,000 rats earned a ticket in a lottery with a top prize of 10 yen. This voluntary system was soon supplemented by an involuntary one. In Taipei, households were required to submit to the police 5–10 rats per month, depending on the size of the household. Those who exceeded the quota were rewarded with money or farm animals, while households failing to meet the quota were fined 0.25 yen per missing rat. An average of 4.6 million rats were captured yearly this way during the height of the rat-catching campaign, from 1904 to 1908; in all, 41,923,644 rats were caught and subjected to analysis by the GGT's bacteriologists by 1912. In conjunction with these efforts to catch as many rats as possible, Japanese authorities aimed to prevent their proliferation by maintaining hygienic living environments. Regulations for Great Household Cleaning, adopted in 1905, instructed people to clean their property semiannually by pulling weeds, exposing bedding and clothing to the sun, cleaning drains and sewers, and disposing of any rubbish that had accumulated on the property. It was the responsibility of hokō officials to inspect each household and ascertain their compliance with these regulations. Households that failed to meet the expected standards of cleanliness were compelled to redo their efforts until they reached a satisfactory state. Hosei were also instructed to report to the police any individual who showed symptoms of the plague so that he or she could be examined by a health official. If it was determined that the individual had in fact been infected with the plague, hokō officials assisted the police in enforcing a quarantine and preventing the sick from coming into contact with anyone other than health officials.[66]

Hokō's involvement in policy enforcement and mobilization of manpower went beyond political and economic realms and into the cultural. In return for their services to the state, hokō officials were rewarded with lucrative opium sales permits; yet, hokō units were simultaneously tasked with monitoring and containing the use of opium as part of the GGT's policy of eradicating "evil" Taiwanese customs and habits. The GGT also targeted the practices of female footbinding—whereby girls would have their feet tightly bound as children to prevent growth—and men's wearing of hair in queues. Finally, hokō were involved in campaigns to spread the use of the Japanese language. In particular, hosei were encouraged to recruit traditional elites, such as themselves (that is, those who had either received schooling before the Japanese period or attended private Confucian schools after 1895), to form nighttime Japanese-language study groups (*yagakkai*). By 1917, membership in yagakkai had expanded beyond the traditional elite to farmers, urban laborers, and those belonging to aboriginal tribes.[67]

In these ways, hokō allowed the colonial state to penetrate Taiwanese society and compel its compliance with various rules and regulations. This was indeed the purpose for which Gotō revived baojia and reconstituted it into hokō in 1898; its usefulness as an instrument of policy enforcement was why hokō continued to operate as the principal institution of sociopolitical organization until the final months of Japanese colonial rule. Yet, if hokō had only served the interests of the state and was nothing more than a mechanism through which the state substantiated its disciplinary power over the subject population, as some have argued,[68] then it is unlikely that hokō would have been able to mediate between the state and social forces so effectively. A fourth function of hokō was therefore to serve the interests of the local community within the constraints imposed on it by the colonial state.

Indeed, while the primary function of the allied hokō meetings was for the police to inform the hosei of new rules and regulations and to coordinate their efforts in enforcing various policy initiatives, they also served as a forum for hokō elites to discuss matters that were important to the local community, such as planning for festivals and soliciting funds for renovating and building temples and schools. The hokō system was also designed to allow hosei to make suggestions to the authorities on matters of policy implementation. In this process, hokō leaders were able to exhibit agency by voicing their own personal (and class) interests and concerns as well as those of their constituents.

During the antiplague campaign, for example, Zhang Lijun, a hosei in the town of Huludun in central Taiwan, did what he could to lessen the impact of the draconian measures that the GGT was taking to contain the plague epidemic. When the number of deaths from the plague spiked in March 1908, Zhang was ordered by the Japanese subdistrict police to isolate those infected and burn their dwellings. Zhang performed his official duties as best he could (being under the close watch of the colonial police), but he was also aware of the interests of villagers to keep infections of family members a secret from the authorities as long as possible, so that loved ones would not be sent to quarantine camps to die alone. When the daughter of one of his tenants fell ill, Zhang first sought medical help from a local Chinese doctor rather than alerting the area's public physician. Only when the Chinese doctor refused to cooperate did Zhang contact the Japanese physician to make a diagnosis—a diagnosis that luckily confirmed the young woman to be plague-free.[69] Later, Zhang served as the principal mediator between representatives of the colonial bureaucracy and local community members in the renovation of the Fengyuan Tzuchi Temple. It was largely due to his efforts that the local government canceled its plan to demolish part of the temple to make way for a new road.[70]

The fifth and final contribution of hokō was to facilitate the structural transformation and modernization of Taiwanese society: It was by taking advantage of the organizational structure of the hokō system that Japanese officials succeeded in thoroughly rationalizing and depersonalizing Taiwan's political sphere above the village and neighborhood levels. Specifically, the hokō system's inherent malleability allowed statebuilders to subdivide and reorganize natural villages and neighborhoods into new and rationally constructed local administrative structures. Here, each hokō unit acted as something akin to a Lego brick that could be flexibly combined and recombined into larger administrative aggregations. In 1909, Taiwan's existing towns and villages were aggregated into 454 sections (*ku*), and in 1920, these sections were further consolidated into 263 urban and rural townships. In support of these administrative reforms, hokō units were merged via hosei-led coordinating committees, first at the level of the ku, and later at that of the administrative townships.[71] In this way, it was hokō's cellularizing qualities that, paradoxically, allowed the GGT to integrate and unify Taiwanese society into a single imagined community— albeit one imagined via administrative structures rather than through nationalist narratives.[72]

Similarly, just as hokō served as the building blocks of the GGT's new system of local government in the 1920s, it became the primary instrument through which the policy of rapid and forceful assimilation (*kōminka*) was instituted in the following decade to finally realize Tokyo's long-standing goal of culturally, politically, and administratively integrating Taiwan into the Japanese nation-state. In the 1930s, as the collapse of the global financial system, assassinations and coup attempts in Tokyo, and the escalation of conflict between Japan and China transformed Japan from a dysfunctional democracy into a military dictatorship,[73] Japan's colonial policy in Taiwan also took a militaristic turn. A series of coercive policies aimed at transforming the Taiwanese people into loyal Japanese subjects was implemented so that the Taiwanese could be mobilized to support Japan's war against China and its Western allies. Many Taiwanese temples were demolished and Japanese shrines built in their place, the teaching of classical Chinese was discontinued in public schools as various measures promoting Japanese-language learning were instituted, and the adoption of Japanese names by Taiwanese subjects was strongly encouraged.[74]

Such efforts to forcefully assimilate the Taiwanese people from the inside out were accompanied by the creation of a number of government-administered mass organizations.[75] Examples of such organizations could be found in all areas of colonial life: Societies for Conforming Customs, Village Arousing Societies, Youth Corps, Health and Sanitation Unions, and Taiwan Federation of Agricultural Cooperatives. Most important of them was the all-encompassing Kōmin Hōkōkai (Association of Imperial Subjects for Patriotic Services, or ISPS). Branches of ISPS were founded at the prefectural, county, township, ward, neighborhood, and village levels. Perhaps unsurprisingly, local-level branches of the ISPS were organized around the hokō system, and hokō officials, as well as cadres of the sōteidan, came to take up leadership positions in village alliances and public service teams, which were the two lowest units of the ISPS organization.[76]

It was precisely because ISPS could be grafted onto the existing hokō structure that it succeeded in subsuming the entire Taiwanese population under its umbrella. Ironically, however, hokō's very contribution to the establishment of a fascist state in Taiwan immediately made it anachronistic. ISPS covered not only all hokō units but occupational groups, public and private corporations, and Taiwanese and Japanese subjects alike. Having both ISPS and hokō only added to the administrative burden of local governments and produced confusion in responsibility among community leaders, who served simultaneously as hosei under the hokō structure and as heads of village alliances and public service teams under ISPS. Moreover, the hokō system was in direct contradiction of the spirit of kōminka: If the state desired the complete assimilation of Taiwanese subjects into the Japanese national identity, how then was the existence of hokō, which excluded Japanese subjects, justifiable? By the early 1940s, hokō had therefore become superfluous at best and an obstacle to the realization of Japan's wartime goals at worst.[77] On June 17, 1945, hokō was abolished, and the transformation of Taiwan into a strong and modern state was complete.

Conclusion: The Contemporary Relevance of Colonial Taiwan

Japan's statebuilding project came to an abrupt end in August 1945 with its unconditional surrender to the Allied Powers and Taiwan's subsequent retrocession to the Republic of China. Thereafter, Taiwan, led by Chiang Kai-shek, underwent rapid industrialization and became one of the region's most stable and effectively governed polities. Speculating on whether Taiwan's postwar emergence as one of East Asia's economic powerhouses would have been possible without the institutional foundations established by the Japanese is beyond the objective of this book. However, what can be said with some certainty is that Taiwan, once a shallowly and unevenly governed province of the Qing Empire, was thoroughly altered under Japanese rule into a strong and modern state. Japan's commitment to forging a large bureaucratic apparatus was certainly an important contributor to Taiwan's transformation. Yet, at least as consequential were reforms directed at mediational institutions at the interface of state and society. Through formalizing and cellularizing Taiwan's traditional system of state-society mediation, colonial officials were able to obtain systematic cooperation of the island's village- and neighborhood-level community leaders, weaken the power of the traditional landed elite, and integrate a society fragmented along a multitude of lineage and ethnic cleavages into a single administered community of obedient subjects.

What makes this case particularly relevant for the larger study of statebuilding are the similarities observed between the underlying structural conditions characterizing Taiwan in the late nineteenth century and those found in today's ungoverned and undergoverned spaces. Similar to territories where the United States, the United Nations, and the World Bank have recently engaged in statebuilding, Taiwan was an agrarian, socioeconomically unequal, and ethnically diverse society where coercive power and political authority were concentrated in the hands of a landed elite. Moreover, statebuilding in Taiwan, like contemporary campaigns to construct strong states in the peripheral regions of the world, was pursued via the imposition of Western-inspired institutional models amid widespread resistance from both elites and non-elites alike. Yet, despite the presence of such adverse antecedent conditions, Japanese colonial officials transformed Taiwan into a strong state in Japan's modernist image. The case of colonial Taiwan thus helps us to understand what it may actually take to succeed in statebuilding under the type of structural, institutional, and political conditions found in the ungoverned and undergoverned spaces of the contemporary era.

In suggesting the contemporary relevance of Taiwan under Japanese rule, I do not argue that the United States, international peacekeeping and development organizations, or rulers of developing countries should necessarily mimic the authoritarian governance structure of the GGT. As pointed out in the previous chapter, when statebuilding is undertaken amid widespread resistance, its success depends on an abundance of coercive capacity by way of a large bureaucratic presence within the locality. Moreover, in order to discipline community leaders as obedient intermediaries, statebuilding by imposition necessitates the illiberal act of reconfiguring the very fabric of society into an administered community. Hence, even if policymakers have the resources, time, and political will to apply the "lessons" of colonial Taiwan to the problem of state weakness and failure in the present era, they should be cognizant of the social and normative costs that a successful statebuilding effort will inevitably entail.

Yet, even if we reject the Taiwan model as a viable template for contemporary statebuilding, the foregoing findings are not without important policy implications. Precisely because the Japanese approach to statebuilding in Taiwan contradicts prevailing beliefs on how modern state institutions can and should be constructed, colonial Taiwan serves as an important corrective to the dominant narrative on statebuilding that reduces it to democracy building. Because it does not fit the story so often told by American policymakers and United Nations peacekeepers—that is, how strong states are constructed through the establishment of representative government, the holding of free and fair elections, the liberalization of the economy, and the enactment of laws to protect private property and advance personal liberties—it forces us to reexamine our fundamental assumptions and commonly invoked templates in the contemporary practice of statebuilding.[78] If Taiwan is what successful statebuilding by imposition looks like, this begs the question of whether Western countries and international organizations should even attempt this endeavor in today's ungoverned and undergoverned spaces, regardless of underlying normative or strategic imperatives.

Nonetheless, before accepting the tentative conclusion that successful statebuilding by imposition necessitates reform strategies and institutional models that are inherently illiberal and undemocratic, it is necessary to examine an actual case in which statebuilding and democracy building were pursued simultaneously amid resistance. Moreover, such a case, from a methodological perspective, should be similar to that of Taiwan in its underlying structural and institutional conditions, as well as time, resources, and manpower invested in the service of statebuilding. For reasons discussed in chapter 1, the Philippines under U.S. rule (1898–1941) presents such a case.

THE AMERICAN WAY

Can America build strong and modern states in ungoverned and undergoverned spaces?[1] Evidence thus far—as observed from America's occupation of the Philippines, its attempt to make South Vietnam into a viable state, and more recently, its endeavors to transform Iraq and Afghanistan into stable and prosperous democracies—suggests otherwise. There are indeed examples of the United States successfully imposing a modern democratic government under military occupation, most notably in post–World War II Germany and Japan, but they are the exceptions that reveal a more general pattern: America can contribute to rebuilding and democratizing an occupied state that, before being destroyed by war, was already a strong state with some experience in democracy, but not when modern political, bureaucratic, and judicial institutions must be built anew in a territory long characterized by state weakness or where traditional systems of power and authority prevail.[2]

Yet, it is important to not assume that simply because America has consistently failed in statebuilding by imposition that a top-down transformation of an ungoverned or undergoverned space into a strong and modern state is impossible. As the case of Taiwan under colonial rule demonstrates, statebuilding success also does not require some right set of structural conditions, be it navigable rivers, temperate climate, mass literacy, relative equality in wealth, or ethnic homogeneity; nor does it succeed only in places where protomodern institutions have already begun to emerge. It also demonstrates that interelite unity and commitment to political modernization are not preconditions and that it is possible to successfully impose modern governance institutions on a subject population amid widespread resistance. Favorable structural conditions and unity among elites will certainly make statebuilding more attainable, but they are neither necessary, nor sufficient, for successful statebuilding.

Why, then, has the United States, one of the world's foremost economic and military powers, demonstrated such inability to build states by imposition? If the Japanese were able to transform Taiwan into a strong and modern state under conditions similar to those that Americans found in the Philippines, what was the cause of the stark divergence in outcome? Insofar as Taiwan and the Philippines at the turn of the twentieth century were structurally, socioeconomically, institutionally, and politically comparable, why did not or could not American officials adopt reforms that would have led to statebuilding success? The aim of this chapter is to address questions regarding why U.S. colonial officials proved (and continue to prove) to be ineffective statebuilders and to analyze exactly how America's attempt to remake the Philippines in its image led instead to a weak state with dysfunctional democratic institutions.

The destruction wrought by the 1899–1902 Philippine-American War, coupled with the expatriation of all Spanish colonial officials and religious figures from the territory, provided the Americans with a unique opportunity to impose their vision of good government on the subject population. This did not mean, however, that U.S. statebuilders were unconstrained in their effort to remake the Philippines into a strong and modern state. Rather than structural and institutional constraints, they faced obstacles that were political and ideational in nature; these constraints did not originate in the Philippines, but instead, in America itself. Precisely because U.S. colonial officials were so successful in neutralizing Filipino opposition to America's annexation of the archipelago, political concerns and calculations from Washington, as well as the statebuilders' own stubbornly held ideas about how modern states should be structured institutionally and how to go about establishing these institutions, came to guide America's actions.

This analysis begins with the domestic political debate surrounding the U.S. decision to annex the Philippine Islands in 1899. Facing an electorate that was skeptical of foreign entanglements, as well as a vocal anti-imperialist movement, President William McKinley and his allies were compelled to characterize U.S. expansionary designs in the Caribbean and the Pacific as civilizing missions—a duty bestowed on the American people by an act of Providence. Yet, it was not just political calculations and concern over backlash by American voters that led U.S. policymakers to pursue an ill-conceived statebuilding strategy during the initial years and to stubbornly stay the course thereafter. From Secretary of War Elihu Root, who devised the overall American strategy in the Philippines, to William Howard Taft, who served as the first U.S. civil governor of the archipelago, policymakers were themselves ideologically committed to mimicking American institutions in the Philippines.

Moreover, the determination demonstrated by U.S. officials to transfer American-inspired political, administrative, and judicial institutions to the Philippines went beyond a belief in the superiority of the U.S. political model and the universality of the rights and freedoms protected by the U.S. Constitution. Having lived their lives in a modern state characterized by a democratic system of government and a robust tradition of rule of law, they possessed little understanding of the norms, mores, and biases of a people who had long suffered under a state that taxed heavily but provided little in the way of public goods and services. Accustomed to a government that was more or less accountable to voters and that provided (or was expected to provide) a wide array of public goods, U.S. policymakers could not fathom the fear, anxiety, and distrust that attempts to rapidly expand the scope of government would generate among Filipinos used to being oppressed by a predatory state. American officials, as a result, could not foresee that compliance, especially to rules and regulations they believed to be just, would become a problem. Believing that people would naturally come to follow good laws and abide by sensible regulations that advanced their wealth and welfare, no effort was put into creating a robust system of local rule to oversee administrative intermediaries and compel their cooperation in policy enforcement. With little awareness that their statebuilding mission in the Philippines was regarded by Filipinos as an act of imposition, American officials simply could not imagine why the populace would not see that it was in their best interest to comply with the new and "enlightened" rules and regulations.

Basic American beliefs and norms about good government would also come to guide how U.S. officials reacted to mounting evidence that their plan for remaking the Philippines in the American image was failing. Once the realization set in that the establishment of good political, administrative, and judicial institutions would not in itself lead to statebuilding success, U.S. officials chose to blame perceived Filipino backwardness and ignorance for their setbacks. Lessons were not learned because statebuilding failure in the Philippines ultimately did not shake American confidence in the superiority of the U.S. political system. U.S. officials reasoned that in due time, as the Filipinos became more civilized with increased education and wealth, they would come to abide by the good laws and regulations established under American tutelage. Most critically, for both the case at hand and for America's subsequent efforts at statebuilding around the globe, the beliefs and biases of U.S. officials prevented them from realizing that the weakness of the Insular Government of the Philippine Islands (IGP) and the dysfunction of Philippine democracy were not legacies of enduring Spanish-era cultural norms and practices, but rather were outcomes of the new American institutional

order that unwittingly provided ample opportunities for administrative intermediaries to aggrandize wealth and power and weaken the state from below and
within.

The Politics and Ideology of American Statebuilding

The Cuban War of Independence of 1895 was a perfect pretext for the transformation of the United States from a continental, and largely isolationist, power
into one with an overseas empire. First, there were the Cuban revolutionaries,
whose brutal repression by the Spanish colonial government garnered the sympathy of the American public. Their quest for self-rule was further amplified by
American commercial interests in Cuba, whose representatives lobbied President
McKinley to intervene and bring the conflict to a swift end. With the sinking of
the USS *Maine* off of Havana on February 15, 1898, and blame for this tragic
incident placed squarely on the Spanish, America's declaration of war against
Spain was all but inevitable.[3] The first battle of the Spanish-American War, however, did not take place in Cuba, or for that matter the Caribbean. Instead, the war
began with Commodore George Dewey's decimation of the Spanish armada in
Manila Bay on May 1.

The Spanish-American War could not have gone any better for the United
States. In a single stroke, U.S. forces crippled Spanish power in the Pacific,
liberating the Filipinos from what they saw as three centuries of Iberian mis-
government. Thoroughly demoralized, Spanish forces also quickly capitulated
in Cuba, leaving the United States in control of Puerto Rico, Spain's other possession in the Caribbean, as well. Seemingly guided by Providence,[4] America was
now poised to extend liberty and freedom—along with its exports—not only to
the Caribbean and the Pacific but also to the rest of Asia. It was an opportunity
to realize American military and economic prowess on the world stage for which
the expansionists, led by New York Governor Theodore Roosevelt, Admiral Alfred Thayer Mahan, and Senator Henry Cabot Lodge, had been patiently waiting
and preparing.[5] Yet, while the American public was electrified by news of Dewey's
victory in Manila Bay and celebrated Cuban independence from Spanish rule,
unease and ambivalence characterized the U.S. emergence as a great power. Support for isolationism ran deep, and many Americans believed that the best course
of action was to bring troops home as quickly as possible and let the liberated
peoples manage their own affairs.

At the center of the debate over the future of the United States as a great
power was the Philippine Islands—significant not only for its size and strategic

importance but also because it presented the greatest challenge to the narrative of America as a force of liberty and democracy in the world. A homegrown revolution predated the U.S. intervention in the Philippines by two years, and the archipelago, except for Manila (under the occupation of the U.S. Army) and the southern territory of Mindanao and Sulu (governed by autonomous sultanates since before the Spanish era), was under the control of Emilio Aguinaldo's revolutionary forces in the months succeeding the Battle of Manila Bay. Having finally rid themselves of the Spanish, Aguinaldo and his compatriots were not about to submit to American colonial rule. Unlike in Cuba, Guam, or Puerto Rico, the United States therefore had to overthrow a government led by native elites in order to exert direct control over the Philippines.[6] It was a proposition that seemingly transformed America from liberator to conqueror, and from a critic of imperialism to its newest practitioner.

The coalition against annexation of the Philippine Islands included a diverse set of actors and interests. At one end of the spectrum was the Anti-Imperialist League, composed of former abolitionists, who drew parallels between the enslavement of African Americans and the proposition to forcefully place Filipinos under U.S. rule. Ironically, they were united in their goal to prevent American takeover of the Philippines with the southern Democrats, who similarly viewed the Philippine issue as a continuation of past struggles over the rights and freedoms of black and white Americans, but from the perspective of preventing further erosion of America's "whiteness." Also siding with the anti-imperialists were a number of Republicans, including House Speaker Thomas Reed, Senator George Hoar, and industrialist Andrew Carnegie, who, though each for his own reasons, argued that it was best to leave the Filipinos alone.[7]

The various arguments against Philippine annexation that filled the pamphlets of the Anti-Imperialist League and the halls of Congress can be categorized into one of three general themes. The first sought to defend American republicanism from moral decay. Our Founding Fathers, argued Senator Hoar, "knew what caused the downfall of the mighty Roman Republic. They read . . . the history of freedom, of the decay, and the enslavement of Greece. . . . They learned from her the doctrine that while there is little else that a democracy can not accomplish it can not rule over vassal states or subject peoples without bringing in the elements of death into its own constitution."[8] To rule foreign people through conquest was in direct contradiction of the spirit of the Declaration of Independence and the U.S. Constitution, and Congress had no authority to act against the intentions of its Founding Fathers and the nation's most cherished principles.[9]

Other anti-imperialists challenged annexation for reasons of race.[10] Former Republican senator Carl Schurz most notably argued that if the United States were to remain true to its republican principles, it could not rule over alien peoples undemocratically; hence, if any new territory were to be annexed, it should be placed on a clear path toward statehood. However, the incorporation of "tropical races" into the federal union, especially one as large as the Filipinos, would dilute America's Anglo-Saxon (and Protestant) national identity. From these premises, it followed that the best course of action was to let the Filipinos govern themselves.[11] Senator Benjamin Tillman, the white supremacist senator of South Carolina, enthusiastically agreed. When the Treaty of Paris—which called for Spain to relinquish control over its Caribbean and Pacific colonies to the United States—received Senate ratification on February 6, 1899, Tillman pointed out that he and other southern Democrats had voted against the treaty because "we understand and realize what it is to have two races side by side that can not mix or mingle without deterioration and injury to both and the ultimate destruction of the civilization of the higher."[12]

In their more noble moments, anti-imperialists attacked annexation out of consideration for the wishes of the Filipinos. They questioned what right the United States had to deny Filipinos the freedom to choose their own form of government. Quipping that the constitutional argument for slavery was in fact stronger than that for annexation of the Philippines, Hoar invoked Abraham Lincoln's famous line that "no man was ever created good enough to own another" and declared, "No nation was ever created good enough to own another."[13] Intellectual leaders such as Moorfield Storey and William James expressed similar sentiments. In his keynote speech during the first meeting of the anti-imperialists at Faneuil Hall on June 15, 1898, Storey argued that "to seize any colony of Spain and hold it as our own, without the free consent of its people is a violation of the principles upon which this government rests."[14] Furthermore, as James argued, annexing the Philippines would destroy "the one sacred thing in the world, the spontaneous budding of a national life." American intervention would nip at its bud the formation of a new and prosperous nation, for "we can destroy their old ideals, but we can't give them ours."[15]

In response to these potent charges, the McKinley administration and its allies sought to characterize annexation of the Philippines as a continuation of America's continental expansion, and akin to Thomas Jefferson's Louisiana Purchase of 1803.[16] As Senator Orville Platt noted wryly, the literal application of the anti-imperialist doctrine that no people may be governed without their consent would have "turned back the *Mayflower* from our coast and would have prevented our expansion westward to the Pacific Ocean."[17] Others, such as Senator Henry Teller, argued that the anti-imperialists' interpretation of the Declaration of Independence was not based on an accurate reading of history: "There is no government in the world, and there never has been one, founded upon a strict observance of [the principle of the consent of the governed], and there can not be. . . .

Because the interests of the few must give way to the interests of the great mass; because it might be dangerous to the body politic to allow a certain class to participate in the affairs of the government."[18] If senators were to be true to the vision of the Founding Fathers, expansionists declared, they ought to ratify the Treaty of Paris and extend America's democratic principles and republican institutions to the seven million Filipino souls who had previously known only despotism and oppression. Since the Filipinos were not ready for self-government, to leave them to their own devices would be an act of cowardice and an abandonment of America's God-given duty.[19]

In this way, the expansionists turned the table on the anti-imperialists: Extension of American sovereignty into the Philippine Islands was not an act of imperialism but one of emancipation; America was not building an empire, but rather spreading republicanism. Soon after the Treaty of Paris was adopted by a single vote (57 to 27) over the necessary two-thirds majority in the Republican-controlled Senate in February 1899, McKinley traveled to Boston—the home of the anti-imperialist movement—and stated to an enthusiastic audience, "No imperial designs lurk in the American mind. They are alien to American sentiment, thought, and purpose." What his administration had done was to "commit the free and enfranchised Filipinos to the guiding hand and the liberalizing influences, the generous sympathies, the uplifting education, not of their American masters, but of their American emancipators."[20] This was the storyline that not only united the Republican coalition of big business and evangelical Christians in support of the administration's Philippine policy but also turned the Democrats' early opposition to annexation into a political liability in the 1900 presidential election. So powerful was the rhetoric of "benevolent assimilation" (as McKinley's Philippine policy came to be known) that it would not only come to be embraced by the Republican administrations of McKinley, Roosevelt, and Taft but would also later become the policy of Woodrow Wilson—albeit with less direct American involvement in the internal affairs of the archipelago—when he assumed the presidency in 1913.[21]

With the United States fully committed to statebuilding in the Philippines, it was now up to McKinley's advisers to determine what exactly benevolent assimilation entailed. Unfortunately, not only were American policymakers inexperienced in statebuilding,[22] but the United States at the time had a dearth of expertise on the Philippines. When McKinley organized a commission led by Jacob Schurman, the president of Cornell University, to investigate prevailing political and socioeconomic conditions in the archipelago and to hear the views of Filipinos themselves on the question of good government, finding experts to join the commission proved to be a challenge. Schurman, a professor of Christian ethics and moral philosophy, had no experience with the Philippines—a vocal anti-imperialist, he was most likely appointed to lead the First Philippine Commission in order to mollify critics of the administration—and the closest thing the commission had to a Philippine expert was zoologist Dean Worcester, who had conducted research in the archipelago a few years earlier. Otherwise, the commission included Admiral Dewey, General Elwell Otis (commander of the U.S. Army in the Philippines), and Charles Denby, former U.S. minister to the Qing court.[23]

Compounding this lack of expertise among the commissioners, their fact-finding mission, which took place during spring and summer of 1899, was conducted largely through interviews undertaken in Manila with those belonging to the class of highly educated and Europeanized urban elites known as the *ilustrado*.[24] Whether by design or coincidence, reliance on ilustrados as their primary source of information led Schurman and his colleagues to discover exactly what they had hoped: that Filipinos predominantly welcomed American tutelage and preferred U.S. occupation to that of a revolutionary government led by Emilio Aguinaldo; that Aguinaldo had the backing of only a small segment of the Tagalog people, and the majority of the population saw the ilustrados as their true leaders; and that any resistance on the part of the larger Filipino population to American rule was due to falsehoods being spread by the revolutionaries.[25] Moreover, most reassuring to the American commissioners—at least according to the testimonies of the ilustrados—was the existence of a "perfect coincidence between the theory and practice of our government on the one hand, and the aspirations and ideals of the Filipinos on the other."[26]

The commission also conveniently discovered that the greatest evil of the Spanish system was centralized despotism. As a result of excessive centralization, "the local institutions of the archipelago had fallen into such decay and confusion that their several members were atrophied and useless, if not indeed transformed into instruments of corruption." The problem, the commission explained, was that because Spanish governors could admonish, fine, or suspend Filipino municipal officials at will, these officials had little incentive to undertake "vigorous initiative in office." Rather than working for the benefit of the townspeople, the municipal mayor was "in truth a political representative of the general government [in Manila] and, as it were, an arbitrary governor of the town."[27] The Filipinos were in fact perfectly capable of democratically governing themselves at the local level if given the opportunity and the right set of institutions. This implied that the United States could administer the Philippines through a small bureaucratic apparatus. By the commission's estimation, only one American provincial official for every two hundred fifty thousand Filipinos would be needed to govern the archipelago. With the population of the Philippines roughly seven million at the time, this amounted to just twenty-eight American administrators outside of

Manila. As such, not only would the Filipinos welcome U.S. forces as their liberators, the occupation itself was unlikely to burden the American taxpayer.[28]

For the first year of the U.S. occupation of the Philippines, events unfolded (at least as reported by General Otis) as McKinley and his advisers had been led to expect, giving them little reason to question Schurman's findings.[29] The revolutionary army seemed largely defeated by the end of 1899, and relative calm characterized the Philippine Islands for the first half of 1900. Aguinaldo and his generals remained at large but were seen to pose little threat to the United States.[30] Confident of imminent military victory, McKinley appointed the second Philippine Commission, this time headed by Taft (then a circuit court justice in Ohio), to replace the U.S. military as the new executive and legislative body in the archipelago. In June 1900, Taft and his fellow commissioners arrived in the Philippines and reported to Secretary of War Root that the insurrection was practically over and the effort to reconstruct the Philippines under civilian leadership could be implemented immediately.[31]

Yet, soon after Taft penned his optimistic report, hostilities between the United States and the Filipino revolutionaries resumed. Aguinaldo and his generals had spent the early months of 1900 regrouping and consolidating their power base in the localities and were now ready to demonstrate how little support the United States actually enjoyed in the archipelago. If the United States sought to remake the Philippines in its image, it would have to do so by suppressing widespread resistance and compelling systematic compliance with rules and regulations that the Filipinos had no interest in abiding by.

The Counterinsurgency Campaign

The self-serving findings of the Schurman Commission informed not just discussions in Washington on how best to modernize and democratize the government structure of the archipelago; they also guided America's initial strategy for defeating Aguinaldo and his forces and obtaining Filipino support for the U.S. occupation. This strategy had two parts. On one hand, the U.S. military would engage Aguinaldo's conventional forces in a relentless pursuit to defeat what Americans characterized as the Tagalog insurrection. On the other, U.S. forces would counteract Aguinaldo's propaganda and dispel any rumors of American maliciousness by demonstrating through deeds and actions that the United States had only benevolent intentions. Accordingly, once localities were "liberated," municipal governments were organized under military auspices and existing local officials were retained and embraced as partners. General Otis also dispersed his army into small garrisons throughout the archipelago and instructed his officers to assist Filipinos in providing much needed public goods and services. Under the guidance of the U.S. military, roads and bridges were built, health and sanitation codes were enforced, and primary education was provided.[32]

Not all U.S. military officials agreed with Schurman's optimistic prognosis, nor believed Otis's so-called policy of attraction to be enough to establish American control throughout the archipelago. General Arthur MacArthur, who took over the Philippine command in May 1900, was one such skeptic and suspected that despite the apparent calm, the war was far from over. Nonetheless, MacArthur at first clung to the hope that a display of benevolence could prove sufficient to end the war, for he understood that the American public, and hence politicians in Washington, would be uneasy with an aggressive counterinsurgency campaign that some of his commanders were advocating. MacArthur was also sensitive to the fact that any sign that America's occupation of the Philippines was going badly could lead to a Democratic victory in the 1900 presidential election and make William Jennings Bryan, who was running on an anti-imperialist platform, the commander in chief.[33]

Yet, as the months went by, and with the death toll rising, it became harder to ignore that the United States was losing the war. Ilustrado assurances that *principales*—that is, the class of municipal-level Filipino political elites—would quickly switch allegiance from Aguinaldo to the American regime were discovered to be untrue. As MacArthur reported, "Most towns secretly organized complete insurgent municipal governments, to proceed simultaneously and in the same sphere as the American governments, and in many instances through the same personnel." He surmised that in some instances principales and villagers cooperated with the insurgents out of intimidation and the threat of assassination, "but fear as the only motive is hardly sufficient to account for the united and apparently spontaneous action of several millions of people. One traitor in each town would effectually destroy such a complex organization."[34] MacArthur's full report of the insurrection was filled with hyperbole and exaggeration in order to convince lawmakers in Washington of the need for additional troops and greater patience with the Philippine campaign. He was nonetheless largely correct in his assessment that the resistance went far beyond the Tagalog people, and that most Filipino elites preferred self-rule under Aguinaldo's revolutionary government to American tutelage.

On December 20, 1900, with McKinley safely reelected to a second term, MacArthur announced his new counterinsurgency strategy: Any refusal to accept American benevolence would be met with harsh reprisal.[35] Moreover, all individuals suspected of aiding the insurgency would be tried by a military tribunal, and insurgents captured in civilian garb would no longer receive the privileges afforded to prisoners of war. Since guerrilla warfare could be sustained only through the cooperation of the principales, measures that directly threatened their well-being were formally sanctioned. When principales were found aiding the insurgents, their crops were destroyed and their houses burned; they also faced the threat of imprisonment and deportation. In addition, the number of garrisons was increased from 400 before the campaign to 502 within a few months, so that security could be adequately provided to Filipino collaborators and their behavior closely monitored. The system of intelligence gathering was revamped, and a robust network of spies and informants established. "Water cure," which involved forcing gallons of water into the victim's stomach, was widely used to obtain intelligence. MacArthur also increased the number of native troops, known as the Philippine Scouts, and began organizing municipal police forces to bolster the security of the garrisoned towns. U.S. troops, now numbering seventy thousand, were continuously deployed in a relentless offensive campaign to exhaust the guerrilla forces into submission.[36]

Most controversially, "reconcentration" was adopted as a strategy for intensive control and surveillance in areas with considerable insurgent activity. Under this policy, select municipalities were designated as "safe zones" and heavily guarded by U.S. troops. All inhabitants in the affected regions were ordered to abandon their homes and fields and relocate to one of the reconcentrated towns. They could travel outside of these safe zones only when accompanied by American troops. Harbors were closed and all trade between municipalities ceased. Outside of the reconcentrated towns, soldiers were authorized to shoot indiscriminately at all adult males and to destroy crops as they pleased. This policy not only cut off the insurgents from their source of food and shelter but also made life unbearable for both ordinary Filipinos and principales alike. The mortality rate skyrocketed from lack of food and unsanitary conditions. Although clearly inhumane, the strategy nonetheless proved highly effective and compelled both insurgents and their principales supporters to seek peace.[37]

America's campaign to establish control over the archipelago did not rely on brute force alone. MacArthur's heavy-handed and coercive counterinsurgency tactics were supplemented, initially against his wishes, with increased efforts to win over the support of Filipino elites through the establishment of a patronage structure akin to the spoils system in the United States.[38] To this end, Taft and wealthy ilustrados founded the Federal Party in the summer of 1900 on the platform of close American-Filipino collaboration and eventual incorporation of the archipelago into the federal union. Ilustrados who had collaborated closely with Americans from the very beginning, such as Benito Legarda, Trinidad Pardo de Tavera, and José Ruiz de Luzuriaga, were rewarded for their loyalty with appointments to the newly expanded eight-member Philippine Commission, which served as both the legislative and executive branch of the colonial government. The next tier of ilustrado collaborators was appointed in the provinces as governors, fis-cals, and judges of first instance. Finally, party leaders accompanied Taft and his fellow commissioners on a series of island-wide trips in 1901 to help organize municipal governments in "liberated" provinces so that they could flaunt their friendship with the American commissioners and impress on the principales their role as power brokers in the new regime. The aim was to expand the base of the Federal Party beyond Manila and the surrounding provinces such that it would become the sole organization for distributing patronage in the archipelago.[39]

What therefore developed in the Philippines was similar to the *baoliangju* scheme advanced by the scholar-gentry in Taiwan. But rather than reject a gov-ernance system centered around wealthy and regionally prominent elites as the Japanese did in Taiwan, American authorities wholeheartedly embraced the Fed-eral Party due to their familiarity with such a system,[40] as well as for reasons of expediency. When the Federal Party was created in 1900, there was a sense that the United States could very well lose the war, or at minimum, become embroiled in a costly guerilla campaign that the American people were unlikely to support. McKinley's narrative for occupying and annexing the Philippines was, after all, based on the premise that the Filipinos would embrace the Americans as libera-tors and teachers. This narrative was already being undermined by the magni-tude of the armed resistance, and the counterinsurgency tactics adopted by MacArthur—even if necessary from a military standpoint—threatened to further erode support for the administration's expansionist policy. Senators voiced grave concerns when the administration asked Congress to authorize a one-hundred-thousand-strong army composed of sixty-five thousand regulars and thirty-five thousand volunteers in February 1899,[41] and now, MacArthur was proposing to increase the number of American troops deployed in the Philippines even fur-ther and to keep a large American military presence there for the foreseeable future. A successful patronage system—especially one centered on a Filipino-led political party that called for the permanent incorporation of the archipelago into the United States—was exactly the kind of evidence that the McKinley admin-istration needed to keep its critics at bay. Moreover, insofar as this proved suc-cessful in helping to bring about an end to the war and maintaining American control over the islands, it would allow the United States to govern the Philippines with a much smaller military deployment and with material incentives replacing coercion as the primary instrument for obtaining collaboration.

The combination of MacArthur's counterinsurgency campaign and Taft's patronage scheme ultimately proved successful in suppressing resistance and es-tablishing American control over the Philippines. On March 15, 1901, the United States scored its first and most important victory in the counterinsurgency cam-paign when Mariano Trías, the charismatic commander of revolutionary forces

MAP 5.1. Administrative Divisions of the Philippines, 1903

Note: Only island groups (e.g., Visayas), islands (e.g., Negros), and provinces (e.g., Batangas) discussed in the text are labeled.

in southern Luzon, came to terms with the United States, triggering a rush of sur-
renders.[42] Aguinaldo's capture on March 28 and his subsequent declaration of
support for the American regime (in exchange for patronage) delivered a further
blow to the insurgency, leading most of the revolutionary leaders to lay down their
arms. By the end of 1901, the only notable rebel commanders left in the field were
Vicente Lukbán in Samar and Miguel Malvar in Batangas. (See Map 5.1.) Lukbán, widely feared after orchestrating the annihilation of the seventy-four-person
garrison in Balangiga, was the first to capitulate. Sick and malnourished, he was
captured on February 18, 1902. Malvar and his men endured the relentless American offensive for several months more, but with his followers starving, his am-
munition depleted, his wife ill with a newborn child, and the people of his home
region suffering in the reconcentrated towns, Malvar finally surrendered on
April 16.[43]

Although sporadic fighting continued for the next few years, the Philippine-
American War was essentially over, with more than four thousand Americans
and an estimated fifty thousand Filipino soldiers dead.[44] Military victory hardly
meant that the U.S. effort to remake the Philippines in its image would proceed
smoothly, however. Territorial control did not ensure statebuilding success, and
a willingness to collaborate in maintaining American authority over the archipelago did not imply that Filipino elites would obediently enforce the colonial
state's new rules and regulations. Finally, as evident in the ensuing analysis, strategies that helped the United States win the war—in particular, the establishment
of a patronage system centered around wealthy and regionally influential elites—
were precisely what stood in the way of the construction of a modern and strong
state.

The American Way of Statebuilding

When Root was appointed war secretary in August 1899 and placed in charge of
crafting the government's policy regarding the newly acquired territories, he had
no relevant experience in government administration and policymaking. Other
than serving as New York State's district attorney, his professional background
was largely in corporate law. Regarded by his peers as a brilliant lawyer, what he
did possess was a highly analytical mind and a strong interest in fundamental
questions on power and authority. In devising America's basic statebuilding strategy for the Philippine Islands, Root began by poring over his collection of books
on European colonialism. It did not take long for him to determine that while
there might have been general lessons for the United States to learn from the British and the Dutch—the two colonial powers that governed, like the United

States, by "the spirit of liberty and freedom"[45] at home—their experience in colonial administration appeared largely irrelevant to the task at hand. After all, what the United States was trying to accomplish was quite different and special. Unlike Britain and the Netherlands, which possessed colonies across the globe for the purposes of protecting trade routes and extracting valuable resources, the United States was attempting to transform the Philippines into a modern, and ultimately democratic, state.

Moreover, British and Dutch administrators employed despotic practices in their respective colonies that the United States could not mimic if it was to respect the principles and beliefs embodied in the U.S. Bill of Rights and because "moral law . . . prevents the Government doing certain things to any man whatever."[46] Familiar with the classic texts on liberty and democracy, and most important, Alexis de Tocqueville's *Democracy in America*, Root was guided by strong convictions on what government should and should not do for the people and how the state ought to be structured institutionally to allow for the development of a prosperous and democratic citizenry.[47] Spanish-era laws and informal institutions and practices would be respected as much as possible in designing new governmental institutions, but Americans should not lose sight of their own values and principles on good government.

The "Instruction of the President to the Philippine Commission"[48] of April 7, 1900—which, despite the title, was written by Root—was indeed an embodiment of this belief in the universality of the basic principles undergirding the U.S. Constitution, as well as America's own experience in democracy building from below. Channeling Tocqueville's argument that norms, mores, and habits of a democratic citizenry can only be fostered through civic and political engagement at the level of villages, towns, and urban neighborhoods, the instructions charged the Philippine Commission to devote its attention to the "establishment of municipal governments, in which the natives of the islands . . . shall be afforded the opportunity to manage their own local affairs to the fullest extent of which they are capable, and subject to the least degree of supervision and control."[49]

Yet, although the main arena for Filipino self-development was to be the localities, there were a number of things that the IGP could do directly to support this process. In the first place, Root emphasized the necessity of establishing judicial institutions aimed at protecting the rights and freedoms of the Filipinos. Unsurprisingly, given Root's training in American jurisprudence, his list of particularly important rights and freedoms reflected the U.S. Bill of Rights: No one shall be deprived of life, liberty, or property without due process; people shall have the right to a speedy and fair trial and receive counsel for their defense; excessive fine or punishment shall not be inflicted; one would not be tried twice for the same offense, or subjected to unreasonable searches and seizures; freedom of speech shall be protected, as well as freedom of religion; etc. What Root had in mind for the Philippines was essentially a judicial system modeled after America's own.[50]

Root also believed that the United States could directly contribute to the material and intellectual progress of the Filipinos in two ways. First was the establishment of a clear property rights regime, so that people would be motivated to invest in their land and come to appreciate the importance of a robust rule of law regime for their material well-being. The commission was thus instructed to investigate complaints of land-grabbing and ensure the just settlement of any past wrongdoings by large landowners.[51] Second, Root called for the commission to institute a system of primary education that would be "free to all, and which shall tend to fit the people for the duties of citizenship and for the ordinary avocations of a civilized community."[52] Root, like many of his contemporaries, believed that the fostering of an enlightened citizenry started in the classroom. It was there that people would be taught the basic skills—the ability to read, write, express one's opinion, and understand the point of view of others—to participate in representative government. The classroom was also where children would be exposed to the works of liberal philosophers and statesmen, and by studying these texts, they would become inculcated with the beliefs, norms, and mores undergirding a democratic polity.[53]

With Root's instructions as the ultimate guide for its statebuilding effort and believing—thanks to the Schurman report—that it already possessed all of the information necessary for designing new political and administrative institutions in the archipelago, the second Philippine Commission, led by Taft, began its work as the Philippines's soon-to-be legislative and executive body even before it left for Manila. The first order of business was to hire Fred Atkinson (a thirty-five-year old high school principal in Springfield, Massachusetts) as the archipelago's new general superintendent of public instruction, so that the process of recruiting teachers and devising a plan for a new public school system could commence immediately.[54] Following Root's instructions, the language of instruction was set as English, and in accordance with the principle of separation of church and state, the public school curriculum offered no classes on religion. Although a few public schools had been built in areas directly controlled by the U.S. military in the preceding year, this was regarded as inadequate both numerically and pedagogically. Atkinson thus proceeded to hire hundreds of American teachers to serve in the Philippines, and in August 1901, the first group of teachers arrived aboard the USAT *Thomas*—more than five hundred Thomasites, as they came to be known—with hundreds more to follow in the coming months.[55]

The work of creating a new judicial structure, meanwhile, began on September 1, 1900, when all legislative powers, previously held by General MacArthur in his capacity as military governor, were formally transferred to the commission. Determining that the Spanish court system, which remained in operation under the U.S. military regime, was unsuitable for a modern and (eventually) democratic state, as well as injurious to the rights and freedoms of the Filipinos, the commission set out to undertake a wholesale replacement of the existing system of court procedure. After months of careful study and discussion among the commissioners, and between them and leading ilustrados, the new system, consisting of a seven-person supreme court and fourteen judicial districts (each with one or more judges of first instance) came into being on June 11, 1901. Cayetano Arellano, an ilustrado who had offered invaluable legal advice to the commission throughout the process, was named the first chief justice of the Philippine Supreme Court. However, for the most part, those appointed to the bench at the national and provincial levels were Americans, given the assumption that Filipinos still needed considerable tutelage in Western jurisprudence: Four out of seven in the Supreme Court and eleven out of seventeen in the courts of first instance came to be occupied by those with legal training and experience in the United States. Yet, out of practical considerations, this practice of appointing Americans to the bench was not extended to the selection of hundreds of justices of the peace, with whom the average Filipino would primarily interact.[56]

Following the procedure observed in the United States—specifically, in the state of Massachusetts—the courts also assumed responsibility over resolving any land disputes and issuing indefeasible (Torrens) titles to those who could display clear evidence of ownership. A special tribunal, the Court of Land Registration, was created in 1902 and began work the following year. However, because only two justices were initially appointed to the Court of Land Registration (this would increase to three in 1909 and six in 1910), because the registration of titles was not made compulsory, because many individuals lacked the basic literacy necessary to file paperwork to have their case reviewed by the land court, and because most landowners did not possess sufficient documentation for the issuance of Torrens titles in the first place, the work of land registration proceeded slowly and unevenly, with only the rich and powerful obtaining secure titles. In light of such shortcomings, the work of the land courts was supplanted by a cadastral survey system in 1913.[57]

Among all of the statebuilding work undertaken by the commission during its first year in the Philippines, none compared in significance to Act No. 82, "a general act for the organization of municipal governments in the Philippine Islands."[58] Known as the Municipal Code, this document outlined how hundreds of Philippine municipalities would be turned into self-governing entities. Starting from the assumption (found in Schurman's report, and eventually reflected in Root's instructions) that many of the Spanish-era laws—except for those pertaining to court procedure—were wisely framed, even if corruptly administered, the commission's plan for municipal organization retained key elements from Spanish precedent. The Municipal Code limited the franchise to men over twenty-three years of age who possessed one of the following qualifications: had held political office under the Spanish regime; owned property worth five hundred pesos or paid over thirty pesos in taxes annually; or could speak, read, and write in English or Spanish. The Municipal Code thus left unchanged the system whereby municipal officeholders largely attended to the interests of those with wealth and education. With so small a number of individuals participating, elections essentially became contests between competing cliques for control over the spoils associated with office.[59]

Yet, although the internal organization of the municipalities, as well as the selection method of its officeholders, underwent little modification, the Municipal Code dramatically expanded the duties and responsibilities of municipal officials and attempted to specify the correct ways by which officeholders would carry out their duties. Composed of nine chapters and one hundred five sections, the act specified the types of taxes that municipalities should collect and how local finances should be maintained and audited. Particularly notable was the extensive list of tasks—thirty-six in total—that the municipal council was expected to perform. They included construction and upkeep of streets, sidewalks, bridges, viaducts, public drains, sewers, and cesspools; maintenance of sanitary conditions by keeping streets and public spaces clean, providing for the collection of garbage, and inspecting the quality of meat, fruits, poultry, milk, and vegetables sold in markets; establishment of police departments, prisons, post offices, and schools; prohibition of gambling, opium consumption, public intoxication, vagrancy, and cruelty against animals (such as cockfighting); and enforcement of proper weights and measures. Furthermore, departing from Spanish precedent, municipalities were reimagined as autonomous and self-governing entities. No longer would *presidentes* (mayors) be under the constant surveillance of the parish priest, and as long as municipal officials did not engage in demonstrably illegal behavior, they were left alone to perform their duties with little interference from the central government.[60]

In most areas targeted for reform, the desire to remake the Philippines into a strong and modern state led, as the foregoing examples demonstrate, American statebuilders to draw inspiration from, and even mimic, institutional models and practices found in the United States itself. An important deviation from this general trend was the design of the insular (central) bureaucracy, whereby the spoils system (which governed the selection and promotion of civil servants in the United States) was explicitly rejected as a model for staffing the administrative organs of the central government, even as it was employed as a mechanism for mediating relations between U.S. colonial officials and Filipino elites and for making political appointments in the provinces. Instead, closely following the ideals of good government as expressed in the writings of such leading Progressive thinkers as Frank Goodnow and Woodrow Wilson,[61] the 1900 Civil Service Act called for "the establishment and maintenance of an efficient and honest civil service in all the executive branches of the government of the Philippine Islands . . . by appointments and promotions according to merit and by competitive examinations where the same are practicable."[62]

Accordingly, bureaucratic examinations were held annually in both Spanish and English and their passage was made necessary, in principle, for all full-time bureaucratic appointments. Top administrative appointments made directly by the governor-general and the commission, such as chiefs and deputy chiefs of government agencies, were excluded from the examination system, as well as those requiring technical, professional, or scientific knowledge. In the latter case, a demonstration of such knowledge, rather than passage of the civil service exam, became the criterion for meritocratic appointment. As a general rule, these examinations were competitive (with many more people taking the exam than the number of positions available), and the process involved three parts: first, individuals had to apply to take the examination; the second part was the examination itself; and third, there was a six-month probationary period before one was assigned to a bureaucratic agency. Proscriptions and injunctions were instituted against inquiry into the political or religious opinions and affiliations of the examinees to counteract any biases, prejudices, and favoritism throughout the process. Finally, a Civil Service Board was created to oversee the examination process and to monitor the behavior of bureaucrats—in particular, to ensure that they did not engage in solicitation or receipt of political contributions—once they were appointed.[63]

These rules, at least for the duration of the American period, were strictly followed to the extent possible. In this way, the bureaucratic apparatus of the IGP came closer to the Weberian ideal than its counterpart in Taiwan, where rules concerning meritocratic hiring were routinely flaunted given shortages in personnel. This was made possible in part by the priority that the United States placed on public education. Another important variable was America's commitment to the "Filipinization" of the colonial administration. As a result of this policy, U.S. officials tapped into the large pool of educated and technically trained individuals from the local population to staff the bureaucracy in a way that the Japanese regime did not. Between 1901 and 1913 (the period from which data are readily available), a total of 66,342 individuals (8,673 Americans and 57,669 Filipinos) took the civil service exam, and 4,967 Americans (57 percent) and 17,494 Filipinos (30 percent) passed the exam, ensuring that there were plenty of qualified

TABLE 5.1.   Regularly and Permanently Appointed Bureaucrats in Colonial Taiwan, the Philippines, and Korea

	TAIWAN		THE PHILIPPINES		KOREA	
	TOTAL	PER THOUSAND INHABITANTS	TOTAL	PER THOUSAND INHABITANTS	TOTAL	PER THOUSAND INHABITANTS
1900	7,088	2.52	—	—	—	—
1905	8,333	2.67	7,330	0.95	—	—
1910	11,941	3.62	7,272	0.88	9,287	0.60
1915	13,714	3.84	9,816	1.06	13,911	0.84
1920	15,282	4.07	13,143	1.26	28,166	1.61
1925	16,838	4.06	16,845	1.44	29,109	1.55
1930	19,219	4.11	21,704	1.66	31,617	1.56
1935	20,222	3.80	22,411	1.52	34,339	1.57

Sources: Corpuz, *The Bureaucracy in the Philippines*, 183; Mizoguchi and Umemura, *Kyū Nihon shokuminchi keizai tōkei*, 256; Okamoto, *Shokuminchi kanryō no seiji shi*, 51, 60; Philippines, Bureau of the Census and Statistics, *Yearbook of Philippine Statistics, 1940*, 13; Philippines, Commissioner of Civil Service, *First Annual Report of the Commissioner of Civil Service, 1936*, 44.

candidates to staff the bureaucracy. Hence, there is good reason to believe that the quality of the colonial civil service was in fact higher in the Philippines than in Taiwan. At minimum, there is no empirical basis on which to claim that it was lower—an interpretation also supported by the largely positive assessments of postwar Filipino scholars regarding the training, integrity, and professionalism of the civil service during the American period.[64]

Another distinguishing feature of the colonial bureaucracy was its size. Table 5.1 compares the number of regularly and permanently appointed bureaucrats of the colonial government in Taiwan, the Philippines, and Korea in five-year intervals starting in 1900. As seen here, the Philippine colonial bureaucracy, with a bureaucratic density averaging 1.3 full-time officials per thousand inhabitants across the years shown, was certainly smaller than its Japanese counterpart in Taiwan, which averaged 3.6 per thousand. Yet, by no means can the Philippine colonial service be characterized as small in an absolute sense; it was larger than most colonial bureaucracies in Southeast Asia, and, as can be seen from this data, comparable in size to the Japanese colonial administration in Korea—arguably the epitome of a large, intrusive, and effective bureaucracy[65]—which also boasted an average bureaucratic density of 1.3 per thousand.[66] Indeed, this relatively large bureaucratic presence was what allowed American colonial officials to micromanage the aforementioned highly centralized public school system[67] and institute a top-down health regime that sought to closely monitor the sanitary habits of the local population.

In sum, what emerged was a government structure that reflected, at least on the surface, both the ideals of democratic government and good bureaucratic administration. On one hand, a system of autonomous municipal governments, inspired by Tocquevillian beliefs, was instituted whereby Filipinos had the opportunity to acquire the norms and habits of a democratic citizenry through practical experience with local self-rule. On the other, colonial officials established a large and meritocratic bureaucracy that incorporated practices of good government long advocated by Progressive reformers in the United States. Yet, as shown in chapter 1, this seemingly well-designed government apparatus did not function as intended. Rather than becoming a model of good governance, the colonial state exhibited acute weakness in its capacity to see and mobilize. The problem was that, contrary to the attention and thought put into designing formal *governmental* institutions, little care was paid to establishing mediational structures between state and society, such that administrative intermediaries could be made into obedient and effective enforcers of rules and regulations.

Designing an Ineffective System of State-Society Mediation

Local autonomy was to be the fundamental principle of the new governance structure in the Philippine Islands. This did not mean that Taft, or even Root, believed that municipal officeholders should enjoy unfettered freedom from administrative oversight. Unlike the Spanish administrators of the previous regime, U.S. officials would not interfere in the day-to-day governance of municipalities, but it was the responsibility of the United States, as teachers of democratic principles and values, to ensure that Filipino community leaders did not abuse their greatly expanded authority. Indeed, although Root was unequivocal in insisting that municipal governments should be given considerable autonomy and discretion to manage their own affairs, he was careful to note in his instructions that "there are also certain practical rules of government which we have found to be essential to the preservation of these great principles of liberty and law, and . . . these principles and these rules of government must be maintained in their islands for the sake of their liberty and happiness, however much they may conflict with the customs or laws of procedure with which they are familiar."[68] Root remained silent, however, on how this was to be done, leaving it to the commission to design a system of central oversight over local Filipino officials.

The commission's plan for overseeing the behavior of local officeholders had two parts. First, provincial governments were placed in charge of monitoring the performance of municipal officials and investigating any complaints of maladministration made against them. "The provincial governor is," in the words of Joseph Hayden, who later served as vice governor-general, "the great local official. His legal authority reaches into every barrio in his province and at the same time makes him the intermediary between the municipalities and the central government."[69] He was responsible for directly overseeing the conduct of municipal officers and councillors by visiting each municipality in his province at least once every six months. During such visits, he was to hear all complaints made against local-level officials. If these complaints were found to be credible, the governor possessed the authority to suspend the official in question, and refer the matter to the governor-general or to the provincial fiscal, depending on the nature of the charges and the rank of the official in question, for further investigation and judgment, which could include removal from office.[70] The governor, as head of his political party's provincial organization and elected to office by the province's municipal officeholders, was also the province's political leader and "almost invariably a man of substance with influential family and business connections."[71] He was therefore uniquely positioned to aggregate the interests and concerns of municipal officials and the wider public and to present them to the central government in Manila.

The remaining two members of the provincial board—treasurer and supervisor—were both directly appointed by the Philippine Commission. As members of the provincial board, they assisted the governor in drafting and enacting resolutions. Much of their time, however, was spent not on matters of general governance and oversight within the province, but on fulfilling specific functional tasks associated with their portfolios. For the provincial treasurer, this was the appraisal and assessment of property in the municipalities and the collection of all central- and provincial-level taxation that had been locally accumulated during the course of the fiscal year. As for the supervisor, he was to oversee the construction, repair, and maintenance of the province's roads and bridges, except for those within the boundaries of a municipality.[72] Moreover, in addition to these formal responsibilities, the treasurer and the supervisor were to informally serve as the eyes and ears of the Philippine Commission at the provincial level. If these officials felt that the governor was failing to fulfill his duties as an administrative intermediary, they were to tactfully pressure him to alter his behavior.[73] Given their informal oversight functions, treasurer and supervisor positions were typically occupied by Americans.

Yet, while the provincial government was assigned considerable responsibility in overseeing the behavior of municipal officials, its institutional structure was insufficient for undertaking a task of such complexity and importance.[74] Composed of little more than a three-member executive-cum-legislative board made up of the governor, treasurer, and supervisor, "the provincial government [was] a government of supervision and record, and [was] maintained with all possible economy."[75] In 1904, for instance, only 173 American and 626 Filipino full-time government officials served in the *entire* provincial service—that is, in all thirty-nine provinces combined. This was an average of 20.5 officials per provincial government. In comparison, the city government of Manila, which was indeed a full-fledged government body, employed 575 American and 1,022 Filipino civil servants, while 2,583 Americans and 1,723 Filipinos served in the insular (central) government.[76] Furthermore, while the provincial governor possessed the formal authority to oversee the conduct of municipal officials, and the treasurer and supervisor the informal responsibility of monitoring the behavior of the provincial governor, none of these members of the provincial board actually were empowered to remove an elected or appointed official from office. This authority belonged to the governor-general alone.[77]

Such limitations in the organization and powers of the provincial government led U.S. officials to innovate a second oversight mechanism centered around the office of the governor-general, and in particular the Executive Bureau. Originally established in 1901 to do little more than provide administrative assistance to the governor-general, the Executive Bureau underwent a number of reorganizations in the ensuing years with the aim of giving the bureau the necessary capacity to supervise provincial and municipal governments. In 1903, the position of law clerk was created so that the Executive Bureau would have the expertise to process formal complaints made against Filipino officeholders and recommend any punitive action.[78] It also became the responsibility of the bureau's Law Division to examine the text of all provincial resolutions, as well as the titles of municipal ordinances, to ensure that they did not exceed the bounds of proper government authority at these levels.[79] The bureau's oversight functions over local government were further expanded in 1905 when supervision of provincial treasurers was transferred from the insular treasurer to the executive secretary.[80] This granted the Executive Bureau broad authority to scrutinize provincial and municipal budgets, the salaries of local officials, and the collection of various minor fees and taxes. It also placed the bureau in charge of reviewing any revisions associated with land assessments and valuation for the purposes of taxation—a politically contentious process that was prone to considerable corruption.[81]

However, as was the case with the provincial government, the small size of the Executive Bureau constrained its ability to perform these vital oversight functions. During the 1903–04 fiscal year, when the position of law clerk was created, the Executive Bureau had a staff of 128 full- and part-time officials. Ten years later in 1913 the bureau employed 208 individuals. This was simply not enough for the Executive Bureau, by the bureau chief's own assessment, to effectively monitor the behavior of hundreds of provincial and municipal officeholders, investigate charges of wrongdoing, ascertain the lawfulness of provincial resolutions and municipal ordinances, ensure that land assessments followed proper procedures, and audit local budgets for possible misuse of funds.[82] The bureau therefore had little choice but to rely on provincial and municipal officeholders—that is, the very individuals it was tasked with overseeing—for information and logistical assistance.[83]

Many instances of corruption and maladministration therefore went unnoticed by the Executive Bureau. In particular, if local politics was monopolized by a single clique, or if the dominant political force had considerable coercive capacity with which to intimidate potential witnesses, it was highly unlikely that unlawful behavior on the part of municipal or provincial officials would be reported to the governor-general.[84] Without a large staff supporting the vast responsibilities of the Executive Bureau, there was also nothing systematic or routine about the way in which it handled charges against provincial and municipal officials. Whether someone was punished or declared innocent depended on who provided the executive secretary and his staff information about local political conditions. According to Hayden, "A stroll down the second-floor corridor of the picturesque old *Ayuntamiento* and a pause in the Secretary's anteroom would always enable one to greet two or three provincial governors, numerous *presidentes*, and other political figures from every part of the Archipelago. . . . In discussing the amount and character of central control over the provinces and municipalities . . . this element of political influence cannot be left out of account."[85]

Further contributing to the dysfunction of the mediational system were perverse incentives that emerged from the various representative and patronage institutions designed to legitimate the IGP in the eyes of Filipino elites. For instance, the provincial governors, beginning in 1902, were chosen by a selectorate composed entirely of municipal officeholders, rather than by the larger voting public. As a result, governors were incentivized to keep the majority of members of the selectorate—who also happened to be the very individuals that governors were tasked with overseeing—content so that they could continue to win reelection every two years.[86] Equally problematic was the relationship of codependence that emerged between top American administrators and leading Filipino elites. Having assumed control over most provinces in 1901 while fighting continued between U.S. forces and remnants of the revolutionary army, the Philippine Commission relied heavily on the Federal Party, and later provincial elites outside of the Manila-based Federal Party's patronage network, to maintain peace and stability in the localities.[87] Under the emerging collaborative framework, American administrators in the provinces would help cooperative elites in their bids to win gubernatorial elections. In return, the insular government obtained their loyal support in suppressing insurrections by former revolutionaries, messianic movements, and peasant uprisings, and with their help decreased U.S. military presence in the archipelago to a level acceptable to U.S. congressmen and senators and the American public. The most notable product of this arrangement was Manuel Quezon of Tayabas, who won the 1906 gubernatorial election with considerable assistance from American constabulary officers and advanced through the political hierarchy to eventually become the first president of the Philippine Commonwealth in 1935. But he was certainly not alone.[88] American administrators therefore hesitated to punish even manifestly corrupt governors, so long as they contributed to the continuance of U.S. control over the archipelago.

Consequently, despite being assigned the role of overseeing the conduct of the governors, provincial treasurers, supervisors, and constabulary officers who failed to "get along" with the local elite were transferred to another province or dismissed outright.[89] In 1906, for example, during the height of the bitter election campaign between the *Federalista* incumbent Pablo Tescon of Bulacan and his primary opponent Teodoro Sandiko—who ran on a platform of Philippine independence from the United States—news of Tescon's rape of a fifteen-year-old girl came to light. Sandiko seized on this information and initiated litigation against the incumbent in the district court, where Tescon was found guilty of charges and sentenced to six months' imprisonment. Yet, Governor-General Henry Ide decided not to suspend Tescon, a staunch American ally, from the Bulacan governorship until the Philippine Supreme Court could rule on the appeal. Several days before the election, the girl and her parents dropped the case altogether, presumably bowing to pressure placed on them by the embattled governor. Despite such efforts by Tescon's American patrons, Sandiko won the election anyway, but fortunately for them, Sandiko's fiery rhetoric against the U.S. occupation would not dictate how he behaved as governor. Soon after winning the governorship, Sandiko traveled to Manila to express his desire to collaborate with the Americans in promoting peace and prosperity in the archipelago.[90]

It was not until the 1910s that the Philippine Constabulary, often with the direct help of provincial governors, succeeded in suppressing the array of large-scale insurrections in eastern and central Visayas and in central and southern Luzon. By that point, however, collaborative relations between American colonial officials, especially officers of the constabulary, and local Filipino elites were firmly entrenched through informal ties and mutually beneficial political arrangements. Yet, this was hardly the only outcome that was available to American officials. U.S. military forces, like their Japanese counterparts in Taiwan, possessed the capacity to establish territorial control over the archipelago *without* the support of powerful provincial-level elites like Quezon, Tescon, and Sandiko. The decision to shield governors from rigorous oversight in exchange for their support in the counterinsurgency campaign was therefore not a product of strategic necessity. It was a *choice* born out of political considerations and ideo-logical biases.

In fact, when given the opportunity, U.S. security forces demonstrated that they were quite capable of defeating rebel groups through their efforts alone. When confronted with renewed rebel activity in Samar and Leyte in 1902 and Cavite and Batangas in 1904, the U.S. Army (in the former) and the Philippine Constabulary (in the latter) employed counterinsurgency strategies and tactics that mimicked those innovated by General MacArthur at the height of the Philippine-American War. Yet, despite thoroughly alienating the provincial elite through the use of highly coercive measures, these campaigns ultimately succeeded in suppressing the insurgencies and reestablishing American control in affected territories.[91] Meanwhile, in defeating the messianic movement led by Dionisio Sigobela—who went by the title Papa Isio—on the island of Negros, constabulary officers, who identified widespread abuse of peasants by municipal office-holders as the primary cause of the uprising, directly interjected themselves in matters of local governance to punish wrongdoers. In this process, constables became well acquainted with local residents and were able to obtain their cooperation in capturing Papa Isio in 1907.[92]

The brutal counterinsurgency campaigns in eastern Visayas and southern Luzon and the policy of attraction that was pursued in Negros might have been polar opposites in the tactics employed to bring peace to these regions. However, they similarly demonstrate that had the U.S. military maintained a large troop presence in the archipelago as MacArthur advocated, or had colonial officials established a provincial bureaucracy with the capacity and manpower to actually monitor and discipline local Filipino officeholders, the IGP would not have become so beholden to provincial elites in sustaining U.S. authority in the Philippines. Such an administrative structure would have allowed colonial officials to organize mediational institutions at the level of *pueblos* and *barrios* and to rely on local community leaders as their primary administrative intermediaries. Instead, an ideological commitment to local autonomy, as well as fear of domestic political backlash in the United States against a large U.S. military presence in the Philippines, prevented U.S. statebuilders from choosing this path.

Conclusion: The Ideational Origin of Statebuilding Failure

A distinguishing feature of the U.S. statebuilding campaign in the Philippines, like its Japanese counterpart in Taiwan, was that it took place at a critical juncture in the archipelago's institutional development.[93] With the disintegration of

the Spanish colonial regime following defeat of its forces by Aguinaldo's revolutionary army, the Philippines no longer had a functioning administrative structure, at least above the municipal level, that the United States could have retained
even if it had so desired. The Catholic priests, who had played an instrumental
role in maintaining Spanish authority in the localities, hoped to remain on the
islands and maintain their estates at first, but, with U.S. officials fearing that their
continued presence would become an enduring source of local conflict, they were
soon expelled from the archipelago and their valuable land holdings sold off to
Filipinos. As for the native landed elites, they had been excluded from participation in the administration of the colony under Spanish rule and were happy to
see Spanish governmental institutions thoroughly dismantled. When Taft and his
fellow commissioners arrived in Manila with Root's instructions in hand, they
therefore possessed considerable leeway to impose whatever institutions they
deemed necessary to reshape the islands into a strong and modern state.

Paradoxically, precisely because U.S. statebuilders enjoyed such freedom in designing and imposing new governmental institutions, they became prisoners of
their strong views as to how a modern and well-governed state should be structured. What stands out across the multitude of public and private pronounce-
ments by U.S. policymakers in both Washington and Manila was an unwavering
belief in the superiority and universality of the U.S. political, judicial, and administrative systems. Root might have stressed the importance of showing sensitivity
toward the customs and habits of the Filipinos, but he was unequivocal in his view
that there were certain principles and practices of good government beyond com-
promise. Friendly interactions between U.S. policymakers and the ilustrados
further padded this confidence in the U.S. statebuilding model and helped per-
petuate the myth that the vision of good government espoused by Filipino elites
was in perfect harmony with American political principles and practices.

The ways in which such beliefs shaped the design of formal administrative institutions were discussed earlier, but the effects of America's ideological commitments and biases did not end there. As demonstrated in chapter 6, the American
mindset also affected how statebuilders reacted to early setbacks. Specifically, it
provided the cognitive framework to interpret failures in local government as
manifestations of Filipino backwardness, rather than as the results of flawed institutional design. If a municipal mayor or provincial governor turned out to be
corrupt or ineffective, the obvious (though not always permissible) solution, from
the U.S. perspective, was to replace the offending individual with someone who
was loyal to the regime and willing to work diligently to carry out its mission.
Widespread failure in policy implementation, meanwhile, was perceived as a sign
that Filipinos had yet to acquire the norms, habits, and mores of a civilized people.
Since lack of compliance with good laws was a cultural problem and not an

institutional one, the solution was to wait for the Filipino civilization to modernize through decades of economic development and enlightened education. It did not occur to U.S. officials that corruption and misbehavior on the part of Filipino politicians, as well as the general unevenness in compliance with rules and regulations, could in fact be the product of institutionally generated incentives—a manifestation of the dysfunctional system of state-society mediation that they themselves had created.

The United States failed in its attempt to transform the Philippines into a strong and democratic state not because of insufficient time, resources, or manpower, nor because the Philippines was socioeconomically or culturally unready for this endeavor. Confident that their own experience as politicians, professors, lawyers, jurists, and businessmen in an established democracy gave them the necessary expertise for the task at hand, and constrained by domestic political pressures and by their own ideologically informed biases, U.S. statebuilders simply did not know, nor seek to learn, how to construct a strong and modern state by imposition amid widespread resistance.

STATE INVOLUTION

The Municipal Code was arguably the most important legislation that the Philippine Commission enacted during its seventeen years as the primary lawmaking body of the archipelago.[1] As William Howard Taft, president of the Philippine Commission and soon-to-be civil governor of the Philippines, explained at the occasion of the law's passage in January 1901, "The town is the unit, or ought to be the unit, of all good government. If one reads [Alexis de] Tocqueville's history of the United States, he will find that [the] great writer devotes much of what he has to say to the town conditions of New England and other parts of the country. Civil liberty and a free government [find their] formulation in that part of the government." Taft, moreover, expressed great confidence that the Filipino people were ready to embrace the rights and freedoms, along with the duties and responsibilities, espoused in the Municipal Code. With sufficient guidance, they would work together with American administrators to transform the Philippines into a modern and democratic state: "Now we find in the islands the town spirit and the elements of a town government. It is these elements that give us the greatest hope of success in obtaining for these islands a self-sustaining and self-administering government."[2]

It did not take long for Taft to backtrack on his lofty expectations. Within two years, he had seen enough to conclude that the municipalities were failing to serve as the engine of statebuilding and democratic development in the archipelago as hoped. "The truth," Taft reported in 1903, "is that the municipal governments have not been as satisfactory in their operations as could be wished."[3] Yet, despite dismissive statements by Taft, as well as by his American colleagues in the commission, it was not the case that municipal governments failed in every aspect of local governance. They performed dismally in the campaign against cholera during the 1902–04 epidemic, but they effectively assisted the Philippine Constabulary in capturing rebels during the counterinsurgency campaign and helping to maintain peace and stability thereafter. Such unevenness was also found within each policy area. No difficulty was reported in the collection of the *cédula*, a flat one-peso tax on all men ages eighteen to fifty-five, but irregularities and noncompliance routinely accompanied payment of the real estate tax.

The problem, therefore, was not one of local capacity per se, but one of willingness (or lack thereof) on the part of municipal officials to collect a certain type of tax or to provide some public good or service. Indeed, whenever a rule or regulation benefited the local elite, enforcement was not an issue, as municipal officials possessed various coercive, normative, and remunerative sources of power to compel the people to abide by their commands. What was missing in the Philippine locality was an effective system of state-society mediation whereby government officials could obtain systematic cooperation from administrative intermediaries in the enforcement of rules and regulations that were unpopular, logistically onerous, or went against individual or class interests. Moreover, having failed to develop effective mediational institutions, U.S. officials became increasingly reliant on the assistance of a select number of Filipino provincial elites to maintain even a modicum of governability in the localities. In turn, as these elites grew in importance and influence, they misused government resources for private gain and carved out spheres of influence within the localities to weaken the state at its foundation. While *caciquism* (bossism) had existed in the Philippines for centuries, it was under American rule that petty local-level despots were turned into powerful provincial bosses.

The U.S. statebuilding mission in the Philippines thus serves as an ideal-typical example of what Prasenjit Duara has aptly termed "state involution":[4] Instead of state weakness being a function of a society's cultural composition, or an enduring legacy of traditional institutions, it is the product of the statebuilding process itself, whereby the construction of modern, yet dysfunctional, governance institutions allows administrative intermediaries to become uncontrollable elements of society. The following discussion details how this outcome came to be even though U.S. officials were well aware of this problem and proactively tried to improve the governability of the archipelago by reforming and expanding the state's bureaucratic apparatus.

At the center of this dynamic is an inescapable link between bureaucracy building and the development of a territory's mediational institutions. Whereas formalized and cellularized institutions of state-society mediation made it possible for Japanese colonial bureaucrats to compel Taiwanese community leaders to behave as obedient administrative intermediaries, mediational institutions established by U.S. statebuilders had the opposite effect in the Philippines. Having enabled the development of a provincial political class of autonomous powerholders, the collaborative regime also served as a mechanism for Filipino elites to lobby top colonial officials, intervene in the everyday duties of bureaucrats, and ultimately corrupt the state from below and within. The Philippine case therefore demonstrates that the effect that mediational institutions have on the functioning of formal governmental institutions is never neutral, especially in the context of statebuilding by imposition. When interests of statebuilders and societal elites diverge, mediational institutions will necessarily be used as an instrument for either the state or society to impose its vision of political modernity onto the other.

Failure of Local Government as Failure in State-Society Mediation

The local governance structure of the American colonial state, as detailed in chapter 5, consisted of two components. The first was the Executive Bureau, which was the foremost government agency responsible for overseeing the conduct of local Filipino officeholders. However, its staff was small and did not possess the capacity to actually oversee and discipline local officials. The second component was the institution of state-society mediation centered around the provincial governor. In addition to his official duties, it was the governor's responsibility to use his personal influence and resources to ensure local compliance with rules and regulations and to help the Executive Bureau collect data and investigate wrongdoing. Most important, governors were tasked with assisting the Philippine Constabulary in suppressing any remaining rebel activity and thereafter in maintaining peaceful and stable conditions under U.S. colonial rule. As such, this was a system that perfectly suited the ideological commitments of American policymakers—that is, their Tocquevillian belief in the need to provide considerable autonomy to municipal governments—as well as the political necessity of upholding the narrative that Americans came to the Philippines as liberators and educators, and not as European-style imperial overlords. It was also one that quickly proved to be thoroughly ineffective in advancing statebuilding by imposition.

Largely left to their own devices, municipal officials did little to enforce systematic assessment of property values and collection of taxes on real estate; to properly fund and maintain the newly established public schools; or to cooperate with health officials to suppress cholera and other deadly epidemics. Yet, failing to realize that these suboptimal outcomes were a product of the flawed design of mediational institutions, U.S. officials placed the blame on what they perceived as civilizational backwardness of the Filipinos. Although it was necessary to grant them sufficient autonomy in their own local affairs for the purpose of political education, it had been far too premature, the statebuilders concluded, to entrust Filipinos with the enforcement of rules and regulations in key policy areas. Given its urgency, the fight against the cholera epidemic of 1902–04 marked the first time this lesson was applied. Thereafter, as a consequence of the struggle of U.S. administrators to reconcile this tension between their commitment to Tocquevillian ideals of local self-rule and their perceived need for more direct bureaucratic enforcement in key policy areas, the Philippine governance structure evolved into a dysfunctional mix of political decentralization, a weak system of local oversight, and a selectively interventionist central bureaucracy.

Elite-Driven Noncompliance in Taxation and Public Education

The tax regime initially adopted by U.S. officials departed from the centralized Spanish system in two important ways. First, reflecting the American governance philosophy that stressed local self-rule and administrative decentralization, all internally collected revenue (*cédula*, business tax, stamp tax and so on) was retained by local authorities, with half of it going to the provincial governments and the other half to the municipalities. Revenue for the central government meanwhile came exclusively from import and export duties. Second, mimicking practices found in the United States, a new real estate tax was introduced whereby local governments levied 0.375 percent on any privately owned land's assessed market value, of which one-third went to the provinces to pay for the construction of roads and bridges and two-thirds to the municipalities for public schooling.[5] The two most important tasks of local governments during the initial period of American rule—the construction of roads and the provision of free primary education for all—were therefore to be financed, at least in theory, entirely through the land tax.[6]

Local reception of the new tax code, which otherwise retained much of the Spanish system, was mixed. On one hand, Filipino elites welcomed their newly obtained freedom to expend tax revenue as they saw fit.[7] On the other, the Insular Government of the Philippine Islands (IGP) faced considerable opposition when it came to the land tax—despite its being set at a considerably low rate to ease its introduction—and Filipino landowners routinely fell delinquent. Yet, rather than punish such acts of blatant noncompliance with what was designed to be the single most important source of tax revenue for the localities, Filipino officeholders defended the landowners. Filipinos were a conservative people, local officials reported, and it would take time for them to accept a new form of taxation. They also claimed that the destruction wrought by war and the counterinsurgency campaign, as well as the rinderpest (a disease that decimated the islands' draft animal population) epidemic, led to years of poor harvests, compelling landowners to fall behind in their tax payments.[8]

Many Filipinos were indeed on the brink of starvation during the early years of U.S. rule. Complaints against the land tax, however, made little mention of the fact that, as an inherently progressive form of taxation, it did not apply to most Filipinos. Recognizing that a large number of Filipino landowners were small-scale farmers engaged in subsistence farming, the commission had exempted from taxation those whose property was valued at fifty pesos (which equaled twenty-five dollars) or less. The real estate tax therefore affected only the wealthy.[9] Moreover, the cédula (head tax), despite its highly regressive nature, was dutifully collected. No plea was made on behalf of the poor tenant farmers, who had lost their farm animals to war and disease and were in fact starving. In short, municipal officials demonstrated their willingness and ability to squeeze tax revenue out of the poor, while simultaneously complaining that wealthy landowners, due to economic hardship, could not pay taxation on real estate—which amounted, for the average property owner, to a levy that was less than the cédula.[10] What local Filipino officials lacked was not the logistical capacity to collect the land tax or the coercive instruments to overcome local resistance, but the desire to do so.

The harm done by municipal officials in the collection of taxation went beyond their propensity to tax the poor heavily while sanctioning nonpayment by the rich. Given that the land tax was based on the assessed value of real estate, its collection depended on detailed knowledge of the size of individual lots and their productive capacity. However, the IGP made little effort to collect systematic information on land ownership through a cadastral survey until 1913, leaving it to local authorities to maintain a land registry on their own and with little central supervision. In turn, with the municipal assessment board dominated by officials elected to office under a restricted franchise, the work of the appraisers necessarily reflected the interests of the landed elite and especially those who belonged to the municipal president's patronage network.[11]

Indeed, evidence of the *presidentes'* (mayors') abusing their control over the assessment process by rewarding their political supporters while punishing those who voted for their opponents was easy to come by. In 1904, Rámon Santos, governor of Samar, noted that collection of land tax suffered because "numerous holdings throughout the province are not declared as to their owners."[12] His report thus implied that presidentes and municipal treasurers aided their supporters in concealing ownership of property. David Shanks, a major in the Virginia volunteers before he was appointed governor of the volatile province of Cavite, made a similar observation in his 1905 report: "Still more important in foment-ing and maintaining the opposition to the land tax" than the agricultural depres-sion of the past few years "was the arbitrary and oftentimes outrageous valuation upon which the taxation was based. . . . Oftentimes the basis of assessment was not the value of the property, but whether the owner did or did not belong to the same faction as the majority of the board of assessors."[13] Unlike the flat one-peso head tax, collection of the land tax necessitated considerable capacity on the part of the state to "see" its people and quantify their wealth. Without such capacity, there were ample opportunities for individuals to escape payment of land taxes through their own efforts or, as was often the case, in collaboration with local pol-iticians in their role as administrative intermediaries.

With little to no tax revenue being generated from land ownership, the con-struction of provincial roads and bridges, as well as the provision of public edu-cation, suffered. Yet, at least at the municipal level, the failure of local officials to provide these vital public goods and services also reflected their propensity to al-locate what little tax revenue they collected to handsome salaries for them-selves.[14] Another casualty of misallocation of public funds was the municipal police, which, in addition to being denied fair pay, was largely used as personal servants and bodyguards for the presidente.[15] Such blatant acts of corruption re-sulted in a large number of complaints against municipal officials across the ar-chipelago, typically by elites who belonged to the losing faction in local elections. During the first decade of the U.S. period, the Executive Bureau investigated more than twenty-three thousand complaints, with nearly 65 percent of those investi-gations resulting in some type of punitive action.[16]

Just as consequential as revenue shortages and corruption in generating un-derprovision of public goods and services were fundamental disagreements be-tween American administrators and local Filipino officials on matters of public policy. Take education, for example, in which U.S. statebuilders invested consid-erable time and resources to establish a free public school system aimed at pro-viding primary and secular education to the masses in English. In the first place, wealthy Filipino parents, who had been educated in schools run by Catholic priests, believed that instruction in Catholic teachings should be an integral com-ponent of education, and thus they resisted sending their children to the new public schools, where religion was explicitly excluded from the curriculum.[17] Meanwhile, presidentes and other municipal officials—out of their own belief in the importance of Catholic education, as well as to ensure that they did not make enemies out of the locally influential parish priests—did little to financially or lo-gistically support public schools, let alone attempt to convince the landed elite to send their children to them. It also did not help that, seeing education as a privi-lege of the elite, municipal officials believed that any available public and private funds should be used for secondary education, rather than to furnish a large number of primary schools in the *barrios*.[18]

Consequently, even as enrollment in the new public schools suffered, private schools—which focused on Catholic teachings and, because they charged a hefty tuition, were attended predominantly by the landed elite—sprung up across the archipelago at a rapid pace. By 1903, to the government's knowledge, there were at least 1,329 private schools in operation (325 of which were managed directly by Catholic parishes). Meanwhile, despite the tremendous effort, time, and resources put into developing a system of public education by American officials, the number of public schools in operation was only slightly greater, at 1,663.[19] Eventually, the number of public schools multiplied rapidly with the support of elected officials, and they proved popular among poorer Filipinos who did not have the means to send their children to private schools.[20] However, this shift in the attitude of local officials toward public education reflected a change in the way it was funded: from a system where public schools were primarily financed through taxation on real estate to one supported by a massive transfer of tax revenue from the insular government to the localities. Under this new funding structure, funding for education became a vital source of patronage.[21]

Cholera and the Failure of Direct Bureaucratic Enforcement

As frustrated as the Americans were with municipal officials over taxation and education, this paled in comparison to the contempt and anger expressed by U.S. health officials toward local Filipino leaders during the cholera epidemic of 1902 to 1904—the deadliest epidemic in Philippine history, with reported deaths totaling 109,461. In turn, it was in the area of health and sanitation that the impetus for the bureaucratization and centralization of the provision of public goods and services, through the establishment of a large bureaucratic apparatus, would advance the furthest. Yet, in the absence of an effective system of state-society mediation, such investment in bureaucracy building ultimately proved self-defeating.

According to Major E. C. Carter of the U.S. Army Medical Corps, who, as the commissioner of public health, oversaw the IGP's effort to contain the horrific cholera epidemic, Filipinos obstructed efforts by health officials at every turn. During the initial phase of the epidemic, health officials, aided by the U.S. military, attempted to quarantine Manila to prevent the epidemic from spreading to the provinces. This proved futile, however, because the "natives generally could not be made to appreciate the necessity for quarantine, and there were always many who were so opposed to it as to destroy any chances of successfully limiting the disease by this means."[22] Once it became clear that quarantining entire cities and towns was impossible, Carter attempted to isolate the sick, as well as those who came into contact with them, in hospitals and detention camps. However, this policy proved highly unpopular, leading many to flee from their homes to escape detainment.[23] Meanwhile, in localities where at-home confinement of the sick was attempted, a red flag would be raised to signal that people were prohibited from freely entering and leaving the house and that access to the sick was limited to health officials and designated caregivers. However, as Capt. L. B. Sandall, who was stationed in Ibaan, Batangas, reported, "The natives gave no heed to this warning and to them the presence of the flag was seemingly only a kind of joke."[24] Even more problematic, Filipinos concealed the sickness from authorities, and when family members died from cholera, bodies were secretly buried under houses or discarded in nearby rivers or lakes at night. The chief surgeon of the Bureau of Health estimated that not more than one-fourth or one-fifth of cholera cases were reported as a result.[25]

Alongside such acts of blatant disobedience, Filipinos magnified the scale of the epidemic, in the view of American health officials, through their ignorance, uncivilized customs, and backward habits.[26] Despite efforts to educate the local population on how cholera was primarily spread via contaminated water, people did not take any measures to ensure the safety of their drinking water and carelessly bought and ate foods prone to contamination in the markets.[27] While disregarding the rule against visiting the sick was bad enough, "having no knowledge of the infectious nature of the disease, those who attended the sick took no precautions for their own safety, and frequently died."[28] Filipinos also preferred to see traditional healers when they exhibited symptoms of cholera and flocked to sacred springs for cure. Given that epidemics were believed to have supernatural causes, the parish priest was regarded as the foremost authority on the subject, as he alone could save the community from the devil's evil acts or the wrath of God. The last person that an average Filipino would turn to was a doctor trained in Western medicine, especially one employed by the U.S. Army or the IGP.[29]

Local Filipino officials, meanwhile, did little to counteract such apparent ignorance and backwardness, infuriating U.S. health officials. It was the responsibility of the presidente to quarantine infected houses, but as noted above, people moved freely in and out of dwellings where cholera patients received care. Municipal boards of health were instructed to disinfect the houses of cholera victims and clean up markets, but their cooperation was hard to obtain.[30] As Carter noted in his 1903 report, "The history of cholera in the small towns during the present epidemic has presented instances over and over again where the disease has been stamped out by proper measures applied by American physicians, even after it had secured a strong foothold, but in the vast majority of cases no intelligent and comprehensive effort was made by the natives to eradicate the infection."³¹ More-over, the hard work by American doctors was often wasted, for, according to Dean Worcester (among the original members of the commission and long-time secretary of interior), even after towns were "put in decent sanitary condition," they would quickly relapse "to their original state of uncleanliness," thus making it likely that cholera would return in the future. "The less said of the work of our present presidents of municipal boards of health the better. They *exist* in 257 of the 655 municipalities of the Philippines, and that is about all."³² Worcester's crit-icism of the provincial board of health was equally scathing in content and de-meaning in tone.³³

Without a doubt, American health officials faced considerable difficulty in their campaign to eradicate cholera. However, it is important not to take their charac-terizations of Filipinos as ignorant and backward, and their leaders as lazy and corrupt, at face value. Placing acts of resistance in a proper context provides a better understanding of the key political dynamics that led to tremendous human suffering during the epidemic as well as why American statebuilding efforts in the Philippines failed more broadly. Being unable to rely on community leaders as effective intermediaries, U.S. officials attempted to substitute state-society me-diation with direct bureaucratic enforcement. However, rather than improve compliance with rules and regulations, this made the epidemic far worse. Sub-jected to culturally insensitive and coercive methods by U.S. health officials, Fili-pinos fled the infected areas, concealed information, and engaged in various forms of everyday resistance as rational reactions to the hardship and injustice they suf-fered at the hands of overzealous bureaucrats.

For instance, it was customary for Filipinos to care for the sick in their own homes—a preference reinforced by the poor state of hospitals during the Span-ish era. Yet, U.S. authorities, at least initially, forcefully took the sick to cholera hospitals. As described by Victor Heiser, who would later become the chief of the Bureau of Health, "uniformed men clattered up with ambulances and without ceremony lifted the sick from their mats and carted them away from their wail-ing families. . . . Four out of five this was the last they ever saw of their loved ones until shortly they received a curt notice to come to the hospital to claim their dead."³⁴ This was not even the most abusive act committed by U.S. health inspec-tors. Although it was well known to the authorities that the religious beliefs of Filipinos prohibited them from cremating the dead, this was exactly what Amer-ican health officials mandated, due to fear that bodies of cholera victims could contaminate underground water sources.³⁵ This American proclivity to use in-cineration to solve the cholera crisis also applied to the dwellings of those suffer-ing: seeing the simple houses of the poor as having little value, U.S. officials viewed burning them as an efficient approach to containing the spread of cholera. This act of cruelty was further compounded by the inability of health officials to contain the fires they started. In a town in Batangas, the attempt to set fire to one house resulted in the destruction of eighty-one others; in Dagupan, Pangasinan, the burning of houses became so uncontrollable that the whole town was nearly destroyed.[36]

Furthermore, to force Filipinos to comply with new rules on sanitation, a health official patrolled the streets with "a gun on his shoulder in order to intimidate the people to make them obey sanitary laws."[37] When such threats failed to generate the desired behavior, some officials even engaged in punitive house burning. It also did not help that the colonial government enlisted Americans of all stripes—clerks, schoolteachers, former soldiers, and so on—to assist the Bureau of Health in containing the epidemic. Indeed, even Worcester, who authored some of the most contemptuous characterizations of the Filipino people, complained that among the Americans thus mobilized were some "who had slight regard for the natives and who enforced the already distasteful regulation in an unwarranted manner, increasing the popular opposition."[38] Also significant, such acts of violence were committed across the archipelago while memories of the brutal counterinsurgency campaign were still fresh.[39] As such, it is not surprising that neither the Filipino populace nor its local leaders were eager to cooperate with health officials. Although the IGP ended or loosened some of its most offensive policies a few months into the anticholera campaign—people were eventually allowed to care for the sick in their homes and to bury the dead, for example— much damage had already been done.

Tragically, all this suffering could have been avoided. Had Worcester, Carter, and Heiser's views on the causes of the cholera epidemic not been so strongly colored by their belief in Filipino ignorance and cultural backwardness, they would have realized that when U.S. officials partnered with locally trusted community leaders, such as traditional healers, priests, and even former rebels, they were much more likely to obtain local compliance with rules and regulations. U.S. officials simply failed to understand that what the archipelago lacked was an effective institution of state-society mediation; a large bureaucratic presence was no substitute for the authority, knowledge, and information that community leaders wielded in the locality.

Diverging examples of similar villages suffering from the cholera epidemic illustrate this point. As early as March 26, 1902, the town of Binan in Laguna Province established a local board of health and divided its population of 9,500 into health districts, each led by a Filipino physician. Binan's first cholera case appeared on April 22, when a woman from Rizal Province died the night she arrived. No further instances of cholera appeared for a month, but the commencing of the local fiesta and the resulting influx of people and foodstuffs from outside the *pueblo* led to an outbreak. The people of Binan initially cooperated with the local board of health by disinfecting their houses and quarantining cholera patients in their homes. However, after the arrival of Dr. R. A. Wilson, who was sent to Binan by the Central Board of Health, the situation rapidly deteriorated. Wilson ended the practice of letting the sick be cared for in their own homes and established cholera hospitals and detention camps. He threatened to burn the home of any individual who intentionally disregarded his orders. From then on, it became impossible for health officials to locate cholera victims, as no one would talk to the authorities; terrified, inhabitants fled to all parts of the pueblo and the surrounding barrios, taking the disease with them. According to official figures, the fatality rate among cholera patients in Binan reached an astonishing 88.2 percent, with 1,451 cases and 1,281 deaths of Filipinos reported. In all, nearly one-fifth of the town's population perished in 1902 due to cholera or as a result of other infections that their weakened bodies could not withstand.[40]

This contrasts with how events unfolded in the town of Balayan, with a population of 8,500, in the neighboring province of Batangas. This province was among the final places where fighting continued between the U.S. Army and revolutionary forces, and when the epidemic reached Balayan in June, the province was still under the direct control of General J. Franklin Bell and his garrison commanders. Bell had been an early proponent of the use of coercive tactics to suppress cholera, but paradoxically he was also among the first to realize that these measures were making matters worse. It was thanks to his intervention in Binan a few months earlier that its inhabitants were spared the tragedy of punitive house burning, despite the insistence of Dr. Wilson. And when the epidemic reached Batangas, Bell adopted a more hands-off approach to fighting cholera. Under Bell's orders, the commanding officer in Balayan made sure that no detention camps were created, no houses were burned, and policy implementation was left to local health officials. This did not mean that compliance with rules and regulations was without issue: When U.S. soldiers ordered people to stay away from the homes of cholera victims, they would not listen; the use of locally hired guards to enforce the quarantine also proved futile. Yet, this outcome was far better than the alternative observed in Binan, where attempts by U.S. health officials to directly stamp out the epidemic led to active concealment of the disease and to the flight of townspeople to the countryside. As the disease naturally ran its course in Balayan, its toll was much less than in Binan, with 300 cases and 173 deaths reported.[41]

Balayan was slightly smaller than Binan, and there are indeed many variables that could account for differences in the number of cholera cases and deaths between these two towns. It is nonetheless clear that direct policy enforcement by colonial bureaucrats made matters worse, due to the underlying fears and anxieties of the Filipino people. Moreover, a comparison across these towns provides some sense of what an effective system of state-society mediation would have done to contain the cholera epidemic and improve the governability of Philippine municipalities more broadly.

The Period of Reform and the Weakening of the Colonial State

In the American occupation of the Philippines, 1903 emerges as something of a watershed. This was the final year of Taft's governorship, Taft having been recalled by President Theodore Roosevelt to serve as war secretary. Thereafter, while Taft would remain engaged in Philippine affairs and would return to the archipelago in 1905 to address an emerging crisis in Filipino-American relations, his involvement in the day-to-day matters of the insular government ended. Taft's successor in the Philippines, Luke Wright, shared Taft's view on the need for political education—that is, giving Filipinos considerable autonomy to practice self-government at the local level—but Wright was skeptical that this alone was sufficient to transform the Philippines into a modern and democratic state. While Taft had been away from the islands for much of 1902 and was not there to witness firsthand the breakdown in local governance as cholera swept across the archipelago, Wright, as the secretary of commerce and police and acting civil governor, directly oversaw and was deeply affected by the failed campaign against the cholera epidemic.

Through this experience, along with the many difficulties that the IGP faced in enforcing rules and regulations on taxation, education, and much else, Wright became convinced that what the Philippines needed was a much larger and direct bureaucratic presence and role in local governance. Thus, along with an overall expansion in the size of the colonial service, the number of Americans employed in the Insular Civil Service was increased from 2,777 in 1903 to 3,307 in 1905 during Wright's three-year tenure as governor-general.[42] In addition, the administration of taxation, public works, and health and sanitation underwent a complete overhaul such that bureaucratic agents of the central government thereafter directly enforced (or at least attempted to) rules and regulations in these key policy areas.

However, such efforts to strengthen the state through the centralization and expansion of the colonial bureaucracy, while improving government performance in some areas (most notably tax collection and road building), largely served to highlight the basic flaw in the U.S. approach to statebuilding. In particular, it demonstrated the weakness of a bureaucracy that was unsupported by effective and obedient administrative intermediaries. Because provincial elites, whom the Americans relied on as enforcers of rules and regulations, possessed autonomous sources of coercive, remunerative, and normative power, they could not be easily disciplined by the colonial state. Moreover, as Wright soon discovered, any vigorous attempt to punish corrupt or ineffective provincial elites—due to the fact that the insular government had become so dependent on these individuals to maintain peace—placed the entire governance structure in peril and threatened the very ability of the United States to exercise control over the archipelago. This was a risk the Americans were simply unwilling to take, even if it implied the perpetuation of state weakness and the entrenchment of provincial elites as powerful *caciques*.

Addressing State Weakness through Bureaucratization and Centralization

The move toward bureaucratization and centralization of the governance structure began with a comprehensive reform of the taxation system. As originally conceived, the Municipal Code made the municipal treasurer an elected official—a decision that created a conflict of interest between the treasurer's obligations to his political patrons within the landowning class and his official responsibilities as the collector of taxes, custodian of municipal funds, and appraiser of real estate. As demonstrated earlier, among the negative consequences of this arrangement was politically motivated assessment of real estate and an ensuing severe shortfall in provincial income that compelled the IGP to provide a loan to nearly a third of the provinces (twelve in total) to keep them financially afloat.[43]

To remedy this situation, the commission reduced the number of municipalities from 1,035 to 623 in the spring of 1903. The assumption was that municipalities were financially distressed because the tax base was not large enough to finance all of the public goods and services mandated by law; by combining two or three smaller municipalities into one, the logic went, fiscal health should improve.[44] The commission also sought to directly resolve the conflict of interest plaguing the municipal treasurer by making this position into an appointed one and by placing it under the protection of the civil service law. Under this new arrangement, the municipal treasurer, at least in theory, would be primarily accountable to the provincial treasurer, who in turn was accountable to the central government.[45]

Shortly following these reforms in the administration of tax collection, the tax code itself underwent a complete overhaul. The commission, as related earlier, had initially intended the central budget to be financed predominantly through import and export duties, with provincial and municipal governments splitting any revenue generated from internal sources of taxation. The new internal revenue law, enacted in July 1904, in addition to increasing the number of goods and businesses subject to taxation (notably, tobacco and liquor), turned the previous decentralized fiscal system on its head.[46] From then on, all locally collected sources of internal revenue, with the exception of the cédula (divided equally between the municipalities and the provinces as before), would first be deposited into the central treasury. Ten percent of internal revenue was then automatically dispensed to the provinces, the municipalities received 15 percent (this was later increased to 20 percent, with 5 percent earmarked for expenditure on public schools), and the remainder was retained by the center.[47] The greatest consequence of the new internal revenue law was that it provided the IGP with the resources to increase its staff and hence expand its role in policy implementation in the localities. In addition, with a centralized collection of revenue, American administrators could now appropriate funds to the provinces in a targeted way to promote the government's priorities.

Taxation on real estate, due to widespread resistance against its collection, was left outside of the scope of the 1904 internal revenue law. This did not mean, however, that the dysfunctional land tax system was left unaltered. By making the municipal treasurer a de facto subordinate of the provincial treasurer, and by placing this individual under civil service protection, it was hoped that the process of property valuation would become less prone to politicization and corruption. A central assessment board was also created in 1906 to standardize the procedure for determining the tax valuation on properties already contained within local land registries; the board did not, however, possess the mandate or the manpower to actually conduct cadastral surveys and to adjudicate any competing ownership claims over land.[48]

Despite these reforms, the entire land tax regime still had glaring issues. Real estate tax rates were still far too low to sufficiently cover the costs of public education in the municipalities and road building at the provincial level. Due to the failure of the voluntary and court-based land survey and registration system, and in the absence of government-led cadastral surveying, officials still lacked any comprehensive knowledge of private land ownership. This created ample opportunities for the wealthy and well-connected to obscure their ownership of land and evade tax obligations.[49] Nonetheless, the new institutional structure was at least more equitable than the old and helped to rectify some of the injustices found in the original system of land assessment and taxation.

The second policy area to undergo considerable institutional reform in the direction of bureaucratization and centralization was public works, especially road building. In 1905, the position of provincial supervisor was abolished and the superintendent of education replaced the supervisor as the third member of the provincial board. From then on, road building at the provincial level was over-seen by the district engineer, who served as the provincial-level agent of the Bureau of Public Works.[50] Even more significant were reforms made to the funding of road building. Having largely given up on land taxes as a reliable source of revenue for public works, the commission enacted a law in 1907 that authorized provinces to collect an additional one peso in cédula per adult male, to be spent exclusively on roads. Those who were too poor to pay the additional peso had to contribute five days of labor to road construction and maintenance.[51]

To compel provincial governors to enact the one-peso increase in the cédula tax, the commission provided a number of financial incentives. First, cooperating provinces would receive an additional 10 percent of the internal revenue, thus doubling their take from the central treasury. Second, 1.2 million pesos in supplementary funding was appropriated to the Bureau of Public Works for the purpose of provincial road construction and maintenance.[52] These funds were used as a means of motivating provincial boards to expend their own resources on the priorities of the Bureau of Public Works—that is, if a provincial board was willing to go along with the district engineer's plan for road construction and maintenance, a portion of the project's cost would be paid directly by the Bureau of Public Works.[53]

Finally, it was in the area of health and sanitation that bureaucratization and centralization were carried out with the greatest vigor. Deeply dissatisfied with the performance of the provincial and municipal boards of health during the cholera epidemic, the Bureau of Health lost little time in enacting a permanent system of health surveillance by training a small army of sanitary inspectors. Their task was to make routine inspections of municipalities across the archipelago and to prepare detailed reports on the condition of the water supply, the cleanliness of markets and other public spaces, and the sewage system. They took note of local habits and customs concerning hygiene, the extent to which health and sanitation regulations were being observed, as well as basic statistics on the spread of infectious diseases. It was also their duty to help educate the population in correct sanitary practices by giving public lectures and holding demon-strations.[54] The goal was to compile "a sanitary map of the Philippines"[55] so the bureau could more effectively and efficiently contain epidemics in the future, while working to gradually improve the population's overall level of health and hygiene.

Following the establishment of a centralized sanitary inspector system in 1906, provincial boards of health were disbanded; in 1912, with the Bureau of Health having reached a size of over three thousand employees (with two hundred of them being physicians), the municipal boards of health were also discontinued. From then on, presidents of sanitary divisions made weekly inspections within the municipalities under their jurisdiction (daily during an epidemic) and worked directly with local officials and doctors in times of health crises.[56]

Empowerment of the Provincial Elite

The net effect of the foregoing reforms, which all took place between 1903 and 1913—the year the United States effectively relinquished control over policymaking to elected Filipino officials—was to alter the archipelago's administrative structure from a highly decentralized system to a more centralized and bureaucratized one. Yet, although agents of the central bureaucracy took charge of overseeing policy implementation in areas such as taxation, public works, and health and sanitation, actual enforcement of rules and regulations continued to rely on Filipino administrative intermediaries. Even in the area of health and sanitation, where institutional reforms between 1903 and 1913 underwent the greatest shift toward centralization, sanitary inspectors remained dependent on municipal officeholders to compel the inhabitants of cities, towns, and villages to adopt hygienic habits and to enforce emergency measures during epidemics. As before, direct interactions between bureaucrats and the average Filipino were minimal.[57]

This outcome was to be expected. During the initial stages of statebuilding, rulers have little choice but to rely on administrative intermediaries to enforce rules and regulations, due to suspicion and opposition to expansion in the scope of government, as abundantly demonstrated during the 1902–04 cholera crisis. Nonetheless, given widespread noncompliance during the initial years of American rule, it would not have been surprising—and perhaps even expected—for some changes to be made to the way in which state-society mediation was organized and managed. This was not to be the case, however, in the Philippines. So entrenched were American beliefs and biases concerning how relations between state and society ought to be organized, and so reliant had U.S. officials become on provincial elites to maintain peace and security in the archipelago, that despite systematic failure in local compliance with rules and regulations, the provincial governor remained the principal administrative intermediary as before. If anything, the outstanding features of the original system of state-society mediation were reinforced during the 1903 to 1913 period: provincial boards were assigned greater regulatory powers over the municipalities, while they came to enjoy even more political autonomy and less administrative scrutiny from the center.

The first step toward strengthening the authority and autonomy of the provincial governor ironically began with a reform intended to increase the supervisory power of the central government over the municipalities. As detailed in chapter 5, the position of law clerk was created within the Executive Bureau in 1903 to oversee the constitutionality of provincial resolutions and municipal ordinances.[58] However, with the Executive Bureau already struggling to review the legality of provincial resolutions with its small staff, it was far beyond its means to actually determine whether municipal councils were behaving in a manner consistent with the letter and spirit of the acts of the Philippine Commission. The Executive Bureau was therefore compelled to depend on provincial boards to review ordinances and orders enacted by municipal councils and alert the law clerk to any that were found to be problematic. The next major area to come under provincial supervision during this period of reform was the municipal police. A 1912 act of the Philippine Commission mandated that the notoriously corrupt and ill-trained municipal police would be bound by new regulations on the minimum qualifications of police personnel. Under the new system, the presidente continued to possess the sole authority to appoint individuals to the municipal police, but the governor now selected the police chief on the presidente's recommendation.[59]

Paradoxically, such expansion of the provincial government's authority to oversee and discipline municipal officeholders was advanced alongside the dismantling of a key instrument of central control over the governor: the American majority on the provincial board. In 1906, the third member of the board (who was typically an American) was replaced by an elected Filipino official. With this, two out of its three members were now chosen by a selectorate of municipal officials. The treasurer remained an appointed position, and with his power over provincial and municipal budgets and tax collection, the IGP retained some control over local governance. However, no longer would Americans have the numbers to veto resolutions of the provincial board that they found to be problematic, forcing them to rely more than ever on the understaffed and overextended Executive Bureau to reign in any acts of abuse at the provincial level.[60]

The surrender of the provincial board to Filipino control was not the only concession made to provincial political elites during this period. In October 1906, a governors' convention was convened in Manila—a spectacle of tremendous symbolic meaning, as it allowed provincial governors to demonstrate to their countrymen their rising status as indispensable power brokers. The governors' convention was also an event of practical importance for the participants, many of whom were elected to office for the first time in 1906 and being unaffiliated with the Federal Party had yet to cultivate the close collaborative ties that Manila ilustrados enjoyed vis-à-vis top American administrators. The convention provided the ideal opportunity for provincial elites to showcase their knowledge and political skills to the American audience and to forge direct working relations with members of the commission.[61]

Furthermore, the governors' convention served as a prelude to the most important concession to the Filipino provincial political elites during this period: the inauguration of the Philippine Assembly in 1907 as the lower legislative body of the archipelago. From this point forward, Filipinos would have a direct say in policymaking, as legislative bills would have to be approved by both the commission and the assembly to become law. Equally important, if not more so, a seat in the assembly, under the newly centralized bureaucratic structure, provided provincial elites with greater capacity to distribute patronage than they would have had as governor.[62] This fact was certainly not lost on the provincial elites. When elections for the Philippine Assembly were held for the first time in 1907, most of those who had risen as leaders of the 1906 governor class— namely, Sergio Osmeña of Cebu, Manuel Quezon of Tayabas, Jaime Carlos de Veyra of Leyte, and Isauro Gabaldón of Nueva Ecija—resigned their gubernatorial posts to seek seats in the assembly.[63] Thereafter, the most powerful political dynasties emerged in places where the governor and the provincial representative to the assembly were close allies, such that they could work in tandem to monopolize control over coercive and remunerative instruments of power on their home turf.[64]

As notable as the concessions made to the provincial elites were reforms abandoned for fear of antagonizing them. Among the most obvious failures of local government, in addition to those already discussed, was policing. Year after year, chiefs and division commanders of the Philippine Constabulary would report along the lines of "the present municipal police organization, as a whole, is worse than useless"[65] and that "the most effective remedy might be to abolish the municipal police and increase the strength and enlarge the scope of the constabulary sufficiently to enable it to handle the municipalities in addition to its other duties."[66]

To remedy this unsatisfactory state of affairs, the Sheriff Bill was introduced for debate during the commission's 1906–7 legislative session. Strongly supported by leaders of the Philippine Constabulary, this bill would have abolished the municipal police system (with total manpower of around nine thousand) and in its place create district-level sheriff's offices (each exercising jurisdiction over several municipalities). It would have expanded the constabulary from a force of approximately seven thousand to ten thousand in order to staff the new sheriff's offices, but it also would have resulted in considerable cost savings, especially for the municipalities.[67] The Sheriff Bill was never put up for a vote, however, due to fear among the majority of the commissioners (including the governor-general) that it would generate considerable opposition from the governors. It was, after all, obvious to anyone who read the bill that the newly proposed system would have encroached on the immense political authority that the governor exercised within his province by placing a constabulary officer in charge of overseeing the conduct of local policing.[68]

In the abstract, it may be puzzling as to why American officials were so hesitant toward doing anything that would have angered the provincial elite, especially given that the proposed system was likely to be far more effective and efficient than the dysfunctional status quo. Yet, the demise of the Sheriff Bill would not have been surprising to any observer that closely followed Philippine politics at the time. Despite the advancement of centralization and bureaucratization in key areas of administration and the constabulary's own efforts to exercise greater control over local policing, the overall trend during this period in the provision of internal security was toward decentralization and greater provincial autonomy. Most notably, in 1908, Governor-General James Smith, who championed both the 1906 governors' conference and the 1907 creation of the Philippine Assembly, approved Bulacan governor Teodoro Sandiko's request to withdraw the constabulary from the province so that the governor could directly and autonomously manage its security.[69] This experiment was terminated in 1909 with the deterioration of conditions in Bulacan, but an important precedent had been set.[70]

In 1917, the Provincial Code was formally amended to authorize governors to hire special agents as needed to maintain peace and security within the province. The ostensible justifications for adding a large number of special agents to the provincial payroll varied across locales. In Albay, it was to provide the governor the means to conduct "personal and close observations of the different municipalities in connection with the execution of the general laws and municipal ordinances." In Camarines Sur, special agents were needed, the governor explained, to "detect prohibited gambling games and illegal use of opium and misuse of funds for road materials." In Masbate, special agents would "aid the Provincial Governor in his campaign against cattle thieves."[71] Whatever the specific justification might have been, the real purpose of the special agents was to allow the governor to maintain control over his clientelistic network and punish any local officeholder or private citizen who dared challenge his authority.[72] Such willingness on the part of American administrators to forfeit the state's claim to the monopoly of coercive power would eventually lead to the development of provincial-level private militias in the 1920s, such as the National Volunteers (in Cavite) and Knights of Peace (in Pampanga)—collectively known by the innocuous label of rural police.[73]

What explains these major concessions to the provincial political elites during a period when the overall administrative structure underwent bureaucratization and centralization? The proximate cause was the breakdown in relations between leading members of the Federal Party, especially Trinidad Pardo de Tavera and Benito Legarda—who, as members of the Philippine Commission, were America's foremost ilustrado collaborators—and top U.S. officials in 1905. The aforementioned 1904 internal revenue law included taxes on tobacco manufacturers and liquor distillers, which were without precedent under Spanish rule. Most problematic, both Pardo de Tavera and Legarda had considerable investments in the tobacco industry; Legarda was also the islands' largest manufacturer of alcoholic beverages. Out of their own personal financial interests, as well as genuine concern that these new taxes would hurt the islands' overall business climate, they mounted a vehement political campaign against the adoption of the new internal revenue law.[74] It also did not help that Wright had stopped the previous practice of appointing only members of the Federal Party to key posts in the insular and provincial governments and that he and other top American officials were starting to forge direct collaborative ties with governors and other provincial elites from outside of the Federal Party's patronage network—the culmination of which was the 1906 governors' conference.[75]

The tension that had been gradually building since the adoption of the new internal revenue law finally reached a breaking point after the Philippine Constabulary mounted a violent counterinsurgency campaign in Cavite and Batangas in January 1905 to suppress a revolt led by Macario Sakay, a former revolutionary officer. Habeas corpus was suspended in the affected provinces, at least a third of the inhabitants were reconcentrated inside designated "safe zones," and three thousand troops led by the constabulary terrorized the local population into submission. When the nationalist newspaper *El Renacimiento* published an exposé on the cruelty exhibited by some constabulary officers toward the local population—in one instance, a former prisoner recounted how hot wax was dripped into his eyes during an interrogation—rather than hold those who committed such barbarous acts accountable, the constabulary, then led by General Henry Allen, arrested the editors of *El Renancimiento* on charges of criminal libel. Finally, adding insult to injury, Pedro Roxas, a prominent plantation owner in Batangas and a close associate of Pardo de Tavera and Legarda, was arrested on sedition charges. According to Roxas's *Federalista* allies, Roxas might have given aid to the insurgents, but it was to pay for protection of his property at a time when law and order had completely broken down.[76]

While all of this was taking place, Pardo de Tavera and Legarda sent a barrage of letters to Secretary of War Taft informing him of these events and the overall deterioration in collaborative relations between the Manila ilustrados and the American commissioners.[77] In early 1905, as the counterinsurgency campaign in Cavite and Batangas raged, Taft decided that he had heard enough and returned to the Philippines to evaluate the situation firsthand. Taft arrived in the midst of the *El Recacimiento* libel trail, which eventually ended in the defendants being cleared of charges. He quickly came to the conclusion that there was much truth to the accusations lodged by Pardo de Tavera and Legarda against the American commissioners, and in particular Governor-General Wright.[78] Taft removed

Wright—by arranging for him to become U.S. ambassador to Japan—and the re-maining commissioners were ordered to repair strained relationships with Fili-pino elites and reestablish the collaborative regime.[79]

The aforementioned concessions were all made in response to Taft's order, but the 1904–05 crisis was itself a symptom of a fundamental contradiction in insti-tutional design that had plagued the IGP since its creation in 1901. As originally designed, provincial governors were to be formally subjected to considerable oversight by the Executive Bureau: The bureau possessed the mandate to oversee local budgets, annul any problematic provincial resolutions and municipal ordi-nances without consulting the judiciary, and suspend any elected or appointed official from office. The colonial government, moreover, had broad authority to intervene in local affairs in times of crisis. This was how the Bureau of Health was able to sidestep the provincial and municipal boards of health during the cholera epidemic and how rights and freedoms of Filipinos were so easily suspended in Cavite and Batangas in 1905. American dominance over policymaking was also initially made possible at the provincial level with the governor-general appoint-ing two out of the three provincial board members. The formal administrative system in the Philippines was thus designed to be hierarchical, and even dictato-rial, so as to give the colonial government the power to discipline Filipinos into internalizing modern democratic habits, norms, and mores.

In contrast, the system of state-society mediation, as originally designed by Taft, was based on a model that reflected both the Tocquevillian principle of democratic education through local autonomy as well as the democratic notion that, as elected representatives, Filipino provincial elites should be treated as part-ners. Moreover, if these beliefs led Americans to forge close working relations with Manila ilustrados and provincial elites, the colonial government's reliance on the landed elite for the archipelago's peace and security, in the place of a large U.S. military presence, made the health of the collaborative regime an impera-tive. Consequently, if there were any disputes between the governor and one of the American officials on the provincial board, the commission typically sided with the governor.[80] For these reasons, although the governor-general might have possessed the formal authority to punish any uncooperative provincial-level elite, he typically chose not to—that is, until the Roxas affair.

As a member of the Philippine Commission from the very beginning, Governor-General Wright, more than anyone else, understood the inherent con-tradiction at the foundation of the American governance system. His centraliz-ing reforms, as well as the highly coercive tactics he authorized in Cavite and Batangas, were intended to strengthen the bureaucracy so that the insular gov-ernment could bypass the provincial governor and overcome this contradiction in key policy areas. Ironically, however, Wright's actions laid bare how entrenched the patronage-based system of state-society mediation had become and how costly it would be for American statebuilders to change course by adopting any measures that threatened the authority and autonomy of the provincial elite. In the aftermath of the 1905 crisis and Taft's intervention, bureaucratization and centralization would continue in key policy areas. However, this would now be accompanied by reforms designed to appease the provincial elite by further reinforcing and entrenching their authority and autonomy, thus weakening the colonial state in the process.

The New Collaborative Regime

Having tried and failed to solve the contradiction in governance structure through bureaucratic centralization and expansion during Wright's governor-generalship, U.S. colonial officials opted instead to further strengthen and institutionalize collaborative ties with the provincial elites, who had become too politically powerful to bypass and too integral to the peace and security of the archipelago to alienate. This is not to suggest that an alternative outcome was impossible in the abstract, but a course similar to the one pursued by the Japanese in Taiwan was simply inconceivable to American statebuilders, given their ideological beliefs and the constraints placed on them by the dynamics of U.S. electoral politics.

In addition to the reforms already discussed, the post-1905 collaborative regime saw two institutional innovations that would critically shape the development of the IGP in succeeding decades. The first was the rise of the Nacionalista Party, which was founded in 1907 under the leadership of Quezon and Osmeña— the young and ambitious duo who would dominate Philippine politics for the next forty years as partners and rivals.[81] In essence, the Nacionalista Party replaced the Federal Party as the principal organ for coordinating interelite relations and distributing patronage in the aftermath of the latter's demise. No longer able to appoint Federalistas to governorships with the introduction of gubernatorial elections in 1902, and with American commissioners increasingly deferring to the governors and other provincial elites (rather than Manila ilustrados) in doling out patronage, the Federal Party had lost its raison d'être by the time Pardo de Tavera and Legarda openly feuded with Wright. Federalistas would continue to exert influence on the central government and in the administration of the City of Manila, but without the ability to distribute patronage throughout the archipelago, their influence in the provinces had all but vanished by 1905.[82] It was in light of this development that Governor-General Smith convened the governors' convention in 1906, which in turn provided the opportunity for provincial elites from across the archipelago to meet one another, forge collaborative ties with U.S. officials, and found the Nacionalista Party the following year.

The elevation of the Nacionalista Party as the new ruling party alone was not sufficient to address inconsistencies in administrative design, however. There still remained the problem of reconciling the perceived need of direct policy implementation by a large interventionist colonial bureaucracy with a mediational structure organized around the provincial elite, who demanded both respect and autonomy from American officials. Paradoxically, the institution that emerged to play this critical role of assuaging relations between colonial bureaucrats and Filipino community leaders was none other than the Philippine Constabulary, which had been at the center of Governor-General Wright's campaign to assert bureaucratic dominance, but now, under the leadership of Harry Bandholtz, had been transformed into a willing facilitator of the collaborative regime.

From the very beginning of his thirteen-year career in the Philippines, Bandholtz, who replaced General Allen as chief of the constabulary in 1907, demonstrated his capability as a liaison between the American colonial regime and Filipino elites. A West Point graduate and veteran of the 1898 Cuba campaign, he came to Tayabas Province as an officer in the U.S. Army in 1900. Critical of fellow army officers for their insensitivity toward the local population and brutality against revolutionary leaders, he engineered an end to the military campaign in Tayabas by cultivating alliances with local elites and negotiating with insurgent generals for their surrender. By the time Tayabas was pacified, Bandholtz had become a trusted figure in the province. He was a person who could be relied on by local elites to maintain the balance of power among the prominent families of Tayabas, while attracting patronage to the province from the central government. When Tayabas held its first provincial governor's election in February 1902, Bandholtz was the surprising victor. He was seen as one of them: an American cacique.[83]

With his military background, fluency in Spanish, and ability to work closely with Filipino elites, there was perhaps no individual in the archipelago better suited to become a commanding officer in the Philippine Constabulary after its establishment in 1901. In April 1903, he resigned his post as governor of Tayabas and joined the constabulary as the commander of the Second District in Southern Luzon (where Tayabas was located). As a constabulary officer, Bandholtz was Allen's antithesis. Whereas Allen believed that the duty of the constabulary was to eliminate corrupt elites and enlighten the masses (through force if need be), Bandholtz happily mingled with the landed elite and even encouraged their corruption by showering his Filipino protégés with gifts, lucrative government contracts, and political appointments.[84] Allen was an ambitious military man, dreaming of becoming a field general in the regular U.S. Army; Bandholtz was a consummate politician, who sought a position in the Department of War, perhaps en route to even higher political office.[85]

The differences between the two men were clearly manifested in their approaches to providing security. If the 1905 campaigns in Cavite and Batangas were quintessential Allen, Bandholtz's policing-through-collaboration was displayed in Albay, where he faced a rebellion led by Siméon Ola. Instead of relying exclusively on military force to hunt down Ola, Bandholtz enlisted the support of local elites—in particular, Rámon Santos, whom Bandholtz later assisted in becoming elected as governor of Albay—to convince the rebel leader to surrender. Bandholtz's strategy paid off, and a province that had seemed at the brink of complete meltdown was largely pacified just a few months after Bandholtz's arrival.[86] His success in Albay boosted his credentials not only as a seasoned counterinsurgency tactician but also as someone who could work effectively with Filipino elites. Subsequently, this reputation led to his reassignment in late 1905 from the Second District to the First, which included Cavite and Batangas, as well as Manila. As commander of the First District, he rounded up remaining insurgents in the two volatile provinces and restored cooperative relations between American officials and provincial elites as Taft had instructed.[87]

Placed in charge of overhauling the constabulary's approach to policing in the aftermath of Taft's visit, Bandholtz lost no time in extending the model that had served him well in southern Luzon to the entire archipelago. According to guidelines he drafted, constabulary officers were to "visit the different provinces in their districts as often as possible" as a means of "securing the coöperation of the officials and people of the provinces, without which the Constabulary work can not be considered successful." They were also to become "personally well acquainted with the governors and the other members of the provincial boards in their districts as well as with the officials of the towns and the principal citizens thereof." Constabulary officials were first and foremost "political agents" and "their ability to get on with the provincial governors and other [Filipino] officials will in a great degree measure their success."[88]

In 1912, Dean Worcester, by then the sole remaining member of the original group of American commissioners, wrote the following to Taft on the constabulary under Bandholtz's leadership:

> In so far as [the constabulary's] present popularity is due, and it is in no small degree, to improved discipline and the resulting cessation of abuses, [Bandholtz] is entitled to a very great credit for what he has done, but I have always been suspicious of a police force which was too *generally* popular, and General Bandholtz has carried politics into the work of his Bureau until the public service has been seriously prejudiced.[89]

Worcester wrote this as a critique of Bandholtz, yet the passage also captures why Bandholtz was so successful as police chief in the post-1905 environment and why the constabulary—with Bandholtz's collaborative policing strategy now engrained into its ethos—could keep armed challenges to the colonial government at bay for the remainder of the U.S. period. By 1911, insurgent activity had ended and the islands were largely at peace, except for the administratively separate Muslim-majority island of Mindanao. *Ladronism* (banditry), which had inflicted the Philippines since Spanish times, ceased to be a concern. Starting in the 1920s, with rising inequality and land tenancy, rural unrest became the new source of potential instability, but the constabulary, aided by its network of informants, was quick to detect discontent. With the cooperation of local elites, the constabulary suppressed most armed uprisings within a few *hours* of their outbreak. It was not until 1946, when the islands were in a state of disarray following World War II, that the Philippines became embroiled in its first major uprising—the Hukbalahap Rebellion—since those in Samar, Cavite, and Batangas in the early 1900s.[90]

Nonetheless, Worcester was not wrong to be weary of what the constabulary had become under Bandholtz's leadership. With the U.S. Army having been relieved of all governance functions and the Executive Bureau weak and understaffed, the constabulary was the only branch of the colonial government with some capacity to discipline the increasingly powerful provincial elite. Bandholtz's reforms, which reflected the consensus of U.S. policymakers in the aftermath of the Cavite-Batangas crisis, signaled that the constabulary would not attempt to play this disciplinary function. Instead, it would serve as the foremost governmental organ promoting collaboration between U.S. officials and Filipino elites by distributing patronage. Accordingly, the coercive and intelligence capacity of the constabulary would not be used to punish governors for abuse of office for personal gain or inattentiveness to policy enforcement, but rather to defeat common enemies, be it rebellious peasants or messianic movements. The consequence of this was not only continued unevenness in compliance with rules and regulations in the locality, but the politicization of the constabulary and the corruption of the administrative machinery by the way of state involution.

Involution of the Colonial State

As for issues of peace and security, the new system of state-society mediation that developed in the aftermath of the Cavite-Batangas crisis was a resounding success. With the forging of strong collaborative relations between American colonial administrators and Filipino provincial elites and the transformation of the constabulary into an instrument for advancing state-society mediation through informal ties and the distribution of patronage, the United States was able to maintain control over, as well as peace within, the archipelago for the remainder of the American period. All this, moreover, was achieved in a way that was ideologically appealing and politically unproblematic to American voters and taxpayers—that is, by providing Filipinos (at least educated and wealthy men) with increased opportunities for democratic participation and self-rule with minimal American presence in the locality.

Yet, internal peace and external control were not America's only objectives in the Philippines; when the United States decided to annex the archipelago, Secretary of War Elihu Root had explicitly rejected European-style colonialism in favor of "benevolent assimilation." Americans believed it was their mission to better the livelihood of the average Filipino by reducing corruption and abuse by the landed elite, eliminating preventable deaths from infectious diseases, and promoting a more equitable form of economic development. In the long run, the goal was to transform the Philippines into a strong state where a democratically elected legislature would work in concert with an independent judiciary and an effective and accountable bureaucracy. However, as it turned out, although the newly reestablished system of state-society mediation was highly successful in maintaining American territorial control over the archipelago, it left the problem of unsystematic enforcement of rules and regulations unresolved. Maladministration of municipal governments continued as before.

In the area of taxation, the absence of systematic information on landownership allowed for considerable abuse in the way that taxes were collected and delinquencies in their payment were handled.[91] The practice of extracting "voluntary" contributions from the local population, meanwhile, became increasingly common over the years. This informal taxation was ostensibly undertaken to advance priorities that benefitted the community as a whole, but the provision of public goods and services by municipal authorities saw little improvement.[92] Even in the area of public health and sanitation, where the administrative system underwent the greatest degree of bureaucratization and centralization during the 1903 to 1913 period, enforcement of rules and regulations remained highly uneven.[93] With municipal officials largely ignoring the pleas of health officers to enforce basic rules and regulations on sanitation, the most these bureaucrats could do was vent their frustrations in their annual report and lament their powerlessness. Concerning the campaign for sanitary disposal of excreta, the "writer is of the opinion that . . . it is now time to discontinue the policy of persuasion and compel the municipal councils to enforce the provisions of law already existing with reference to this matter."[94] As for the condition of markets and slaughterhouses, "there is still much to be desired in [their] improvement" due to the fact that municipal officials "do not take much interest in keeping them in a sanitary condition."[95] During the 1919 cholera outbreak, which tragically resulted in 25,593 reported cases and 18,052 registered deaths—the second most deadly after the 1902–04 epidemic—the "quarantined house [could not] be strictly guarded, not only on account of lack of police force in the municipalities, but because sometimes the police itself permits the access of contact to the persons quarantined."[96]

Yet, while colonial bureaucrats might have been unable to achieve systematic enforcement of rules and regulations, their administrative decisions were still consequential for the wealth and welfare of individual Filipinos and their communities. The highly centralized bureaucracy, after all, possessed de jure authority over the provision of most public goods and services at the provincial level. The Bureau of Public Works, for instance, determined how much of its substantial budget to spend on what, and which province or municipality would materially benefit from its largesse. The Bureau of Lands controlled all public lands in the archipelago and developed guidelines and procedures for Filipinos to claim ownership over them. It also managed the sale of the "friar lands"—former estates of the Spanish Catholic orders that were purchased by the United States from the Vatican after the Spanish priests were expelled from the archipelago—which included some of the islands' most valuable farmlands.[97] As such, if provincial elites were to truly exercise dominance within their local sphere of influence as political bosses, it was pertinent for them to ensure, often with the help of their American patrons, that the bureaucracy made policy decisions and budget allocations in ways that benefited them and their clientelistic networks.

Illustrative of this dynamic was how Osmeña, the longtime majority leader of the Philippine Assembly, came to enjoy de facto discretion over the sale of friar lands in his home province of Cebu—approximately 10,000 hectares of prime land in metropolitan Cebu as well as in the towns of Talisay and Minglanilla—thus overriding the authority of the Bureau of Lands and ignoring its procedure for how such sales should be handled. In 1918, any pretense that the Bureau of Lands managed the sale of Cebu's friar lands was given up when Governor-General Francis Harrison transferred control over unsold portions of the estates (over 6,000 hectares in total) to the provincial government of Cebu. These valuable agricultural lands were subsequently acquired by Osmeña's relatives and allies, and Talisay and Minglanilla became electoral strongholds for successive generations of Osmeñas.[98] Emilio Aguinaldo, the former leader of the Philippine Revolution turned collaborator, also enjoyed similar privileges in Cavite. Beginning in 1908, the Bureau of Lands allowed him to occupy, without contract, 1,185 hectares of prime sugar fields in the town of Dasmariñas, until he finally purchased the former friar land in 1927 in a "public" auction. In this transaction, Aguinaldo circumvented prohibition of individuals purchasing over 144 hectares of public land—a rule that was instituted to prevent the development of large landed elites—by dividing the land into multiple lots and placing them under the names of his children and grandchildren. Aguinaldo was to pay for his purchase in installments, but even though he withheld the mandatory payments, he avoided delinquency. When the Bureau of Lands finally confiscated his sugar estate in 1934, it was not due to the illegality of the original purchase or subsequent delinquency in payment, but because he fell out of favor with Quezon, whose power as leader of the Nacionalista Party had come to rival the governor-general's.[99]

Filipino elites, as well as American officials who traded favors with them to maintain the collaborative regime, also aided in the politicization of the bureaucracy by intervening in personnel management. Here, with the bureaucracy enjoying rules protecting its members from political meddling, the options available to Filipino elites were limited. They could not easily interfere in the hiring process, as most bureaucratic positions were open only to those who passed the civil service exam; the Civil Service Board, meanwhile, vigilantly monitored bureaucratic employees for evidence of bribery. The area where Filipino elites, as well as politically motivated American colonial administrators, did have control was in transfers and promotions. In 1905, for instance, Bandholtz sought to engineer the transfer of R. H. Wardall, an American principal of the Central School of Lucena, in light of Wardall's opposition to Quezon in the gubernatorial race in Tayabas.[100] While Bandholtz, who had yet to rise to the top of the police hierarchy, failed in this particular attempt, it was much easier for him to engage in the politically motivated transfer of personnel when it concerned his own men. Such was the case when Captain John Swann was moved from Albay to Sorsogon after he failed to get along with the governor.[101]

Initially, transfers of personnel, even when politically motivated, were largely initiated by top American officials, who used them to maintain harmony between colonial bureaucrats and Filipino intermediaries. Yet, as provincial elites became more powerful and entrenched over time, it would be the bureaucratic agency routinely acquiescing to transfer requests made by local bosses—a fact not lost on the broader public, which was fully aware of the caciques' "hidden power to send away an officer at [their] pleasure, any time, with or without justified cause."[102] This in turn created, as Joseph Hayden (vice governor-general from 1933 to 1935) writes, "an environment [that] is admirably adapted to the development and persistence of bossism."[103] With people assuming (rather correctly) that the municipal police, the constabulary, and the justices of peace would have little incentive to punish powerful provincial elites and their local allies for everyday acts of corruption and abuse, most individuals simply paid their share of "voluntary" contributions and kept silent as the landed elite engaged in wide-scale land-grabbing.

In a telling anecdote, Hayden conveys a conversation that he had with a member of the Philippine Senate (which replaced the commission as the archipelago's upper legislative body in 1916) about Manuel Tinio, a former revolutionary general turned provincial governor turned director of the Bureau of Lands, who amassed considerable wealth and influence in his home province of Nueva Ecija:

> I was called to Nueva Ecija to defend certain men who were accused of the murder of one of General Tinio's henchmen. No local lawyer dared to handle the case. I found that although the province was full of witnesses whose testimony might have cleared my client I couldn't get one of them into court. . . . Tinio controlled the entire government: the courts of first instance, the justices of peace, the chiefs of police and the police forces, the mayors and the councils. These, together with a tremendous money and power, were in his hands. No one dared to stand up against him.[104]

Tinio, whom Hayden called as "absolute a boss as ever dominated any ward, city or state,"[105] is often singled out in memoirs by American colonial officials due to the sheer scale of his abuse. However, he was merely the most striking example of how the structure of state-society mediation, which American colonial officials themselves *designed* and *managed*, provided Filipino provincial elites with the incentives and means to control key administrative organs of the state for personal benefit. Indeed, with the governor-general possessing the authority to veto any law and to discipline all appointed and elected officials for any reason (until 1935), corrupt and violent behavior on the part of Filipino elites, especially at the level described by Hayden, was only possible with implicit (and sometimes explicit) American support. Both Osmeña and Tinio enjoyed close personal ties with Governor-General W. Cameron Forbes (1909–13) as they amassed wealth and influence in Cebu and Nueva Ecija, respectively.[106] Aguinaldo, meanwhile, became a trusted ally of Governor-General Leonard Wood (1921–27), who regularly took Aguinaldo's advice on executive appointments and allowed the former revolutionary hero to interfere in the government's management of friar lands.[107]

The initial difficulties experienced by U.S. colonial administrators in collecting taxes, suppressing the spread of infectious diseases, or getting school-aged children to attend public schools may perhaps be interpreted as symptomatic of new state institutions having not yet taken root, or a function of statebuilders still tinkering with structures of state-society mediation. After all, Japan's statebuilding campaign also went disastrously for the first few years, prompting Japanese officials to consider abandoning Taiwan altogether. Due to an acute lack of information, unfamiliarity with local customs and traditions, and most significant, widespread armed resistance, the difficulties faced by the U.S. colonial regime in establishing new governance institutions were to be expected.

Yet, in contrast to Japanese colonial officials, who pragmatically reassessed their initial assumptions and learned from their mistakes to construct a highly effective institution of state-society mediation, U.S. colonial officials stayed the course. Ultimately, rather than attempt to contain or dismantle the influence of the provincial elites—America's chosen administrative intermediaries within the new governance structure—colonial officials further reinforced their power and autonomy. This decision certainly helped the United States maintain peace and security with a minimal U.S. military presence, but it did little to solve the problem of unevenness in compliance with rules and regulations within the locality. Moreover, it set into motion the process of state involution, whereby provincial elites took advantage of their position as indispensible administrative intermediaries to not only dominate local political and economic affairs, but also to influence the government's administration of rules and regulations in their favor.

By the time the United States granted political autonomy to the Philippines in 1935 and handed complete control over internal affairs to Quezon's commonwealth government, the archipelago had made considerable achievements in socioeconomic indicators of development: Its population was better educated, its farmlands were more productive, and its GDP per capita was among the highest in Asia (and not much different from that of Taiwan).[108] However, the state was hardly any stronger than it had been in 1898, and to a great extent institutional factors contributing to its weakness were now far more ingrained in the political, economic, and social fabric. Caciquism, as noted in chapter 1, was a long-standing feature of the archipelago, but it was limited to the level of villages, towns, and urban neighborhoods. The landed elite exercised considerable control over the local economy and the lives of the peasantry before American rule; yet, they had previously enjoyed little political power above the local level and their coercive capacity was limited. The Spanish regime had various disciplinary instruments at its disposal, including the Guardia Civil and the Catholic Church, and while they failed to systematically enforce rules and regulations for a variety of reasons, an uncontrollable native elite stratum was not to blame. The U.S. attempt to transform the Philippines into a strong and modern state was a failure, not because it could not strengthen the state's capacity to enforce rules and regulations beyond that which the Spanish achieved, but because state weakness became more institutionalized and thus harder to reverse under U.S. tutelage.

Conclusion: Perpetuating the Cycle of Statebuilding Failure

Former colonial officials, especially those who served in the Philippines during the initial years, such as Worcester and Forbes, typically blame "Filipinization"—in particular the practice, starting in 1913, of replacing American administrators with Filipinos as chiefs of bureaucratic agencies—for the corruption and weakening of the colonial state.[109] As a result of Filipinization, influential provincial elites, such as Tinio, indeed assumed top administrative positions in the colonial government, but it was certainly not the case that Filipinos were the only ones engaging in clientelism. U.S. colonial officials behaved as political bosses themselves by cultivating clients within the provincial elite stratum and materially rewarding those who demonstrated loyalty and effectiveness in implementing the government's priorities. It was politically and normatively convenient for American administrators to blame the Filipinos and their "backward" culture and norms for the weakness of the colonial state. Yet, the underlying cause of the insular government's inability to systematically enforce rules and regulations was the local governance structure—in particular the system of state-society mediation revolving around the provincial elites—that was designed and managed by the Americans themselves to satisfy their own ideological beliefs and domestic political needs.

All this was not inevitable. As noted in chapters 3 and 4, Taiwan, although having background conditions similar to the Philippines'—ethnic diversity, prevalence of bossism in the locality, and the like—came to be characterized by a system of state-society mediation that cellularized administrative intermediation at the village and neighborhood levels. In the Philippines, mediational practices similar to those found in Taiwan were in fact successfully employed on a limited scale, as during the campaign to defeat the insurgency in Negros and the cholera epidemic in Batangas. A reorganization of the constabulary that would have allowed for wider application of a more cellularized system of state-society mediation was introduced in 1907—the Sheriff Bill—but was never enacted. There were in fact multiple occasions for colonial administrators to institute a different and arguably more effective structure of state-society mediation during the first decade of American rule, but such a course of action was purposefully not chosen. Ideological beliefs and political constraints, combined with American administrators' growing dependence on the provincial elite for internal peace and security, would instead lead them to adopt measures that buttressed the very institutional features that made the IGP into a weak state.

Most problematically, despite having failed to transform the Philippines into a strong and democratic state, U.S. officials congratulated themselves for a job well done in face of difficult circumstances. After all, how could they have prevented the rise of provincial bosses and the politicization of the bureaucracy, when caciquism was so entrenched in Filipino culture? Was it not simply better to respect local customs and traditions concerning political interactions and behaviors? Is not such an approach more in line with American liberal and democratic values? As Hayden argued after the end of his tenure as vice governor-general of the Philippine Islands, the U.S. statebuilding effort in the Philippines simply created a political order that "has the virtue and the defects which arise from its being fundamentally a *natural* government. Its form may be alien and the new procedures and standards introduced by the Americans unfamiliar. But it has been worked by genuinely representative Filipinos who have made it in a real sense a Filipino government."[110]

Lost in this narrative was the fact that the United States had completely remade the political and socioeconomic landscape of the Philippines since annexing the archipelago in 1899. Having elevated petty caciquism to the provincial level and turned it into an entrenched attribute of Philippine politics, U.S. officials conveniently reimagined Philippine politics and socioeconomic institutions as having always exhibited these features. The United States would thereafter move on to other statebuilding missions in Japan, South Korea, South Vietnam, and, more recently, Iraq and Afghanistan. Having convinced themselves that the weak state they created in the archipelago was the best they could have achieved, U.S. officials unabashedly applied their strategies and models for political modernization to other polities seemingly in need of U.S. tutelage. Repeating the same mistakes they committed in the Philippines, and once again learning little from them, the United States thus perpetuated this cycle of statebuilding failure into the next century.

FROM THE COLONIAL PAST
TO THE FUTURE OF STATEBUILDING

My investigation of statebuilding by imposition began with a puzzle. At the turn of the twentieth century, two territories of the East Asian littoral—Taiwan and the Philippines—became the site of parallel statebuilding campaigns by the world's latest imperialist powers: Japan and the United States. They were parallel in the sense that Taiwan and the Philippines were neighboring islands, and their annexation occurred at the same moment in history, with Japan's invasion of Taiwan (1895) preceding the U.S.'s of the Philippines (1898) by a mere three years. The socioeconomic and political conditions found in Taiwan and the Philippines were comparable as well. Due to their ethnic diversity and stark inequality, both societies were prone to conflict, and their landed elites exercised considerable power and autonomy in the locality. Furthermore, Japanese and U.S. occupiers faced widespread resistance, and neither territory was fully pacified until the 1910s. Mere pacification, however, did not mean that the Taiwanese and the Filipinos had accepted the statebuilders' visions of modernity. Statebuilding in both Taiwan and the Philippines, therefore, necessitated institutional imposition, whereby compliance with new rules and regulations had to be obtained in the face of local opposition, both overt and otherwise.

Yet, despite similarities in underlying structural, socioeconomic, and political conditions across Taiwan and the Philippines, the outcomes of Japanese and U.S. statebuilding campaigns were vastly different. Comparing state strength across a number of indicators, including the government's ability to gather information, collect taxes, and combat epidemics, a clear and consistent gap emerged between the Government-General of Taiwan (GGT) and the Insular Government of the Philippine Islands (IGP). In Taiwan, the colonial government obtained systematic compliance with its rules and regulations in spite of its illegitimacy, largely as a result of cooperation by the island's community leaders in their capacity as administrative intermediaries. In contrast, policy enforcement in the Philippines was highly uneven because Filipino socioeconomic elites lent their assistance only when a rule or regulation advanced their own personal or class interests. They abused their authority as administrative intermediaries to aggrandize wealth and power, carve out autonomous spheres of influence in the localities, and infiltrate and politicize the administrative and judicial machineries of the state. What explains this variation in statebuilding across Taiwan and the Philippines? Why were the Japanese able to obtain the obedience of community leaders in enforcing rules and regulations, whereas in the Philippines, administrative intermediaries became the very cause of state weakness?

The preceding chapters argue that a key cause of this variation was the structure of mediational institutions. In Taiwan, state-society mediation was formalized and cellularized. Having dislodged the urban scholar-gentry and the rural strongmen from positions of political authority, the Japanese revived and reconstituted an alternative local governance structure centered around village- and neighborhood-level community leaders—that is, locally authoritative individuals who could be easily disciplined due to their limited power and wealth. The community leaders' duties and responsibilities as administrative intermediaries were clarified and codified, and an explicit set of rewards and punishments was instituted so that their behavior could be monitored and sanctioned in a routine and rule-bound manner. The mediational system in colonial Philippines was the exact opposite. Rather than structuring state-society mediation at the lowest level of sociopolitical organization, Americans carried it out at the provincial level. Broad rules governing the duties and responsibilities of administrative intermediaries existed on paper, but in practice, relations between government officials and provincial elites were managed through personal ties and obligations. Consequently, while mediational institutions in Taiwan served as effective instruments for making community leaders into obedient intermediaries, the institutional equivalent in the Philippines functioned primarily as a mechanism for maintaining clientelistic exchanges and, in the process, entrenching provincial elites as powerful political bosses.

What remains to be addressed is the question of why colonial Taiwan and the Philippines became characterized by such contrasting mediational institutions. This concluding chapter argues that Japan's and America's divergent approaches to organizing institutions of state-society mediation were driven more by domestic political and ideological factors than by structural and institutional conditions found in the colonized societies. Simply stated, Japan succeeded at statebuilding by imposition because it was an *autocracy*, and America failed because of its commitment to *democratic* institutions and processes at home and abroad. This has important implications for how we think about statebuilding in today's so-called ungoverned and undergoverned spaces.

Similarly to how statebuilding took the form of imposition in colonial Taiwan and the Philippines, so too have recent statebuilding campaigns by Western countries and organizations in the peripheral regions of the world—that is, territories where modern state institutions were never fully established under colonialism or postcolonialism. The rhetoric surrounding statebuilding has certainly changed since the colonial period; statebuilders now eschew direct control of target territories, preferring to indirectly exert influence on local collaborators by way of military, economic, and technical aid and assistance, and the expected time frame for statebuilding has also been drastically reduced, from several generations to a decade at most. Yet, despite these differences, the fact remains that, like the Japanese and American statebuilders a century earlier, contemporary statebuilders are *imposing* their vision of good governance on target territories amid widespread resistance from local communities and their leaders.

As such, just as the observed variation in statebuilding outcomes across colonial Taiwan and the Philippines hinged on the capacity and effectiveness of mediational institutions as *disciplinary instruments*, so too does the success of today's statebuilding missions. We may, for ideological or ethical reasons, be tempted to imagine statebuilding and democracy building as perfectly compatible, and even complementary, objectives. But what the past teaches us is that a societal structure most conducive to the establishment of a strong and modern state is rarely one that is democratic or liberal in its basic constitution.

This is not to suggest, however, that those subjected to statebuilding would be better off if Western countries and organizations dispensed with their commitment to democracy building and adopted strategies and institutional models similar to those the Japanese employed in Taiwan. Sustainable and equitable economic development requires strong governmental institutions, and authoritarian regimes, once they have achieved a certain level of wealth, have historically tended to undergo democratization.[1] Yet, the potential for long-term prosperity does not justify denying basic human rights, freedoms, and dignity to the majority of the people in the short term as the Japanese did in Taiwan. At the heart of statebuilding by imposition, therefore, lies an ethical conundrum—a conundrum that must be explored in contemplating the broader implications of the foregoing analysis for statebuilding today.

Antecedent Conditions and Statebuilding in Taiwan and the Philippines

The outcome of any institutional reform is a function of two sets of variables: (1) a polity's antecedent conditions that limit the range of possible outcomes and (2) beliefs, practices, and strategies, as well as resources and manpower, that reformers bring to the table. In applying this general insight to the question of why development of mediational institutions in colonial Taiwan and the Philippines varied so considerably, one would want to first know the extent to which differences in various underlying structural conditions, as well as each polity's stock of political, administrative, and socioeconomic institutions, might have produced this outcome. And second, one would want to compare and contrast how Japanese and American statebuilders went about reforming existing institutions and imposing new ones, and why. There were indeed important differences in antecedent conditions, especially in formal governmental institutions, that arguably made the Philippines *more* conducive to statebuilding success. But ultimately, such differences mattered less than Japan and America's contrasting visions of modernity and how they went about designing and establishing a new governance system.

As demonstrated in chapter 1, late nineteenth-century Taiwan and Philippines were comparable in important structural variables, such as climate, factor endowments, and level of socioeconomic inequality. The Philippines was more ethnically diverse, but any perceived ethnic differences were far more politicized, and violently so, in Taiwan. In contrast, governmental institutions under the Qing and Spanish regimes, particularly the structure of the formal administrative apparatus, varied considerably. The Qing bureaucracy in Taiwan, staffed by individuals who had passed the highly competitive civil service examination after years of study, was more professionalized than its counterpart in the Philippines. The Spanish colonial bureaucracy was nonetheless much larger and more organizationally differentiated into departments and agencies with specialized functions. The scope of government was also greater in the Philippines, and, unlike in Taiwan where socioeconomic elites fielded their own militia armies, the Spanish colonial state more or less monopolized coercive power. These differences, however, had little effect on the development of governance structures during the Japanese and American periods, because existing governmental institutions were thoroughly displaced at the outset of the respective statebuilding campaigns. There was also little continuity in government personnel. In Taiwan, the Japanese were determined to largely exclude the Taiwanese people, including those belonging to the Qing bureaucratic class of gentry degree holders, from employment in the GGT. The American strategy, unlike the one adopted by the Japanese, was to nurture an indigenous civil service. However, Filipinos thus employed as bureaucrats in the IGP did not come with prior experience in the corrupt and dysfunctional Spanish administration, given Spain's long-standing practice of staffing its colonial bureaucracies exclusively with individuals from Europe.[2]

Yet, even if transition in sovereignty in Taiwan and the Philippines resulted in wholesale transplantations of new administrative institutions, practices, and personnel, there was a certain degree of stability, at least initially, in the two territories' societal structures: The wars of conquest, despite their destructiveness, produced very few internally displaced persons—with the important exception of the scholar-gentry in Taiwan—and long-standing communal institutions and relations remained largely undisturbed, especially outside the urban centers. With Qing- and Spanish-era societal structures, including those regulating relations between government officials and administrative intermediaries, having survived the war, to what extent did they carry over into the Japanese and American periods? Did existing societal structures in Taiwan or the Philippines make it easier or harder for statebuilders to forge effective mediational institutions?

Superficially, there was much continuity in institutions of state-society mediation between the Qing and the Japanese periods, given that *hokō*, which served as the foundation of the Japanese governance system, was ostensibly modeled after the Qing-era institution of *baojia*. In addition to borrowing its name—"hokō" being the Japanese pronunciation of the same Chinese characters—Japanese reformers seemingly mimicked baojia's system of governing the Taiwanese population as aggregations of households rather than as individuals. Japanese colonial administrators themselves even claimed that their decision to govern Taiwan via hokō was inspired by their investigation of Qing administrative practices and local customs. In reality, however, there was little institutional continuity between baojia, as *actually* organized and practiced in Taiwan, and hokō.

The system of structuring households in units of ten, one hundred, and one thousand was never instituted under Qing rule, with baojia units reflecting the size and organization of organically formed settlements. Moreover, even this indigenized version of baojia had largely atrophied by the time Taiwan was annexed by Japan in 1895. In place of baojia, what developed during the nineteenth century, as discussed previously, was a mediational system organized around rural strongmen (*tuhao*) and the urban scholar-gentry. The strongmen, who had been bestowed the semiofficial rank of *zongli* (overseer), were typically heads of lineage groups composed of several rural towns and villages and controlled militias of a few dozen men. The scholar-gentry, meanwhile, helped mediate affairs between state and society at a higher level of sociopolitical organization through their appointment in quasi-governmental bureaus (*ju*) in areas such as land reclamation, pacification of aborigines, and management of the camphor monopoly.

The number and variety of tasks assigned to hokō under Japanese rule, moreover, went far beyond what seventeenth-century Qing officials had intended for baojia. Whereas baojia essentially had only two functions—collection of rudimentary census data and the organization of a local militia—hokō contributed to every aspect of colonial governance, from eradicating "evil" customs and habits, to keeping streets clean of waste and rubbish, to enforcing quarantines during epidemics. As such, the Japanese decision to govern the Taiwanese people through hokō was hardly a continuation of previous governance practices, or a conversion of existing institutions to perform new ends. Rather, it entailed the displacement of Taiwan's mediational institutions organized around the strongmen and scholar-gentry under the guise of institutional continuity. Formalization and cellularization of mediational institutions during the Japanese period thus constituted a break with the past and were designed not only to improve the governability of the island but also to undermine the power and influence of Taiwan's traditional elites.

In contrast, there was actual continuity in the local governance system of the Philippines across the Spanish and American periods. The *gobernadorcillo*—the municipal mayor under Spanish rule—might have been given the new title of *presidente* by the Americans, as well as responsibility for enforcing a much greater array of rules and regulations, but little changed in the municipalities' administrative structures and practices. As before, the mayor received the input and assistance of a municipal council in exercising his duties and relied on the *cabezas de barangay* (neighborhood/village captains) to enforce rules and regulations in each of the municipality's subdistricts (*barrios*). Despite this institutional continuity in local governance, however, U.S. statebuilders made significant modifications to the larger system of state-society mediation, with far-reaching implications for the archipelago's governability.

An important, while imperfect, disciplinary instrument of the Spanish colonial regime was the parish priest, who not only exercised considerable normative authority in his religious capacity but also directly controlled the lives of Filipinos as landlord. As formally recognized agents of the colonial state, priests participated in various municipal councils and were tasked with overseeing the conduct of municipal officials. American statebuilders—guided by their commitment to the principle of separation of church and state—immediately dismantled this system of monitoring and disciplining Filipino administrative intermediaries via the Catholic Church, thus creating an administrative void between the newly established insular government in Manila and the hundreds of municipalities spread across the archipelago. This void was subsequently filled by wealthy landed elites, empowered as administrative intermediaries at the provincial level.

In this way, rather than extend the colonial administration down to the level of urban neighborhoods and rural townships to ensure local enforcement of rules and regulations, U.S. officials aggregated society through a hierarchy of patron-client relations. At first, the selection of individuals as provincial governors was managed by the Federal Party—a patronage machine founded by Manila-based *ilustrados*, with Civil Governor William Howard Taft's blessing—but soon these appointed *Federalista* governors were replaced by those elected to office by a selectorate composed of municipal officeholders. A polity once characterized by a cellularized system of state-society mediation was thereafter governed by an institutional structure that amassed power and authority of Filipino community leaders at the provincial level; the centralized despotism of the Spanish state was thus replaced by the decentralized and privatized despotism of Filipino elites.

It was the Philippines, rather than Taiwan, that arguably possessed an institutional foundation more conducive to statebuilding. But this ultimately did not matter in the development of institutions of state-society mediation during the Japanese and American periods, with both statebuilders committed to imposing on the subject population their own vision of modernity. The mediational structure that the Japanese constructed in Taiwan, ironically enough, would in turn come to resemble—at least in terms of the level of sociopolitical aggregation at which state-society mediation took place—the one found in the Philippines under Spanish rule. The new U.S. system, meanwhile, became more or less a modernized version of what had prevailed in Qing-era Taiwan, with Filipino provincial governors assuming the functional role once performed by the scholar-gentry in Taiwan. To understand this reversal and why mediational institutions conducive to statebuilding success developed in Taiwan but not in the Philippines, one must go beyond antecedent structural conditions and examine the beliefs, practices, and strategies of the statebuilders themselves.

Why Democratic Statebuilding Fails

At a basic level, Japan and the United States were comparable in their approach to governing their colonies. Albeit for entirely different reasons, both countries rejected the European practice of ruling nonsettler colonies through indirect rule, whereby colonized peoples, at least in theory, were governed through their *own* rulers, institutions, laws, and customs, with minimal European presence and intervention in daily life.[3] (It must be noted that in practice indirect rule thoroughly reconfigured the political and socioeconomic institutions of the colonies to create highly despotic, violent, and patriarchal systems that were quite unlike what had existed in many African and Asian territories prior to the arrival of the Europeans.[4]) Indeed, the objective of Japanese and American colonial officials went beyond maintaining control over their territories for strategic and commercial reasons. What they sought to achieve was the imposition of their vision of modernity onto subject populations: what the Japanese called *naichi enchō shugi* (homeland extensionism) and *dōka* (cultural assimilation) and the Americans called benevolent assimilation.

Moreover, not only did Japanese and American policymakers engage in the discourse of culturally and politically assimilating local inhabitants to behave as modern subjects, they actually committed time, manpower, and resources to realize these goals.[5] In both Taiwan and the Philippines, among the most important institutional manifestations of commitment to political modernity was the establishment of a large, professional, and functionally differentiated bureaucracy, as well as the enactment of hundreds of new laws and regulations that reflected the state's greatly expanded scope over the subject population. In short, despite the colonial setting in which they operated, Japanese and American officials in Taiwan and the Philippines perceived themselves as statebuilders and behaved accordingly.

Nonetheless, while sharing a commitment to statebuilding, Japanese and American colonial administrators held very different beliefs as to how best to transform a polity into a modern state. At the time of Taiwan's annexation, Japan was an autocracy—specifically, a bureaucratic dictatorship ruled by an oligarchy composed of former revolutionaries turned elder statesmen—and Japanese officials naturally turned to their own institutions and experiences for inspiration in modernizing Taiwan's governance structure. In contrast, the United States—its discrimination and exclusion of women and nonwhite men from politics notwithstanding—was a democracy. This not only shaped ideas held by American policymakers as to how best to govern the Filipinos and lead them to become modern democratic citizens but also placed constraints on how colonial officials could undertake statebuilding. Ultimately, American statebuilders were accountable to voters and taxpayers at home in a way that their Japanese counterparts were not. Actions taken by U.S. officials in the Philippines would thus remain within the boundaries of what the American people believed to be ethically and financially acceptable.

This observation, in light of Japan's success and America's failure at statebuilding by imposition, raises an intriguing question, with implications that go far beyond these two cases: Were Japan's autocratic institutions and the beliefs that undergirded them more conducive to statebuilding than America's liberal democratic ones? In general, are autocracies more likely than democracies to succeed at statebuilding? If so, what does this imply for the prospects of statebuilding in today's ungoverned and undergoverned spaces? Although the comparative-historical methodology employed in the foregoing analysis limits the generaliz-ability of its findings, the case studies nonetheless provide support to the hypoth-esis linking regime type to statebuilding outcomes. In particular, one can identify at least two distinct causal pathways through which the statebuilders' regime type and associated political ideologies shape how they go about structuring institu-tions of state-society mediation in the target territory, with lasting consequences for the development and strength of the state.

The first concerns the relationship between statebuilding and warfare. State-building missions, when pursued by way of imposition, typically begin with a campaign to pacify armed resistance. However, military strategies that minimize the human and financial costs of war tend to be those that *undermine* the construction of effective mediational institutions in the conflict's aftermath. Democratically accountable statebuilders, to the extent that their domestic au-dience demands that war be fought in the most economical and least violent manner possible, are therefore likely to make strategic choices during the pacifica-tion campaign that put into place institutional structures and practices that hurt statebuilding in the long run.[6] Second, and more directly, the statebuilder's vision of how a modern and well-governed polity should be organized—based on domestic political institutions or derived from strongly held beliefs on what modernity ought to look like—are not necessarily those that lead to the success-ful establishment of a modern state. Although this insight applies to all state-building missions, this divergence is likely to be the widest—and irreconcilably so—when the statebuilder is a liberal democracy.

The following pages, drawing from historical narratives found in the preced-ing chapters, substantiate these claims. The aim here, moreover, is to raise broader questions on whether it is even possible for democracies, as well as international and transnational organizations imbued with liberal and democratic principles, to transfer their own political institutions, practices, and ideals to ungoverned and undergoverned spaces by way of imposition. For the most part, statebuilding cam-paigns have been pursued in the contemporary era under the assumption that *democratic* statebuilding is a viable proposition. It is also commonly believed that the difficulties Western countries and organizations have encountered in build-ing strong and democratic states were consequences of insurmountable obsta-cles on the ground; the statebuilder's lack of commitment in money, time, and manpower; or failure on the part of reformers to take into account local customs, traditions, and power relations in designing new governance institutions. As such, so the argument goes, under the right circumstances, with enough commitment, and through the employment of better reform strategies, it should be possible to impose democratic governance on peoples who suffer from misrule and insecu-rity. On the contrary, this analysis suggests that democratic statebuilding, at least by way of imposition, is impossible: No matter how hard statebuilders try, un-governed and undergoverned spaces simply cannot be transformed into strong *and* democratic states when there is widespread resistance from local communities and their leaders.

The Pacification Campaign and Statebuilding

Territorial control and suppression of armed resistance are more easily obtained when statebuilders receive the cooperation of powerful provincial bosses and warlords, whose support can single-handedly ensure peace in a region. The problem, however, is that such actors hardly make for ideal collaborators in statebuilding. Their material self-interests may lead provincial bosses and warlords to ally with statebuilders during the pacification campaign, but this does not mean that their preferences and their vision of how the postwar political order should be organized are aligned with those of the modernist reformers. Provincial bosses and warlords, whose wealth and power are derived from private and communal sources, are in fact likely to view the construction of a strong state, with its capacity to monopolize coercive and rule-making authority, as a threat to their economic and political interests. Moreover, the very things that made them into effective wartime allies—control over large areas of land, those who work their land as tenants, and local militia forces—are precisely those that furnish provincial bosses and warlords with the means to challenge and obstruct statebuilding later on.

In contrast, village- and neighborhood-level community leaders, due to their limited authority and power, are far more controllable and disciplinable. Hence, even if community leaders do not see the construction of modern state institutions as being in their best interests, they can be compelled to behave as obedient enforcers of rules and regulations. As discussed in the analysis of colonial Taiwan, however, the transformation of community leaders into effective intermediaries is an institutionally produced outcome predicated on statebuilders having suppressed the insurgency, achieved territorial control, and constructed a large bureaucratic apparatus able to monitor and discipline administrative intermediaries. Without such institutional structures already in place, statebuilders will struggle, especially without the help of provincial bosses or warlords, to manage relationships with, and coordinate the actions of, hundreds of local community leaders, all with their own sets of interests and sympathies. Furthermore, even if statebuilders somehow succeed in managing and coordinating community leaders under the fog of war, the actual capacity of local communities to contribute to the pacification campaign is likely to be limited—especially in comparison to provincial bosses and warlords—compelling statebuilders to expend more of their own resources and manpower to win the war.

Strategic choices that minimize the cost of war, at least in terms of selection of local allies, are therefore not necessarily those that lead to long-term statebuilding success. Insofar as statebuilders are accountable to domestic constituents who seek to fight the war as cheaply and quickly as possible, they will be compelled to ally with, and thus empower, regionally influential societal elites that can contribute to the war effort in the immediate term, at the cost of statebuilding's success in the long run. In theory, it may be possible for statebuilders who relied on provincial bosses and warlords during the pacification campaign to abandon their mercurial wartime allies and organize the postwar mediational structure around village- and neighborhood-level elites instead. In practice, however, the alliance that helped to win the war, especially when this involves elites at higher levels of sociopolitical aggregation, is likely to endure and undergird the postwar governance system. Alienating wealthy and powerful elites immediately after the secession of hostilities—when memories of violence committed during the pacification campaign are still fresh, and hatred and discontent toward statebuilders simmer beneath the surface—would pose considerable risks to peace and stability. After all, the very characteristics that made provincial bosses and warlords into effective wartime allies will allow them to push entire regions, and even the occupied territory as a whole, back into a state of war. Yet, the longer statebuilders wait to dislodge wartime allies from positions of power, the more they become entrenched in the new political order and the harder their removal becomes. This is indeed what happened in the Philippines.

The superiority of U.S. military power was never in doubt during the course of the Philippine-American War. Soon after the opening of hostilities in February 1899, the United States easily defeated the revolutionary army in Manila and then relentlessly pursued the retreating forces until they were compelled to formally disband by the year's end. However, despite U.S. military superiority, controlling territory proved far more challenging than anticipated once the nature of the conflict changed from a conventional war to a guerilla campaign, given the sympathies that the revolutionaries enjoyed across much of the archipelago. U.S. generals initially believed that a display of benevolence, in the form of providing much needed public goods and services, would convince Filipinos to accept, and even welcome, American rule and induce people to turn against the rebels. Under the stern guidance of the U.S. military, roads and bridges were built, health and sanitation codes were enforced, and primary education was provided. Yet, it soon became apparent that this was not enough to win over the "hearts and minds" of the local population. Regardless of whether they were actually committed to the revolutionary cause, or simply feared reprisals for collaborating with the Americans, local community leaders secretly aided the revolutionaries, even as they outwardly expressed loyalty to the U.S. colonial regime.

If local community leaders could not be trusted to remain loyal to the United States even when treated benevolently, as General Arthur MacArthur surmised, the only way for the United States to maintain control over the Philippines was to flood the archipelago with U.S. troops and coerce Filipinos to behave obediently. To this end, he expanded the number of U.S. garrisons during his first year as commander of the U.S. forces in the Philippines, so that there was one in or near every municipality. He also dramatically increased the cost of disloyalty to the U.S. regime by adopting harsh punishments against any Filipino elite who assisted the rebels. In provinces that proved particularly difficult to control, he implemented a policy of reconcentration, whereby the province's entire population was relocated to, and confined in, a few heavily fortified "safe zones," so as to deny revolutionaries access to food and shelter. U.S. military officials also interfered in local governance to ensure that municipal officials fully cooperated with the enforcement of new rules and regulations, much in the same way parish priests had done under Spanish rule. They approved election results, supervised the conduct of municipal councils, and enforced new rules on sanitation, gambling, prostitution, and the like.[7]

Militarily, MacArthur's brutal counterinsurgency campaign was a resounding success, but it was politically untenable and unsustainable with respect to the American electorate. At its core, his strategy relied on maintaining control over the territory through a large military presence, but U.S. lawmakers, reflecting the sentiments of their constituents, had little appetite for this kind of military commitment. The Army Bill of February 1899, which created a 65,000-strong regular army and a 35,000-man volunteer army for service in the Philippines, generated considerable opposition from U.S. senators across party lines. Most prominently, Senator George Vest (Democrat, Missouri) noted how strange it was that if U.S. forces were in the Philippines as liberators and emancipators, the president would need "100,000 missionaries with rifles to shoot his good resolution into effect."[8] The Army Bill passed 55 to 13, but it was not without a crucial amendment making the increase in the size of the army a temporary measure to expire in July 1901. When the bill to reauthorize this expansion was introduced in Congress the following year, senators from both parties again wondered aloud why such a large army was needed. Although the Republican-controlled Congress approved the 1901 bill, which set the maximum size of the army at 100,000 men, President Theodore Roosevelt, aware of the sensitivity of the matter, immediately reduced its strength to the bill's minimum of 56,989 when the war was officially declared over in 1902.[9]

Also problematic were MacArthur's highly violent and inhumane counterinsurgency tactics, which departed considerably from the narrative of "benevolent assimilation"—a narrative that President William McKinley was compelled to champion as a way of convincing the American electorate to support his party's expansionist foreign policy. As reports of atrocities by U.S. military personnel against Filipinos filled the news, and as congressmen and senators demanded formal investigations regarding American misconduct in the archipelago, Republican leaders feared that public opinion would sour against the Philippine occupation and that they would be punished electorally.[10] On February 26, 1901, a mere two months after MacArthur initiated his new counterinsurgency strategy, Secretary of War Elihu Root made it clear to General Adna Chaffee (who was slated to succeed MacArthur) that it was his intention to establish civil government under Taft and to transfer all executive and legislative authority from the U.S. military commander to the IGP as quickly as possible "because we wish the army to avoid the prejudice which always arises when military government is too long continued, and because we want to get the Army out of the governing business and get its officers back to the performance of their proper function as soldiers."[11] For this to be possible, however, something had to take the place of the U.S. military's 502 garrisons in maintaining control over the archipelago.

This alternative was first the Federal Party and later the Nacionalista Party. From this point onward, American colonial officials worked to forge close collaborative ties with provincial elites and relied on these individuals and their clientelistic networks to suppress any uprisings (which continued well into the 1910s) in officially pacified territories. Instead of U.S. garrison commanders directly overseeing and disciplining local community leaders, the provincial governor—elected by the province's municipal officeholders—would thereafter ensure that the province remained at peace. In return, provincial elites were afforded various economic privileges that allowed them to aggrandize tremendous wealth and came to enjoy near-complete political autonomy in the locality. The result of this dynamic, as discussed, was the involution of the Philippine state into an "anarchy of families."

In contrast, the Japanese counterinsurgency model, just like the governance structure that followed, was one of relying on village- and neighborhood-level community leaders to maintain order and governability. When Japanese ground forces arrived in Taiwan in 1895, however, this was hardly the most obvious approach to pacifying the island, or one that was likely to succeed militarily. As previously noted, Taiwan at the end of the nineteenth century had an established landed class that dominated politics and socioeconomic interactions at the island-wide level. Although these powerful elites had initially mobilized to resist Japan's annexation of Taiwan, once the Japanese demonstrated their military superiority on the battlefield, many signaled their willingness to collaborate with the Japanese in exchange for special political, economic, and social privileges. Most prominently, soon after Japanese forces entered Taipei, the city's scholar-gentry presented to Governor-General Kabayama Sukenori a plan for indirectly administering Taiwan though gentry-led quasi-governmental offices named *bao-liangju*—a plan that was not so different from the one that would emerge in the Philippines a few years later, with the baoliangju serving as the institutional equivalent of the Federal and Nacionalista Parties. However, the baoliangju system never took hold: After briefly experimenting with this plan in northern Taiwan, the colonial government shifted course. Japanese officials feared that the baoliangju system, especially if it proved effective, would facilitate the entrenchment of the scholar-gentry in the colonial governance structure. They therefore determined to politically sideline these powerful individuals and sought to pacify the island through the efforts of the imperial army alone.

It remains a question whether the Japanese would have established their authority over the island less violently and with a smaller military deployment had they decided to retain the baoliangju system and expand it throughout Taiwan. Given the island's long-standing north-south split in political alliances and socioeconomic ties, the scholar-gentry in southern Taiwan could have refused to participate in a collaborative structure developed by elites in the north and chosen instead to fight the Japanese or flee to the Chinese mainland regardless. The fact remains, however, that the possibility of a less costly option—one derived directly from administrative practices in late nineteenth-century Taiwan—existed and had contributed to the imperial army's swift pacification campaign of northern Taiwan. Yet, this option was rejected by the Japanese, who regarded the scholar-gentry as posing a long-term threat to their statebuilding agenda, and instead looked for societal allies at lower levels of sociopolitical aggregation in fighting the insurgency and building a postwar governance structure. Thus emerged the proposal to revive baojia in 1896 and its reconstitution as hokō in 1898.

As it turned out, hokō units proved thoroughly *ineffective* at defending towns and villages against rebel attack or rooting out insurgents from a rebellious province. Peace and stability would have to be obtained by a combination of the imperial army's violent counterinsurgency campaign and the deployment of a large police presence—that is, by transforming Taiwan into a *polizeistaat*. However, although hokō did not do much to help the Japanese pacify Taiwan, it later proved highly valuable as a mediational institution once the remaining rebel forces were defeated. As in the Philippines, an institution that was originally established as an instrument for controlling territory and gaining the loyalty of the local population during the counterinsurgency campaign would thus come to dictate the organizational structure of state-society mediation in the war's aftermath, though in Japan's case, with profound implications for the *success* of statebuilding.

Democracy Building and Statebuilding

In retrospect, the statebuilder's initial blueprint for restructuring the target territory in its modernist image will almost always appear to have been misguided. To the extent that the vision of how best to govern the subject population is ideologically derived, it will necessarily conflict with the complexities of real socioeconomic relationships and interactions found in the target territory, as well as people's long-standing habits, customs, traditions, and practices.[12] Foreignness of the statebuilder's institutional model is another reason that even the most well thought out plan often goes awry: When new governance institutions are fashioned after those found in established states, they will be without the larger set of political, economic, and social organizations, as well as the practices, norms, mores, beliefs, and customs, that allow these institutions to function effectively in their original setting.[13] Institutions that contribute to an *established* state's security, wealth, and prosperity are also not the same as those that lead to the *establishment* of a strong and modern state, thus making direct institutional transfer a poor strategic choice for statebuilding.[14]

As such, in order for statebuilding to succeed, institutional reformers will, at minimum, have to adapt new institutions to local conditions so that they can function alongside, or be layered on, the target territory's existing set of formal and informal institutions. Insofar as a key institutional element cannot be transplanted, local substitutes will need to be found; this, in turn, will necessitate the conversion of a territory's existing institutions to perform new functions. Statebuilders may also have to abandon their initial designs for institutional reform altogether, if their vision of modernity is fundamentally incompatible with political and socioeconomic realities on the ground, or if its realization leads to the entrenchment of the very causes of state weakness.

Successful statebuilders are therefore those that are ideologically flexible and pragmatic in their approach—characteristics more likely to be associated with results-oriented reformers, who enjoy considerable freedom to experiment, innovate, and change direction as needed. Japanese statebuilders in Taiwan exemplified this dynamic, yet autonomy and insularity from their own national government in Tokyo, as well as societal interests and social forces in Japan and in Taiwan, were not the only reasons why Japanese colonial officials proved to be more effective statebuilders than their American counterparts. Just as important was the fact that the aforementioned gap between the statebuilder's vision of modernity and the realm of possible was much greater between the United States and the Philippines than between Japan and Taiwan. The "problem" was that the United States, unlike Japan, was a democracy and steadfastly sought to modernize the Philippines by mimicking its own democratic institutions and practices.

Consequently, American statebuilders were unable to construct governance institutions in the Philippine locality, especially institutions of state-society mediation, in a way that allowed for the archipelago's transformation into a strong and modern state.

When statebuilding is imposed on a subject population amid widespread resistance by local communities and their leaders, the principal function of mediational institutions is to serve as instruments of discipline. This is made possible, as demonstrated in the preceding chapters, by four factors. The first two are the primary focus of this study and concern the organizational structure of mediational institutions themselves: (1) *formalization* of institutions of state-society mediation makes the actions of administrative intermediaries more visible to, and hence controllable by, the state; and (2) *cellularization*, whereby the level at which state-society mediation takes place is scaled down to the most basic units of sociopolitical organization, reduces the risk of community leaders becoming an uncontrollable force in society. In addition to these changes to the structure of mediational institutions, the government's own administrative institutions and practices must also be altered to enable frontline bureaucrats to effectively discipline community leaders into obedient intermediaries. To this end, statebuilders must (3) establish a large bureaucratic apparatus with considerable presence in the locality and (4) be willing to act on the belief that the government has the right and responsibility (at least during the initial stages of statebuilding) to penetrate society, interfere in people's private lives and social interactions, and compel subject peoples to adopt behaviors that go against their self-interest. Although formalization and cellularization of mediational institutions make it easier for the state to observe and punish administrative intermediaries, behavioral change in the subject population also requires that a credible and constant threat of punishment for disobedient behavior be applied throughout the realm.

As leaders of an autocratic state, Japanese policymakers were predisposed to accept all four of the above factors that make statebuilding by imposition possible. In fact, Japanese society had itself been governed through a formalized and cellularized set of mediational institutions known as *goningumi* (five-person group) since the early seventeenth century, and this institution, which contributed greatly to Japan's own statebuilding efforts, was still in effect in Japan's countryside when Taiwan was annexed in 1895.[15] Japan's modernist rulers moreover believed that government had an obligation to spearhead the nation's political, economic, and cultural modernization and accordingly invested considerable resources into developing the Japanese state's disciplinary capacity.[16] The most obvious manifestation of this belief was the powerful Home Ministry, which, in addition to appointing all of Japan's prefectural governors and overseeing the national police, fostered and managed various grassroots organizations—such as neighborhood associations and women's groups—as enforcers of the government's various priorities.[17] Hence, even as Chief Civil Administrator Gotō Shimpei and his associates rejected Tokyo's preference for naichi enchō shugi and dōka and stressed the need to found Taiwan's new governance institutions on local customs and traditions, Gotō's reforms were not major departures from the autocratic institutions and practices found in Japan itself. Indeed, in reinventing baojia as hokō, and reconstituting Taiwan into a polizeistaat, Gotō created a system of local governance that was much closer to Japan's own administrative structure than anything that had existed, in practice or in theory, in Taiwan under Qing rule.

The American experience with state-society relations and mediational institutions, at least as it was understood in the popular imagination at the time, could not have been any more different from what prevailed in Japan. As observed by the French philosopher Alexis de Tocqueville during his 1831 visit to the United States, the outstanding feature of the American governance system was its robust associational life: the sheer number of political, economic, and social associations found in America, people's fervent participation in these associations, the diversity of functions they performed, and, most important, the freedom and autonomy they enjoyed from the state. It was by participating in various democratically constituted associations—which ranged from free and independent townships to the plethora of secondary associations that were spontaneously and voluntarily organized to advance common political, economic, and social interests—that people acquired the social mores, political culture, and habits of collective action that were necessary for a democratic polity to flourish.[18]

The vibrancy of associationalism in America, Tocqueville argued, taught people to value liberty, embrace public spiritedness, internalize the norm of generalized reciprocity, trust fellow citizens, and guard against the tyrannical tendencies of centralized power; it also contributed to America's prosperity and lawfulness. Through their participation in secondary associations, people were empowered and motivated to govern themselves and to solve societal problems without relying on the state.[19] "No doubt," Tocqueville noted, the common person "is often less successful than the state would have been in his place, but in the long run the sum of all private undertakings far surpasses anything the government might have done."[20] In short, the American governance system, which substituted direct enforcement of rules and regulations by the central government with autonomous and self-governing towns and secondary associations, not only contributed to the health of its democracy but was also what made America a strong state.

The validity of Tocqueville's argument that the vibrancy of associational life was at the root of America's political, economic, and social achievements is debatable.[21] Yet, the fact remains that Tocqueville was widely read by American intellectuals, and his observations, insights, and conclusions were accepted as truths by the very individuals who were responsible for designing and implementing America's statebuilding strategy in the Philippines. The highly impactful 1900 report by Jacob Schurman, while it does not mention Tocqueville by name, was thoroughly Tocquevillian in its analysis that the reason why Philippine municipalities were so poorly governed was because of their subordination to the Spanish colonial administration. It thus followed that the best way to end corruption and to improve the public spiritedness of local officials was to allow municipalities to fully manage their own affairs.[22] The Tocquevillian belief that good governance and prosperity would naturally result from diminishing government's role in the provision of public goods and services and letting localities govern themselves to the fullest extent possible also pervaded Secretary Root's instructions to the Philippine Commission for organizing the archipelago's governance system.[23] Taft, meanwhile, explicitly invoked Tocqueville, and in particular his analysis of New England towns, in explaining the logic behind the commission's decision to afford Philippine municipalities considerable political and fiscal autonomy.[24]

The gap between what McKinley and Root presented to the public as America's vision for the Philippines and the mediational structure that would have led to statebuilding success in the archipelago was therefore considerable. At various points during the first decade of U.S. rule, some, having come to realize this incongruence, sought to abandon (or at least modify) Washington's commitment to Tocquevillian principles in organizing local governance. General MacArthur's decision to establish over five hundred army garrisons throughout the archipelago during the pacification campaign and his insistence that the Philippines continue to be governed via these garrisons after the end of hostilities was the most notable example of this; also significant was Governor-General Luke Wright's attempt to expand the size as well as the duties of the colonial bureaucracy and to curtail the autonomy of Filipino provincial and municipal officeholders. However, these challenges to the Tocquevillian ideal were met with strong condemnation from Washington, each resulting in the removal of those who had advocated the policy reversal, as well as explicit orders for their successors to redouble commitment to local self-rule and to "get along" with Filipino elites.

Ultimately, unlike in Taiwan, where the sole agenda of the modernist reformers was the construction of a strong state, the goal in the Philippines was to establish a state that was both strong *and* democratic. When these two objectives collided, the inclination of policymakers in Washington, as well as most of America's colonial agents in the Philippines, was to favor the latter at the expense of the former. As Joseph Hayden, who served as vice governor-general, wrote in his memoir:

> It should not be forgotten that compared with the colonies of Japan or of the Netherlands, local government in the Philippines is a government by the people for the people. In Formosa [Taiwan], for instance, the police make the rounds once a year and compel every householder to move everything out of his home and give the place a thorough cleaning. This is autocracy. In the Philippines "clean-up week" occurs once each year. Posters, printed propaganda, newspaper feature stories, and speakers are sent to all parts of the Islands. A vigorous campaign is carried on through the public and private schools. Municipal, provincial, and insular contests are conducted. Local and national pride is aroused. The intelligence and patriotism of the people are appealed to. A nation is educated in community cleanliness and sanitation. This is Democracy. Democracy in the Philippines is not as efficient as autocracy in Formosa. But few Americans or few Filipinos would exchange the former for the latter. Thus it is irrational to make efficiency the sole, or even the chief, test in judging local government in the American possession.[25]

Hayden had a point. He was indeed right to question that efficiency, or what I call "state strength," should be the sole objective in constructing modern governmental institutions. Life in a strong state may be preferable to life in a weak one, but so too is a democracy preferable to an autocracy. As such, if the successful construction of a democratic state leads to a weaker state, is this not a worthy trade-off? While Japan might have been more successful in constructing a *strong* state in Taiwan, would it be correct to label America's statebuilding mission in the Philippines as a failure? If we employ different standards for evaluating success and failure, could an argument not be made that it was the United States, rather than Japan, that was more successful in statebuilding?

The problem with Hayden's analysis, like those of other former colonial officials who sought to defend America's statebuilding record in the Philippines and elsewhere, is that it is based on faulty premises: that the institutions imposed by the United States on the subject population actually contributed to making the Philippines more democratic; that more than anything else, the corruption and misrule that characterized local governance under American rule were legacies of deep-rooted culture and thus unavoidable consequences of Filipinos governing themselves as they saw fit.[26] Yet, as noted in the preceding chapters, the various defects in the system of state-society mediation that developed under U.S. rule, in particular the emergence of a powerful class of landed elites as provincial bosses, were not features of Philippine customs and traditions or a continuation of

Spanish-era institutions and practices. They were instead products of an institutional design that regarded centralization of government administration as a threat to democracy but was completely oblivious to the fact that concentration of wealth and power among a handful of socioeconomic elites could be just as tyrannical and repressive, especially in a weak state, as an all-powerful Leviathan.

What U.S. policymakers failed to understand was that a mediational structure that led to a prosperous and well-governed polity in the American political, socioeconomic, and historical setting was not one that would produce state strength *or* democratic governance in a context where new and modern institutions were imposed on an unequal society dominated by a predatory landed elite. In places like the New England towns that Tocqueville observed in 1831, where rulers and the subject population share a common understanding on the proper scope of government, local autonomy and self-rule may indeed facilitate effective implementation of public policy; where the state is seen as legitimate, people are more likely to comply with its rules and regulations, even if they go against their own selfish interests; where the state possesses the capacity to identify and punish wrongdoers, citizens will be deterred from engaging in unlawful behavior and trust one another to contribute to the public good; where relative equality in wealth and social status pertain and community members feel morally obligated to one another's well-being, then secondary associations that reflect the interests of the wider community may form to provide much needed public goods and services on behalf of, or in partnership with, the state.

Yet, none of these conditions were met in the Philippines under U.S. rule. The intention of American policymakers was to prioritize democratization over the government's efficiency, and in doing so they rejected proposals to increase the government's disciplinary capacity over administrative intermediaries. However, given the political and socioeconomic context in which the United States pursued statebuilding in the Philippines, the outcome of its commitment to the Tocquevillian vision of state-society relations was, paradoxically, both to weaken the state's capacity to govern *and* to engender and entrench the institutional features that have since stymied democratic development and consolidation in the Philippines.

Conclusion: The Ethics of Statebuilding

Statebuilding by imposition is made possible by a mediational structure that can only be described as authoritarian. It may very well be that the statebuilder's vision of modernity is one where the government and its administrative machinery are accountable to the public, laws are made by a democratically elected body, and the rule of law is upheld by an independent judiciary. However, insofar as local communities and their leaders reject *any* attempt by statebuilders to expand the scope of government and regard the modernist state's new rules and regulations as illegitimate, it is unlikely that statebuilders will be aided in their efforts by spontaneous and voluntary cooperation on the part of the subject population. To the extent that the interests and objectives of rulers and the governed diverge, and community leaders cannot be trusted to carry out their duties and responsibilities as administrative intermediaries on their own volition, effective enforcement of rules and regulations is achievable only when people are disciplined to outwardly behave as if they support the ruler's modernist agenda. Statebuilding by imposition is therefore an *inherently* undemocratic and illiberal proposition— one that is made possible by overcoming local opposition and compelling people to engage in behaviors that go against their self-interest. When this basic insight is forgotten or ignored and statebuilders attempt to govern society through mediational institutions that treat local communities and their leaders as though they are reliable partners in the pursuit of modernity, statebuilding fails.

Yet, while U.S. statebuilding efforts in the Philippines have been characterized as a failure throughout this work, one should not lose sight of the fact that colonial Philippines was not a failed state. From the 1910s, the Philippines was relatively stable and peaceful; it was also booming economically, at least for the landed elite. A comparison of commonly used indicators of socioeconomic development in the archipelago right before the onset of the Pacific War (1941–45) and those of Taiwan, Korea, and other East and Southeast Asian colonies shows that the Philippines ranks near the top.[27] Indeed, the Philippines under U.S. rule in all likelihood represents the best-case scenario of a Tocquevillian approach to statebuilding by imposition. But this is also precisely why the weakness of the Philippine state, as well as the dysfunction of its representative and judicial institutions, should give contemporary statebuilders pause.

Like early twentieth-century U.S. colonial officials, today's statebuilders are committed to the Tocquevillian model of state-society relations. With enough investment in time, money, and manpower, contemporary statebuilders may be able to match what American colonial officials achieved in the Philippines a century ago and remake target territories into stable, albeit weak and dysfunctional, democracies. Such an outcome, despite its negative effects on the welfare of the wider population, will be perfectly acceptable to the statebuilders themselves. After all, to the extent that statebuilding is initially motivated by the threats that ungoverned or undergoverned spaces pose to regional and global security, a "Philippines" is certainly preferable to whatever political order existed before. However, if one truly cares about the welfare of those living in territories characterized by state weakness, a "Philippines" is not good enough. To the extent that a statebuilding campaign inadvertently entrenches power structures and abusive socioeconomic practices and relations that prevent the construction of a more just and prosperous polity, this may arguably leave people worse off than in a state that has completely collapsed, such that communities have the opportunity to develop nonstate systems of local governance in the absence of a corrupt or tyrannical state. How then *should* statebuilders proceed?

Mimicking Japan's statebuilding strategy in Taiwan, even if this is the only way to establish strong and modern states by way of imposition, is not a viable option for Western countries and organizations in the contemporary era. The political and normative constraints that prevented the United States from transforming mediational institutions into effective instruments of discipline remain ever so present today, not just in the United States but across all Western democracies. Even Japan—where society was long subjected to varying degrees of bureaucratic oversight and management and the development of an autonomous associational sphere lagged behind other established democracies—has come to embrace the Tocquevillian model in recent decades.[28] Its approach to statebuilding abroad, as well as its vision of modernity at home, are also now largely in concert with that of its Western allies.[29] This is not to suggest that commitment to the Tocquevillian model is now universal. Nonetheless, all of the major international and transnational actors involved in statebuilding today have more or less internalized this model, and Tocquevillian theories and assumptions pervade the contemporary practice of statebuilding, from direct U.S.- or United Nations–led statebuilding missions to the array of projects initiated and administered by the World Bank and various international development agencies.[30]

While the West may be committed to the Tocquevillian model, modernist rulers and rebel leaders of ungoverned and undergoverned spaces, to the extent that they become incentivized to pursue statebuilding themselves, could adopt institutional models and statebuilding strategies employed by the Japanese in Taiwan.[31] Moreover, such statebuilding strategies need not lead to a highly oppressive and discriminatory authoritarian regime in the long run. Because Taiwan was a colonial state in which maintenance of Japanese political supremacy was predicated on the exclusion and subjugation of the Taiwanese people, Japanese government officials feared, with good reason, that democratization would lead to demands for, and movement toward, Taiwan's independence. In contrast, there is no reason why formalization and cellularization of mediational institutions and their use as disciplinary instruments during the initial stages of statebuilding would not allow for the eventual establishment of democratic institutions in today's ungoverned and undergoverned spaces. The critical word here, however, is *eventual.* In statebuilding by imposition, the quest for political modernity is, by definition, the aspiration of a small subset of domestic elites and their foreign collaborators and enablers. Statebuilding success therefore requires that the majority of people and their leaders be prevented from participating in politics and policymaking.

Moreover, as noted, the very process through which statebuilding by imposition is achieved locally—that is, by formalizing and cellularizing institutions of state-society mediation—contradicts norms and beliefs associated with liberal democracy and necessarily leads to the curtailment of universally recognized human rights and freedoms. When it comes to statebuilding, it is certainly important to design institutions with an eye toward their long-term effects, but does this justify a governance system characterized by oppression, discrimination, and indignity in the short term? We may challenge Hayden's characterization of colonial Philippines as a democracy, but it is hard to find fault with the contention that the objective of statebuilders should go beyond maximizing government efficiency. If statebuilding by imposition ultimately comes down to a choice between two ethically problematic outcomes, should such an endeavor even be engaged in to begin with?

This leads to the true alternative to statebuilding in addressing problems of insecurity and misrule in today's ungoverned and undergoverned spaces—that of anarchy properly understood.[32] Territories that are commonly characterized by Western countries and organizations as ungoverned or undergoverned spaces are not without some kind of political order. Local governance structures that take the place of states are oftentimes far from being democratic or liberal; in the contemporary era, ungoverned and undergoverned spaces are more likely than not characterized by insecurity and despotism in one form or another. Yet, there are also pockets of security and localized forms of democracy in areas where the state is absent. It is in such places that one might possibly find a viable model of governance to take the place of the Leviathan.[33] Given the seemingly irreconcilable ethical conundrum associated with statebuilding by imposition, is it time to start exploring and embracing nonstate solutions to governance? If one is inclined to reject both the authoritarianism of colonial Taiwan and the weakness of the Philippine state as ethically unacceptable visions of modernity, is there little choice but to see what the ungoverned and undergoverned spaces themselves have to offer as alternatives to statebuilding for the improvement of human security and welfare?

Despite the allure of nonstate governance systems, it would be a mistake to abandon statebuilding altogether. Once one dispenses with romanticized notions of how communities self-organize in the "state of nature,"[34] what one finds is that nonstate governance systems are unlikely to satisfy what have come to be universally accepted as basic human rights. In the world today, nonstate governance systems, even if they are socioeconomically egalitarian and politically democratic, are almost always patriarchal communities wherein women are not granted the same rights as men. People living in such places are likely bound by strict social norms concerning proper behavior as husbands, wives, children, and sexual partners. While the majority of nonstate peoples might have lived longer, eaten better, and enjoyed greater freedoms in centuries past, such is no longer the case.[35] Moreover, no matter how egalitarian and democratic nonstate governance systems may be, they are likely to lack a true public sphere where individuals can fully exercise their autonomy from political, religious, and economic forces. Only modern states have universities, independent news agencies, and the variety of associations that inform people of their rights as well as produce ideas, identities, and narratives that empower them and ensure that public policy serves the people rather than the narrow interests of those with power. It is indeed hardly coincidental that the notion that humans have universal rights, and that all people should be treated equally and respectfully regardless of who they are and what they believe in, was developed in strong and modern states.[36]

How then are we to proceed? To the extent that statebuilding is pursued out of a desire to advance human welfare, security, and dignity, what are we to do? There are simply no easy or good answers to these questions. When undertaken amid widespread resistance, statebuilding will inevitably lead to one outcome or another that violates contemporary liberal values on justice and fairness. Yet, the alternative—that is, to seek nonstate solutions to the problem of governance—is also highly problematic.

It is for this reason that whether or not we ought to pursue or support statebuilding is inherently a political question, rather than a technical issue. But in order to have an informed debate on statebuilding, we must first firmly understand what it would take to successfully impose new and modern governmental institutions amid resistance. All too often the discourse surrounding statebuilding is carried out under the assumption that strong states can be created in today's ungoverned and undergoverned spaces through liberal and democratic means. It is only when we dispense with this myth and understand what successful statebuilding by imposition actually entails that we can make ethically defensible decisions about whether and how to undertake this enterprise.

Notes

1. TAIWAN, THE PHILIPPINES, AND THE PUZZLE OF STATEBUILDING

1. Matt Andrews, *The Limits of Institutional Reform in Development* (New York, 2013); Stewart Patrick, *Weak Links* (New York, 2011).

2. James Scott, *Seeing Like a State* (New Haven, 1998), 4.

3. Stephen Krasner and Jeremy Weinstein, "Improving Governance from the Outside In," *Annual Review of Political Science* 17 (2014): 123–45; David Lake, *Statebuilder's Dilemma* (Ithaca, 2016); Jennifer Murtazashvili, *Informal Order and the State in Afghanistan* (New York, 2016); Astri Suhrke, *When More Is Less* (New York, 2012).

4. On statebuilding in Maoist China, see Vivienne Shue, *The Reach of the State* (Stanford, 1988); Helen Siu, *Agents and Victims in South China* (New Haven, 1989); Patricia Thornton, *Disciplining the State* (Cambridge, MA, 2007), 127–217. On statebuilding in Soviet Russia, see Mark Beissinger, *Scientific Management, Socialist Discipline, and Soviet Power* (Cambridge, MA, 1988); Richard Stites, *Revolutionary Dreams* (New York, 1989).

5. See, for example, Paul Miller, *Armed State Building* (Ithaca, 2013); Roland Paris, "Saving Liberal Peacebuilding," *Review of International Studies* 36 (2010): 337–65.

6. This concept of scope should be differentiated from what Huntington terms "degree of government," which refers to the development and strength of formal political and bureaucratic institutions, rather than the extent to which government intervenes in people's lives. Samuel Huntington, *Political Order in Changing Societies* (New Haven, 1968), 1.

7. Michael Mann, *The Sources of Social Power: Volume 2* (New York, 1993); Scott, *Seeing Like a State*.

8. Catherine Boone, *Property and Political Order in Africa* (New York, 2014); Evan Lieberman and Prerna Singh, "Census Enumeration and Group Conflict," *World Politics* 69, no. 1 (2017): 1–53; Mahmood Mamdani, *Citizen and Subject* (Princeton, 1996); Crawford Young, *The African Colonial State in Comparative Perspective* (New Haven, 1994).

9. This notion of strength is similar to what Mann calls "infrastructural power." Michael Mann, "The Autonomous Power of the State," *European Journal of Sociology* 25, no. 2 (1984): 189.

10. Scott, *Seeing Like a State*.

11. Tong Lam, *A Passion for Facts* (Berkeley, 2011); Melissa Lee and Nan Zhang, "Legibility and the Informational Foundations of State Capacity," *Journal of Politics* 79, no. 1 (2017): 118–32; Scott, *Seeing Like a State*.

12. This logic is what Levi calls "quasi-voluntary compliance." See Margaret Levi, *Of Rule and Revenue* (Berkeley, 1988), 52–67.

13. Timothy Tsu, "Japanese Colonialism and the Investigation of the Taiwanese Old Customs," in *Anthropology and Colonialism in Asia and Oceania*, ed. Jan van Bremen and Akitoshi Shimizu (Surrey, UK, 1999); Jen-to Yao, "The Japanese Colonial State and Its Forms of Knowledge in Taiwan," in *Taiwan under Japanese Colonial Rule*, ed. Ping-hui Liao and David Der-wei Wang (New York, 2006).

14. Irrigable and dry fields each had ten grades specific to the respective land type; there were seven grades of fishpond. For further details on the data collected through the

cadastral survey, see Canute VanderMeer and Paul VanderMeer, "Land Property Data on Taiwan," *Journal of Asian Studies* 28, no. 1 (1968): 144–50.

15. This assessment is based on a comparison of the 1939 Census of the Philippines, in which the total hectares of privately owned land reported by respondents was 6,690,594, and the 1935 report of the Bureau of Lands stating that the total hectares of land surveyed was 3,893,552. See Philippines, Commission of the Census, *Census of the Philippines: 1939*, vol. 2 (Manila, 1940–1943), 968; Philippines, Bureau of Lands, *Annual Report of the Director of Lands, 1935* (Manila, 1936), 44.

16. In Korea under Japanese rule, which was comparable in size to portions of the Philippine archipelago directly governed by the insular government (the large southern island of Mindanao was administered instead by the U.S. military), Japanese officials completed the cadastral survey in nine years (1910 to 1918). Atul Kohli, "Where Do High Growth Political Economies Come From?," *World Development* 22, no. 9 (1994): 1275.

17. United States, Bureau of the Census, *Census of the Philippine Islands: 1903*, vol. 4 (Washington, DC, 1905), 254–66; Philippines, Census Office, *Census of the Philippine Islands: 1918*, vol. 3 (Manila, 1920–1921), 72–94; Philippines, Commission of the Census, *Census of the Philippines: 1939*, vol. 2, 968.

18. It should be noted, however, that the percentage of farms tilled by owners versus tenants remained constant in Taiwan during the 1920s and 1930s even though Taiwan was also directly affected by this commodity boom, and, as in the Philippines, sugar was its most valuable export. Chih-ming Ka, *Japanese Colonialism in Taiwan* (Boulder, CO, 1995), 149.

19. Philippines, Bureau of Lands, *Report of the Director of Lands, 1924* (Manila, 1925), 22; Lewis Gleeck Jr., *Nueva Ecija in American Times* (Manila, 1981), 104, 117–18; Joseph Hayden, *The Philippines* (New York, 1942), 278; Theodore Roosevelt Jr., "Land Problems in Puerto Rico and the Philippine Islands," *Geographical Review* 24, no. 2 (1934): 182–204.

20. For data on deaths during the Japanese colonial period, see Taiwan, Tong ji shi, *Tai wan sheng wu shi yi nian lai tong ji ti yao* (Taipei, 1946), 270–76.

21. Joseph Wicentowski, "Policing Health in Modern Taiwan" (PhD diss., Harvard University, 2007), 54–65; Jen-to Yao, "Governing the Colonised" (PhD diss., University of Essex, 2002), 118–28.

22. Wicentowski, "Policing Health in Modern Taiwan," 60.

23. Wicentowski, "Policing Health in Modern Taiwan," 70–73.

24. Reynaldo Ileto, "Cholera and the Origins of the American Sanitary Order in the Philippines," in *Imperial Medicine and Indigenous Societies*, ed. David Arnold (New York, 1988), 125–48; Dean Worcester, *A History of Asiatic Cholera in the Philippine Islands* (Manila, 1908). In contrast, when the sixth cholera pandemic struck Taiwan in 1902, the GGT swiftly contained the disease, limiting the number of deaths to 613 individuals. Although cholera was eradicated from the island soon after it arrived in 1902, it returned in 1912 and again in 1919—due to cholera's persistence in nearby territories—resulting in 256 and 4,336 deaths, respectively. Taiwan, Tong ji shi, *Tai wan sheng wu shi yi nian lai tong ji ti yao*, 270–76.

25. Ileto, "Cholera and the Origins of the American Sanitary Order in the Philippines"; United States, Department of War, *Annual Report of the Philippine Commission, 1903*, pt. 2 (Washington, DC, 1904), 105–6.

26. Philippines, Philippine Health Service, *Report of the Philippine Health Service, 1919* (Manila, 1920), 181.

27. Warwick Anderson, *Colonial Pathologies* (Durham, NC, 2006), 70; W. Cameron Forbes, *The Philippine Islands*, vol. 1 (Boston, 1928), 356.

28. For more on these strategies of institutional reform, see James Mahoney and Kathleen Thelen, "A Theory of Gradual Institutional Change," in *Explaining Institutional Change*, ed. James Mahoney and Kathleen Thelen (New York, 2010), 1–37.

29. Daron Acemoglu, Simon Johnson, and James Robinson, "The Colonial Origins of Comparative Development," *American Economic Review* 91, no. 5 (2001): 1369–1401; Jeffry Herbst, *States and Power in Africa* (Princeton, 2000).

30. Marcus Kurtz, *Latin American State Building in Comparative Perspective* (New York, 2013).

31. Robert Bates, *Markets and States in Tropical Africa* (Berkeley, 1981); Nicolas van de Walle, *African Economies and the Politics of Permanent Crisis* (New York, 2001).

32. Ronald Knapp, *China's Island Frontier* (Honolulu, 1980); Dale Miyagi, "Neo-Caciquismo," *Pacific Asian Affairs* 1 (1976): 20–34.

33. See Dan Slater, *Ordering Power* (New York, 2010) and Tuong Vu, *Paths to Development in Asia* (New York, 2010) for a comparative analysis of the strength of these states.

34. United States, Bureau of the Census, *Census of the Philippine Islands: 1903*, vol. 1, 468.

35. Taiwan, Bureau of Aboriginal Affairs, *Report on the Control of Aborigines in Formosa* (Tokyo, 1911), 1; Stevan Harrell, "From *Xiedou* to *Yijun*, the Decline of Ethnicity in Northern Taiwan," *Late Imperial China* 11, no. 1 (1990), 110.

36. Chiukun Chen, "From Landlords to Local Strongmen," in *Taiwan*, ed. Murray Rubinstein (New York, 1999), 133–62; Harrell, "From *Xiedou* to *Yijun*"; Reynaldo Ileto, *Pasyon and Revolution* (Manila, 1979); David Sturtevant, *Popular Uprisings in the Philippines* (Ithaca, 1976).

37. Mahoney and Thelen, "A Theory of Gradual Institutional Change."

38. Abhijit Banerjee and Lakshmi Iyer, "History, Institutions, and Economic Performance," *American Economic Review* 95, no. 4 (2005): 1190–1213; Atul Kohli, *State-Directed Development* (New York, 2004); Matthew Lange, *Lineages of Despotism and Development* (Chicago, 2009); James Mahoney, *Colonialism and Postcolonial Development* (New York, 2010).

39. Roberto Stefan Foa, "Persistence or Reversal of Fortune?," *Politics and Society* 45, no. 2 (2017): 301–24; Stelio Michalopoulos and Elias Papaioannou, "Pre-Colonial Ethnic Institutions and Contemporary African Development," *Econometrica* 81, no. 1 (2013): 113–52; Martha Wilfahrt, "Precolonial Legacies and Institutional Congruence in Public Goods Delivery," *World Politics* 70, no. 2 (2018): 1–35.

40. Inō Yoshinori, *Taiwan bunka shi*, vol. 1 (Tokyo, 1928), 751.

41. Robert Gardella, "From Treaty Ports to Provincial Status, 1860–1894," in *Taiwan*, ed. Murray Rubinstein (New York, 2007), 163–200; Knapp, *China's Island Frontier*.

42. Benjamin Elman, *Civil Examinations and Meritocracy in Late Imperial China* (Cambridge, MA, 2013); Ramon Myers, "Taiwan under Ch'ing Imperial Rule," *Journal of the Institute of Chinese Studies of the Chinese University of Hong Kong* 4, no. 2 (1971): 495–520.

43. Max Weber, *Economy and Society*, ed. Guenther Ross and Claus Wittich (Berkeley, 1978), 956–1005.

44. Mark Allee, *Law and Local Society in Late Imperial China* (Stanford, 1994); John Watt, *The District Magistrate in Late Imperial China* (New York, 1972).

45. Harry Lamley, "The Taiwan Literati and Early Japanese Rule" (PhD diss., University of Washington, 1964), 101–32; Johanna Meskill, *A Chinese Pioneer Family* (Princeton, 1979), 199–213, 232–76.

46. Meskill, *A Chinese Pioneer Family*, 103–98.

47. Allee, *Law and Local Society in Late Imperial China*, 65–94.

48. Eliodoro Robles, *The Philippines in the Nineteenth Century* (Quezon City, PH, 1969), 210.

49. Onofre Corpuz, *The Bureaucracy in the Philippines* (Quezon City, PH, 1957), 22–45; Robles, *The Philippines in the Nineteenth Century*, 199–201.

50. Robles, *The Philippines in the Nineteenth Century*, 141–45, 211–14, 195–96, 201–6.

51. Greg Bankoff, *Crime, Society, and the State in the Nineteenth-century Philippines* (Quezon City, PH, 1996), 134–37; Alfred McCoy, *Policing America's Empire* (Madison, WI, 2009), 30–33.

52. In Manila and the four surrounding provinces of Cavite, Laguna, Bulacan, and Rizal, where the church was most entrenched, the Catholic orders owned more than half of the total agricultural lands. Peter Gowing, "The Disentanglement of Church and State Early in the American Regime in the Philippines," in *Studies in Philippine Church History*, ed. Gerald Anderson (Ithaca, 1969), 203–22.

53. Greg Bankoff, "Big Fish in Small Ponds," *Modern Asian Studies* 26, no. 4 (1992): 685–88; Robles, *The Philippines in the Nineteenth Century*, 199–200; John Blanco, *Frontier Constitutions* (Berkeley, 2009), 64–94.

54. Ken De Bevoise, *Agents of Apocalypse* (Princeton, 1995), 94–97; Robles, *The Philippines in the Nineteenth Century*, 217–18.

55. De Bevoise, *Agents of Apocalypse*, 102–08, 166–67.

56. Alfred McCoy, "A Queen Dies Slowly," in *Philippine Social History*, ed. Alfred McCoy and Ed. C. de Jesus (Quezon City, PH, 1982), 320–22.

57. Bankoff, *Crime, Society, and the State in the Nineteenth-century Philippines*, 77–79; McCoy, "A Queen Dies Slowly," 320–22; Marshall McLennan, "Changing Human Ecology on the Central Luzon Plain," in *Philippine Social History*, ed. Alfred McCoy and Ed. C. de Jesus (Quezon City, PH, 1982), 69–70; Miyagi, "Neo-Caciquismo."

58. For example, between 1841 and 1865, when Negros Occidental underwent its rapid transformation from a densely forested backwater province into the archipelago's foremost sugar-growing province, a total of twenty-two individuals served as gobernador-cillo of the municipality of Molo in Iloilo Province (which, along with Jaro, was where most of Negros Occidental's mestizo landed elite had originated); of these twenty-two former municipal officials, eighteen had family names that appeared on the official roster of Negros Occidental's landowners in 1897. Furthermore, whereas most Filipino landowners at the time owned lots of less than two hectares, the average holdings of these former gobernadorcillos was seven hundred seventy-four hectares. They were therefore among the very elite of the province's planter class. McCoy, "A Queen Dies Slowly," 315.

59. Here I mean a strong society in the manner defined by Joel Migdal, *Strong Societies and Weak States* (Princeton, 1988).

60. This methodological approach is commonly known as the method of difference. See John Stuart Mill, "Two Methods of Comparison," in *Comparative Perspectives*, ed. Amitai Etzioni and Frederic Du Bow (Boston, 1969), 205–13; Adam Przeworski and Henry Teune, *The Logic of Comparative Social Inquiry* (New York, 1970).

61. On this point, see Mahoney and Thelen, "A Theory of Gradual Institutional Change."

62. James Dobbins et al., *America's Role in Nation-Building* (Santa Monica, CA, 2003); James Fearon and David Laitin, "Neotrusteeship and the Problem of Weak States," *International Security* 28, no. 4 (2004): 5–43; Stephen Krasner, "Sharing Sovereignty," *International Security* 29, no. 2 (2004): 85–120.

63. For works that take a similar approach, see Severine Autesserre, *Peaceland* (New York, 2014); Scott, *Seeing Like a State*.

64. Tony Smith, *America's Mission* (Princeton, 1994); Jeremi Suri, *Liberty's Surest Guardian* (New York, 2011).

2. A THEORY OF STATEBUILDING BY IMPOSITION

1. Max Weber, *Economy and Society*, ed. Guenther Ross and Claus Wittich (Berkeley, 1978), 956–1005.

2. Michael Mann, "The Autonomous Power of the State," *European Journal of Sociology* 25, no. 2 (1984): 185–213; Hendrik Spruyt, *The Sovereign State and Its Competitors* (Princeton, 1994); Max Weber, "Politics as a Vocation," in *From Max Weber*, ed. H. H. Gerth and C. Wright Mills (New York, 1946), 77–128.

3. Eugen Weber, *Peasants into Frenchmen* (Stanford, 1976).

4. Warwick Anderson, *Colonial Pathologies* (Durham, NC, 2006); Ruth Rogaski, *Hygienic Modernity* (Berkeley, 2004).

5. Theodore Porter, *Trust in Numbers* (Princeton, 1995), 35–36.

6. At the eve of the First World War in 1910, the size of the civilian bureaucracy, as a percentage of total population, in various European countries was as follows: Austria-Hungary, 3.15; France, 2.14; Great Britain, 2.60; and Germany, 1.57. Data on size of the bureaucracy from Michael Mann, *The Sources of Social Power: Volume 2* (New York, 1993), 393.

7. Merilee Grindle, *Jobs for the Boys* (Cambridge, MA, 2012), 37–71; Weber, *Economy and Society*, 1006–69.

8. Francis Fukuyama, *The Origins of Political Order* (New York, 2011), 110–38.

9. Grindle, *Jobs for the Boys*, 72–93; Bernard Silberman, *Cages of Reason* (Chicago, 1993), 120–56.

10. Margaret Levi, *Of Rule and Revenue* (Berkeley, 1988), 48–55.

11. For the various strategies of resistance available to the weak, see James Scott, *Weapons of the Weak* (New Haven, 1985).

12. Atul Kohli, *State-Directed Development* (New York, 2004); Erik Kuhonta, *The Institutional Imperative* (Stanford, 2011); Joel Migdal, *Strong Societies and Weak States* (Princeton, 1988); Hillel Soifer, *State Building in Latin America* (New York, 2015); Charles Tilly, *Coercion, Capital, and European States* (Cambridge, MA, 1990).

13. Levi, *Of Rule and Revenue*, 48–55.

14. James Scott, *The Art of Not Being Governed* (New Haven, 2009), 7.

15. Here, I borrow Thomas Hobbes's words, if not his argument. See Thomas Hobbes, *Leviathan,* ed. Richard Tuck (New York, 1991), 89.

16. Crawford Young, *The African Colonial State in Comparative Perspective* (New Haven, 1994), 1–2.

17. Nicholas Dirks, *Castes of Mind* (Princeton, 2011), 201.

18. Tong Lam, *A Passion for Facts* (Berkeley, 2011), 77.

19. Scott, *The Art of Not Being Governed.*

20. Benedict Anderson, *Imagined Communities* (New York, 1991), 83–111; Weber, *Peasants into Frenchmen*, 303–38.

21. James Scott, *Seeing Like a State* (New Haven, 1998).

22. Herbert Kitschelt and Steven Wilkinson, eds., *Patrons, Clients and Policies* (New York, 2007).

23. Harumi Befu, "Village Autonomy and Articulation with the State," *Journal of Asian Studies* 25, no. 1 (1965): 19–32; Benjamin Read, *Roots of the State* (Stanford, 2012).

24. Gregory Kasza, *The Conscription Society* (New Haven, 1995).

25. On the role intermediaries play as translators of modernist ideas and practices within local communities, see David Lewis and David Mosse, *Development Brokers and Translators* (Bloomfield, CT, 2006).

26. For further analysis of this dynamic, see Daniel Mattingly, "Elite Capture," *World Politics* 68, no. 3 (2016): 383–412.

27. John Haley, *Authority without Power* (New York, 1991), 51–65.

28. Lily Tsai, *Accountability without Democracy* (New York, 2007). See also Philip Gorski, *The Disciplinary Revolution* (Chicago, 2003), 34–77, for an example of a solidary group in early modern Dutch Republic.

29. For illustrations of this dynamic in two different settings, see Prasenjit Duara, *Culture, Power, and the State* (Stanford, 1988), 42–57; Mahmood Mamdani, *Citizen and Subject* (Princeton, 1996), 37–61.

30. It is on this point that my analysis departs from Foucauldian analyses of disciplinary power. See Michel Foucault, *Discipline and Punish*, trans. Alan Sheridan (New York, 1977).

31. This point is stressed by Kate Baldwin in her conceptualization of chiefs and their functions within the local community in Africa. Kate Baldwin, *The Paradox of Traditional Chiefs in Democratic Africa* (New York, 2015), 20–52. When state-society mediation is primarily undertaken through a clientelistic system, the foremost function of an intermediary becomes the distribution of state-controlled resources to the government's supporters. On clientelism, see Susan Stokes et al., *Brokers, Voters, and Clientelism* (New York, 2013).

32. See, for example, Luke Roberts, *Performing the Great Peace* (Honolulu, 2012).

33. John Brehm and Scott Gates, *Working, Shirking, and Sabotage* (Ann Arbor, 1997); Gary Miller, "The Political Evolution of Principal-Agent Models," *Annual Review of Political Science* 8 (2005): 203–25.

34. See, for example, Eduardo Dargent et al., "Greater State Capacity, Lesser State," *Politics and Society* 45, no. 1 (2017): 3–34; Duara, *Culture, Power, and the State*, 42–57; Frances Hagopian, *Traditional Politics and Regime Change in Brazil* (New York, 1996), 36–72; Nicholas Van de Walle, *African Economies and the Politics of Permanent Crisis* (New York, 2001), 113–87.

35. Mark Allee, *Law and Local Society in Late Imperial China* (Stanford, 1994); Johanna Meskill, *A Chinese Pioneer Family* (Princeton, 1979), 103–98.

36. Spruyt, *The Sovereign State and Its Competitors*. For a similar argument linking statebuilding to the representation of commercial interests within the governing coalition in Latin American and African countries, see Ryan Saylor, *State Building in Boom Times* (New York, 2014).

37. James Mahoney, *Colonialism and Postcolonial Development* (New York, 2010); Marcus Kurtz, *Latin American State Building in Comparative Perspective* (New York, 2013); Kenneth Sokoloff and Stanley Engerman, "History Lessons," *Journal of Economic Perspectives* 14, no. 3 (2000): 217–32.

38. Richard Bensel, *Yankee Leviathan* (New York, 1990); Miguel Centeno, *Blood and Debt* (University Park, PA, 2002); Tilly, *Coercion, Capital, and European States*.

39. Dan Slater, *Ordering Power* (Cambridge, 2010).

40. Tuong Vu, *Paths to Development in Asia* (New York, 2010).

41. Stathis Kalyvas, *The Logic of Violence in Civil War* (New York, 2006), 111–45; James Scott, *Domination and the Arts of Resistance* (New Haven, 1990).

42. Timur Kuran, *Private Truths, Public Lies* (Cambridge, MA, 1995); Lisa Wedeen, *Ambiguities of Domination* (Chicago, 1999).

43. I borrow the term *cellularization* from Helen Siu. See Helen Siu, *Agents and Victims in South China* (New Haven, 1989).

44. On the importance of monitoring capacity in obtaining compliance, see Michael Hechter, *Principles of Group Solidarity* (Berkeley, 1987), 51.

45. Scott, *Seeing Like a State*.

46. On the importance of sanctioning capacity to obtaining compliance, see Hechter, *Principles of Group Solidarity*, 50.

47. Karen Barkey, *Bandits and Bureaucrats* (Ithaca, 1996), 55–84; Duara, *Culture, Power, and the State*, 168–93; Mamdani, *Citizen and Subject*, 37–61.

48. Arguably this is why communist parties excelled as statebuilders, due to their emphasis on building local party cells and cultivating local leaders as a means of achieving their revolutionary, and ultimately statebuilding, goals. See Victor Nee, "Between Center and Locality," in *State and Society in Contemporary China*, ed. Victor Nee and David Mozingo (Ithaca, 1983), 223–43; Siu, *Agents and Victims in South China*.

49. Theda Skocpol, *States and Social Revolutions* (New York, 1979), 29.

50. Joshua Cohen and Joel Rogers, "Secondary Associations and Democratic Governance," *Politics and Society* 20, no. 4 (1992): 393–472; Robert Putnam, *Making Democracy Work* (Princeton, 1993); Mark Warren, *Democracy and Association* (Princeton, 2001).

51. Alfred McCoy, ed., *An Anarchy of Families* (Madison, WI, 2009). On this point, see also John Sidel, *Capital, Coercion, and Crime* (Stanford, 1999).

3. THE *POLIZEISTAAT*

1. What makes this especially puzzling, from a historical perspective, is that it departed from Japan's own statebuilding strategy of mimicking successful European institutions and practices. On this point, see D. Eleanor Westney, *Imitation and Innovation* (Cambridge, MA, 1987). After all, other than in places where European settlers dominated the territory's political and economic institutions, indirect rule was the method through which all European powers—even the French, who superficially pursued a strategy of direct rule—governed their colonial territories. See Raymond Betts, *Assimilation and Association in French Colonial Theory* (New York, 1960).

2. For details on the Sino-Japanese War, the Treaty of Shimonoseki, and the Triple Intervention, see S. C. M. Paine, *The Sino-Japanese War of 1894–1895* (New York, 2003).

3. Quotation found in Stewart Lone, *Army, Empire and Politics in Meiji Japan* (London, 2000), 46. For the original document, see Katsura Tarō, "Taiwan tōchi hōshin [Taiwan governing policy]," July 1896, in Katsura Tarō kankei monjo [Documents related to Katsura Tarō], reel 9, no. 84.1 (National Diet Library, Tokyo).

4. Edward I-te Chen, "The Attempt to Integrate the Empire," in *The Japanese Colonial Empire*, ed. Ramon Myers and Mark Peattie (Princeton, 1984), 240–74.

5. Montague Kirkwood, "Taiwan seido, tennō no taiken, oyobi Teikoku Gikai ni kansuru ikensho [Opinion paper on the issue of the Taiwan system, the authority of the emperor, and the Imperial Diet]," in *Taiwan shiryō*, ed. Kaneko Kentarō (Tokyo, 1970 [1895]), 78–107.

6. Montague Kirkwood, "Shokuminchi seido [Colonial systems]," in *Taiwan shiryō*, 108–48.

7. Michel Revon, "Ryōtō oyobi Taiwan tōchi ni kansuru tōgi [Response to the question of governing Liaodong and Taiwan]," in *Taiwan shiryō*, 407. For Revon's entire opinion paper, see 399–409.

8. On this point, see also the recommendation provided by Henry Denison, an American who served as legal advisor to successive Japanese foreign ministers and was the author of the clause concerning Taiwan in the Treaty of Shimonoseki. Asano Toyomi, *Teikoku Nihon no shokuminchi hōsei* (Nagoya, JP, 2008), 66–72.

9. Richard Siddle, "Colonialism and Identity in Okinawa before 1945," *Japanese Studies* 18, no. 2 (1998): 122.

10. Government officials were deeply troubled by the possible effects of Japan's Taiwan policy on the new Commerce and Navigation Treaty, which had just been concluded with Great Britain in July 1894. A key requirement of the treaty was for Japan to adopt a new law code in accordance with Western legal standards and practices. With annexation,

Taiwan was now formally a part of the territory where a new Western legal code was to be adopted; Japan thus had to be careful not to allow its Taiwan policy to derail the treaty. Asano, *Teikoku Nihon no shokuminchi hōsei*, 24–25; Oguma Eiji, *"Nihonjin" no kyōkai* (Tokyo, 1998), 86–93.

11. Hara Takashi, "Taiwan mondai nian [Two proposals for the Taiwan problem]," in *Taiwan shiryō*, 32–34.

12. Quotation found in Oguma, *"Nihonjin" no kyōkai*, 86.

13. This policy was inspired by Germany's approach to determining citizenship status in Alsace-Lorraine. Asano, *Teikoku Nihon no shokuminchi hōsei*, 30–50.

14. Oguma, *"Nihonjin" no kyōkai*, 93–100.

15. Asano, *Teikoku Nihon no shokuminchi hōsei*, 85–99; Tay-sheng Wang, *Legal Reform in Taiwan under Japanese Colonial Rule* (Seattle, 2000).

16. Izawa Shūji, "Taiwan kōgakkō setchi ni kansuru iken [Opinion on the establishment of public schools in Taiwan]," in *Izawa Shūji senshū*, ed. Shinano Kyōikukai (Nagano, JP, 1958), 608–26.

17. Lori Watt, *When Empire Comes Home* (Cambridge, MA, 2010), 20–34.

18. Haruyama Meitetsu, "Taiwan kyūkan chōsa to rippō kōsō," *Taiwan kingendaishi kenkyū* 6 (1988): 81–114.

19. Mochiji Rokusaburō, *Taiwan shokumin seisaku* (Tokyo, 1912), 282–93; Chen Peifeng, *"Dōka" no dōshō imu* (Tokyo, 2001), 75–78.

20. E. Patricia Tsurumi, *Japanese Colonial Education in Taiwan* (Cambridge, MA, 1977), 22–26; Taiwan Kyōikukai, *Taiwan kyōiku enkakushi* (Taihoku [Taipei], 1973[1939]), 229–36; Yoshino Hidekimi, *Taiwan kyōiku shi* (Taihoku [Taipei], 1927), 237.

21. Kō Shōdō, *Taiwan Minshukoku no kenkyū* (Tokyo, 1970); Harry Lamley, "The Taiwan Literati and Early Japanese Rule" (PhD diss., University of Washington, 1964), 143–73.

22. Ōe Shinobu, "Shokuminchi sensō to Sōtokufu no seiritsu," in *Iwanami kōza kindai Nihon to shokuminchi*, vol. 2, ed. Ōe Shinobu (Tokyo, 1992), 3–33.

23. Lamley, "The Taiwan Literati and Early Japanese Rule," 224–27.

24. Lamley, "The Taiwan Literati and Early Japanese Rule," 228–30.

25. Ching-chih Chen, "Japanese Socio-political Control in Taiwan, 1895–1945" (PhD diss., Harvard University, 1973), 19–26; James Davidson, *The Island of Formosa Past and Present* (New York, 1903), 314–70; Ōe, "Shokuminchi sensō to Sōtokufu no seiritsu." A description of this area can be found in Johanna Meskill, *A Chinese Pioneer Family* (Princeton, 1979).

26. Davidson, *The Island of Formosa Past and Present*, 323.

27. Chen, "Japanese Socio-political Control in Taiwan," 23–24.

28. Lamley, "The Taiwan Literati and Early Japanese Rule," 261–65; Mukōyama Hiroo, *Nihon tōchika ni okeru Taiwan minzoku undō shi* (Tokyo, 1987).

29. Chen, "Japanese Socio-political Control in Taiwan," 32.

30. Quotation found in Chen, "Japanese Socio-political Control in Taiwan," 33–34.

31. Chen, "Japanese Socio-political Control in Taiwan," 34–36; Wang, *Legal Reform in Taiwan under Japanese Colonial Rule*, 107.

32. Stevan Harrell, "From *Xiedou* to *Yijun*," *Late Imperial China* 11, no. 1 (1990): 99–127; Mukōyama, *Taiwan minzoku undō shi*; Ōe, "Shokuminchi sensō to Sōtokufu no seiritsu."

33. Chen, "Japanese Socio-political Control in Taiwan," 283–84.

34. Hui-yu Caroline Ts'ai, "One Kind of Control" (PhD diss., Columbia University, 1990), 19; Lamley, "The Taiwan Literati and Early Japanese Rule," 237.

35. Taiwan's civil administration alone cost six to seven million yen a year. To this must be added the amount required to maintain a large military presence on the island. Hirai Hirokazu, *Nihon shokuminchi zaisei shi kenkyū* (Kyoto, 1997), 26–53.

36. Tsurumi Yūsuke, *Seiden Gotō Shimpei*, vol. 2, ed. Ikkai Tomoyoshi (Tokyo, 2004), 647.

37. When an influential leader in the district of Yilan failed to pay a license fee for a mining operation, he was executed for his disobedience, leading inhabitants to rebel in anger. Chen, "Japanese Socio-political Control in Taiwan," 30–31.

38. Okamoto Makiko, *Shokuminchi kanryō no seiji shi* (Tokyo, 2008), 51.

39. Chen, "Japanese Socio-political Control in Taiwan," 158–59; Hiyama Yukio, "Taiwan tōchi no kikō kaikaku to kanki shinshuku mondai," in *Taiwan Sōtokufu monjo mokuroku*, vol. 2, ed. Chūkyō Daigaku Shakai Kagaku Kenkyūjo (Tokyo, 1995), 326–31; Mukōyama, *Taiwan minzoku undō shi*, 123–25.

40. Chen, "Japanese Socio-political Control in Taiwan," 159–60.

41. Chen, "Japanese Socio-political Control in Taiwan," 200–01; Hiyama, "Taiwan tōchi no kikō kaikaku to kanki shinshuku mondai," 330–31.

42. Chen, "Japanese Socio-political Control in Taiwan," 204–08; Yosaburō Takekoshi, *Japanese Rule in Formosa*, trans. George Braithwaite (New York, 1907), 144–45.

43. Okamoto, *Shokuminchi kanryō no seiji shi*, 155–225.

44. Hiyama, "Taiwan tōchi no kikō kaikaku to kanki shinshuku mondai," 326–27; Mukōyama, *Taiwan minzoku undō shi*, 123; Takekoshi, *Japanese Rule in Formosa*, 144–45; Jen-to Yao, "Governing the Colonised" (PhD diss., University of Essex, 2002), 171.

45. Lamley, "The Taiwan Literati and Early Japanese Rule," 340, 348, 355–56.

46. Lamley, "The Taiwan Literati and Early Japanese Rule," 325–43.

47. Hung Chiu-fen, "Ri ju chu qi tai wan de bao jia zhi du," *Jin dai shi yan jiu suo ji kan* 21 (1991): 437–71; Lee Shinn-cherng, "Qing dai yi lan de 'baojia' yu 'qingzhuanglianjia' zhi yan jiu," *Xing da ren wen xue bao* 43 (2009): 219–55; Ts'ai, "One Kind of Control," 48–49.

48. Hung, "Ri ju chu qi tai wan de bao jia zhi du"; Mukōyama, *Taiwan minzoku undō shi*, 124–25; Ts'ai, "One Kind of Control," 48–49.

49. The text of the 1896 imperial decree establishing the military governor-general system can be found in Yamazaki Tanshō, *Gaichi tōchi kikō no kenkyū* (Tokyo, 1943), 185–86.

50. Tsurumi, *Seiden Gotō Shimpei*, vol. 2, 647–48.

51. Finance Minister Inoue Kaoru was in fact so baffled by the choice that he requested that Gotō submit a policy paper on Taiwan so that the elder statesman could judge for himself whether Gotō was up to the task. Tsurumi, *Seiden Gotō Shimpei*, vol. 2, 649–50.

52. For Gotō's career before his appointment as chief civil administrator of Taiwan, see Tsurumi, *Seiden Gotō Shimpei*, vols. 1 and 2. Gotō's Taiwan opium policy can be found in vol. 2, 589–626.

53. Gotō Shimpei, "Taiwan tōchi kyūkyū an [A proposal for the rehabilitation of the Taiwan administration]," 1898, in Gotō Shimpei monjo, reel 12, no. 4.33 (Mizusawa Shiritsu Gotō Shimpei Kinenkan, Iwate, JP), 1.

54. For a discussion of the concept of polizeistaat, see Marc Raeff, "The Well-Ordered Police State and the Development of Modernity in Seventeenth- and Eighteenth-Century Europe," *American Historical Review* 80, no. 5 (1975): 1221–43. For this model's later development in Prussia, see Alf Lüdtke, *Police and State in Prussia*, trans. Pete Burgess (New York, 1989).

55. Gotō, "Taiwan tōchi kyūkyū an," 1.

56. Chen, "Japanese Socio-political Control in Taiwan," 197–98.

57. Tsurumi, *Seiden Gotō Shimpei*, vol. 3, 57–58.

58. Chen, "Japanese Socio-political Control in Taiwan," 200–03.

59. Mochiji, *Taiwan shokumin seisaku*, 72–73; Yoshihara Jōji, *Nihon tōchika Taiwan keisatsu seido oyobi hokō seido nōto* (Tokyo, 1998), 33–38; Washinosu Atsuya, *Taiwan keisatsu yonjūnen shiwa* (Tokyo, 2000[1938]), 97–115.

60. Chen, "Japanese Socio-political Control in Taiwan," 203–11; Taiwan Sōtokufu Keimukyoku, *Taiwan Sōtokufu keisatsu enkakushi*, vol. 1 (Taihoku [Taipei], 1933), 810; Yao, "Governing the Colonised," 176.

61. Mochiji, *Taiwan shokumin seisaku*, 73; Mukōyama, *Taiwan minzoku undō shi*, 226–27; *Taiwan Sōtokufu keisatsu enkakushi*, 506–07, 513–15; Ts'ai, "One Kind of Control," 43–45, 175; E. Patricia Tsurumi, "Taiwan Under Kodama Gentarō and Gotō Shimpei," *Papers on Japan, Harvard University, East Asian Research Center* 4 (1967), 117–18; Yao, "Governing the Colonised," 184–88.

62. Yao, "Governing the Colonised," 190–95.

63. Chen, "Japanese Socio-political Control in Taiwan," 42–63; Tsurumi, *Seiden Gotō Shimpei*, vol. 3, 57–58; Wang, *Legal Reform in Taiwan under Japanese Colonial Rule*, 110–11.

64. Wang, *Legal Reform in Taiwan under Japanese Colonial Rule*, 107–08.

65. Mukōyama Hiroo, "Shokuminchi Taiwan no chian hōsei," *Kokugakuin hōgaku* 5, no. 2 (1967): 97–147; Wang, *Legal Reform in Taiwan under Japanese Colonial Rule*, 108–10.

66. Wang, *Legal Reform in Taiwan under Japanese Colonial Rule*, 119–23.

67. Francis Fukuyama, *The Origins of Political Order* (New York, 2011); Michael Mann, *The Sources of Social Power: Volume 2* (New York, 1993); Charles Tilly, *Coercion, Capital, and European States* (Cambridge, MA, 1990).

68. Max Weber, *Economy and Society*, ed. Guenther Ross and Claus Wittich (Berkeley, 1978).

69. In comparison, the size of the entire civilian bureaucracy within Japan itself was a much more modest 1.6 per thousand during this period. Okamoto, *Shokuminchi kanryō no seiji shi*, 43, 51, 60.

70. Chen, "Japanese Socio-political Control in Taiwan," 257–59.

71. Suzuki Tetsuzō, "Ri zhi chu nian tai wan zong du fu wei sheng xing zheng zhi du zhi xing cheng," *Shi da tai wan shi xue bao* 4 (2011): 128–59; Tsai Lung-pao, "Ri zhi chu qi tai wan zong du fu de ji shu ren li zhi zhao mu," *Guo li zheng zhi da xue shi xue bao* 35 (2011): 75–143; Jen-to Yao, "The Japanese Colonial State and Its Forms of Knowledge in Taiwan," in *Taiwan under Japanese Colonial Rule*, ed. Ping-hui Liao and David Der-wei Wang (New York, 2006).

72. Chalmers Johnson, *MITI and the Japanese Miracle* (Stanford, 1982); Bernard Silberman, *Cages of Reason* (Chicago, 1993).

73. Okamoto, *Shokuminchi kanryō no seiji shi*, 249–50.

74. Okamoto, *Shokuminchi kanryō no seiji shi*, 52–55.

75. Max Weber, "Politics as a Vocation," in *From Max Weber*, ed. H. H. Gerth and C. Wright Mills (New York, 1946), 78.

4. THE ADMINISTERED COMMUNITY

1. James Scott, *Seeing Like a State* (New Haven, 1998).

2. The concept of administered community should be distinguished from that of the "administered society," which Allen Kassof developed for the post-totalitarian Soviet Union. The political system Kassof describes is that of direct bureaucratic rule over society, rather than one characterized by state-society mediation. He also sees society as having no autonomy from the state, which is unlike the system I describe in this chapter. See Allen Kassof, "The Administered Society," *World Politics* 16, no. 4 (1964): 558–75.

3. I borrow the concept of imagined communities from Benedict Anderson, *Imagined Communities* (New York, 1991). On identity formation under Japanese rule, see Leo Ching, *Becoming "Japanese"* (Berkeley, 2001); Ming-cheng Lo, *Doctors within Borders* (Berkeley, 2002).

4. Hsu Shih-chia, "Zhi min zheng quan dui tai wan min jian zi zhu xing de fang ren yu shou bian," *Xin shi xue* 24, no. 3 (2013): 53–94; Miriam Kingsberg, *Moral Nation* (Berkeley, 2014), 20–28; Miao Yen-wei, "Cong tian ran zu hui dao jie chan hui," *Tai wan she hui yan jiu* 91 (2013): 125–74.

5. The defense of dōka as the primary goal of public education in Taiwan is made most explicitly and forcefully in the writings of Izawa Shūji, who served as GGT's first chief of Education Affairs. See Izawa Shūji, "Shin hanto jinmin kyōka no hōshin [Policy for educating subjects of the new territory]," in *Izawa Shūji senshū*, ed. Shinano Kyōikukai (Nagano, JP, 1958), 632–41. For further discussion of Izawa's education policy, see Chen Peifeng, *"Dōka" no dōshō imu* (Tokyo, 2001), 36–59; Komagome Takeshi, *Shokuminchi teikoku Nihon no bunka tōgō* (Tokyo, 1996), 52–57.

6. For a collection of government documents pertaining to the debate on colonial policy in Taiwan, see Itō Hirobumi, *Taiwan shiryō*, ed. Kaneko Kentarō (Tokyo, 1970).

7. Oguma Eiji, *"Nihonjin" no kyōkai* (Tokyo, 1998), 86–93.

8. Quotation found in Oguma, *"Nihonjin" no kyōkai*, 94.

9. For analyses of Gotō's ideas on colonial governance, see Mizobe Hideaki, "Gotō Shimpei ron," *Hōgaku ronsō* 100, no. 2 (1976): 62–96; Nakamura Akira, "'Nihon shokuminchi seisaku ippan' kaidai," in *Nihon shokuminchi seisaku ippan*, ed. Nakamura Akira (Tokyo, 1944), 8–10.

10. Gotō demonstrated particular interest in the German effort to assimilate the French-speaking population of Alsace-Lorraine, as he viewed this case as being the closest parallel to the pursuit of assimilation in Taiwan. See "Doitsu ryōyū zengo no Eruzasu-Rōtoringen" [Alsace-Lorraine before and after Germany's possession], in Gotō Shimpei monjo, reel 31, no. 7–76 (Mizusawa Shiritsu Gotō Shimpei Kinenkan, Iwate, JP).

11. Gotō Shimpei, *Nihon shokuminchi ron* (Tokyo, 1915).

12. Tsurumi Yūsuke, *Seiden Gotō Shimpei*, vol. 3, ed. Ikkai Tomoyoshi (Tokyo, 2004), 52. For further elaboration of this perspective in Japanese colonial policy, see Ching, *Becoming "Japanese."*

13. Quoted in Tsurumi, *Seiden Gotō Shimpei*, vol. 3, 39.

14. Quoted in Tsurumi, *Seiden Gotō Shimpei*, vol. 3, 45.

15. This argument is presented most thoroughly by Okamatsu Santrō, who advised Gotō on legal matters and led the GGT's effort to collect information on Taiwanese customary law. See Okamatsu Santrō, "Taiwan no seido ni kansuru ikensho [Opinion paper concerning Taiwan's system]," 1901, in Gotō Shimpei monjo, reel 25, no. 7–38; Okamatsu Santrō, "Nippon minpō no ketten wo ronji te Taiwan rippō ni taisuru kibō ni oyobu," *Taiwan kanshū kiji* 5, no. 3 (1905): 13–26.

16. Ishizuka Eizō, "Kokumin-teki seizonkyōsō oyobi dōka zetsumetsu," *Taiwan Kyōkai kaihō* 27 (1900): 1–10; Gotō Shimpei, "Gotō Chōkan no kunji," *Taiwan Kyōikukai zasshi* 27 (1904): 2–3; Mochiji Rokusaburō, "Kenchi kanken [My humble opinion on provincial governance]," in Gotō Shimpei monjo, reel 31, no. 7.73. For an analysis of education policy under the Gotō administration, see Chen, *"Dōka" no dōshō imu*, 73–97.

17. This undertaking was led by Nakamura Zekō, who later became the president of the South Manchurian Railway Company (Mantetsu). For the official English translation of the report that came out of this early effort to understand Taiwanese customs, see Taiwan, Committee of the Formosan Special Census Investigation, *The Special Population Census of Formosa, 1905* (Tokyo, 1909).

18. Haruyama Meitetsu, "Hōgaku Hakase Okamatsu Santarō," *Taiwan kingendaishi kenkyū* 6 (1988): 197–216; Timothy Tsu, "Japanese Colonialism and the Investigation of the Taiwanese," in *Anthropology and Colonialism in Asia and Oceania*, ed. Jan van Bremen and Akitoshi Shimizu (Surrey, UK, 1999), 201–8.

19. Haruyama Meitetsu, "Taiwan kyūkan chōsa to rippō kōsō," *Taiwan kingendaishi kenkyū* 6 (1988): 81–114; Tsu, "Japanese Colonialism and the Investigation of the Taiwanese," 203–11.

20. This began in earnest in the 1920s during the administration of Prime Minister Hara Takashi, who had advocated the pursuit of dōka and naichi enchō shugi as vice foreign minister in 1895 and again as home minister in 1906. Now that he was prime minister, he could finally implement his long-standing policy of administratively, politically, and culturally assimilating Taiwan into the Japanese nation-state. For Hara's 1895 position paper on Taiwan, see Hara Takashi, "Taiwan mondai nian [Two proposals for the Taiwan problem]," in *Taiwan shiryō*, ed. Kaneko Kentarō (Tokyo, 1970[1896]), 32–34. See also Haruyama Meitetsu, "Kindai Nihon no shokuminchi tōchi to Hara Kei," in *Nihon shokuminchi shugi no seiji-teki tenkai*, ed. Haruyama Meitetsu and Wakabayashi Masahiro (Tokyo, 1980), 1–75; Haruyama Meitetsu, "Meiji kenpō taisei to Taiwan tōchi," in *Iwanami kōza kindai Nihon to shokuminchi*, vol. 4, ed. Ōe Shinobu (Tokyo, 1993), 31–50.

21. Tay-sheng Wang, *Legal Reform in Taiwan under Japanese Colonial Rule* (Seattle, 2000), 140–45.

22. On notions of good government and the rightful responsibilities of the state in Qing China, see Robert Antony and Jane Leonard, eds., *Dragons, Tigers, and Dogs* (Ithaca, 2002); Susan Mann, *Local Merchants and the Chinese Bureaucracy* (Stanford, 1986).

23. Lee Shinn-cherng, "Qing dai yi lan de 'baojia' yu 'qingzhuanglianjia' zhi yan jiu," *Xing da ren wen xue bao* 43 (2009): 219–55.

24. Mark Allee, *Law and Local Society in Late Imperial China* (Stanford, 1994), 197–98; Lee, "Qing dai yi lan de 'baojia' yu 'qingzhuanglianjia' zhi yan jiu."

25. Johanna Meskill, *A Chinese Pioneer Family* (Princeton, 1979), 86–87.

26. Inō Yoshinori, *Taiwan bunka shi*, vol. 1 (Tokyo, 1928), 751.

27. John Shepherd, *Statecraft and Political Economy on the Taiwan Frontier* (Stanford, 1993).

28. Although the Hakka, who migrated to Taiwan from Guangdong, remained a relatively cohesive group, at least in terms of ethnic self-identification, the Hokkienese from Fujian were divided between those from Quanzhou and Zhangzhou. Quanzhou migrants were further subdivided into ethnic categories of Anxi, Tongan, and Sanyi. Stevan Harrell, "From *Xiedou* to *Yijun*, the Decline of Ethnicity in Northern Taiwan," *Late Imperial China* 11, no. 1 (1990): 110.

29. Allee, *Law and Local Society in Late Imperial China*, 31–51; Chiukun Chen, "From Landlords to Local Strongmen," in *Taiwan*, ed. Murray Rubinstein (New York, 2007); Harrell, "From *Xiedou* to *Yijun*"; Harry Lamley, "Subethnic Rivalry in the Ch'ing Period," in *The Anthropology of Taiwanese Society*, ed. Emily Martin Ahern and Hill Gates (Stanford, 1981), 282–318.

30. Allee, *Law and Local Society in Late Imperial China*, 196–215.

31. Allee, *Law and Local Society in Late Imperial China*, 196–215; Chen, "From Landlords to Local Strongmen"; Lee, "Qing dai yi lan de 'baojia' yu 'qingzhuanglianjia' zhi yan jiu"; Meskill, *A Chinese Pioneer Family*, 117–34.

32. Robert Gardella, "From Treaty Ports to Provincial Status," in *Taiwan*, ed. Murray Rubinstein (New York, 2007); Harry Lamley, "The Taiwan Literati and Early Japanese Rule" (PhD diss., University of Washington, 1964), 101–32; Ramon Myers, "Taiwan under Ch'ing Imperial Rule," *Journal of the Institute of Chinese Studies of the Chinese University of Hong Kong* 4, no. 2 (1971): 495–520.

33. Lamley, "The Taiwan Literati and Early Japanese Rule," 101–32; Meskill, *A Chinese Pioneer Family*, 179–98.

34. See chapter 1 on Lin Wencha's exploits.

35. Meskill, *A Chinese Pioneer Family*, 135–54.

36. Lamley, "The Taiwan Literati and Early Japanese Rule," 101–32; Li Wen-liang, "Wan qing tai wan qing fu shi ye de zai kao cha," *Han xue yan jiu* 24 (2006): 387–416; Meskill, *A Chinese Pioneer Family*, 179–98; William Speidel, "The Administrative and Fiscal Reforms of Liu Ming-ch'uan in Taiwan," *Journal of Asian Studies* 35, no. 3 (1976): 441–59.

37. Harumi Befu, "Village Autonomy and Articulation with the State," *Journal of Asian Studies* 25, no. 1 (1965): 19–32; Philip Brown, *Formation of Early Modern Japan* (Stanford, 1993); Herman Ooms, *Tokugawa Village Practice* (Berkeley, 1996); Thomas Smith, "The Japanese Village in the Seventeenth Century," *Journal of Economic History* 12, no. 1 (1952): 1–20.

38. Gotō Shimpei, "Taiwan tōchi kyūkyū an [A proposal for the rehabilitation of the Taiwan administration]," 1898, in Gotō Shimpei monjo, reel 12, no. 4.33; Tsurumi, *Seiden Gotō Shimpei*, 194.

39. The text of the 1898 Hokō Bylaw can be found in Tsurumi, *Seiden Gotō Shimpei*, vol. 3, 194.

40. Hung Chiu-fen, "Ri ju chu qi tai wan de bao jia zhi du," *Jin dai shi yan jiu suo ji kan* 21 (1991): 437–71; Mochiji Rokusaburō, *Taiwan shokumin seisaku* (Tokyo, 1912), 75–76; Suzuki Masuhito, "Taiwan no hokō seido," pt. 1, *Toshi mondai* 39.5/6 (1944), 7–9; Hui-yu Caroline Ts'ai, "One Kind of Control" (PhD diss., Columbia University, 1990), 66–86; Hui-yu Caroline Ts'ai, *Taiwan in Japan's Empire Building* (London, 2009), 98–105; Yoshihara Jōji, *Nihon tōchika Taiwan keisatsu seido oyobi hokō seido nōto* (Tokyo, 1998), 62–73.

41. Ching-chih Chen, "Japanese Socio-political Control in Taiwan" (PhD diss., Harvard University, 1973), 218–32; Hung, "Ri ju chu qi tai wan de bao jia zhi du"; Suzuki, "Taiwan no hokō seido," pt. 2, 30; Ts'ai, *Taiwan in Japan's Empire Building*, 105–8; Washinosu Atsuya, *Taiwan hokō kōminka dokuhon* (Tokyo, 2000[1941]), 106–13.

42. Hung, "Ri ju chu qi tai wan de bao jia zhi du."

43. On the importance of impartiality in inducing compliance, see Bo Rothstein, *The Quality of Government* (Chicago, 2011).

44. For a full list of issues typically covered in a *hokō* code and thus subject to such fines, see Yoshihara, *Nihon tōchika Taiwan keisatsu seido oyobi hokō seido nōto*, 74–76.

45. Hung, "Ri ju chu qi tai wan de bao jia zhi du"; Ts'ai, "One Kind of Control," 93–94; Ts'ai, *Taiwan in Japan's Empire Building*, 99–102; Wang, *Legal Reform in Taiwan under Japanese Colonial Rule*, 135–36; Washinosu, *Taiwan hokō kōminka dokuhon*, 107.

46. Chen, "Japanese Socio-political Control in Taiwan," 208–9, 227, 257–59.

47. Hung, "Ri ju chu qi tai wan de bao jia zhi du."

48. Hung, "Ri ju chu qi tai wan de bao jia zhi du"; Ts'ai, "One Kind of Control," 85–86.

49. Ts'ai, "One Kind of Control," 85–86, 94–95; Ts'ai, *Taiwan in Japan's Empire Building*, 104–5.

50. Ts'ai, *Taiwan in Japan's Empire Building*, 98–99, 102–8.

51. Hung, "Ri ju chu qi tai wan de bao jia zhi du"; Ts'ai, "One Kind of Control," 85–86, 229–35.

52. Ts'ai Hui-yu, "Baozheng, baojia shu ji, jiezhuangyichang-kou shu li shi," *Tai wan yan jiu shi* 2, no. 2 (1995): 187–214.

53. Hung Chiu-fen, "Ri zhi shi qi zhi min zheng fu he di fang zong jiao xin yang zhong xin guan xi zhi tan tao," *Si yu yan: ren wen yu she hui ke xue za zhi* 42, no. 2 (2004): 1–41.

54. Chen, "Japanese Socio-political Control in Taiwan," 284; Ts'ai, "Baozheng, baojia shu ji, jiezhuangyichang-kou shu li shi"; Ts'ai, *Taiwan in Japan's Empire Building*, 137–38.

55. Yosaburō Takekoshi, *Japanese Rule in Formosa*, trans. George Braithwaite (New York, 1907), 128.

56. Takekoshi, *Japanese Rule in Formosa*, 128.

57. Takekoshi, *Japanese Rule in Formosa*, 129.

58. Takekoshi, *Japanese Rule in Formosa*, 129.

59. Ts'ai, *Taiwan in Japan's Empire Building*, 125; Tsai Lung-pao, "Ri zhi chu qi tai wan zong du fu de ji shu ren li zhi zhao mu," *Guo li zheng zhi da xue shi xue bao* 35 (2011): 75–143; Jen-to Yao, "The Japanese Colonial State and Its Forms of Knowledge in Taiwan," in *Taiwan under Japanese Colonial Rule*, ed. Ping-hui Liao and David Der-wei Wang (New York, 2006), 47–52.

60. Chiang Ping-k'un, *Taiwan chiso kaisei no kenkyū* (Tokyo, 1974), 155–65.

61. Taiwan, Committee of the Formosan Special Census Investigation, *The Special Population Census of Formosa, 1905*; Yao, "The Japanese Colonial State," 52–56.

62. Meguro Gorō, *Genkō hokō seido sōsho* (Taichū [Taichung], 1936), 21–22; Jen-to Yao, "Governing the Colonised" (PhD diss., University of Essex, 2002), 259–62.

63. Ts'ai, "One Kind of Control," 236–39, 378–82; Yao "Governing the Colonised," 254–55.

64. Ts'ai, "One Kind of Control," 335–42; Tsai Lung-pao, "Ri zhi shi qi tai wan dao lu shi ye de tui jin," *Guo shi guan xue shu ji kan* 6 (2005): 61–108; Tsai Lung-pao, "Ri zhi chu qi tai wan de dao lu shi ye," *Guo shi guan xue shu qi kan* 7 (2006): 85–129.

65. Ting Wen-hui, "Tai wan ri zhi shi qi nue ji fang zhi zhi tui xing," *Ren wen yan jiu xue bao* 42, no. 2 (2008): 75–89; Suzuki Tetsuzō, "Ri zhi chu nian tai wan wei sheng zheng ce zhi zhan kai," *Tai wan shi da li shi xue bao* 37 (2007): 143–80; Ts'ai, *Taiwan in Japan's Empire Building*, 108–113.

66. Ts'ai, *Taiwan in Japan's Empire Building*, 108–13; Joseph Wicentowski, "Policing Health in Modern Taiwan" (PhD diss., Harvard University, 2007), 54–65; Yao, "Governing the Colonised," 118–28.

67. Hsu, "Zhi min zheng quan dui tai wan min jian zi zhu xing de fang ren yu shou bian"; Miao, "Cong tian ran zu hui dao jie chan hui"; Ts'ai, *Taiwan in Japan's Empire Building*, 114–17, 128–36; Hui-yu Caroline Ts'ai, "Engineering the Social or Engaging 'Everyday Modernity'?" in *Becoming Taiwan*, ed. Ann Heylen and Scott Sommers (Wiesbaden, DE, 2010), 83–100.

68. Yao, "Governing the Colonised," in particular, adopts an explicitly Foucauldian approach in his analysis of hokō. Although Ts'ai presents a much more complex and multidimensional analysis of hokō in her various works, her theoretical analysis, expressed most clearly in *Taiwan in Japan's Empire Building*, borrows heavily from Michel Foucault.

69. Wicentowski, "Policing Health in Modern Taiwan," 69–74.

70. Hung, "Ri zhi shi qi zhi min zheng fu he di fang zong jiao xin yang zhong xin guan xi zhi tan tao."

71. Ts'ai, "One Kind of Control," 127–76.

72. This is not to deny the existence of various cultural associations that emerged in the 1920s and 1930s that sought to articulate the meaning of being Taiwanese, as opposed to Chinese or Japanese. Membership in these associations, however, did not go beyond the small group of Taiwanese professionals and intellectuals. Rwei-ren Wu, "The Formosan Ideology" (PhD diss., University of Chicago, 2003).

73. Peter Duus and Daniel Okimoto, "Fascism and the History of Pre-War Japan," *Journal of Asian Studies* 39, no. 1 (1979): 65–76; Janis Mimura, *Reform Bureaucrats and the Japanese Wartime State* (Ithaca, 2011). For a portrayal of Japan's cultural transformation during this period, see Louise Young, *Japan's Total Empire* (Berkeley, 1998).

74. Ching, *Becoming "Japanese"*; Wan-yao Chou, "The 'Kōminka' Movement" (PhD diss., Yale University, 1991).

75. For analyses of the characteristics of government-administered mass organizations and their development in Japan in the 1930s, see Gregory Kasza, *The Conscription Society* (New Haven, 1995).

76. Ts'ai, "One Kind of Control," 452–56, 485–91.

77. Ts'ai, "One Kind of Control," 456–66, 493–513; Suzuki, "Taiwan no hokō seido," pt. 2, 34–36.

78. For recent articulations of this narrative, see Daron Acemoglu and James Robinson, *Why Nations Fail* (New York, 2012); Timothy Besley and Torsten Persson, *Pillars of Prosperity* (Princeton, 2011); Roland Paris, "Saving Liberal Peacebuilding," *Review of International Studies* 36 (2010): 337–65.

5. THE AMERICAN WAY

1. This question is inspired by Jason Brownlee's review essay on the topic: Jason Brownlee, "Can America Nation-Build?" *World Politics* 59, no. 2 (2007): 314–40.

2. Here, it is important to note the difference between statebuilding and the rebuilding of a strong and modern state that has been destroyed by war. On this point, see S. C. M. Paine, "Introduction," in *Nation Building, State Building, and Economic Development*, ed. S. C. M. Paine (New York, 2010), 8.

3. Julius Pratt, *Expansionists of 1898* (Baltimore, 1936).

4. Religious symbolism was ubiquitous throughout the debate on the Philippine Islands given that the late nineteenth century was a time of Christian revival in America. Gerald Anderson, "Providence and Politics behind Protestant Missionary Beginnings in the Philippines," in *Studies in Philippine Church History*, ed. Gerald Anderson (Ithaca, 1969), 279–300; Kenton Clymer, *Protestant Missionaries in the Philippines* (Urbana, Il, 1986).

5. Pratt, *Expansionists of 1898*.

6. Brian Linn, *The Philippine War* (Lawrence, KS, 2000), 26–41.

7. Robert Beisner, *Twelve Against Empire* (New York, 1968); E. Berkeley Tompkins, *Anti-Imperialism in the United States* (Philadelphia, 1970).

8. Senator Hoar on acquisition of territory, U.S. Senate, *Congressional Record*, 55th Cong., 3d sess. (January 9, 1899), 494. For his entire argument, see 493–502.

9. Senator Hoar on acquisition of territory, 495.

10. Paul Kramer, *The Blood of Government* (Chapel Hill, NC, 2006), 117–19; Stuart Miller, *"Benevolent Assimilation"* (New Haven, 1982), 124–25.

11. Beisner, *Twelve against Empire*, 22–23.

12. Senator Tillman on policy regarding the Philippine Islands, U.S. Senate, *Congressional Record*, 55th Cong., 3d sess. (February 7, 1899), 1532. For his entire argument, see 1529–33.

13. Senator Hoar on acquisition of territory, U.S. Senate, *Congressional Record*, 55th Cong., 3d sess. (January 9, 1899), 501. For his entire argument, see 493–502.

14. Quoted in Tompkins, *Anti-Imperialism in the United States*, 124.

15. Quoted in Beisner, *Twelve against Empire*, 44.

16. This argument, although presented by various Republican senators, was most clearly articulated by Orville Platt of Connecticut. See Senator Platt on acquisition of territory, U.S. Senate, *Congressional Record*, 55th Cong., 3d sess. (December 19, 1898), 287–97.

17. Senator Platt on acquisition of territory, U.S. Senate, *Congressional Record*, 55th Cong., 3d sess. (January 9, 1899), 502.

18. Senator Teller on acquisition of territory, U.S. Senate, *Congressional Record,* 55th Cong., 3d sess. (December 20, 1898), 328. For his entire argument, see 325–30.

19. John Foreman, "Spain and the Philippine Islands," *Contemporary Review* 74 (1898): 29–30; Senator Platt on acquisition of territory, U.S. Senate, *Congressional Record,* 55th Cong., 3d sess. (January 9, 1899), 502–03.

20. William McKinley, "Speech at Dinner of the Home Market Club, 16 February 1899," in *Speeches and Addresses of William McKinley* (New York, 1900), 192.

21. The so-called benevolent assimilation proclamation was delivered by President McKinley as an executive order to the Secretary of War on December 21, 1898. The order may be found in James Richardson, *A Compilation of the Messages and Papers of the President,* vol. 10 (Washington, DC, 1899), 219–21.

22. This was certainly not the first time the U.S. government sought to impose its institutions onto conquered peoples. However, unlike past instances of institutional imposition, such as those pursued against the Native American populations and the Southern states during Reconstruction, the Philippine occupation entailed the establishment of the entire machinery of government.

23. Kenneth Hendrickson Jr., "Reluctant Expansionist," *Pacific Historical Review* 36, no. 4 (1967): 405–21. An account of the activities of the Schurman Commission is described in detail by Dean Worcester in letters to his wife. See Dean C. Worcester Papers, vol. 16 (Special Collections Library, University of Michigan, Ann Arbor).

24. Dean Worcester, *The Philippines Past and Present,* ed. Joseph Hayden (New York, 1930), 253–68. American and European businessmen and professionals living in the Philippines also served as key witnesses in the compilation of the commission's report.

25. Jacob Schurman et al., *Report of the Philippine Commission,* vol. 2 (Washington, DC, 1900), 67–70.

26. Schurman, *Report of the Philippine Commission,* vol. 1, 85.

27. Schurman, *Report of the Philippine Commission,* vol. 1, 61–62.

28. Schurman, *Report of the Philippine Commission,* vol. 1, 97–99.

29. For an example of Otis's optimistic reports, see Elwell Otis to Henry Corbin, June 26, 1899, Dean C. Worcester Papers, vol. 17, Folder p. 124–163 (Special Collections Library).

30. Linn, *The Philippine War,* 160–81.

31. William Howard Taft to Elihu Root, July 14, 1900, William Howard Taft Papers, reel 640 (Library of Congress, Washington, DC). The actual author of the "Instructions" was Elihu Root, and for the duration of his tenure as secretary of war, he kept a close eye over the progress of the statebuilding mission in the Philippines, as seen by Taft's near-weekly reports to Root. For these reports, see William Howard Taft Papers, reel 640.

32. John Gates, *Schoolbooks and Krags* (Westport, CT, 1973), 108–12; Linn, *The Philippine War,* 30–31, 139–59; Kenneth Young, *The General's General* (Boulder, CO, 1994), 249–50.

33. Arthur MacArthur, *Annual Report of Major General Arthur MacArthur, 1900,* vol. 1 (Washington, DC, 1900), 1–21; John Gates, "Philippine Guerillas, American Anti-imperialists, and the Election of 1900," *Pacific Historical Review* 46, no. 1 (1977): 58–59; Linn, *The Philippine War,* 187, 209–11; Young, *The General's General,* 265–66.

34. MacArthur, *Annual Report,* vol. 1, 5–6. This assessment was largely based on Lt. William Johnston's May 21, 1900, report titled "Investigation into the Methods Adopted by the Insurgents for Organizing and Maintaining a Guerrilla Force." For a discussion of this report, see Brian Linn, *The U.S. Army and Counterinsurgency in the Philippine War* (Chapel Hill, NC, 1989), 40–43, 124–26.

35. Linn, *U.S. Army and Counterinsurgency in the Philippine War,* 42–61. For the full text of the December 20, 1900, proclamation, see Arthur MacArthur, *Annual Report of Major General Arthur MacArthur, 1901,* vol. 1 (Washington, DC, 1901), 6–9.

36. Gates, *Schoolbooks and Krags*, 204–11; Henry Graff, ed., *American Imperialism and the Philippine Insurrection Testimony* (Boston, 1969), 64–134; Linn, *The U.S. Army and Counterinsurgency in the Philippine War*, 143–47; Linn, *The Philippine War*, 208–16; Young, *The General's General*, 280–81. For documents pertaining to MacArthur's plan for organizing local policing under the auspices of the U.S. military, see War Department, Bureau of Insular Affairs, RG 350, General Files 1898–1914, box 173, number 1184, entry 5 (National Archives and Records Administration, College Park, MD).

37. Gates, *Schoolbooks and Krags*, 206–11; Linn, *U.S. Army and Counterinsurgency in the Philippine War*, 57–60, 152–61; Glenn Anthony May, *Battle for Batangas* (New Haven, 1991), 242–69.

38. Patricio Abinales, "Progressive-Machine Conflict in Early-Twentieth-Century U.S. Politics and Colonial-State Building in the Philippines," in *The American Colonial State in the Philippines*, ed. Julian Go and Anne Foster (Durham, NC, 2003), 148–81.

39. United States, Senate Committee on the Philippines, *Affairs in the Philippine Islands* (Washington, DC, 1902), 3–67; Michael Cullinane, *Ilustrado Politics* (Quezon City, PH, 2003), 66–72; James LeRoy to Harry Coleman, February 8, 1901, James Alfred LeRoy Papers, box 1 (Bentley Historical Library, University of Michigan, Ann Arbor); Peter Stanley, *A Nation in the Making* (Cambridge, MA, 1974), 68–72.

40. Taft was himself a product of the powerful Ohio-based Republican patronage network. See Abinales, "Progressive-Machine Conflict."

41. Senator George Vest (Democrat from Missouri) most prominently noted how strange it was that if U.S. forces were in the Philippines as liberators and emancipators, the president would need "100,000 missionaries with rifles to shoot his good resolution into effect." Quotation found in "Senate for Army Increase," *New York Times*, February 28, 1899.

42. MacArthur, *Annual Report, 1901*, vol. 1, 77–85.

43. Linn, *The Philippine War*, 310–21; Linn, *U.S. Army and Counterinsurgency in the Philippine War*, 59–61, 148–61; May, *Battle for Batangas*, 242–69; Resil Mojares, *War Against the Americans* (Quezon City, PH, 1999), 5–16; Norman Owen, "Winding Down the War in Albay," *Pacific Historical Review* 48, no. 4 (1979): 566; Young, *The General's General*, 286–88.

44. Kramer, *The Blood of Government*, 157. This figure does not include the countless Filipino civilian deaths.

45. Philip Jessup, *Elihu Root*, vol. 1 (New York, 1939), 345.

46. Jessup, *Elihu Root*, vol. 1, 345.

47. His views on government are most clearly presented in Elihu Root, *Experiments in Government and the Essentials of the Constitution* (Princeton, 1913).

48. "Instructions of the President to the Philippine Commission, April 7, 1900." A digital copy can be found at University of Michigan Library's Southeast Asia collection: https://quod.lib.umich.edu/p/philamer/ACQ0871.0001.001.

49. "Instructions of the President to the Philippine Commission," 5–6.

50. "Instructions of the President to the Philippine Commission," 9. In his 1900 annual report, Root discusses the creation of a new court system as the most important undertaking of the Philippine Commission during its first year. See Elihu Root, *The Military and Colonial Policy of the United States*, ed. Robert Bacon and James Scott (Cambridge, MA, 1916), 241.

51. "Instructions of the President to the Philippine Commission," 9.

52. "Instructions of the President to the Philippine Commission," 9.

53. On this point, see also Schurman et al., *Report of the Philippine Commission*, vol. 1, 17.

54. Atkinson was recommended to Taft by Charles Eliot, President of Harvard University, whom Taft coincidentally met on the train ride from Washington to Boston on

March 1, 1900. Glenn Anthony May, *Social Engineering in the Philippines* (Westport, CT, 1980), 80.

55. May, *Social Engineering in the Philippines*, 78–96; Peter Tarr, "The Education of the Thomasites," vol. 1 (PhD diss., Cornell University, 2006), 159–209.

56. W. Cameron Forbes, *The Philippine Islands*, vol. 1 (Boston, 1928), 292–314; Worcester, *The Philippines Past and Present*, 323–28. For a list of judicial appointments in 1901, see United States, Department of War, *Public Laws and Resolutions Passed by the United States Philippine Commission, 1901* (Washington, DC, 1901), 737–46.

57. Enrique Altavás, *Land Registration in the Philippine Islands* (Manila, 1923); Forbes, *The Philippine Islands*, vol. 1, 314–22; Frank Sherman, *What's Wrong with the Lands Bureau?* (Manila, 1929), 6–9. For a firsthand account of the failures of the 1902 system, see D. R. Williams to Taft, January 17, 1905, William Howard Taft Papers, reel 48.

58. United States, Department of War, *Public Laws and Resolutions Passed by the Philippine Commission, 1901*, 133–67.

59. Benedict Anderson, "Cacique Democracy and the Philippines," *New Left Review* 169 (1988): 3–31; Michael Cullinane, "Implementing the 'New Order,'" in *Compadre Colonialism*, ed. Norman Owen (Ann Arbor, MI, 1971), 24; Henry Willis, *Our Philippine Problem* (New York, 1905), 74–75.

60. United States, Department of War, *Public Laws and Resolutions Passed by the Philippine Commission, 1901*, 145–47.

61. Frank Goodnow, *Politics and Administration* (New York, 1900); Woodrow Wilson, "The Study of Administration," *Political Science Quarterly* 2, no. 2 (1887): 197–222.

62. United States, Department of War, *Public Laws and Resolutions Passed by the Philippine Commission, 1901*, 15.

63. United States, Department of War, *Public Laws and Resolutions Passed by the Philippine Commission, 1901*, 14–20; Onofre Corpuz, *The Bureaucracy in the Philippines* (Quezon City, PH, 1957), 164–68.

64. Corpuz, *The Bureaucracy in the Philippines*, 182–83, 195–213.

65. Bruce Cumings, "Colonial Formations and Deformations," in *Parallax Visions*, ed. Bruce Cumings (Durham, NC, 1999), 69–94; Atul Kohli, *State-Directed Development* (New York, 2004).

66. Philippines, Commissioner of Civil Service, *First Annual Report of the Commissioner of Civil Service, 1936* (Manila, 1937); Okamoto Makiko, *Shokuminchi kanryō no seiji shi* (Tokyo, 2008), 51, 60.

67. Philippines, Board of Educational Survey, *A Survey of the Educational System of the Philippine Islands* (Manila, 1925), 521–27.

68. "Instructions of the President to the Philippine Commission," 8–9.

69. Joseph Hayden, *The Philippines* (New York, 1942), 284.

70. United States, Department of War, *Annual Report of the Philippine Commission, 1905*, pt. I (Washington, DC, 1906), 178. Henceforth, RPC. See also, Hayden, *The Philippines*, 265–66; RPC, 1901, pt. 1, 9–10. As W. Cameron Forbes, who would join the commission in 1904 as secretary of commerce and police, explained to his friend Lloyd Griscom, this right by the governor-general to remove a municipal president was rarely exercised in practice. Forbes to Griscom, May 7, 1906, W. Cameron Forbes Papers, Outgoing Correspondences, vol. 4 (Houghton Library, Harvard University, Cambridge, MA).

71. Hayden, *The Philippines*, 284.

72. United States, Department of War, *Public Laws and Resolutions Passed by the Philippine Commission, 1901*, 168–77.

73. For example, Harry Bandholtz, who was the second in command of the Philippine Constabulary at the time, wrote to E. E. Garnett, treasurer of Tayabas: "It will be up to

you to keep careful watch on [Governor] Quezon to prevent his ear running away with his head. He oozes good intentions from every pore and his main defect is youth which is more than counterbalanced by his great mental capacity. He has a high opinion of you, and between [Supervisor] Muerman and yourself on the [Provincial] Board and Colonel Harbord in the [Second Constabulary] District, I predict for Tayabas a prosperous and progressive two years of government." Bandholtz to Garnett, February 27, 1906, Harry H. Bandholtz Papers, reel 1 (Bentley Historical Library, University of Michigan, Ann Arbor).

74. For details on the organization of the provincial government, see "A general act for the organization of provincial governments in the Philippine Islands," enacted on February 6, 1901, in United States, Department of War, *Public Laws and Resolutions Passed by the Philippine Commission, 1901*, 168–77.

75. RPC, 1905, pt. I, 178.

76. Philippines, Civil Service Board, *Fourth Annual Report of the Philippine Civil Service Board, 1904* (Manila, 1904), 76–87.

77. Cullinane, "Implementing the 'New Order'," 23.

78. RPC, 1904, pt. I, 341.

79. Hayden, *The Philippines*, 272.

80. Philippines, Executive Bureau, *Annual Report of the Executive Secretary of the Philippine Islands, July 1, 1905, to June 30, 1906* (Manila, 1906), 9–10.

81. Hayden, *The Philippines*, 272–73.

82. Paul Hutchcroft, "Colonial Masters, National Politicos, and Provincial Lords," *Journal of Asian Studies* 59, no. 2 (2000): 287; RPC, 1904, pt. I, 312; RPC, 1913, 77.

83. Cullinane, "Implementing the 'New Order'," 26–27.

84. For example, see Hayden's discussion of politics in Nueva Ecija in Hayden, *The Philippines*, 278–79.

85. Hayden, *The Philippines*, 275.

86. Cullinane, "Implementing the 'New Order'," 28.

87. Cullinane, *Ilustrado Politics*, 97–111, 143–244; Stanley, *A Nation in the Making*.

88. Cullinane, *Ilustrado Politics*, 153–67; Hayden, *The Philippines*, 285; Alfred McCoy, *Policing America's Empire* (Madison, WI, 2009), 142–48. A less well-known example of Constabulary intervention in gubernatorial elections occurred in Albay in 1904. In this case, members of the Philippine Commission, along with most Americans in Albay, supported one of the two Americans who ran for governor against Ramón Santos, the eventual victor. Harry Bandholtz, the Constabulary district commander, secretly supported Santos, however, to reward him for his help in capturing insurgent leader Simeón Ola the previous year. Willis, *Our Philippine Problem*, 140–42.

89. See Edgar Bellairs, *As It Is in the Philippines* (New York, 1902), 109–51, for Amzi Kelly's account of how he was dismissed from his position as treasurer of Nueva Ecija by Taft for attempting to bring to light the corrupt behaviors of the provincial governor. In another example, Captain John Swann, the provincial head of the Philippine Constabulary in Albay, was transferred to Sorsogon after falling out with the provincial governor. Learning from his mistakes in Albay, Swann later happily reported how he helped reelect Governor Monreals of Sorsogon in 1906, thus cementing his collaborative ties with the governor. Bandholtz to Santos, June 19, 1905, and Swann to Bandholtz, February 6, 1906, Harry H. Bandholtz Papers, reel 1.

90. Cullinane, *Ilustrado Politics*, 163.

91. McCoy, *Policing America's Empire*, 132–36; David Sturtevant, *Popular Uprisings in the Philippines* (Ithaca, 1976), 127–31.

92. Sturtevant, *Popular Uprisings in the Philippines*, 121–25.

93. On the concept of critical juncture, see Giovanni Capoccia and R. Daniel Kelemen, "The Study of Critical Junctures," *World Politics* 59, no. 3 (2007): 341–69; Hillel Soifer,

"The Causal Logic of Critical Junctures," *Comparative Political Studies* 45, no. 12 (2012): 1572–97.

6. STATE INVOLUTION

1. From 1900 to 1907, the Philippine Commission was the sole legislative body in the colony. After the Philippine Assembly was formed in 1907, until its displacement by the Philippine Senate in 1916, it would serve as the more powerful upper legislative chamber with the power to veto any legislation put forth by the assembly.

2. Quotation found in Glenn Anthony May, *Social Engineering in the Philippines* (Westport, CT, 1980), 41. Taft's speech during a public session of the Philippine Commission was originally published in the *Manila Times* on January 31, 1901.

3. United States, Department of War, *Annual Report of the Philippine Commission, 1903*, pt. I (Washington, DC, 1906), 84. Henceforth, RPC.

4. On the concept of state involution, see Prasenjit Duara, *Culture, Power, and the State* (Stanford, 1988), 73–77.

5. If local governments sought to fund other expenses via the land tax, provincial and municipal authorities were authorized to collect up to an additional 0.25 percent of property valuation in taxation for this purpose.

6. W. Cameron Forbes, *The Philippine Islands*, vol. 1 (Boston, 1928), 254–56; RPC, 1901, pt. I, 26–27.

7. For more on Filipino elite reception of American rule, see Julian Go, *American Empire and the Politics of Meaning* (Durham, NC, 2008), 93–130.

8. Difficulties in collecting land taxes were extensively reported by provincial governors in their annual reports. See, in particular, RPC, 1904, pt. I, 373; RPC, 1905, pt. I, 177, 215, 323, 364.

9. See Act No. 680 in United States, Department of War, *Acts of the Philippine Commission, 1903*, 437–38. Such pleas for leniency toward the landed elite came amid a net decrease in taxes collected from the wealthy under U.S. rule, as a result of the change in how the cédula was assessed: Rather than its rate increasing with one's wealth, as practiced by the Spanish, cédula became a flat one-peso tax. Overall, only 4.5 million pesos were collected in the 1902–03 fiscal year as opposed to 12 million pesos in the final year the archipelago was under Spanish control. Peter Stanley, *A Nation in the Making* (Cambridge, MA, 1974), 118.

10. An individual would have had to own property valued at over 266 pesos for the property tax to exceed the cédula. According to the assessment board's calculations, the average value of real estate in the Philippines was 154.27 pesos in 1908. RPC, 1908, pt. I, 76.

11. James LeRoy to Dean Worcester, August 3, 1906, James Alfred LeRoy Papers, Philippine Islands Folder, Correspondence 1904–1909 (Bentley Historical Library, University of Michigan, Ann Arbor).

12. RPC, 1904, pt. I, 373.

13. RPC, 1905, pt. I, 215,

14. RPC, 1903, pt. I, 83–84.

15. RPC, 1904, pt. I, 625, 672; RPC, 1905, pt. III, 74–79.

16. Forbes, *The Philippine Islands*, vol. 1, 167.

17. This reflected Secretary of War Elihu Root's strong beliefs on the issue of separation of church and state, as expressed in "Instructions of the President to the Philippine Commission, April 7, 1900." A digital copy can be found at University of Michigan Library's Southeast Asia collection: https://quod.lib.umich.edu/p/philamer/ACQ0871.0001.001.

18. These attitudes were reported by American school administrators across the archipelago. For their reports, see RPC, 1903, pt. III. See, in particular, 705–07, 730, 743, 763,

781, 799, 804, 811–12. See also, May, *Social Engineering in the Philippines*, 93–96; Peter Tarr, "The Education of the Thomasites," vol. 1 (PhD diss., Cornell University, 2006), 185–209.

19. Philippines, Census Office, *Census of the Philippine Islands: 1918*, vol. 4, pt. II (Manila, 1920–1921), 7.

20. Board of Educational Survey, *A Survey of the Educational System of the Philippine Islands* (Manila, 1925), 14–15.

21. Board of Educational Survey, *A Survey of the Educational System*, 561–608.

22. RPC, 103, pt. II, 105.

23. Reynaldo Ileto, "Cholera and the Origins of the American Sanitary Order in the Philippines," in *Imperial Medicine and Indigenous Societies*, ed. David Arnold (New York, 1988), 135.

24. Quoted in Ileto, "Cholera and the Origins of the American Sanitary Order in the Philippines," 139.

25. Ileto, "Cholera and the Origins of the American Sanitary Order in the Philippines," note 60.

26. Luke Wright to Elihu Root, July 20, 1902, Clarence Ransom Edwards Papers, box 2, folder 7 (Massachusetts Historical Society, Boston).

27. RPC, 1903, pt. II, 106.

28. RPC, 1903, pt. II, 106.

29. Ken De Bevoise, *Agents of Apocalypse* (Princeton, 1995), 96–97.

30. RPC, 1903, pt. II, 106.

31. RPC, 1903, pt. II, 105–06.

32. Dean Worcester, *A History of Asiatic Cholera in the Philippine Islands* (Manila, 1908), 130. Italics found in original text.

33. Worcester, *A History of Asiatic Cholera*, 94–95.

34. Quotation found in Ileto, "Cholera and the Origins of the American Sanitary Order in the Philippines," 134.

35. De Bevoise, *Agents of Apocalypse*, 180; Ileto, "Cholera and the Origins of the American Sanitary Order in the Philippines," 137–38.

36. De Bevoise, *Agents of Apocalypse*, 181; Ileto, "Cholera and the Origins of the American Sanitary Order in the Philippines," 136.

37. Quotation found in Warwick Anderson, *Colonial Pathologies* (Durham, NC, 2006), 68. This quotation comes from Trinidad Pardo de Tavera's letter to William Howard Taft. Tavera was a medical doctor by training and one of the three Filipinos on the Philippine Commission.

38. Ileto, "Cholera and the Origins of the American Sanitary Order in the Philippines," 134.

39. Ileto, "Cholera and the Origins of the American Sanitary Order in the Philippines," 140–41.

40. De Bevoise, *Agents of Apocalypse*, 182.

41. De Bevoise, *Agents of Apocalypse*, 183. See also, Ileto, "Cholera and the Origins of the American Sanitary Order in the Philippines," 140–42, for similar contrasts between municipalities that came under the direct control of centrally appointed American health inspectors and those that were allowed to manage the cholera epidemic largely through local efforts.

42. For data on the number of Americans in the Philippine service, see Onofre Corpuz, *The Bureaucracy in the Philippines* (Quezon City, PH, 1957), 183. For contrasting accounts of Wright's attitude toward Filipinos, see Stanley, *A Nation in the Making*, 117–18; Lewis Gleeck Jr., *The American Governors-General and High Commissioners in the Philippines* (Quezon City, PH, 1986), 33–57.

43. Henry Willis, *Our Philippine Problem* (New York, 1905), 80.

44. RPC, 1903, pt. I, 83. Whether this actually helped in improving the fiscal health of municipalities, and local governance more broadly, is a separate matter, however. For a critical assessment of this measure by Governor L. Karmany of Zambales, see RPC, 1904, pt. I, 674–75.

45. See Act No. 999 (enacted March 12, 1903) in United States, Department of War, *Acts of the Philippine Commission, 1904*, 43. Opinions on whether this would help matters diverged among Filipino governors. See RPC, 1904, pt. I, 373; RPC, 1905, pt. I, 365.

46. The new internal revenue law was highly controversial and one of the primary causes of the fallout between the American and Filipino members of the Philippine Commission in 1905 and the subsequent dismissal of Governor-General Wright. See Stanley, *A Nation in the Making*, 118–22.

47. See Act No. 1189 (enacted July 2, 1904) in United States, Department of War, *Acts of the Philippine Commission, 1904*, 319–69.

48. Act No. 1455 (enacted February 19, 1906) in United States, Department of War, *Acts of the Philippine Commission, 1906*, 125–31. On the work of the board, see RPC, 1906, pt. I, 102–04. When its investigation was completed in 1908, authorities found that the properties of some landowners had indeed been grossly overvalued, presumably for political reasons. In 1906, the average valuation of real estate in the entire archipelago was 195.63 pesos. In 1908, it decreased by nearly a quarter to 154.27 pesos. See RPC, 1908, pt. I, 76.

49. RPC, 1906, pt. I, 104–05; LeRoy to Worcester, August 3, 1906, James Alfred LeRoy Papers, Philippine Islands Folder, Correspondence 1904–1909.

50. Forbes, *The Philippine Islands*, vol. 1, 374.

51. Act No. 1652 (enacted May 18, 1907) in United States, Department of War, *Acts of the Philippine Commission, 1907*, 164–66. This act was initially written in such a way that provincial boards had to reauthorize the collection of the road tax every year. Act No. 1979 (enacted April 19, 1910) made the road tax, once adopted, permanent until repealed by the provincial board. See United States, Department of War, *Acts of the Philippine Commission, 1910*, 51–52.

52. Act No. 1688 (enacted August 17, 1907) and Act No. 1695 (enacted August 20, 1907) in United States, Department of War, *Acts of the Philippine Commission, 1907*, 289–94, 303–05.

53. "It was in the use of this part of the money," W. Cameron Forbes, the secretary of commerce and police at the time, explained, "that the general policies of the bureau found expression." Forbes, *The Philippine Islands*, vol. 1, 375. In particular, this was how the Bureau of Public Works compelled provincial boards to expend resources on the maintenance of existing roads, rather than on constructing new ones, even when the latter tended to generate greater local enthusiasm and political support. Forbes, *The Philippine Islands*, vol. 1, 375–78.

54. Anderson, *Colonial Pathologies*, 52. See also Worcester, *A History of Asiatic Cholera*.

55. Quotation by E. C. Carter, Director of the Bureau of Health, found in Anderson, *Colonial Pathologies*, 52.

56. Anderson, *Colonial Pathologies*, 70; Forbes, *The Philippine Islands*, vol. 1, 356. For a discussion of the sanitary inspectors, see Philippines, Philippine Health Service, *Report of the Philippine Health Service, 1924* (Manila, 1926), 29–31. For acts creating the sanitary district system, and discontinuing the previous health boards regime, see Act No. 1487 (enacted May 16, 1906) in United States, Department of War, *Acts of the Philippine Commission, 1906*, 230–34; Act No. 2156 (enacted February 6, 1912) in United States, Department of War, *Acts of the Philippine Commission, 1911–1912*, 121–24.

57. The activities of the health instructors are depicted with considerable detail in the *Report of the Philippine Health Service* between 1919 and 1921, when Vicente de Jesús, as Director of the Philippine Health Service, was responsible for its compilation.

58. On the Executive Bureau and its functions, see chapter 5.

59. See Act No. 676 (enacted March 12, 1903), Act No. 1691 (enacted August 20, 1907), and Act No. 2169 (enacted February 6, 1912) in United States, Department of War, *Acts of the Philippine Commission,* various volumes. On the increasing authority of the provincial governor, see Michael Cullinane, "Implementing the 'New Order,'" in *Compadre Colonialism,* ed. Norman Owen (Ann Arbor, 1971), 21–22.

60. Cullinane, "Implementing the 'New Order,'" 22–23.

61. Michael Cullinane, *Ilustrado Politics* (Quezon City, PH, 2003), 251–56. It was during this event that Sergio Osmeña of Cebu, who emerged as the young leader of the governors, met then Secretary of Commerce and Police W. Cameron Forbes for the first time to forge a political alliance that would prove highly valuable to both. Osmeña would become the first speaker of the Philippine Assembly in 1907, and Forbes was appointed governor-general in 1909 in large part thanks to Osmeña's support.

62. For examples of how Osmeña used his position to benefit his political allies and associates in Cebu as speaker of the Philippine Assembly, see John Sidel, *Capital, Coercion, and Crime* (Stanford, 1999), 133–36. On the corrupt lending practices of the Philippine National Bank, see Paul Hutchcroft, *Booty Capitalism* (Ithaca, 1998), 65–71; Stanley, *A Nation in the Making,* 239–48.

63. Cullinane, *Ilustrado Politics,* 256–85; Joseph Hayden, *The Philippines* (New York, 1942), 167–73. On the reason for the creation of the Philippine Assembly in 1907, see James Smith to William Howard Taft, October 7, 1907, Clarence Ransom Edwards Papers, box 7, folder 2.

64. For various examples of this dynamic, see Sidel, *Capital, Coercion, and Crime.*

65. RPC, 1905, pt. III, 74.

66. RPC, 1905, pt. III, 80.

67. A thorough discussion of the proposals contained within the Sheriff Bill can be found in Harry Bandholtz to Frank Carpenter, May 22, 1905, Harry H. Bandholtz Papers, reel 1 (Bentley Historical Library, University of Michigan, Ann Arbor).

68. Bandholtz to James Harbord, May 9, 1907, Harry H. Bandholtz Papers, reel 2.

69. Bandholtz to A. C. Carson, April 18, 1907, Harry H. Bandholtz Papers, reel 2; Forbes, *The Philippine Islands,* vol. 1, 232–33.

70. RPC, 1909, 137.

71. Emanuel Bajá, *Philippine Police System and Its Problems* (Manila, 1933), 533–37.

72. Pedro Espiritu, for example, upon becoming governor of Cavite in 1931, initiated a campaign to crack down on *jueteng* (an illegal numbers game). Yet, only presidentes who had opposed his candidacy were targeted by his special agents and forced to resign their posts. Espiritu's wealthy ally, Honorio Rojas—who was known as Cavite City's Jueteng King—was not investigated at all and with the governor's blessing used this opportunity to expand his operations. John Sidel, "Walking in the Shadow of the Big Man," in *An Anarchy of Families,* ed. Alfred McCoy (Madison, WI, 2009), 123.

73. Bajá, *Philippine Police System and Its Problems,* 532, 539–40; David Sturtevant, *Popular Uprisings in the Philippines* (Ithaca, 1976), 249–50.

74. Cullinane, *Ilustrado Politics,* 102–09; Stanley, *A Nation in the Making,* 117–23.

75. Wright to Bandholtz, January 22, 1909, Harry H. Bandholtz Papers, box 8.

76. Alfred McCoy, *Policing America's Empire* (Madison, WI, 2009), 132–38.

77. For a sampling of these letters, see Pardo de Tavera to Taft, February 7, 1905, William Howard Taft Papers, reel 48 (Library of Congress, Washington, DC); Legarda to Taft, February 28, 1905, William Howard Taft Papers, reel 48; Legarda to Taft, April 14, 1905,

William Howard Taft Papers, reel 49; Pardo de Tavera to Taft, April 17, 1905, Clarence Ransom Edwards Papers, box 5, folder 10; Legarda to Taft, April 27, 1905, Clarence Ransom Edwards Papers, box 5, folder 12; Pardo de Tavera to Taft, May 19, 1905, William Howard Taft Papers, reel 50.

78. Cullinane, *Ilustrado Politics*, 131–42; LeRoy to Worcester, August 3, 1906, James Alfred LeRoy Papers, Philippine Islands Folder, Correspondence 1904–1909.

79. Henry Ide to Taft, February 4, 1906, William Howard Taft Papers, reel 55; Taft to Ide, January 22, 1906, and March 21, 1906, William Howard Taft Papers, reel 487; Smith to Taft, October 7, 1907, Clarence Ransom Edwards Papers, box 7, folder 2.

80. See chapter 5, note 89.

81. Cullinane, *Ilustrado Politics*, 287–94.

82. Cullinane, *Ilustrado Politics*, 97–111.

83. Cullinane, *Ilustrado Politics*, 184–95; McCoy, *Policing America's Empire*, 178. Quezon, who emerged as among the most powerful Filipino politician during the American colonial period and later became president of the Philippine Commonwealth, was in fact an early Bandholtz protégé.

84. See, for example, correspondences between Anicento Medel, Bandholtz, and Horace Higgins from February 25, 1907, to March 5, 1907, Harry H. Bandholtz Papers, reel 1. Here, Bandholtz recommends the appointment of Don Medel, a prominent landowner from Albay, as a railroad construction inspector to Higgins, who was then the general manager of Manila and Dagupan Railway. See also Cullinane, *Ilustrado Politics*, 282–85; McCoy, *Policing America's Empire*, 145.

85. McCoy, *Policing America's Empire*, 88–90, 109–11, 177–96.

86. George Yarrington Coats, "The Philippine Constabulary" (PhD diss., Ohio State University, 1968), 93–99; McCoy, *Policing America's Empire*, 144.

87. Coats, "The Philippine Constabulary," 183–88; McCoy, *Policing America's Empire*, 136–37. By the time Bandholtz arrived in Cavite and Batangas, however, these provinces had largely been pacified as a result of General Henry Allen's highly coercive yet effective counterinsurgency campaign.

88. Art Guthrie, "Circular No. 33," September 15, 1905, in William Howard Taft Papers, reel 52, 1–3. See also Art Guthrie, "General Orders No. 66," July 22, 1905, William Howard Taft Papers, reel 52; Allen to Harbord, September 1, 1905, William Howard Taft Papers, reel 52.

89. Worcester to Taft, May 2, 1912, Dean C. Worcester Papers, box 1 (Bentley Historical Library, University of Michigan, Ann Arbor), 3.

90. For an account of the peasant uprisings from 1923 to the end of the American period, see Sturtevant, *Popular Uprisings in the Philippines*, 141–255.

91. LeRoy to Worcester, August 3, 1906, James Alfred LeRoy Papers, Philippine Islands Folder, Correspondence 1904–1909.

92. As Forbes wrote in his journal, "In the centre of the towns where the municipal presidents are supposed to maintain the roads, there were puddles and holes, no ditches and generally a mess. We had to slow up, and still got jolted towards the sky." Journal of William Cameron Forbes, vol. 3, May 31, 1909 entry (Houghton Library, Harvard University, Cambridge, MA), 159. See also Cullinane, "Implementing the 'New Order,'" 32–33; Board of Educational Survey, *A Survey of the Educational System*, 86–87, 595–97.

93. Where the central government bypassed municipal officials and partnered directly with nonstate community organizations, provision of public goods and services tended to see better results. An example of this dynamic was observed in the successful implementation of Clean-up Week, which typically took place a week before Christmas. The Philippine Health Service initially attempted to promote Clean-up Week by working with provincial governors, with little avail. Health officials then decided to try a different strat-

egy: They would call on public schools, women's clubs, and various other charitable organizations to take the lead on Clean-up Week and award cash prizes of one hundred pesos to those groups demonstrating the greatest success. By 1922, Clean-up Week had become well observed throughout the archipelago. On Clean-up Week, see Anderson, *Colonial Pathologies*, 127; Philippines, Philippine Health Service, *Report of the Philippine Health Service, 1920*, 297.

94. Philippines, Philippine Health Service, *Report of the Philippine Health Service, 1920*, 283.

95. Philippines, Philippine Health Service, *Report of the Philippine Health Service, 1920*, 287.

96. Philippines, Philippine Health Service, *Report of the Philippine Health Service, 1919*, 181.

97. Jose Endriga, "The Friar Lands Settlement," *Philippine Journal of Public Administration* 14 (1970): 397–413; Rene Escalante, *The American Friar Lands Policy* (Manila, 2002).

98. Sidel, *Capital, Coercion, and Crime*, 128.

99. Sidel, "Walking in the Shadow of the Big Man," 121–22.

100. Bandholtz's role in this matter can be pieced together from a series of correspondences between Bandholtz, Harbord, Wardall, Muerman, and Balch between December 3, 1905, and January 11, 1906, found in Harry H. Bandholtz Papers, reel 1.

101. Bandholtz to Ramón Santos, June 19, 1905, Harry H. Bandholtz Papers, reel 1.

102. Bajá, *Philippine Police System and Its Problems*, 134. See also 287–90.

103. Hayden, *The Philippines*, 278.

104. Hayden, *The Philippines*, 278.

105. Hayden, *The Philippines*, 278.

106. See Journal of William Cameron Forbes, in particular volume 3, for numerous entries discussing Forbes's collaborative undertakings with Osmeña and Tinio, as well as his thoughts on their character and capabilities.

107. Sidel, "Walking in the Shadow of the Big Man," 120.

108. Anne Booth, *Colonial Legacies* (Honolulu, 2007).

109. This is the central thesis advanced in W. Cameron Forbes and Leonard Wood, *Report of the Special Mission on the Investigation to the Philippines Islands* (Washington, DC, 1921).

110. Hayden, *The Philippines*, 288–89.

7. FROM THE COLONIAL PAST TO THE FUTURE OF STATEBUILDING

1. Daron Acemoglu and James Robinson, *Why Nations Fail* (New York, 2012); Samuel Huntington, *The Third Wave* (Norman, OK, 1991).

2. An important exception was the Guardia Civil, the Spanish-era national police force, which recruited personnel from the local population. When the Philippine Constabulary was established in 1901, U.S. officials not only used the Guardia Civil as an institutional model but also incorporated its veterans into the new police force. Alfred McCoy, *Policing America's Empire* (Madison, WI, 2009), 30–33.

3. On direct versus indirect rule, see Matthew Lange, *Lineages of Despotism and Development* (Chicago, 2009). In contrast to my view that American colonial practices departed considerably from European precedent, Julian Go argues that American and British imperialism were highly comparable. See Julian Go, *Patterns of Empire* (New York, 2011).

4. Mahmood Mamdani, *Citizen and Subject* (Princeton, 1996).

5. This contrasts to colonies of European countries such as Germany, Spain, Italy, and especially France, where colonial administrators did little to substantiate their government's

assimilationist rhetoric. Raymond Betts, *Assimilation and Association in French Colonial Theory* (New York, 1960).

6. This is not to suggest that autocratic governments are completely unaccountable to domestic audiences, and insofar as the autocratic government's ruling coalition and key supporters oppose a costly counterinsurgency campaign, there may be no observed difference in outcome compared to a democracy. Nonetheless, autocratic governments do, on average, exhibit greater autonomy from societal actors and forces in foreign policymaking than democratic ones. On the question of autocratic accountability in foreign policy, see Jessica Weeks, *Dictators at War and Peace* (Ithaca, 2014).

7. For discussion of MacArthur's counterinsurgency campaign, see chapter 5.

8. "Senate for Army Increase," *New York Times*, February 28, 1899.

9. Frank Golay, *Face of Empire* (Madison, WI, 1998), 70; "Reduction of the Army," *New York Times*, October 25, 1902.

10. For reports of abuses by military officers, see George Hunter to William Howard Taft, May 16, 1900, and June 4, 1900, William Howard Taft Papers, reel 30 (Library of Congress, Washington, DC). Congressional hearings regarding U.S. military conduct in the archipelago were eventually held in 1902. For excerpts from the hearings pertaining specifically to the issue of U.S. atrocities, see Henry Graff, ed., *American Imperialism and the Philippine Insurrection Testimony* (Boston, 1969). See also United States, Senate Committee on the Philippines, *Affairs in the Philippine Islands* (Washington, DC, 1902).

11. Elihu Root to Adna Chaffee, February 26, 1901, William Howard Taft Papers, reel 640, 1–2.

12. James Scott, *Seeing Like a State* (New Haven, 1998).

13. Francis Fukuyama, *State-Building* (Ithaca, 2004); Wade Jacoby, *Imitation and Politics* (Ithaca, 2000); D. Eleanor Westney, *Imitation and Innovation* (Cambridge, MA, 1987).

14. For similar approaches, see Douglass North, John Wallis, and Barry Weingast, *Violence and Social Orders* (New York, 2009); Merilee Grindle, *Jobs for the Boys* (Cambridge, MA, 2012).

15. James Baxter, *The Meiji Unification through the Lens of Ishikawa Prefecture* (Cambridge, MA, 1994). On Tokugawa-era village authority structures, see Harumi Befu, "Village Autonomy and Articulation with the State," *Journal of Asian Studies* 25, no. 1 (1965): 19–32; Herman Ooms, *Tokugawa Village Practice* (Berkeley, 1996).

16. This belief was also shared by progressive reformers, allowing for close state-society collaboration in pursuit of state-led modernization. Sheldon Garon, "Rethinking Modernization and Modernity in Japanese History," *Journal of Asian Studies* 53, no. 2 (1994): 346–66; Richard Samuels, *"Rich Nation, Strong Army"* (Ithaca, 1996).

17. Sheldon Garon, *Molding Japanese Minds* (Princeton, 1997); Kenneth Pyle, "The Technology of Japanese Nationalism," *Journal of Asian Studies* 33, no. 1 (1973): 51–65.

18. Alexis de Tocqueville, *Democracy in America*, ed. J. P. Mayer, trans. George Lawrence (New York, 1988), 62–70, 89–98, 513–17.

19. Tocqueville, *Democracy in America*, 513–17.

20. Tocqueville, *Democracy in America*, 95.

21. See, for example, Jason Kaufman, *For the Common Good?* (New York, 2002).

22. Jacob Schurman et al., *Report of the Philippine Commission to the President*, vol. 1 (Washington, DC, 1900), 61–62.

23. "Instructions of the President to the Philippine Commission, April 7, 1900." A digital copy can be found at University of Michigan Library's Southeast Asia collection: https://quod.lib.umich.edu/p/philamer/ACQ0871.0001.001.

24. Glenn Anthony May, *Social Engineering in the Philippines* (Westport, CT, 1980), 41.

25. Joseph Hayden, *The Philippines* (New York, 1942), 282–83.

26. Hayden, *The Philippines*, 288. Italics found in original text.

27. Anne Booth, *Colonial Legacies* (Honolulu, 2007).

28. Robert Pekkanen, Yutaka Tsujinaka, and Hidehiro Yamamoto, *Neighborhood Associations and Local Governance in Japan* (New York, 2017); Susan Pharr and Frank Schwartz, *The State of Civil Society in Japan* (New York, 2003); Benjamin Read, *Roots of the State* (Stanford, 2012), 238–41.

29. David Lehey and Kay Warren, *Japanese Aid and the Construction of Global Development* (New York, 2010).

30. On this point, see Séverine Autesserre, *Peaceland* (New York, 2014); Roland Paris, *At War's End* (New York, 2004).

31. A recent example of this is Rwanda. Filip Reyntjens, *Political Governance in Post-Genocide Rwanda* (New York, 2015); Scott Straus and Lars Waldorf, eds., *Remaking Rwanda* (Madison, WI, 2011).

32. Peter Leeson, *Anarchy Unbound* (New York, 2014); James Scott, *The Art of Not Being Governed* (New Haven, 2009).

33. Ann Clunan and Harold Trinkunas, eds., *Ungoverned Spaces* (Stanford, 2010); Zachariah Mampilly, *Rebel Rulers* (Ithaca, 2011); Jennifer Murtazashvili, *Informal Order and the State in Afghanistan* (New York, 2016).

34. On the state of nature, see Jean-Jacques Rousseau, "Discourse on the Origin and Foundations of Inequality Among Men," in *Rousseau*, ed. Victor Gourevitch (New York, 1997), 111–88.

35. James Scott, *Against the Grain* (New Haven, 2017).

36. Joshua Cohen and Joel Rogers, "Secondary Associations and Democratic Governance," *Politics and Society* 20, no. 4 (1992): 393–472; Jürgen Habermas, *Between Facts and Norms* (Cambridge, MA, 1996); Samuel Moyn, "Barbarian Virtue," *The Nation*, October 5, 2017; Mark Warren, *Democracy and Association* (Princeton, 2001).

Bibliography

ARCHIVAL DOCUMENTS

Henry T. Allen Papers. Library of Congress, Washington, DC.

Harry H. Bandholtz Papers. Bentley Historical Library, University of Michigan, Ann Arbor.

David Prescott Barrows Papers. Bancroft Library, University of California, Berkeley.

Henry C. Corbin Papers. Library of Congress, Washington, DC.

Clarence Ransom Edwards Papers. Massachusetts Historical Society, Boston.

Charles Burke Elliott Papers. Library of Congress, Washington, DC.

William Cameron Forbes Papers. Houghton Library, Harvard University, Cambridge, MA.

Journal of William Cameron Forbes. Houghton Library, Harvard University, Cambridge, MA.

Gotō Shimpei monjo [Documents related to Gotō Shimpei]. Mizusawa Shiritsu Gotō Shimpei Kinenkan, Iwate, JP.

Victor G. Heiser Papers. American Philosophical Society, Philadelphia.

Katsura Tarō kankei monjo [Documents related to Katsura Tarō]. National Diet Library, Tokyo.

Frank Lamson-Scribner Papers. Library of Congress, Washington, DC.

James A. LeRoy Papers. Bentley Historical Library, University of Michigan, Ann Arbor.

Ministry of Foreign Affairs of Japan. Takushokushō setchi ni kansuru ken [The case pertaining to the establishment of the Ministry of Colonial Affairs]. The Diplomatic Record Office of the Ministry of Foreign Affairs of Japan, Tokyo.

Bernard Moses Papers. Bancroft Library, University of California, Berkeley.

Elihu Root Papers. Library of Congress, Washington, DC.

Saitō Makoto kankei monjo [Documents related to Saitō Makoto]. National Diet Library, Tokyo.

Shimomura Kainan Taiwan Minsei Chōkan jidai chōsa fukumeisho [Reports by Shimomura Kainan during his tenure as Chief Civil Administrator of Taiwan]. Tenri University Library, Tenri, Japan.

Suzuki Saburō monjo [Documents related to Suzuki Saburō]. National Diet Library, Tokyo.

United States. War Department. Bureau of Insular Affairs. RG 350. National Archives and Records Administration, College Park, MD.

William Howard Taft Papers. Library of Congress, Washington, DC.

Leonard Wood Papers. Library of Congress, Washington, DC.

Dean C. Worcester Papers. Bentley Historical Library, University of Michigan, Ann Arbor.

Dean C. Worcester Papers. Special Collections Library, University of Michigan, Ann Arbor.

PUBLISHED PRIMARY AND SECONDARY SOURCES

Abinales, Patricio N. "Progressive-Machine Conflict in Early-Twentieth-Century U.S. Politics and Colonial-State Building in the Philippines." In *The American Colonial*

State in the Philippines: Global Perspectives, edited by Julian Go and Anne L. Foster. Durham, NC: Duke University Press, 2003, 148–81.

Acemoglu, Daron, and James A. Robinson, *Why Nations Fail: The Origins of Power, Prosperity, and Poverty*. New York: Crown Business, 2012.

Acemoglu, Daron, Simon Johnson, and James A. Robinson. "The Colonial Origins of Comparative Development: An Empirical Investigation." *American Economic Review* 91, no. 5 (2001): 1369–1401.

Allee, Mark A. *Law and Local Society in Late Imperial China: Northern Taiwan in the Nineteenth Century*. Stanford: Stanford University Press, 1994.

Altavás, Enrique. *Land Registration in the Philippine Islands*. Manila: Oriental Commercial Co., 1923.

Anderson, Benedict. "Cacique Democracy and the Philippines: Origins and Dreams." *New Left Review* 169 (1988): 3–31.

——. *Imagined Communities: Reflections on the Origin and Spread of Nationalism*, revised edition. New York: Verso, 1991.

Anderson, Gerald H. "Providence and Politics behind Protestant Missionary Beginnings in the Philippines." In *Studies in Philippine Church History*, edited by Gerald H. Anderson. Ithaca: Cornell University Press, 1969, 279–300.

Anderson, Warwick. *Colonial Pathologies: American Tropical Medicine, Race, and Hygiene in the Philippines*. Durham, NC: Duke University Press, 2006.

Andrews, Matt. *The Limits of Institutional Reform in Development: Changing Rules for Realistic Solutions*. New York: Cambridge University Press, 2013.

Antony, Robert J., and Jane Kate Leonard, eds. *Dragons, Tigers, and Dogs: Qing Crisis Management and Boundaries of State Power in Late Imperial China*. Ithaca: Cornell University Press, 2002.

Asano Toyomi. *Teikoku Nihon no shokuminchi hōsei: hōiki tōgō to teikoku chitsujo* [Imperial Japan and colonial legal system: unification of legal jurisdiction and imperial order]. Nagoya, JP: Nagoya Daigaku Shuppan, 2008.

Autesserre, Séverine. *Peaceland: Conflict Resolution and Everyday Politics of International Intervention*. New York: Cambridge University Press, 2014.

Bajá, Emanuel Agrava. *Philippine Police System and Its Problems*. Manila: Pobre's Press, 1933.

Baldwin, Kate. *The Paradox of Traditional Chiefs in Democratic Africa*. New York: Cambridge University Press, 2015.

Banerjee, Abhijit, and Lakshmi Iyer. "History, Institutions, and Economic Performance: The Legacy of Colonial Land Tenure Systems in India." *The American Economic Review* 95, no. 4 (2005): 1190–213.

Bankoff, Greg. "Big Fish in Small Ponds: The Exercise of Power in a Nineteenth-century Philippine Municipality." *Modern Asian Studies* 26, no. 4 (1992): 679–700.

——. *Crime, Society, and the State in the Nineteenth-century Philippines*. Quezon City, PH: Ateneo de Manila University Press, 1996.

Barkey, Karen. *Bandits and Bureaucrats: The Ottoman Route to State Centralization*. Ithaca: Cornell University Press, 1996.

Bates, Robert. *Markets and States in Tropical Africa*. Berkeley: University of California Press, 1981.

Baxter, James C. *The Meiji Unification through the Lens of Ishikawa Prefecture*. Cambridge, MA: Harvard University Press, 1994.

Befu, Harumi. "Village Autonomy and Articulation with the State: The Case of Tokugawa Japan." *Journal of Asian Studies* 25, no. 1 (1965): 19–32.

Beisner, Robert L. *Twelve Against Empire: The Anti-Imperialists, 1898–1900*. New York: McGraw-Hill, 1968.

Beissinger, Mark R. *Scientific Management, Socialist Discipline, and Soviet Power.* Cambridge, MA: Harvard University Press, 1988.

Bellairs, Edgar G. *As It Is in the Philippines.* New York: Lewis, Scribner & Co., 1902.

Bensel, Richard Franklin. *Yankee Leviathan: The Origins of Central State Authority in America, 1859–1877.* New York: Cambridge University Press, 1990.

Besley, Timothy, and Torsten Persson. *Pillars of Prosperity: The Political Economics of Development Clusters.* Princeton: Princeton University Press, 2011.

Betts, Raymond F. *Assimilation and Association in French Colonial Theory, 1890–1914.* New York: Columbia University Press, 1960.

Blanco, John D. *Frontier Constitutions: Christianity and Colonial Empire in the Nineteenth-Century Philippines.* Berkeley: University of California Press, 2009.

Boone, Catherine. *Property and Political Order in Africa: Land Rights and the Structure of Politics.* New York: Cambridge University Press, 2014.

Booth, Anne E. *Colonial Legacies: Economic Development in East and Southeast Asia.* Honolulu: University of Hawai'i Press, 2007.

Brehm, John, and Scott Gates. *Working, Shirking, and Sabotage: Bureaucratic Response to a Democratic Public.* Ann Arbor: University of Michigan Press, 1997.

Brown, Philip C. *Formation of Early Modern Japan: The Case of Kaga Domain.* Stanford: Stanford University Press, 1993.

Brownlee, Jason. "Can America Nation-Build?" *World Politics* 59, no. 2 (2007): 314–40.

Capoccia, Giovanni, and R. Daniel Kelemen. "The Study of Critical Junctures: Theory, Narrative, and Counterfactuals in Historical Institutionalism." *World Politics* 59, no. 3 (2007): 341–69.

Centeno, Miguel Angel. *Blood and Debt: War and the Nation-State in Latin America.* University Park: Pennsylvania State University, 2002.

Chen, Ching-chih. "Japanese Socio-political Control in Taiwan, 1895–1945." PhD diss., Harvard University, 1973.

Chen, Chiukun. "From Landlords to Local Strongmen: The Transformation of Local Elites in Mid-Ch'ing Taiwan, 1780–1862." In *Taiwan: A New History*, edited by Murray Rubinstein. New York: M. E. Sharpe, 1999, 133–62.

Chen, Edward I-te. "The Attempt to Integrate the Empire: Legal Perspectives." In *The Japanese Colonial Empire, 1895–1945*, edited by Ramon H. Myers and Mark R. Peattie. Princeton: Princeton University Press, 1984, 240–74.

Chen Peifeng. *"Dōka" no dōshō imu: Nihon tōchika Taiwan no kokugo kyōiku shi saikō* [Strange bedfellows of Japan's "assimilation policy": Japanese language education in colonial Taiwan revisited]. Tokyo: Sangensha, 2001.

Chiang Ping-k'un. *Taiwan chiso kaisei no kenkyū: Nihon ryōyū shoki tochi chōsa no honshitsu* [Study of Taiwanese land-tax reform: the true nature of Japan's early colonial land investigation]. Tokyo: Tokyo Daigaku Shuppankai, 1974.

Ching, Leo T. S. *Becoming "Japanese": Colonial Taiwan and the Politics of Identity Formation.* Berkeley: University of California Press, 2001.

Chou, Wan-yao. "The 'Kōminka' Movement: Taiwan under Wartime Japan, 1937–1945." PhD diss., Yale University, 1991.

Clunan, Ann, and Harold Trinkunas, eds. *Ungoverned Spaces.* Stanford: Stanford University Press, 2010.

Clymer, Kenton J. *Protestant Missionaries in the Philippines, 1898–1916: An Inquiry into the American Colonial Mentality.* Urbana: University of Illinois Press, 1986.

Coats, George Yarrington. "The Philippine Constabulary: 1901–1917." PhD diss., Ohio State University, 1968.

Cohen, Joshua, and Joel Rogers. "Secondary Associations and Democratic Governance." *Politics and Society* 20, no. 4 (1992): 393–472.

Corpuz, Onofre D. *The Bureaucracy in the Philippines*. Quezon City, PH: Institute of Public Administration, University of the Philippines, 1957.

Cullinane, Michael. "Implementing the 'New Order': The Structure and Supervision of Local Government During the Taft Era." In *Compadre Colonialism: Studies on the Philippines under American Rule*, edited by Norman Owen. Ann Arbor: University of Michigan Center for South and Southeast Asian Studies, 1971.

——. *Ilustrado Politics: Filipino Elite Responses to American Rule, 1898–1908*. Quezon City, PH: Ateneo de Manila University Press, 2003.

Cumings, Bruce. "Colonial Formations and Deformations: Korea, Taiwan, and Vietnam." In *Parallax Visions: Making Sense of American-East Asian Relations at the End of the Century*, edited by Bruce Cumings. Durham, NC: Duke University Press, 1999, 69–94.

Dargent, Eduardo, Andreas E. Feldmann, and Juan Pablo Luna. "Greater State Capacity, Lesser State: Lessons from the Peruvian Commodity Boom." *Politics and Society* 45, no. 1 (2017): 3–34.

Davidson, James W. *The Island of Formosa Past and Present: History, People, Resources, and Commercial Prospects*. New York: Macmillan Company, 1903.

De Bevoise, Ken. *Agents of Apocalypse: Epidemic Disease in the Colonial Philippines*. Princeton: Princeton University Press, 1995.

Dirks, Nicholas B. *Castes of Mind: Colonialism and the Making of Modern India*. Princeton: Princeton University Press, 2011.

Dobbins, James, John G. McGinn, Keith Crane, Seth G. Jones, Rollie Lal, Andrew Rathmell, Rachel Swanger, and Anga Timilsina, *America's Role in Nation-Building: From Germany to Iraq*. Santa Monica, CA: Rand, 2003.

Duara, Prasenjit. *Culture, Power, and the State: Rural North China, 1900–1942*. Stanford: Stanford University Press, 1988.

Duus, Peter, and Daniel I. Okimoto. "Fascism and the History of Pre-War Japan: The Failure of a Concept." *Journal of Asian Studies* 39, no. 1 (1979): 65–76.

Elman, Benjamin A. *Civil Examinations and Meritocracy in Late Imperial China*. Cambridge, MA: Harvard University Press, 2013.

Endriga, Jose N. "The Friar Lands Settlement: Promise and Performance." *Philippine Journal of Public Administration* 14 (1970): 397–413.

Escalante, Rene R. *The American Friar Lands Policy: Its Framers, Context, and Beneficiaries, 1898–1916*. Manila: De La Salle University Press, 2002.

Fearon, James D., and David D. Laitin. "Neotrusteeship and the Problem of Weak States." *International Security* 28, no. 4 (2004): 5–43.

Foa, Roberto Stefan. "Persistence or Reversal of Fortune? Early State Inheritance and the Legacies of Colonial Rule." *Politics and Society* 45, no. 2 (2017): 301–24.

Forbes, William Cameron. *The Philippine Islands*. Boston: Houghton Mifflin, 1928.

Forbes, William Cameron, and Leonard Wood. *Report of the Special Mission on the Investigation to the Philippines Islands to the Secretary of War*. Washington, DC: Government Publishing Office, 1921.

Foreman, John. "Spain and the Philippine Islands." *Contemporary Review* 74 (1898): 20–33.

Foucault, Michel. *Discipline and Punish: The Birth of the Prison*. Translated by Alan Sheridan. New York: Vintage Books, 1977.

Fukuyama, Francis. *State-Building: Governance and World Order in the 21st Century*. Ithaca: Cornell University Press, 2004.

——. *The Origins of Political Order: From Prehuman Times to the French Revolution*. New York: Farrar, Straus and Giroux, 2011.

Gardella, Robert. "From Treaty Ports to Provincial Status, 1860–1894." In *Taiwan: A New History*, edited by Murray Rubinstein. New York: M.E. Sharpe, 2007, 163–200.

Garon, Sheldon. "Rethinking Modernization and Modernity in Japanese History: A Focus on State-Society Relations." *Journal of Asian Studies* 53, no. 2 (1994): 346–66.

——. *Molding Japanese Minds: The State in Everyday Life.* Princeton: Princeton University Press, 1997.

Gates, John M. *Schoolbooks and Krags: The United States Army in the Philippines, 1898–1902.* Westport, CT: Greenwood Press, 1973.

——. "Philippine Guerillas, American Anti-imperialists, and the Election of 1900." *Pacific Historical Review* 46, no. 1 (1977): 51–64.

Gleeck, Lewis E. Jr. *Nueva Ecija in American Times: Homesteaders, Hacenderos and Politicos.* Manila, Historical Conservation Society, 1981.

——. *The American Governors-General and High Commissioners in the Philippines: Proconsuls, Nation-builders and Politicians.* Quezon City, PH: New Day Publishers, 1986.

Go, Julian. *American Empire and the Politics of Meaning: Elite Political Cultures in the Philippines and Puerto Rico during U.S. Colonialism.* Durham, NC: Duke University Press, 2008.

——. *Patterns of Empire: The British and American Empires, 1688 to the Present.* New York: Cambridge University Press, 2011.

Golay, Frank Hindman. *Face of Empire: United States-Philippine Relations, 1898–1946.* Madison: Center for Southeast Asian Studies, University of Wisconsin, 1998.

Goodnow, Frank Johnson. *Politics and Administration: A Study in Government.* New York: Macmillan Company, 1900.

Gorski, Philip S. *The Disciplinary Revolution: Calvinism and the Rise of State in Early Modern Europe.* Chicago: University of Chicago Press, 2003.

Gotō Shimpei. "Gotō Chōkan no kunji [Instructions of Chief Civil Administrator Gotō]." *Taiwan Kyōikukai zasshi* 27 (1904): 2–3.

——. *Nihon shokuminchi ron* [Essay on Japanese colonialism]. Tokyo: Kōmin Dōmei, 1915.

Gowing, Peter G. "The Disentanglement of Church and State Early in the American Regime in the Philippines." In *Studies in Philippine Church History*, edited by Gerald H. Anderson. Ithaca: Cornell University Press, 1969, 203–22.

Graff, Henry F., ed. *American Imperialism and the Philippine Insurrection Testimony taken from Hearings on Affairs in the Philippine Islands before the Senate Committee on the Philippines, 1902.* Boston: Little, Brown and Company, 1969.

Grindle, Merilee S. *Jobs for the Boys: Patronage and the State in Comparative Perspective.* Cambridge, MA: Harvard University Press, 2012.

Habermas, Jürgen. *Between Facts and Norms: Contributions to a Discourse Theory of Law and Democracy.* Cambridge, MA: MIT Press, 1996.

Hagopian, Frances. *Traditional Politics and Regime Change in Brazil.* New York: Cambridge University Press, 1996.

Haley, John Owen. *Authority without Power: Law and the Japanese Paradox.* New York: Oxford University Press, 1991.

Hara Takashi. *Hara Takashi nikki* [Journal of Hara Takashi]. Edited by Hara Keiichirō. Tokyo: Kangensha, 1950–1951.

Hara Takashi Monjo Kenkyūkai, ed. *Hara Takashi kankei monjo* [Documents related to Hara Takashi]. Tokyo: Nihon Hōsō Shuppan Kyōkai, 1984.

Harrell, Stevan. "From *Xiedou* to *Yijun*, the Decline of Ethnicity in Northern Taiwan, 1885–1895." *Late Imperial China* 11, no. 1 (1990): 99–127.

Haruyama Meitetsu. "Kindai Nihon no shokuminchi tōchi to Hara Takashi [Modern Japanese colonial rule and Hara Takashi]." In *Nihon shokuminchi shugi no seiji-teki tenkai 1895–1934: sono tōchi taisei to Taiwan no minzoku undō* [Political development of Japanese imperialism, 1895–1934: its governance structure and Taiwanese nationalist movement], edited by Haruyama Meitetsu and Wakabayashi Masahiro. Tokyo: Ajia Seikei Gakkai, 1980, 1–75.

———. "Hōgaku Hakase Okamatsu Santarō [Law Professor Okamatsu Santarō]." *Taiwan kingendaishi kenkyū* 6 (1988): 197–216.

———. "Taiwan kyūkan chōsa to rippō kōsō: Okamatsu Santarō ni yoru chōsa to ritsuan wo chūshin ni [Investigation of Taiwanese laws and customs and the legislative framework: with a focus on Okamatsu Santarō's research and legislative proposals]." *Taiwan kingendaishi kenkyū* 6 (1988): 81–114.

———. "Meiji kenpō taisei to Taiwan tōchi [The Meiji constitutional structure and Taiwanese colonialism]." In *Iwanami kōza kindai Nihon to shokuminchi* [Iwanami series on modern Japan and its colonies], volume 4, edited by Ōe Shinobu. Tokyo: Iwanami Shoten, 1993, 31–50.

Hayden, Joseph Ralston. *The Philippines: A Study in National Development*. New York: Macmillan Company, 1942.

Hechter, Michael. *Principles of Group Solidarity*. Berkeley: University of California Press, 1987.

Hendrickson, Kenneth E. Jr. "Reluctant Expansionist: Jacob Gould Schurman and the Philippine Question." *Pacific Historical Review* 36, no. 4 (1967): 405–21.

Herbst, Jeffry. *States and Power in Africa: Comparative Lessons in Authority and Control*. Princeton: Princeton University Press, 2000.

Hirai Hirokazu. *Nihon shokuminchi zaisei shi kenkyū* [Study of the financial history of Japanese colonies]. Kyoto: Mineruva Shobō, 1997.

Hiyama Yukio. "Taiwan tōchi no kikō kaikaku to kanki shinshuku mondai: Meiji 30-nen no Taiwan tōchi [Reform of the Taiwan colonial administration and the problem of bureaucratic discipline: colonial rule of Taiwan in 1897]." In *Taiwan Sōtokufu monjo mokuroku* [Index to documents related to the Taiwan Government-General], volume 2, edited by Chūkyō Daigaku Shakai Kagaku Kenkyūjo. Tokyo: Yumani Shobō, 1995, 325–440.

Ho, Samuel P. S. *Economic Development of Taiwan, 1860–1970*. New Haven: Yale University Press, 1978.

Hobbes, Thomas. *Leviathan*. Edited by Richard Tuck. New York: Cambridge University Press, 1991.

Hsu Shih-chia. "Zhi min zheng quan dui tai wan min jian zi zhu xing de fang ren yu shou bian: yi ri zhi chu qi duan fa yun dong wei li [The limits of social autonomy under colonialism: the queue-cutting movement in the early Japanese period in Taiwan]." *Xin shi xue* 24, no. 3 (2013): 53–94.

Hung Chiu-fen. "Ri ju chu qi tai wan de bao jia zhi du (1895–1903) [The baojia system in Taiwan, 1895–1903]." *Jin dai shi yan jiu suo ji kan* 21 (1991): 437–71.

———. "Ri zhi shi qi zhi min zheng fu he di fang zong jiao xin yang zhong xin guan xi zhi tan tao: Fengyuan Tzuchi gong de ge an yan jiu [An investigation into the relationship between Japanese colonial government and local religious belief centers: a case study of the Fengyuan Tzuchi Temple]." *Si yu yan: ren wen yu she hui ke xue za zhi* 42, no. 2 (2004): 1–41.

Huntington, Samuel P. *Political Order in Changing Societies*. New Haven: Yale University Press, 1968.

———. *The Third Wave: Democratization in the Late Twentieth Century*. Norman: University of Oklahoma Press, 1991.

Hutchcroft, Paul D. *Booty Capitalism: The Politics of Banking in the Philippines*. Ithaca: Cornell University Press, 1998.

——. "Colonial Masters, National Politicos, and Provincial Lords: Central Authority and Local Autonomy in the American Philippines, 1900–1913." *Journal of Asian Studies* 59, no. 2 (2000): 277–306.

Ileto, Reynaldo C. *Pasyon and Revolution: Popular Movements in the Philippines, 1840–1910*. Manila: Ateneo de Manila University Press, 1979.

——. "Cholera and the Origins of the American Sanitary Order in the Philippines." In *Imperial Medicine and Indigenous Societies*, edited by David Arnold. New York: Manchester University Press, 1988.

Inō Yoshinori. *Taiwan bunka shi* [Cultural history of Taiwan]. Tokyo: Tōkō Shoin, 1928.

Ishizuka Eizō. "Kokumin-teki seizonkyōsō oyobi dōka zetsumetsu [Survival of the fittest among nations and extinction by assimilation]." *Taiwan Kyōkai kaihō* 27 (1900): 1–10.

Itō Hirobumi and Kaneko Kentarō, eds. *Taiwan shiryō* [Taiwan documents]. Tokyo: Hara Shobō, 1970.

Izawa Shūji. *Izawa Shūji senshū* [Selected writings of Izawa Shūji]. Edited by Shinano Kyōikukai. Nagano, JP: Shinano Kyōikukai, 1958.

Jacoby, Wade. *Imitation and Politics: Redesigning Modern Germany*. Ithaca: Cornell University Press, 2000.

Jessup, Philip C. *Elihu Root*. New York: Dodd, Mead and Company, 1939.

Johnson, Chalmers. *MITI and the Japanese Miracle: The Growth of Industrial Policy, 1925–1975*. Stanford: Stanford University Press, 1982.

Ka, Chih-ming. *Japanese Colonialism in Taiwan: Land Tenure, Development, and Dependency, 1895–1945*. Boulder, CO: Westview Press, 1995.

Kalyvas, Stathis. *The Logic of Violence in Civil War*. New York: Cambridge University Press, 2006.

Kassof, Allen. "The Administered Society: Totalitarianism without Terror." *World Politics* 16, no. 4 (1964): 558–75.

Kasza, Gregory J. *The Conscription Society: Administered Mass Organizations*. New Haven: Yale University Press, 1995.

Kaufman, Jason. *For the Common Good? American Civic Life and the Golden Age of Fraternity*. New York: Oxford University Press, 2002.

Kingsberg, Miriam. *Moral Nation: Modern Japan and Narcotics in Global History*. Berkeley: University of California Press, 2014.

Kitschelt, Herbert, and Steven I. Wilkinson, eds. *Patrons, Clients and Policies: Patterns of Democratic Accountability and Political Competition*. New York: Cambridge University Press, 2007.

Knapp, Ronald G. *China's Island Frontier: Studies in the Historical Geography of Taiwan*. Honolulu: University of Hawai'i Press, 1980.

Kō Shōdō. *Taiwan Minshukoku no kenkyū: Taiwan dokuritsu undō shi no ichi danshō* [A study on the Republic of Formosa: a chapter in the history of the Taiwan independence movement]. Tokyo: University of Tokyo Press, 1970.

Kohli, Atul. "Where Do High Growth Political Economies Come From? The Japanese Lineage of Korea's 'Developmental State.'" *World Development* 22, no. 9 (1994): 1269–93.

——. *State-Directed Development: Political Power and Industrialization in the Global Periphery*. New York: Cambridge University Press, 2004.

Komagome Takeshi. *Shokuminchi teikoku Nihon no bunka tōgō* [Cultural integration of the Japanese colonial empire]. Tokyo: Iwanami Shoten, 1996.

Kramer, Paul A. *The Blood of Government: Race, Empire, the United States, and the Philippines*. Chapel Hill: University of North Carolina Press, 2006.

Krasner, Stephen D. "Sharing Sovereignty: New Institutions for Collapsed and Failing States." *International Security* 29, no. 2 (2004): 85–120.

Krasner, Stephen D., and Jeremy M. Weinstein. "Improving Governance from the Outside In." *Annual Review of Political Science* 17 (2014): 123–45.

Kuhonta, Erik Martinez. *The Institutional Imperative: The Politics of Equitable Development in Southeast Asia.* Stanford: Stanford University Press, 2011.

Kuran, Timur. *Private Truths, Public Lies: The Social Consequences of Preference Falsification.* Cambridge, MA: Harvard University Press, 1995.

Kurtz, Marcus. *Latin American State Building in Comparative Perspective: Social Foundations of Institutional Order.* New York: Cambridge University Press, 2013.

Lake, David A. *Statebuilder's Dilemma: On the Limits of Foreign Intervention.* Ithaca: Cornell University Press, 2016.

Lam, Tong. *A Passion for Facts: Social Surveys and the Construction of the Chinese Nation-State, 1900–1949.* Berkeley: University of California Press, 2011.

Lamley, Harry J. "The Taiwan Literati and Early Japanese Rule, 1895–1915: A Study of Their Reactions to the Japanese Occupation and Subsequent Responses to Colonial Rule and Modernization." PhD diss., University of Washington, 1964.

———. "Subethnic Rivalry in the Ch'ing Period." In *The Anthropology of Taiwanese Society*, edited by Emily Martin Ahern and Hill Gates. Stanford: Stanford University Press, 1981, 282–318.

Lange, Matthew. *Lineages of Despotism and Development: British Colonialism and State Power.* Chicago: University of Chicago Press, 2009.

Lee, Alexander. "Redistributive Colonialism: The Long Term Legacy of International Conflict in India." *Politics and Society* 45, no. 2 (2017): 173–224.

Lee, Melissa, and Nan Zhang. "Legibility and the Informational Foundations of State Capacity." *Journal of Politics* 79, no. 1 (2017): 118–32.

Lee Shinn-cherng. "Qing dai yi lan de 'baojia' yu 'qingzhuanglianjia' zhi yan jiu [The study of 'baojia' system and 'Qing-zhuang lian-jia' in Qing Yi-Lan]." *Xing da ren wen xue bao* 43 (2009): 219–55.

Leeson, Peter T. *Anarchy Unbound: Why Self-Governance Works Better than You Think.* New York: Cambridge University Press, 2014.

Lehey, David, and Kay Warren. *Japanese Aid and the Construction of Global Development.* New York: Routledge, 2010.

LeRoy, James A. *Philippine Life in Town and Country.* New York: G. P. Putnam's Sons, 1905.

Levi, Margaret. *Of Rule and Revenue.* Berkeley: University of California Press, 1988.

Lewis, David, and David Mosse. *Development Brokers and Translators: The Ethnography of Aid and Agencies.* Bloomfield, CT: Kumarian Press, 2006.

Li Wen-liang. "Wan qing tai wan qing fu shi ye de zai kao cha: 'jian si liu liu' de jue ce guo cheng yu yi yi [Re-thinking land reform policies in late Qing Taiwan: the significance and policy-making process of 'cutting 40% and retaining 60% of large rents']." *Han xue yan jiu* 24 (2006): 387–416.

Lieberman, Evan S., and Prerna Singh. "Census Enumeration and Group Conflict: A Global Analysis of the Consequences of Counting." *World Politics* 69, no. 1 (2017): 1–53.

Linn, Brian McAllister. *The U.S. Army and Counterinsurgency in the Philippine War, 1899–1902.* Chapel Hill: University of North Carolina Press, 1989.

———. *The Philippine War, 1899–1902.* Lawrence: University Press of Kansas, 2000.

Lo, Ming-cheng M. *Doctors within Borders: Profession, Ethnicity, and Modernity in Colonial Taiwan.* Berkeley: University of California Press, 2002.

Lone, Stewart. *Army, Empire and Politics in Meiji Japan: The Three Careers of General Katsura Tarō.* London: Macmillan Press, 2000.

Lüdtke, Alf. *Police and State in Prussia, 1815–1850*. Translated by Pete Burgess. New York: Cambridge University Press, 1989.

MacArthur, Arthur. *Annual Report of Major General Arthur MacArthur*. Washington, DC: Government Publishing Office, 1900–1901.

Mahoney, James. *Colonialism and Postcolonial Development: Spanish America in Comparative Perspective*. New York: Cambridge University Press, 2010.

Mahoney, James, and Kathleen Thelen. "A Theory of Gradual Institutional Change." In *Explaining Institutional Change: Ambiguity, Agency, and Power*, edited by James Mahoney and Kathleen Thelen. New York: Cambridge University Press, 2010, 1–37.

Mamdani, Mahmood. *Citizen and Subject: Contemporary Africa and the Legacy of Late Colonialism*. Princeton: Princeton University Press, 1996.

Mampilly, Zachariah Cherian. *Rebel Rulers: Insurgent Governance and Civilian Life During War*. Ithaca: Cornell University Press, 2011.

Mann, Michael. "The Autonomous Power of the State: Its Origins, Mechanisms, and Results." *European Journal of Sociology* 25, no. 2 (1984): 185–213.

——. *The Sources of Social Power: Volume 2, The Rise of Classes and Nation States, 1760–1914*. New York: Cambridge University Press, 1993.

Mann, Susan. *Local Merchants and the Chinese Bureaucracy, 1750–1950*. Stanford: Stanford University Press, 1986.

Mattingly, Daniel C. "Elite Capture." *World Politics* 68, no. 3 (2016): 383–412.

May, Glenn Anthony. *Social Engineering in the Philippines: The Aims, Execution, and Impact of American Colonial Policy, 1900–1913*. Westport, CT: Greenwood Press, 1980.

——. *Battle for Batangas: A Philippine Province at War*. New Haven: Yale University Press, 1991.

McCoy, Alfred W. "A Queen Dies Slowly: The Rise and Decline of Iloilo City." In *Philippine Social History: Global Trade and Local Transformations*, edited by Alfred W. McCoy and Ed. C. de Jesus. Quezon City, PH: Ateneo de Manila University Press, 1982, 297–360.

——. *Policing America's Empire: The United States, the Philippines, and the Rise of the Surveillance State*. Madison: University of Wisconsin Press, 2009.

——, ed. *An Anarchy of Families: State and Family in the Philippines*. Madison: University of Wisconsin Press, 2009.

McKinley, William. *Speeches and Addresses of William McKinley, from March 1, 1897 to May 30, 1900*. New York: Doubleday & McClure, 1900.

McLennan, Marshall S. "Changing Human Ecology on the Central Luzon Plain: Nueva Ecija, 1705–1939." In *Philippine Social History: Global Trade and Local Transformations*, edited by Alfred W. McCoy and Ed. C. de Jesus. Quezon City, PH: Ateneo de Manila University Press, 1982, 57–90.

Meguro Gorō. *Genkō Hokō seido sōsho* [The collections on the hokō system]. Taichū [Taichung]: Hokō Seido Sōsho Fukyūjo, 1936.

Meskill, Johanna Menzel. *A Chinese Pioneer Family: The Lins of Wu-feng, Taiwan, 1729–1895*. Princeton: Princeton University Press, 1979.

Miao Yen-wei. "Cong tian ran zu hui dao jie chan hui: ri zhi chu qi tai wan de nü quan zheng zhi [From 'Natural Feet Societies' to 'Footbinding Liberation Societies': the politics of female body in early colonial Taiwan]." *Tai wan she hui yan jiu* 91 (2013): 125–74.

Michalopoulos, Stelio, and Elias Papaioannou. "Pre-Colonial Ethnic Institutions and Contemporary African Development." *Econometrica* 81, no. 1 (2013): 113–52.

Migdal, Joel S. *Strong Societies and Weak States: State-Society Relations and State Capability in the Third World*. Princeton: Princeton University Press, 1988.

Mill, John Stuart. "Two Methods of Comparison." In *Comparative Perspectives: Theories and Methods*, edited by Amitai Etzioni and Frederic L. Du Bow. Boston: Little, Brown, 1969, 205–13.

Miller, Gary J. "The Political Evolution of Principal-Agent Models." *Annual Review of Political Science* 8 (2005): 203–25.

Miller, Paul D. *Armed State Building: Confronting State Failure, 1898–2012*. Ithaca: Cornell University Press, 2013.

Miller, Stuart Creighton. *"Benevolent Assimilation": The American Conquest of the Philippines, 1899–1903*. New Haven: Yale University Press, 1982.

Mimura, Janis. *Reform Bureaucrats and the Japanese Wartime State*. Ithaca: Cornell University Press, 2011.

Miyagi, Dale S. "Neo-Caciquismo: Origins of Philippine Boss Politics, 1875–1896." *Pacific Asian Affairs* 1 (1976): 20–34.

Mizobe Hideaki. "Gotō Shimpei ron: tōsō-teki sekaizō to 'risei no dokusai' [An essay on Gotō Shimpei: a conflict-prone world and 'despotism of reason']." *Hōgaku ronsō* 100, no. 2 (1976): 62–96.

Mizoguchi Yoshiyuki and Umemura Mataji. *Kyū Nihon shokuminchi keizai tōkei: suikei to bunseki* [Basic economic statistics of former Japanese colonies, 1895–1938: estimates and findings]. Tokyo: Tōyō Keizai Shinpōsha, 1988.

Mochiji Rokusaburō. *Taiwan shokumin seisaku* [Colonial policy in Taiwan]. Tokyo: Fuzanbō, 1912.

Mojares, Resil B. *War Against the Americans: Resistance and Collaboration in Cebu, 1899–1906*. Quezon City, PH: Ateneo de Manila University Press, 1999.

Moore, Colin D. *American Imperialism and the State, 1893–1921*. New York: Cambridge University Press, 2017.

Mukōyama Hiroo. "Shokuminchi Taiwan no chian hōsei [Peace preservation laws in colonial Taiwan]." *Kokugakuin hōgaku* 5, no. 2 (1967): 97–147.

——. *Nihon tōchika ni okeru Taiwan minzoku undō shi* [A history of the national movement in Taiwan under the Japanese rule]. Tokyo: Chūō Keizai Kenkyūjo, 1987.

Murtazashvili, Jennifer Brick. *Informal Order and the State in Afghanistan*. New York: Cambridge University Press, 2016.

Myers, Ramon H. "Taiwan under Ch'ing Imperial Rule, 1684–1895: The Traditional Order." *Journal of the Institute of Chinese Studies of the Chinese University of Hong Kong* 4, no. 2 (1971): 495–520.

Nakamura Akira. "'Nihon shokuminchi seisaku ippan' kaidai [An examination of 'A thought on Japanese colonial policy']." In *Nihon shokuminchi seisaku ippan; Nihon bōchō ron* [A thought on Japanese colonial policy; Essay on Japanese expansion], edited by Nakamura Akira. Tokyo: Nihon Hyōronsha, 1944, 3–15.

Nee, Victor. "Between Center and Locality: State, Militia, and Village." In *State and Society in Contemporary China*, edited by Victor Nee and David Mozingo. Ithaca: Cornell University Press, 1983, 223–43.

North, Douglass C., John J. Wallis, and Barry R. Weingast. *Violence and Social Orders: A Conceptual Framework for Interpreting Recorded Human History*. New York: Cambridge University Press, 2009.

Ōe Shinobu. "Shokuminchi sensō to Sōtokufu no seiritsu [Colonial war and the establishment of the Government-General]." In *Iwanami kōza kindai Nihon to shokuminchi* [Iwanami series on modern Japan and its colonies], volume 2, edited by Ōe Shinobu. Tokyo: Iwanami Shoten, 1992, 3–33.

Oguma Eiji. *"Nihonjin" no kyōkai: Okinawa, Ainu, Taiwan, Chōsen shokuminchi shihai kara fukki undō made* [The Boundaries of "Japanese": Okinawa, Ainu, Taiwan,

Korea from colonial domination to recovery movement]. Tokyo: Shinyōsha, 1998.

Okamatsu Santrō. "Nippon minpō no ketten wo ronji te Taiwan rippō ni taisuru kibō ni oyobu [Hopes for Taiwanese legislation through the recognition of the flaws of the Japanese Civil Code]." *Taiwan kanshū kiji* 5, no. 3 (1905): 13–26.

Okamoto Makiko. *Shokuminchi kanryō no seiji shi: Chōsen, Taiwan Sōtokufu to teikoku Nihon* [The political history of the colonial bureaucracy: Korean and Taiwanese Governments-General and the Japanese Empire]. Tokyo: Sangensha, 2008.

Ooms, Herman. *Tokugawa Village Practice: Class, Status, Power, Law.* Berkeley: University of California Press, 1996.

Owen, Norman G. "Introduction: Philippine Society and American Colonialism." In *Compadre Colonialism: Studies on the Philippines under American Rule*, edited by Norman Owen. Ann Arbor: University of Michigan Center for South and Southeast Asian Studies, 1971, 1–12.

——. "Winding Down the War in Albay, 1900–1903." *Pacific Historical Review* 48, no. 4 (1979): 557–89.

Paine, S. C. M. *The Sino-Japanese War of 1894–1895: Perceptions, Power, and Primacy.* New York: Cambridge University Press, 2003.

——. "Introduction." In *Nation Building, State Building, and Economic Development: Case Studies and Comparisons*, edited by S. C. M. Paine. New York: Routledge, 2010.

Paris, Roland. *At War's End: Building Peace after Civil Conflict.* New York: Cambridge University Press, 2004.

——. "Saving Liberal Peacebuilding." *Review of International Studies* 36 (2010): 337–65.

Patrick, Stewart. *Weak Links: Fragile States, Global Threats, and International Security.* New York: Oxford University Press, 2011.

Pekkanen, Robert J., Yutaka Tsujinaka, and Hidehiro Yamamoto. *Neighborhood Associations and Local Governance in Japan.* New York: Routledge, 2017.

Pharr, Susan J., and Frank J. Schwartz. *The State of Civil Society in Japan.* New York: Cambridge University Press, 2003.

Philippines. Board of Educational Survey. *A Survey of the Educational System of the Philippine Islands.* Manila: Bureau of Printing, 1925.

Philippines. Bureau of Health. *Report of the Bureau of Health.* Manila: Bureau of Printing, 1901–1914.

Philippines. Bureau of the Census and Statistics. *Yearbook of Philippine Statistics, 1940.* Manila: Bureau of Printing, 1941.

Philippines. Bureau of Lands. *Report of the Director of Lands.* Manila: Bureau of Printing, 1901–1935.

Philippines. Census Office. *Census of the Philippine Islands: 1918.* Manila: Bureau of Printing, 1920–1921.

Philippines. Civil Service Board. *Fourth Annual Report of the Philippine Civil Service Board to the Civil Governor of the Philippine Islands and the Philippine Commission, 1904.* Manila: Bureau of Printing, 1904.

Philippines. Commission of the Census. *Census of the Philippines: 1939.* Manila: Bureau of Printing, 1940–1943.

Philippines. Commissioner of Civil Service. *First Annual Report of the Commissioner of Civil Service, From the Period from November 15, 1935 to December 31, 1936.* Manila: Bureau of Printing, 1937.

Philippines. Executive Bureau. *Annual Report of the Executive Secretary of the Philippine Islands.* Manila: Bureau of Printing, 1902–1935.

Philippines. Philippine Health Service. *Report of the Philippine Health Service.* Manila: Bureau of Printing, 1915–1935.

Porter, Theodore. *Trust in Numbers: The Pursuit of Objectivity in Science and Public Life.* Princeton: Princeton University Press, 1995.

Pratt, Julius W. *Expansionists of 1898: The Acquisition of Hawaii and the Spanish Islands.* Baltimore: Johns Hopkins University Press, 1936.

Przeworski, Adam, and Henry Teune. *The Logic of Comparative Social Inquiry.* New York: Wiley-Interscience, 1970.

Putnam, Robert. *Making Democracy Work: Civic Traditions in Modern Italy.* Princeton: Princeton University Press, 1993.

Pyle, Kenneth B. "The Technology of Japanese Nationalism: The Local Improvement Movement, 1900–1918." *Journal of Asian Studies* 33, no. 1 (1973): 51–65.

Raeff, Marc. "The Well-Ordered Police State and the Development of Modernity in Seventeenth- and Eighteenth-Century Europe: An Attempt at a Comparative Approach." *American Historical Review* 80, no. 5 (1975): 1221–43.

Read, Benjamin L. *Roots of the State: Neighborhood Organization and Social Networks in Beijing and Taipei.* Stanford: Stanford University Press, 2012.

Reyntjens, Filip. *Political Governance in Post-Genocide Rwanda.* New York: Cambridge University Press, 2015.

Richardson, James D. *A Compilation of the Messages and Papers of the President, 1789–1897.* Washington, DC: Government Publishing Office, 1899.

Roberts, Luke S. *Performing the Great Peace: Political Space and Open Secrets in Tokugawa Japan.* Honolulu: University of Hawai'i Press, 2012.

Robles, Eliodoro G. *The Philippines in the Nineteenth Century.* Quezon City, PH: Malaya Books, 1969.

Rogaski, Ruth. *Hygienic Modernity: Meanings of Health and Disease in Treaty-Port China.* Berkeley: University of California Press, 2004.

Roosevelt, Theodore Jr. "Land Problems in Puerto Rico and the Philippine Islands." *Geographical Review* 24, no. 2 (1934): 182–204.

Root, Elihu. *Experiments in Government and the Essentials of the Constitution.* Princeton: Princeton University Press, 1913.

——. *The Military and Colonial Policy of the United States: Addresses and Reports.* Edited by Robert Bacon and James Brown Scott. Cambridge, MA: Harvard University Press, 1916.

Rothstein, Bo. *The Quality of Government: Corruption, Social Trust and Inequality in a Comparative Perspective.* Chicago: University of Chicago Press, 2011.

Rousseau, Jean-Jacques. "Discourse on the Origin and Foundations of Inequality Among Men." In *Rousseau: The Discourses and Other Early Political Writings*, edited by Victor Gourevitch. New York: Cambridge University Press, 1997.

Samuels, Richard J. *"Rich Nation, Strong Army": National Security and the Technological Transformation of Japan.* Ithaca: Cornell University Press, 1996.

Saylor, Ryan. *State Building in Boom Times: Commodities and Coalitions in Latin America and Africa.* New York: Oxford University Press, 2014.

Schurman, Jacob Gould, George Dewey, Elwell S. Otis, Charles Denby, and Dean C. Worcester. *Report of the Philippine Commission to the President.* Washington, DC: Government Publishing Office, 1900.

Scott, James C. *Weapons of the Weak: Everyday Forms of Peasant Resistance.* New Haven: Yale University Press, 1985.

——. *Domination and the Arts of Resistance: Hidden Transcripts.* New Haven: Yale University Press, 1990.

——. *Seeing Like a State: How Certain Schemes to Improve the Human Condition Have Failed.* New Haven: Yale University Press, 1998.

——. *The Art of Not Being Governed: An Anarchist History of Upland Southeast Asia.* New Haven: Yale University Press, 2009.

——. *Against the Grain: A Deep History of the Earliest States.* New Haven: Yale University Press, 2017.

Shepherd, John Robert. *Statecraft and Political Economy on the Taiwan Frontier, 1600–1800.* Stanford: Stanford University Press, 1993.

Sherman, Frank W. *What's Wrong with the Lands Bureau?* Manila: Kriedt Print Co., 1929.

Shue, Vivienne. *The Reach of the State: Sketches of the Chinese Body Politic.* Stanford: Stanford University Press, 1988.

Siddle, Richard. "Colonialism and Identity in Okinawa before 1945." *Japanese Studies* 18, no. 2 (1998): 117–33.

Sidel, John T. *Capital, Coercion, and Crime: Bossism in the Philippines.* Stanford: Stanford University Press, 1999.

——. "Walking in the Shadow of the Big Man: Justiniano Montano and Failed Dynasty Building in Cavite, 1935–1972." In *An Anarchy of Families: State and Family in the Philippines,* edited by Alfred W. McCoy. Madison: University of Wisconsin Press, 2009, 109–61.

Silberman, Bernard S. *Cages of Reason: The Rise of the Rational State in France, Japan, the United States, and Great Britain.* Chicago: University of Chicago Press, 1993.

Siu, Helen F. *Agents and Victims in South China: Accomplices in Rural Revolution.* New Haven: Yale University Press, 1989.

Skocpol, Theda. *States and Social Revolutions: A Comparative Analysis of France, Russia, and China.* New York: Cambridge University Press, 1979.

Slater, Dan. *Ordering Power: Contentious Politics and Authoritarian Leviathans in Southeast Asia.* New York: Cambridge University Press, 2010.

Smith, Thomas C. "The Japanese Village in the Seventeenth Century." *Journal of Economic History* 12, no. 1 (1952): 1–20.

Smith, Tony. *America's Mission: The United States and the Worldwide Struggle for Democracy in the Twentieth Century.* Princeton: Princeton University Press, 1994.

Soifer, Hillel David. "The Causal Logic of Critical Junctures." *Comparative Political Studies* 45, no. 12 (2012): 1572–97.

——. *State Building in Latin America.* New York: Cambridge University Press, 2015.

Sokoloff, Kenneth L., and Stanley L. Engerman. "History Lessons: Institutions, Factors Endowments, and Paths of Development in the New World." *Journal of Economic Perspectives* 14, no. 3 (2000): 217–32.

Speidel, William M. "The Administrative and Fiscal Reforms of Liu Ming-ch'uan in Taiwan, 1884–1891: Foundation for Self-strengthening." *Journal of Asian Studies* 35, no. 3 (1976): 441–59.

Spruyt, Hendrik. *The Sovereign State and Its Competitors: An Analysis of Systems Change.* Princeton: Princeton University Press, 1994.

Stanley, Peter W. *A Nation in the Making: The Philippines and the United States, 1899–1921.* Cambridge, MA: Harvard University Press, 1974.

Stites, Richard. *Revolutionary Dreams: Utopian Vision and Experimental Life in the Russian Revolution.* New York: Oxford University Press, 1989.

Stokes, Susan C., Thad Dunning, Marcelo Nazareno, and Valeria Brusco. *Brokers, Voters, and Clientelism: The Puzzle of Distributive Politics.* New York: Cambridge University Press, 2013.

Straus, Scott, and Lars Waldorf, eds. *Remaking Rwanda: State Building and Human Rights after Mass Violence*. Madison: University of Wisconsin Press, 2011.

Sturtevant, David. *Popular Uprisings in the Philippines, 1840–1940*. Ithaca: Cornell University Press, 1976.

Suhrke, Astri. *When More Is Less: The International Project in Afghanistan*. New York: Columbia University Press, 2012.

Suri, Jeremi. *Liberty's Surest Guardian: Rebuilding Nations After War from the Founders to Obama*. New York: Free Press, 2011.

Suzuki Masuhito. "Taiwan no hokō seido [Taiwan's *hokō* system]." *Toshi mondai* 39.5/39.6 (1944): 1–9/26–36.

Suzuki Tetsuzō. "Ri zhi chu nian tai wan wei sheng zheng ce zhi zhan kai: yi 'gong yi bao gao' zhi fen xi wei zhong xin [The opening of sanitary policies in early Japanese Taiwan: from the public health physician reports]." *Tai wan shi da li shi xue bao* 37 (2007): 143–80.

———. "Ri zhi chu nian tai wan zong du fu wei sheng xing zheng zhi du zhi xing cheng: yu jin dai ri ben wei sheng xing zheng zhi du bi jiao kao cha [The formation of the sanitary administrative system of Taiwan Governor-General in early colonial Taiwan: a comparison with modern Japanese sanitary administrative system]." *Shi da tai wan shi xue bao* 4 (2011): 128–59.

Takekoshi, Yosaburō. *Japanese Rule in Formosa*. Translated by George Braithwaite. New York: Longmans, Green, and Co., 1907.

Taiwan. Bureau of Aboriginal Affairs. *Report on the Control of Aborigines in Formosa*. Tokyo: Tōyō Printing Co., 1911.

Taiwan. Committee of the Formosan Special Census Investigation. *The Special Population Census of Formosa, 1905*. Tokyo: Imperial Printing Bureau, 1909.

Taiwan. Tong ji shi. *Tai wan sheng wu shi yi nian lai tong ji ti yao* [Statistical summaries of the province of Taiwan for the past fifty-one years]. Taipei: Tai wan sheng xing zheng zhang guan gong shu tong ji shi, 1946.

Taiwan Kyōikukai. *Taiwan kyōiku enkakushi* [History of education in Taiwan]. Taihoku [Taipei]: Kotei Shooku, 1973[1939].

Taiwan Sōtokufu Keimukyoku. *Taiwan Sōtokufu keisatsu enkakushi* [A history of the Taiwan Government-General police department]. Taihoku [Taipei]: Taiwan Sōtokufu Keimukyoku, 1933.

Tarr, Peter James. "The Education of the Thomasites: American School Teachers in Philippine Colonial Society, 1901–1913." PhD diss., Cornell University, 2006.

Thornton, Patricia M. *Disciplining the State: Virtue, Violence, and State-making in Modern China*. Cambridge, MA: Harvard University Press, 2007.

Tilly, Charles. *Coercion, Capital, and European States, AD 90–1990*. Cambridge, MA: Blackwell, 1990.

Ting Wen-hui. "Tai wan ri zhi shi qi nue ji fang zhi zhi tui xing [The prophylaxis and treatment against malaria in colonial Taiwan]." *Ren wen yan jiu xue bao* 42, no. 2 (2008): 75–89.

Tocqueville, Alexis de. *Democracy in America*. Edited by J. P. Mayer. Translated by George Lawrence. New York: Harper Perennial, 1988.

Tompkins, E. Berkeley. *Anti-Imperialism in the United States: The Great Debate, 1890–1920*. Philadelphia: University of Pennsylvania Press, 1970.

Ts'ai, Hui-yu Caroline. "One Kind of Control: The 'Hokō' System in Taiwan under Japanese Rule, 1895–1945." PhD diss., Columbia University, 1990.

———. "Baozheng, baojia shu ji, jiezhuangyichang-kou shu li shi (Li Jinzhen, Chen Rongsong, Chen Jinhe) [A verbal history on yasumasa, baojia secretary, and villages

(Li Jinzhen, Chen Rongsong, Chen Jinhe)]." *Tai wan yan jiu shi* 2, no. 2 (1995): 187–214.

——. *Taiwan in Japan's Empire Building: An Institutional Approach to Colonial Engineering.* London: Routledge, 2009.

——. "Engineering the Social or Engaging 'Everyday Modernity'? Interwar Taiwan Reconsidered." In *Becoming Taiwan: From Colonialism to Democracy*, edited by Ann Heylen and Scott Sommers. Wiesbaden, DE: Harrassowitz Verlag, 2010, 83–100.

Tsai, Lily L. *Accountability without Democracy: Solidary Groups and Public Goods Provision in Rural China.* New York: Cambridge University Press, 2007.

Tsai Lung-pao. "Ri zhi shi qi tai wan dao lu shi ye de tui jin: min li zhi wei yong tai wan ren zhi ju di [The development of the road construction in Taiwan under Japanese rule: the conscription of the local manpower and Taiwanese resistance and adaptation]." *Guo shi guan xue shu ji kan* 6 (2005): 61–108.

——. "Ri zhi chu qi tai wan de dao lu shi ye [The road construction business in Taiwan during the early period of the Japanese reign]." *Guo shi guan xue shu qi kan* 7 (2006): 85–129.

——. "Ri zhi chu qi tai wan zong du fu de ji shu ren li zhi zhao mu: yi tu di diao cha shi ye wei li [The Governor-General of Taiwan's mobilization of technical manpower in the early Japanese colonial period: the case of land surveys]." *Guo li zheng zhi da xue shi xue bao* 35 (2011): 75–143.

Tsu, Timothy Y. "Japanese Colonialism and the Investigation of the Taiwanese Old Customs." In *Anthropology and Colonialism in Asia and Oceania*, edited by Jan van Bremen and Akitoshi Shimizu. Surrey, UK: Cruzon, 1999, 197–218.

Tsurumi, E. Patricia. "Taiwan Under Kodama Gentarō and Gotō Shimpei." *Papers on Japan, Harvard University, East Asian Research Center* 4 (1967): 95–146.

——. *Japanese Colonial Education in Taiwan, 1895–1945.* Cambridge, MA: Harvard University Press, 1977.

Tsurumi Yūsuke. *Seiden Gotō Shimpei* [Official biography of Gotō Shimpei]. Edited by Ikkai Tomoyoshi. Tokyo: Fujiwara Shoten, 2004.

United States. Bureau of the Census. *Census of the Philippine Islands: 1903.* Washington, DC: Government Publishing Office, 1905.

United States. Department of War. *Acts of the Philippine Commission.* Washington, DC: Government Publishing Office, 1902–1916.

——. *Annual Report of the Philippine Commission to the Secretary of War.* Washington, DC: Government Publishing Office, 1900–1916.

——. *Public Laws and Resolutions Passed by the United States Philippine Commission.* Washington, DC: Government Publishing Office, 1901.

United States. Senate Committee on the Philippines. *Affairs in the Philippine Islands: Hearings before the Committee on the Philippines of the United States Senate.* Washington, DC: Government Publishing Office, 1902.

van de Walle, Nicolas. *African Economies and the Politics of Permanent Crisis, 1979–1999.* New York: Cambridge University Press, 2001.

VanderMeer, Canute, and Paul VanderMeer. "Land Property Data on Taiwan." *Journal of Asian Studies* 28, no. 1 (1968): 144–50.

Vu, Tuong. *Paths to Development in Asia: South Korea, Vietnam, China, and Indonesia.* New York: Cambridge University Press, 2010.

Wang, Tay-sheng. *Legal Reform in Taiwan under Japanese Colonial Rule, 1895–1945: The Reception of Western Law.* Seattle: University of Washington Press, 2000.

Warren, Mark E. *Democracy and Association.* Princeton: Princeton University Press, 2001.

Washinosu Atsuya. *Taiwan keisatsu yonjūnen shiwa* [Discussion of the forty-year history of the Taiwan police]. Tokyo: Ryokuin Shobō, 2000[1938].

——. *Taiwan hokō kōminka dokuhon* [A reader on *hokō* and imperialization in Taiwan]. Tokyo: Ryokuin Shobō, 2000[1941].

Watt, John R. *The District Magistrate in Late Imperial China.* New York: Columbia University Press, 1972.

Watt, Lori. *When Empire Comes Home: Repatriation and Reintegration in Postwar Japan.* Cambridge, MA: Harvard University Press, 2010.

Weber, Eugen. *Peasants into Frenchmen: The Modernization of Rural France, 1870–1914.* Stanford: Stanford University Press, 1976.

Weber, Max. "Politics as a Vocation." In *From Max Weber: Essays in Sociology,* edited by H. H. Gerth and C. Wright Mills. New York: Oxford University Press, 1946, 77–128.

——. *Economy and Society: An Outline of Interpretive Sociology.* Edited by Guenther Ross and Claus Wittich. Berkeley: University of California Press, 1978.

Wedeen, Lisa. *Ambiguities of Domination: Politics, Rhetoric, and Symbols in Contemporary Syria.* Chicago: University of Chicago Press, 1999.

Weeks, Jessica L. P. *Dictators at War and Peace.* Ithaca: Cornell University Press, 2014.

Westney, D. Eleanor. *Imitation and Innovation: The Transfer of Western Organizational Patterns to Meiji Japan.* Cambridge, MA: Harvard University Press, 1987.

Wicentowski, Joseph C. "Policing Health in Modern Taiwan, 1898–1949." PhD diss., Harvard University, 2007.

Wickberg, Edgar. "Continuities in Land Tenure, 1900–1940." In *The Anthropology of Taiwanese Society,* edited by Emily Martin Ahern and Hill Gates. Stanford: Stanford University Press, 1981, 212–38.

Wilfahrt, Martha. "Precolonial Legacies and Institutional Congruence in Public Goods Delivery: Evidence from Decentralized West Africa." *World Politics* 70, no. 2 (2018): 1–35.

Willis, Henry Parker. *Our Philippine Problem: A Study of American Colonial Policy.* New York: H. Holt and Company, 1905.

Wilson, Woodrow. "The Study of Administration." *Political Science Quarterly* 2, no. 2 (1887): 197–222.

Worcester, Dean C. *A History of Asiatic Cholera in the Philippine Islands.* Manila: Bureau of Printing, 1908.

——. *The Philippines Past and Present.* Edited by Joseph Ralston Hayden. New York: Macmillan Company, 1930.

Wu, Rwei-ren. "The Formosan Ideology: Oriental Colonialism and the Rise of Taiwanese Nationalism, 1895–1945." PhD diss., University of Chicago, 2003.

Yamazaki Tanshō. *Gaichi tōchi kikō no kenkyū* [A study of the governing institutions of the outer lands]. Tokyo: Takayama Shoin, 1943.

Yao, Jen-to. "Governing the Colonised: Governmentality in the Japanese Colonisation of Taiwan, 1895–1945." PhD diss., University of Essex, 2002.

——. "The Japanese Colonial State and Its Forms of Knowledge in Taiwan." In *Taiwan under Japanese Colonial Rule, 1895–1945,* edited by Ping-hui Liao and David Der-wei Wang. New York: Columbia University Press, 2006.

Yoshihara Jōji. *Nihon tōchika Taiwan keisatsu seido oyobi hokō seido nōto* [A note on the police and *hokō* systems under Japanese colonial rule]. Tokyo: Tsuzukiinshokan, 1998.

Yoshino Hidekimi. *Taiwan kyōiku shi* [History of education in Taiwan]. Taihoku [Taipei]: Taiwan Nichinichi Shinpōsha, 1927.

Young, Crawford. *The African Colonial State in Comparative Perspective.* New Haven: Yale University Press, 1994.

Young, Kenneth. *The General's General: The Life and Times of Arthur MacArthur.* Boulder, CO: Westview Press, 1994.

Young, Louise. *Japan's Total Empire: Manchuria and the Culture of Wartime Imperialism.* Berkeley: University of California Press, 1998.

Index

accountability: autonomous civil society in, 46; in domestic electoral politics (U.S.), 106, 171, 172, 174; in *hokō*, 90–91

agency, local, 94–95, 99–101. *See also* autonomy

Aguialdo, Emilio, 108, 111, 117, 158–59, 160

Albay insurgency, 155

Allen, Henry, 151, 154–55

alternatives to statebuilding, 186–87

American way of statebuilding: constraints on, 24, 105–6, 153, 171, 185; in counterinsurgency, 112–17, 128–29; in ineffective state-society mediation, 124–29, 134–35; politics and ideology of, 23–24, 105–12, 128–31; strategy of, 117–24; weaknesses in, 104–7

anarchy as alternative to statebuilding, 186–87

annexations: of the Philippines, 105–6, 107–12; of Taiwan, 50–52, 54, 58–62

antecedent/structural conditions in statebuilding, 11–21, 167–70

anti-imperialism, American, 105–10

Arellano, Cayetano, 120

assimilation/assimilation models: "benevolent," 110–11, 157, 170–71; *dōka*, 52–57, 78–79, 80, 170–71, 200n20; *hokō* in, 99; *kōminka*, 101; in outcomes, 170–71; rejected by Gotō, 68–69

authoritarianism/autocracy: autonomy in, 214n6; in conflict with liberal democracy, 46–47; contemporary relevance of, 103; and the ethics of statebuilding, 183–86; in statebuilding success, 24, 166, 171–72, 179–80, 181–82

authority: abuse of, 19–20, 65, 157, 159–60, 165; acceptance of, 45; of bureaucracy, 158; in ideal-typical modern states, 28–29; under the IGP, 147–48, 152; in ineffective state-society mediation, 125–26; of intermediaries, 36, 44; local, in cellularization, 42–43

autonomy: in administered communities, 77–78, 89, 92; in American ideology, 129, 134, 180; of autocracies, 178, 214n6; and

cellularization, 43, 77–78, 93; in democratic statebuilding, 176, 180–81, 183; in the ethics of statebuilding, 187; of Filipino elites, 134–35, 152–53, 154, 161, 176; in IGP reforms, 143–44, 147–48, 150, 152–53; in ineffective state-society mediation, 124–25, 129; of Philippine municipalities, 121, 124–25, 134–35, 180–81. *See also* self-government/self-rule

Balayan, Batangas Province (Philippines), 142–43

Bandholtz, Harry, 154–56, 207n88

Bandit Punishment Ordinance (Taiwan), 72–73

baojia (Taiwan), 66–67, 77, 82–83, 86, 89, 168–69, 177

baoliangju (Taiwanese state-society mediation), 59, 63, 65, 177

Batangas insurgency, 129, 151

beliefs and biases: "backwardness" of Filipinos as, 106, 130–31, 134–35, 139, 140–41, 162; on modernization, 171; on the role of government, 179, 181; in statebuilding in the Philippines, 105–12, 129–31, 147, 162–63. *See also* ideology

Bell, J. Franklin, 142

"benevolent" assimilation, 110–11, 157, 170–71

Binan, Laguna Province (Philippines), 141–42

bosses: Filipino provincial, 133, 158–60, 162–63, 165, 173–74, 182–83 (*See also* *caciquism*); Taiwanese, 82; U.S. officials as, 162. *See also* strongmen, local

bubonic plague eradication, 9–10, 98, 100

bureaucracy/civil service: authority of, 158; cellularization of, 43; centralization of, 71, 111, 143–47, 149, 152–53, 183; in discipline of intermediaries, 179; Filipinos in, 167–68; in GGT land surveys, 96; in modernization, 171; politicization of, 159–60, 165; professionalization of, 15, 29–31; in Qing-era Taiwan, 15–17, 167; in Spanish-era Philippines, 17–20, 167; in statebuilding in the Philippines, 111–12, 121–24, 133–34,

Studies of the Weatherhead East Asian Institute

Columbia University

Selected Titles

(Complete list at: http://weai.columbia.edu/publications/studies-weai/)

The Invention of Madness: State, Society, and the Insane in Modern China, by Emily Baum. University of Chicago Press, 2018.

Idly Scribbling Rhymers: Poetry, Print, and Community in Nineteenth Century Japan, by Robert Tuck. Columbia University Press, 2018.

Forging the Golden Urn: The Qing Empire and the Politics of Reincarnation in Tibet, by Max Oidtmann. Columbia University Press, 2018.

The Battle for Fortune: State-Led Development, Personhood, and Power among Tibetans in China, by Charlene Makley. Cornell University Press, 2018.

Aesthetic Life: Beauty and Art in Modern Japan, by Miya Mizuta Lippit. Harvard University Asia Center, 2018.

China's War on Smuggling: Law, Economic Life, and the Making of the Modern State, 1842–1965, by Philip Thai. Columbia University Press, 2018.

Where the Party Rules: The Rank and File of China's Communist State, by Daniel Koss. Cambridge University Press, 2018.

Resurrecting Nagasaki: Reconstruction and the Formation of Atomic Narratives, by Chad R. Diehl. Cornell University Press, 2018.

China's Philological Turn: Scholars, Textualism, and the Dao in the Eighteenth Century, by Ori Sela. Columbia University Press, 2018.

Making Time: Astronomical Time Measurement in Tokugawa Japan, by Yulia Frumer. University of Chicago Press, 2018.

Mobilizing Without the Masses: Control and Contention in China, by Diana Fu. Cambridge University Press, 2018.

Post-Fascist Japan: Political Culture in Kamakura after the Second World War, by Laura Hein. Bloomsbury, 2018.

China's Conservative Revolution: The Quest for a New Order, 1927–1949, by Brian Tsui. Cambridge University Press, 2018.

Promiscuous Media: Film and Visual Culture in Imperial Japan, 1926–1945, by Hikari Hori. Cornell University Press, 2018.

The End of Japanese Cinema: Industrial Genres, National Times, and Media Ecologies, by Alexander Zahlten. Duke University Press, 2017.

The Chinese Typewriter: A History, by Thomas S. Mullaney. The MIT Press, 2017.

Forgotten Disease: Illnesses Transformed in Chinese Medicine, by Hilary A. Smith. Stanford University Press, 2017.

Borrowing Together: Microfinance and Cultivating Social Ties, by Becky Yang Hsu. Cambridge University Press, 2017.

Food of Sinful Demons: Meat, Vegetarianism, and the Limits of Buddhism in Tibet, by Geoffrey Barstow. Columbia University Press, 2017.

Youth For Nation: Culture and Protest in Cold War South Korea, by Charles R. Kim. University of Hawaii Press, 2017.

Socialist Cosmopolitanism: The Chinese Literary Universe, 1945–1965, by Nicolai Volland. Columbia University Press, 2017.

Yokohama and the Silk Trade: How Eastern Japan Became the Primary Economic Region of Japan, 1843–1893, by Yasuhiro Makimura. Lexington Books, 2017.

The Social Life of Inkstones: Artisans and Scholars in Early Qing China, by Dorothy Ko. University of Washington Press, 2017.

Darwin, Dharma, and the Divine: Evolutionary Theory and Religion in Modern Japan, by G. Clinton Godart. University of Hawaii Press, 2017.

Dictators and Their Secret Police: Coercive Institutions and State Violence, by Sheena Chestnut Greitens. Cambridge University Press, 2016.

The Cultural Revolution on Trial: Mao and the Gang of Four, by Alexander C. Cook. Cambridge University Press, 2016.

Inheritance of Loss: China, Japan, and the Political Economy of Redemption After Empire, by Yukiko Koga. University of Chicago Press, 2016.

Homecomings: The Belated Return of Japan's Lost Soldiers, by Yoshikuni Igarashi. Columbia University Press, 2016.

Samurai to Soldier: Remaking Military Service in Nineteenth-Century Japan, by D. Colin Jaundrill. Cornell University Press, 2016.

The Red Guard Generation and Political Activism in China, by Guobin Yang. Columbia University Press, 2016.

Accidental Activists: Victim Movements and Government Accountability in Japan and South Korea, by Celeste L. Arrington. Cornell University Press, 2016.

Ming China and Vietnam: Negotiating Borders in Early Modern Asia, by Kathlene Baldanza. Cambridge University Press, 2016.

Ethnic Conflict and Protest in Tibet and Xinjiang: Unrest in China's West, coedited by Ben Hillman and Gray Tuttle. Columbia University Press, 2016.

One Hundred Million Philosophers: Science of Thought and the Culture of Democracy in Postwar Japan, by Adam Bronson. University of Hawaii Press, 2016.

Conflict and Commerce in Maritime East Asia: The Zheng Family and the Shaping of the Modern World, c. 1620–1720, by Xing Hang. Cambridge University Press, 2016.

Chinese Law in Imperial Eyes: Sovereignty, Justice, and Transcultural Politics, by Li Chen. Columbia University Press, 2016.

Imperial Genus: The Formation and Limits of the Human in Modern Korea and Japan, by Travis Workman. University of California Press, 2015.

Yasukuni Shrine: History, Memory, and Japan's Unending Postwar, by Akiko Takenaka. University of Hawaii Press, 2015

The Age of Irreverence: A New History of Laughter in China, by Christopher Rea. University of California Press, 2015

The Knowledge of Nature and the Nature of Knowledge in Early Modern Japan, by Federico Marcon. University of Chicago Press, 2015

The Fascist Effect: Japan and Italy, 1915–1952, by Reto Hofmann. Cornell University Press, 2015

Empires of Coal: Fueling China's Entry into the Modern World Order, 1860–1920, by Shellen Xiao Wu. Stanford University Press, 2015

CPSIA information can be obtained
at www.ICGtesting.com
Printed in the USA
BVHW030024040219
539312BV00002B/17/P